The Canoe

The Ca

International Marine Publishing Company
Camden, Maine

Kenneth G. Roberts & Philip Shackleton

noe

A History of the Craft from Panama to the Arctic

In Memory of
RON SHACKLETON 1949-1975
...a steady paddler

Copyright © 1983
Philip Shackleton and Kenneth G. Roberts

Library of Congress Card Number 83-48153

International Standard Book Number 0-87742-175-7

Printed and bound in Hong Kong

Published simultaneously in Canada by Macmillan of
Canada, Toronto.

Published by International Marine Publishing Company,
21 Elm Street,
Camden, Maine 04843
(207) 236-4342

Contents

Virginia Indians fishing from a dugout were painted in watercolor by John White, who made several trips to the New World between 1585 and 1590. One of the earliest convincing renderings by a European of an Indian canoe, it illustrates the curved shaping, particularly the symmetrically rounded bow and stern, achieved by a burn-and-scrape technology. The bowman wields a shovel-bladed paddle and the stern man a fishing spear. The significance of the fire amidships is uncertain, but North Americans while afloat sometimes raised a smudge to discourage insects or, while travelling, kindled a small cooking fire on a stone or earthen hearth. Or White may have been attempting to illustrate the distinction between daytime and nighttime fishing, the latter requiring at gunwale level a fire for light and to attract fish. The lettering on the dugout indicates that cannow was the word first used by the English in Virginia.

The manner of their fishing.

A Cannow.

Introduction

WE WERE RELAXING after a long day on the water, lounging by a fire on the shore of a little lake in that Precambrian rock country north of the Great Lakes. Our simple camp chores were finished for the night; the tent was pitched on the one bit of level ground on that rocky point; we had a dry pile of beaver-cut poplar to feed the fire; and our scarred old canvas canoe was turned over and snugged safely among the spruce trees.

There was a chill in the September air and against a dark sky the northern lights flared green in an astonishing display, just for us. It was a magical night, a night for dreams before sleeping, a night when the romantic past melded easily with the living present. Cushioned on a pile of caribou moss, and with a little brandy to stir memory and warm the imagination, we wondered how many Indian hunters of the past might have slipped along our route in their quest for game and fur. Thousands no doubt, in their bark canoes. Through the glow of our camp-fire we could almost see a procession of birch-skin vessels and hear the dipping paddles of warriors, hunters, traders, and women on their way to the wild-rice harvesting.

Even if this water passage had never been a crowded one, certainly we were not far from lake and river ways that had seen a steady bark traffic through a thousand seasons of open water. With two days' paddling to the south, Indian travellers would have crossed the main east-west canoe route of the fur traders, that strand of lakes and streams and ponds that spans the continent. From our tiny lake in its muskeg basin a traveller could paddle to the Atlantic Ocean, or to the Pacific, or to the chill waters of Hudson Bay, or, perhaps by way of the old Chicago Portage, down the Mississippi to the Gulf of Mexico.

As the fire flickered low we conjured a parade of other travellers who might have passed this way: black-robed priests, soldiers, surveyors and prospectors, all dependent on the canoe for their transport. Had this canoe ever been given the prominence it deserved in the telling of North American history? Perhaps not. We agreed that the native peoples had rarely been given full credit for their inventiveness and their craftsmanship, for their skills on the water, and for the very gift of the canoe to European newcomers. Before we slept we decided to do something about it.

We lost little time in transforming a camp-fire reverie into a job of serious research. When we returned to a less magical urban world we continued to ask questions and demand answers of each other. We came to realize that the canoe is a universal vessel but that on our continent it has evolved from ancient to modern forms and has remained in use from the beginnings of recorded

history to the present day. Modern political borders had no significance to earlier inhabitants of North America, and we agreed that they could have no relevance until very late in the canoe story. We acknowledged that the kayaks of the Eskimoan peoples from Greenland to Alaska deserved treatment comparable to that we might devote to Indian craft. As our interest was lured east and west, then south and farther south, we were led from one culture to another until we found ourselves caught up in the story records of the various watercraft of the Middle American peoples. Finally, we drew an arbitrary line at Panama, conceding at the same time that no balanced survey could be achieved without including a study of the vessels of the seafaring peoples who have inhabited that chain of islands that stretches from Cuba to Trinidad and separates the Atlantic from the Caribbean Sea.

The decision allowed us to tell a continental story, one ranging from polar to tropical waters. The limits created, we thought, a neatly severed territory in which to study the canoe. We set off to do so with two great advantages—our enthusiasm and our innocence. The latter provided a brash assurance that enabled us to approach the subject with confidence; the former sustained us as we came gradually to appreciate something of the full scope of that subject.

The research experience was a rewarding pleasure from beginning to end, but as our filing cabinets filled and threatened to overflow, the organization of the material into book form became a serious problem. The manner in which we have arranged and presented our story may not please everyone, but we hope that most readers will find some logic in the form we have chosen. That we have been able to take delight and satisfaction from our research is due in large part to the enthusiasm and generous help of persons all over this continent and abroad. Whether we met them in person or through correspondence, we count them now among our friends.

A first and special acknowledgement must be made to Kirk Wipper, founder and continuing heart and soul of the Kanawa International Museum, near Minden, Ontario, to whose unique collection of historic canoes we have enjoyed free access. Bill Holm, canoe sculptor and curator of Northwest Coast Indian Art at the Thomas Burke Memorial Washington State Museum, Seattle, has shared generously his time, his knowledge, and his insight. David W. Zimmerly of the National Museum of Man, Ottawa, has been an indispensable guide to the skin boats of the Arctic. With infinite patience and good will, Jerry Evans and Raymond F. Willis of the Florida State Museum, Gainesville, have striven to further our understanding of the most ancient of surviving dugouts. Skilled paddlers like Shirley Black of the National Capital Commission, Ottawa, Hugh MacMillan of Rockwood, Ontario, and the Canadian Canoe Association's Fred Johnston of Odessa, Ontario, have alternated discreetly and effectively between goading us and sustaining us in our work. Jack Richardson of Ottawa, an habitué of archival institutions, has been an unfailing and encyclopedic reference source.

We have had many questions considered and resolved by such reliably helpful persons as Marcia Smith, librarian at the Adirondack Museum, Blue Mountain Lake, New York; Harriet Callahan of the Louisiana State Library in Baton Rouge; and Cecile Lund of the James Jerome Hill Reference Library in Saint Paul, Minnesota. In Ottawa, Jim Burand of the Public Archives of Canada and Joyce Banks of the National Library have aided greatly in winnowing from pictorial and documentary records the history of the canoe in Canada. Travis Hudson, curator of anthropology at the Santa Barbara Museum of Natural History, has been a stalwart guide to the story of the marine canoe of the California coast. Without the sure and steady support of Paula J. Fleming in Washington's National Museum of Natural History, Smithsonian Institution, we would have become impossibly lost while prospecting the riches of the National Anthropological Archives.

Marion Brophy provided access to the documentary and pictorial records of the American Canoe Association, now filed with the New York State Historical Association at Cooperstown. Mike Scott of the Rideau Canoe Club, Ottawa, has been a ready reference to matters concerning the history of competitive paddling. Among many generous persons who provided reference data and historical illustrations are: E. Wyllys Andrews V, Director of the Middle American Research Institute at Tulane University, New Orleans; John M. Kochiss of Bridgeport, Connecticut; Francisco R. Onate of Morelia, Mexico; Bobbie Elworth of the Vancouver City Archives; Alika Webber of Victoria; G. A. Aarons of the Jamaica National Trust Commission; John C. Henley III, of the Isla de Roatan, Honduras; Cathy Stewart of the Winnipeg Art Gallery; Roger Wilkinson of the American Canoe Association; and John W. Dudderidge of the British Canoe Union.

Wherever we went, to whomsoever we wrote, we were encouraged by the support and assistance of persons associated with many different libraries, museums, and other institutions. We are sincerely grateful to staff members of the Archives of Ontario; les Archives Nationales du Québec; the Mariners Museum in Newport News, Virginia; the Library of Congress in Washington; the Ottawa Public Library; el Museo Nacional de Antropología e Historia in Mexico; the Peabody Museum of Archeology and Ethnology at Harvard University; the Toronto Public Library Board, and particularly its Photography Unit; the Glenbow-Alberta Institute in Calgary; the British Columbia Provincial Museum; the Provincial Archives of British Columbia; National Maritime Museum of London; and the Library Services Division of the National Museums of Canada.

To the Canada Council, whose Exploration grant has helped so much to underwrite the costs of travel during our research, we offer our sincere thanks. We salute also our editors, Jan Walter and Pat Kennedy, who with the greatest goodwill have been persistent in leading us and driving us along the road towards publication. For much of what is gathered in the pages that follow we owe a debt to historians, archeologists, anthropologists, and illustrators from the fifteenth century to the present day. We have learned much through the willing and patient help of Indian artisans, among them Anderson Dick, the Salish elder who carves racing dugouts at Kulleet Bay on Vancouver Island, and William and Mary Commanda, skilled Algonquin canoe-makers of Maniwaki, Quebec.

To the native peoples past and present who have built and paddled the craft we call canoe, we hope this book may be an acceptable tribute.

What Is a Canoe?

Among the countless paintings and carvings to be seen on rock faces in many parts of North America, possibly the most splendid rendering of a canoe is that to be found above the shoreline of Pictured Lake, not far west of Thunder Bay, Ontario. Such pictographs may date from distant prehistoric to relatively recent times and some of them, no doubt, are the innocent efforts of recording artists. There are other chipped and painted images, however, which incorporate such exotic features as vessel bows in animal form, and still others appear as spirit canoes or solar boats associated with the vital business of aiding the sun in its daily transit.

IN ITS ORIGINAL SENSE the word canoe simply means boat. It comes from the language of the Arawak people and was used to denote the vessel they built and used on the waters of the West Indies. Taken into European languages, the word developed a narrower meaning, but, in the sixteenth century, the earliest American-born writer in Spanish defined it clearly. Garcilaso de la Vega, the son of an Inca mother and a Spanish father, established that canoe in the native language of Hispaniola and neighboring islands meant a boat without decks.

By using the word in his reports of discovery, Christopher Columbus introduced *canoa* to Europeans, and it became the familiar term used by Spanish explorers and historians to denote native dugouts. In Caribbean waters the French used such renderings as *canoua* before making *canot* the accepted word for their dictionary; as their explorers ranged over the continental mainland they applied *canot* without apparent distinction to both dugouts and bark vessels used by native peoples. Records of the period provide such variants as *canaoiia*, *canoo*, and *canno*, and English seamen, for whom literacy was scarcely a requisite to employment, were particularly casual in their interpretations. The Arawak word was carried to Virginia as *cannowa* and applied to the Indian dugouts found there, but the word was modified in time to become *canoe*, and it has been used ever since in English almost as a generic term for the aboriginal boat, whether made of skin or bark or fashioned from a log.

A second American word adopted by Europeans was *pirogue*, taken from the vocabulary of the Carib Indians, hardy marine people who occupied the small islands of the West Indies. The original was twisted by European tongues and pens to appear in their records in every possible and some quite improbable spellings: *piragua*, *piragoa*, *piraquita*, *pirahua*, and *pettyauger*. The Caribs used their term to describe a dugout with sides raised by the addition of boards or washstrakes, a boat larger and more complex in design than the basic hollowed log. Europeans, particularly the French and the British, used the word in different parts of the continent to label dugout vessels of widely varied character, but, except for some latter-day craft made of boards after a shaped-log prototype, it has been applied only to dugout vessels.

As newcomers grew more familiar with the great variety of aboriginal craft, they became more precise in describing them, using European adjectives to supplement Indian and Inuit terms. In the Arctic they learned to call skin boats *kayaks* and *umiaks* or, where the Russians came to trade and colonize, *baidarkas* and *baidars*. On the California coast *tomol* describes a unique native vessel made of split planks. In Middle America *corial*, *bongo*, and *dory* each denote a type of dugout. Explorers came to recognize the distinct qualities of the boats of different peoples and began to refer to Ojibwa and Choctaw and Kootenay canoes. *Canot du maître* and *canot du nord* were the precise names of quite distinctly different bark vessels, both essential to the fur trade.

Thousands of years of experiment and evolution resulted in a bewildering diversity of watercraft manufactured by the original peoples and, as well, a further variety of models inspired by their designs but with European modifications and constructed of both traditional and modern materials. An all-encompassing definition must be a general one: a canoe is an open watercraft of hollow form, generally shaped at each end to improve its hydrodynamic qualities, and designed originally to be propelled by one or more occupants, facing forward and using paddles or push-poles.

Three basic classes—the dugout, the bark craft, and the skin boat—were widely used in aboriginal North America. The dugout in its simplest form was a crude and clumsy vessel, a log hollowed by burning and scraping a cavity from end to end. In its most advanced form it was sculpted from a huge tree trunk into a complex curved hull, designed for speed and capable of withstanding very rough seas.

The bark canoe consists of a long trough of bark with the ends pinched together and the seams secured by lashing or sewing. Indians used any bark that could be stripped from a tree in sheets but some barks proved more manageable than others. That from the big birches seemed ideally suited to shaping light, tough, and speedy boat shells. To prevent a bark trough from folding up under the weight of its paddler some supporting frame was usually required. It is important to understand that almost invariably the bark trough was completed first and only then were the stiffening wooden frame members fitted into it.

The skin boat, in contrast, began with a rigid wooden framework that was completed before animal hides were stretched over it. In its simplest form it appeared as the bowl-shaped bull boat of the plains Indians, used primarily as a river ferry and scarcely distinguishable from the leather coracle of western Europe. In its most sophisticated form it was the long, slim, and incredibly fast hunting kayak of the Arctic people.

Whatever its material, whatever the form, the canoe gave its owner mobility on river, lake, and sea. It put the fisherman out on the water and extended the hunter's range. It carried braves to war and was freight vessel for Indian traders. It was a vehicle for one person to cross a stream or for a migrant people to cross the continent.

The canoe became an object on which the artist could lavish his talents, scraping and scribing emblems in the birch skin, carving his totem on a wooden hull or decorating the skin with mystic designs. Among the young people it was a vessel for boisterous racing competition and among the elders it played a role in ceremonial life. Ancient painted images of canoes, still to be seen on worn rock faces along old canoe routes, make it clear that the vessel had assumed a spiritual significance beyond the limitations of this life. The Indian might be transported to his burial ground in a canoe, or the canoe itself might serve as his sepulcher. Beyond death, it was a spirit canoe that carried him to another world.

The native boat was scarcely less important to many of the first Europeans who established themselves in the New World. In the north the rich harvest of precious furs was carried by Indian canoes from wilderness camps to trading posts and on to salt-water shipping ports. Much of present-day Canada and the United States was first explored by Europeans who found a canoe the only possible mode of transport through what they regarded as a trackless wilderness. Over much of the north there is scarcely a major lake or river whose earliest white visitor did not first view it over the gunwale of a canoe.

With courier canoes French colonists in the eighteenth century maintained communications between Quebec on the St. Lawrence River and New Orleans at the mouth of the Mississippi. Surveyors, map-makers, and prospectors travelled in them from the beginning and some still do. In log and bark vessels Old World missionaries, who saw only devil worship in native practices, carried their faith afield in tropical, temperate, and arctic America.

Through coral-reef waters buccaneers sailed dugouts against Spanish treasure ships and on jungle streams merchant adventurers loaded them with trinkets to bargain with the native peoples for the exotic wealth of a strange land. And even in the later years of the nineteenth century, before the railway link was completed, the "express" canoe remained the fastest means of crossing the northern east-west span of the continent.

A compressed history of the North American canoe is the business of this book. The story that leads eventually to the development of the present-day canoe, which is produced in factories in a diversity of styles, sizes, and materials, begins with the appearance of the simplest ancient native vessels. The story, perhaps, should be opened by asking what came before the canoe.

2

Rafts and Floats

(PREVIOUS PAGE) *For thousands of years after the native people of North America had developed dugouts and skin and bark canoes, the raft persisted as a quick and easy means for river crossings or downstream transport or for short trips on tranquil waters. This Woodland Indian woman was sketched by Dennis Gale about 1860 in bark canoe country. The pole sticking up behind her is likely shoved between the logs and into the mud to hold her craft in position.*

Rafts and Floats

A "man of California fishing on his bark log" was produced for the English seafarer George Shelvocke and first published in London in 1726. With the shortage of wood on some parts of the California coast it is highly likely that such tiny rafts were improvised for short trips to seal and mussel rocks just offshore. Bark log was the English seaman's term for a log raft.

MANKIND'S EARLIEST WATERCRAFT was probably a single log. Certainly it was something that would float on water and could support a person who clung to or straddled it. The first people to cross from Asia to Alaska were no doubt familiar with primitive floats and on the American continents their descendants used whatever buoyant material they found to contrive a great variety of floats and rafts.

Even the most primitive craft provided the means to cross a river that was otherwise a barrier. Mobility upon the water was a boon to hunting and fishing, and coastal rafts probably played a part in group migrations. Native legend attests to the antiquity of such craft, for stories of a great flood persist in many oral histories, and among the Alabama and the Natchez tribes the Indians' Noah was said to have survived by building a raft.

After the development in North America of bark, dugout, and skin canoes, rafts continued in some regions to serve as supplementary craft, quickly contrived to cross a river, to make a one-way downstream run, or to move a heavy load of goods. Some Indians, California coast people in particular, continued to make rafts and floats their primary vessels.

As far north as the Arctic Circle and as late as the end of the nineteenth century, Indians on the Mackenzie River built rafts. The ethnologist A. G. Morice saw them made "of three dry logs bound together, with their larger ends aft, while a slightly tapering shape is given their opposite extremities. The logs are fastened together fore and aft by means of ropes, which, when of truly aboriginal make, are of twisted strips of willow bark, starting from one end of a crossbar placed over them and going round each of the logs and the bar alternately." Some of their log rafts were built in the shape of an A; hunting canoes could be moored in the open end, while on the closed triangular bow the travellers sat around a fire kindled on an earthen hearth.

Travelling in the early eighteenth century in the lower Mississippi country of the Natchez, Chickasaws, and Choctaws, the French writer Antoine Le Page Du Pratz several times crossed that river on what those tribes called a *cajeu*: "They cut a great number of canes, which they tie up into faggots, part of which they fasten together sideways, and over these they lay a row crossways, binding all close together, and then launching it into the water." Before the middle of the sixteenth century, Spanish explorer Hernando de Soto appears to have used a somewhat similar Indian raft of canes and wood to cross the Alabama River.

The Aztecan people, who built the first Mexico City in the shallows of a lake, made static rafts for garden plots. They matted branches and logs together with other vegetation to form buoyant platforms and then dredged up rich silt from the lake bottom in which to plant their maize and beans, squash and tomatoes. These plots began as tethered floating gardens but later settled to become small farm islands.

The Balsas, longest of Mexico's rivers emptying into the Pacific, takes its name from the rafts once so familiar on its waters. As late as 1950, the *balsa*, supported by the shells of a type of gourd called the calabash, and used for fishing, was still to be seen there. It was of complex construction and suggests a long period of development. About one meter square, it was formed by lashing a platform of light stalks over a frame of bamboo called *otate*. Within and beneath the frame eight calabashes fastened by netting gave it buoyancy. Elders recalled times when large rafts made with as many as twenty calabashes could ferry entire families.

When the great sacrificial well at the Maya city of Chichén Itzá in Yucatan was dredged, one of the treasures recovered was a gold disk, and on it is inscribed the scene of a naval battle involving a canoe and three rafts. Each raft is depicted as a straight horizontal line—the bamboo frame—while beneath are two semicircular bulges, no doubt representing calabashes. The artwork is austere in its simplicity but there can be little doubt that the craft represented are what the Spanish called *calabazas*.

In tropical American waters, familiar English terms were "rafter" and "bark log," applied to any float craft up to the huge freight-carrying and sail-powered log craft of the Peruvian coast. *Balsa*, the Spanish word for raft, came into wide general use and was the name given to that tropical South and Central American tree that produces the lightest-weight wood known. Lionel Wafer, an English surgeon who visited Panama in the seventeenth century, called it "Lightwood" and observed the Indians building "Rafters":

They take Logs of this Wood not very big, and bind them together collaterally with *Maho*-Cords, making of them a kind of Floor. Then they lay another Range of Logs across these, at some distance from each other, and peg them down to the former with long Pins of *Macaw*-wood; and the Wood of the Float is so soft, and tenacious withal, that it easily gives admittance to the Peg upon driving, and closes fast about it.

Macaw is a variety of palm with a very hard wood; *maho* or *mahot* refers to a tree or shrub whose stringy bark was widely used to make strong cord, rope, and fish-netting.

The seagoing Peruvian rafts, which the Spanish used early for freighting goods as far north as Panama, were of similar construction. Truly huge, one captured by a fellow freebooter in 1680 was described by the English buccaneer William Dampier: "Captain Knight...took a Bark-log...laden chiefly with Flower. She had other Goods, as Wine, Oyl, Brandy, Sugar, Soap, and Leather of Goat-skins...." Among the islands of the Caribbean, rafts continue in use to the present time. In Jamaica a long raft made by lashing together ten to twelve bamboo stems will carry three to four hundred pounds of produce from the interior down the Rio Grande to the sea. The drifting and poling trip ended, the raft is broken up and the materials are sold. In neighboring Haiti similar rafts are built with a low railing to keep the heaped food produce from falling into the water.

On the California coast, Pomo Indians were reported to venture out on log rafts to harvest mussels from the rocks off San Francisco Bay. Farther south, log rafts were familiar on both sides of Baja California, and in 1539 Francisco de Ulloa, the Spanish admiral, described those of the Cochimi Indians of Cedros Island off the Pacific coast:

They had five or six rafts which they had used in fishing, made of pine or cedar timbers, as long as twelve or fifteen feet and so big that a man could hardly reach around them. The part underwater is rounded, and where the people stand on them is flat. They are not hollow in any part. On each side, to maintain the balance, there are bundles of many cedar poles, closely tied together.... They rowed them with paddles two or three palms long and about three fingers across....

An English adventurer, George Shelvocke, describing the fishermen at the southern point of Baja California in 1721, wrote, "they seldom need want a supply of this [fish], the men being excellent harpooners, they go out to sea on their bark-logs, which are only composed of five logs of light wood, made fast to one another by wooden pegs; on these they venture out rowing with a double paddle, and with their harpoons (which are made of a hard wood) strike the largest Albacores, and bring them in."

The eighteenth-century historian Francesco Saverio Clavijero described Indian fishing expeditions for which

they used a simple raft composed of three, five or seven logs fastened together with sticks and well tied; the log in the middle, which extends farther because of being longer, serves as a prow. The wood from which these rafts are made is cork [probably balsa wood] because it is lightest. On each of them, according to their size, 2 or 3 men take their places and depart 4 or 5 miles from the coast, without fear of the high waves of the Pacific Sea, which at times, seem to lift them as far as the clouds and at times to bury them in the bottom of the sea.

6

In 1923, researcher J. P. Harrington recorded the process of tule construction among the Tachi Indians of California. Bob Trehlawat, then about eighty years old, straddles the tapered ends of three bundles of tule while binding them into a bow shape for his new craft.

A medium-sized tule balsa of the Pomo Indians, made near Clear Lake, California, could carry about four people. The upturned bow is also typical of the craft of the Northern Paiute Indians, who used similar craft on the Owyhee, Snake, Malheur, Crooked, and Humboldt rivers.

The Seri Indians made bundles with the cane butts to the center, overlapping them for longitudinal strength. As the bundle grew, it was rolled to keep it round and was bound spirally with vegetable fiber. The bundles for one vessel were of an equal length of about thirty feet, and at the center they were tied together side by side. Towards the ends the outer bundles came together to form upturned and pointed bow and stern.

Sailing along the California coast in 1792, Captain George Vancouver sighted a "straw canoe" and his observations leave a misleading impression of some inferior native craft of no significance. This tule boat was used primarily in sheltered waters for gathering shellfish, laying nets, and harpooning fish, but it was well designed to absorb rough-water punishment without severe damage and was practically unsinkable. Vancouver's report of such a craft on the open sea is in fact a positive testimonial to the tule's seaworthiness.

The technology of such vessels was simple but by no means simplistic. Floats and rafts were devised and constructed from seemingly insubstantial materials but by such methods as to effectively meet the needs of their builders. During the thousands of years that humans have moved about this continent, the raft has served well as a vehicle for local transport, as a ferry, as an aid to hunting and fishing, and as a vessel for migration.

The rising bow and stern of this cane float give it a distinct boat shape even though it has no interior. When more than one person stood on these craft, the ends rose slightly. The boatman, a Seri Indian from Kino Bay, Mexico, is using a pole, but double paddles were used in deep water.

(OPPOSITE) On their reserve on the West Indian island of Dominica, present-day Carib craftsmen still build seagoing dugouts for their own use and for fishermen of neighboring islands. John Valmond (right) and his brother, St. Hilaire, use steel rather than the stone and shell tools of their ancestors to shape gumwood trunks into hulls ready for spreading. Washstrakes are added to each side to increase freeboard, and the finished vessels are called gommiers.

The Dugout

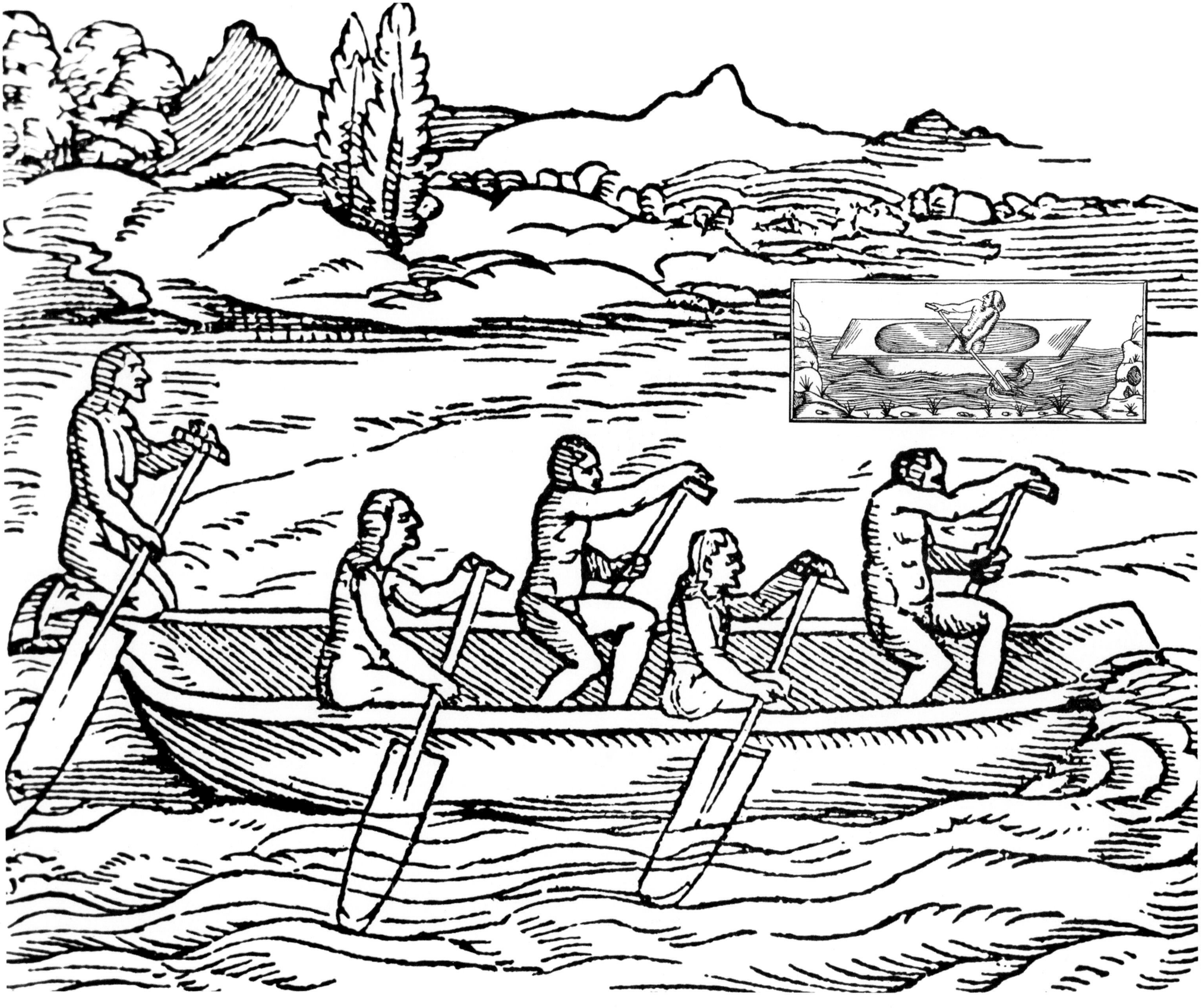

The Caribbean

When Columbus and other early visitors compared the West Indian paddle to a baker's peel, a European illustrator was tempted to render the canoe as a baker's kneading trough. The smaller picture appeared in 1547 in Fernandez de Oviedo's La historia generale de las Indias, *but it reveals that the artist never visited the Americas. The sketch of a vessel with a five-man crew, published in 1563 in Girolamo Benzoni's* La historia del Mondo Nuevo, *is crudely done but it conveys a more convincing impression of the dugout of the Caribbean.*

THE BOAT MADE BY hollowing a log was the most widespread type of canoe in North America. Trees of adequate size were to be found everywhere except in the far north and in parts of the central plain, and most early peoples devised techniques for making a cavity in a tree-trunk section and using the product as a vessel for hunting and fishing and for transport that ranged from local ferry service to the moving of a population from an old to a new settlement area.

The role of the canoe in migrations past is nowhere more apparent than in the West Indies. That chain of coral and volcanic islands, spread in a wide arc from Trinidad in the south to Cuba in the northwest, was first occupied by people with highly developed maritime skills and superior canoes. Successive island cultures have flourished while maintaining communication and trade links between villages and islands with great sea-going dugouts. Although some early island settlers may have originated from the Florida peninsula, anthropological evidence makes it clear that the West Indies were peopled first by groups that came mainly from South America—and they came by canoe.

When the first Europeans arrived, the most primitive islanders, the Ciboney, survived only in a few pockets at the western ends of Cuba and Hispaniola. They had been largely displaced by Arawakan people who had moved gradually northward along the island chain from the South American mainland. The strong northerly current from the mouth of the Orinoco River, combined with prevailing offshore winds, made the inter-island passage a natural route for migrants with adequate watercraft.

With the next island often visible on the horizon, they had moved in strength to occupy much of the West Indies. More technologically advanced than the Ciboney, who probably used only marine shell tools, the Arawaks had developed a kit of sharp stone axes and other cutting implements.

Moving in big dugouts from island to island, Arawak groups became familiar with the full arc of the West Indies probably more than two thousand years before the first European ships reached these waters. But a second major group of South American migrants had moved into the Lesser Antilles, those small islands from the Virgins down to Trinidad, no more than a few hundred years before Columbus landed. These were the Caribs, scourge of the Arawaks and, according to most European accounts, a thoroughly belligerent people. The very name Carib came into European languages to convey more than ethnic identity; the English version is cannibal.

By the fifteenth century the Arawakan group called Tainos occupied Cuba, Hispaniola, and Puerto Rico. There were Arawaks, too, on Jamaica and another group, the Lucayans, among the Bahama Islands. The Caribs controlled all the smaller islands, but there were both Carib and Arawak bases on Trinidad. The mild Arawaks and the fierce Caribs probably attained much the same high level of canoe craftsmanship. If the Caribs gained any greater repute it may simply have come because their paddlers were fearless navigators and bold and bloody fighters, people who seem never to have conceded that on occasion the odds were against them.

The canoe-building methods of these two peoples were apparently the same. A tree was felled by kindling a fire around its base and using wet moss to prevent its spreading upward. To cut, scrape, and break away the charred wood they used stone axes fitted to hardwood handles and secured with thongs. Fist-size rocks were the hammer stones used to pound stone chisels and gouges. With repeated kindling and dousing of the fire, and persistent chipping away of weakened and damaged wood fiber, the tree eventually toppled.

Fire was equally important in shaping the vessel, inside and out. Control of the alternate burning and scraping to preserve a critical thickness of hull was the highest skill of stone-age canoe-manufacturing. Most men were probably capable of making small canoes alone or with a helper or two. A large canoe no doubt required community effort and a work force under central direction. The refining of a crude log down to a sophisticated marine hull having an optimum thickness was almost certainly the responsibility of a master craftsman with long experience at the task.

Their tool kits varied somewhat from island to island. Coral islands offer no hard igneous rock with which to make useful axes, adzes, and chisels. To some islands, trade brought the better stone tools, including South American "green" stone axes highly favored by the Caribs. Archeological work on Barbados has revealed large quantities of cutting tools made from conch shell, while ancient work sites on Antigua have given up celts and chisels made from conch, as well as the pieces of sandstone used to sharpen them and hard stone tools shaped from local igneous rock. Shaped coral pieces probably used as wood rasps have come from island middens, and an early Spanish report suggests that the Indians used shark skin in lieu of sandpaper.

Settled on larger islands and partially dependent on an important farming base, the Arawaks spent relatively little time on the sea. The Caribs, on the other hand, were based on small islands, relied more heavily on fishing, and made frequent raids on Arawak islands. For one reason or another, most male Caribs were almost constantly in their canoes. Their traditions are better known today primarily because the Caribs remained for so long a stubborn force with which Europeans had to contend. The island Arawaks perished almost entirely, and quickly so, as a result of the slave-labor conditions and diseases brought by the Europeans, and much of their history died with them.

The Arawaks did carry on a canoe fishery, principally on the lee shores of their islands, and conducted considerable trade by canoe, some as far as the South American coast, although this ended when the Caribs occupied the Lesser Antilles. The dazzling speed of their larger canoes particularly impressed Christopher Columbus in his first encounters with American people. A letter he wrote concerning the first voyage of 1492-93 refers to the Lucayans and Arawaks:

They have in all the islands very many canoes, after the manner of rowing galleys, some larger, some smaller; and a good many are larger than a galley of eighteen benches. They are not so wide, because they are made of a single log of timber, but a galley could not keep up with them in rowing, for their motion is a thing beyond belief. And with these, they navigate through all those islands which are numberless, and ply their traffic. I have seen some of these canoes with seventy, and eighty, men in them, each one with his oar.

Many European visitors, familiar with the techniques of rowing, used the term "oar" when writing about the New World canoe. The use of a paddle without a fixed fulcrum, like a rowlock, was unfamiliar to them. A European with oars faced the stern of his vessel and the observer, therefore, was diverted to note that the Indian paddlers faced forward. Narratives of the period might devote a page or two to describe in painstaking detail the manner in which Indians manipulated their paddles.

During Columbus' second voyage in 1493 the Spaniards first encountered Caribs. A letter from one of the crew evidently provided the material for a pamphlet published immediately afterward in Italy:

They have larger and smaller vessels, called by them canoes, which they impel with oars. . . . The larger vessels have their sides constructed of timbers fastened together, and are eighty feet long. . . . For oars they have broad boards, such as our bakers use for oven shovels, only a little shorter. With this kind of boats they cross over to the neighboring islands. . . . Sometimes they make longer voyages, even to the distance of a thousand miles, for the purpose of plundering.

This may be the earliest published report of the fact that large dugouts were made more seaworthy by adding boards to build up the gunwales and increase freeboard. These washstrakes constituted a significant development in marine engineering, in that they made dugout canoes sufficiently seaworthy for inter-island travel.

In Cuba Columbus saw an Arawak canoe he said was as large as a *fusta*, a modestly sized Spanish ship of the time. It was sheltered in a *ramada*, a boathouse framed of wood and thatched with palm leaves. Canoes in many sizes were intended for different uses. The smallest carried only one or two persons and were used for personal transport and inshore fishing. The largest were trade and war canoes with built-up bulwarks and carrying large crews of paddlers. Ceremonial vessels used by *caciques* or chieftains on special occasions were carved and decorated and painted. On his second voyage Columbus reported from Jamaica that each *cacique* had his own distinctively decorated canoe and he measured one dugout of ninety-six feet in length.

Indian Houses

Canoes, strikingly similar to some still made by Arawakan Indians of South America, appear in an illustration from the 1740 publication of Antonio de Herrera's The general history of the vast continent and islands of America, published first in Spanish in 1601. The encounter between Indians and Spaniards occurred in Caribbean waters off the coast of what is now Venezuela.

When, during the first voyage, Columbus' principal ship, the *Santa Maria*, was wrecked off Hispaniola, it was a fleet of Arawak canoes that made the rescue. The furious admiral accused his crew of having concern only for their own skins but he praised the local *cacique* who organized his villagers and sent canoes to the disaster site. Arawak paddlers brought every scrap of the cargo to shore, then stored and guarded it under shelter so that Columbus was able to record that not so much as a shoelace was missing.

The Spaniards were greatly impressed with intrepid Indian seamanship and were always amazed to encounter lone paddlers making passage between various islands of the Bahama group. For provisions the Indians carried only cassava bread and a calabash of water. A half-calabash was also a standard bailing-tool, although they were so accustomed to being partly awash that they often bailed simply by rocking the canoe from side to side.

The natives normally followed familiar canoe routes and, although fearless sailors, they were not foolhardy. They were never eager to attempt treacherous waters like those of the channel separating Cuba from the mainland peninsula of Yucatan. That difficult water was an effective barrier between the people of the Antilles and those of mainland Middle America, and the strong current in the channel north of Jamaica discouraged regular contact between the Arawaks of that island and those of Cuba and Hispaniola.

The Spaniard who led the canoe crossing of this channel in 1503 became a hero to his shipmates. Towards the end of his fourth and final voyage, Columbus was forced to beach his two worm-ridden ships on the north coast of Jamaica. The crews were safe but thoroughly marooned more than a hundred miles south of Hispaniola, where help might be sought from Spanish settlements. They lived aboard the grounded ships and traded for food with the Arawaks. When Columbus bought canoes from the Indians one of his men volunteered to try the sea route to Hispaniola.

Evidently more scholar than swashbuckler, Diego Méndez de Segura may have been the first European to attempt a major canoe trip in American waters. The full story remains today imprecise and it isn't certain whether one canoe or two made the journey. Méndez himself wrote that he fastened a false keel to a canoe and "I nailed some boards on the stern and bow as a defence against the sea that it might not come in as it might owing to the low freeboard. And I put up a mast and sail, and laid in the supplies necessary."

17

Spelled at times by Spanish sailors, Jamaican Indians did most of the paddling. The voyage appears to have taken about five days. The rescue mission then hiked overland to the Hispaniola colony capital and, after many delays, Méndez convinced officials to send a ship back to rescue Columbus and his castaways. Mendez achieved only fleeting fame for the exploit, but after his death his family found in his will this singular request for a memorial above his tomb: "In the middle of the said stone, let there be carved a canoe, which is the hollowed tree in which the Indians navigate, for in such a one I navigated three hundred leagues, and above it let them set just the letters which read, 'Canoa.'"

While some sixteenth-century accounts reported native vessels with sails, there is insufficient period evidence to be quite certain that the Indians used sail before contact with Europeans. Thereafter, however, for native Antilleans who survived the first period of European incursion, sail largely replaced paddle power in seagoing dugouts.

Europeans were secure in a cultural tradition which accepted the virtues of the thumbscrew, the rack, and crude and gory execution. They were, however, entirely horrified to learn of the Caribs' sometime practice of eating other humans. Cannibalism appears to have been in part a ritual practice and the Caribs as a rule considered only male adversaries fair game. Captured women were adopted as wives and full members of the community. This practice explains, no doubt, the existence of two principal but quite distinct languages within traditional Carib society, one tongue used exclusively by men, the other by women. The men evidently understood the women's language but never deigned to speak it.

The use of parallel languages has helped increase the confusing variety of Amerindian terms for different watercraft. A vocabulary still used in the small surviving Carib community on the island of Dominica includes the term u'kuni, used by men to indicate dugout canoe, and kuria'la, used by women. Derived from the latter word, probably Arawakan in origin, are curial and corial, dugout terms familiar in some areas in the colonial period.

Perhaps because they were able to establish more amicable relations with the Caribs than anything managed by the Spanish, French missionaries of the seventeenth and eighteenth centuries left more richly detailed reports on the indigenous canoes. Father Jean Baptiste Du Tertre, whose work was published in Paris in 1667, revealed that the Indians by that time were using European axes, adzes, and other tools and suggested that they no longer took "entire years" to finish one of the largest vessels that they called canoua. The smallest dugouts he referred to by the native word couliala. The big dugouts, with a large plank fastened to each side, had a gunwale width of up to seven feet, small pieces of plank being used to enclose the gaps where the washstrakes met at bow and stern.

According to Du Tertre, the largest canoua, or pirogue as the French called it, usually had a second pair of gunwale planks added, planks as much as sixteen inches wide. Nails had not yet been adopted from the Europeans and the planks were fastened together and to the basic dugout with twine made from mahot fiber. Caulking material was made from the beaten bark of this same tropical tree. A long pole was fastened inside the hull along each side, about six inches below the gunwale, and thwarts, which served as seats, were lashed between these poles. The pirogues he saw were about forty feet long and up to eight feet wide, and could carry fifty people together with all their effects. The traditional Caribbean paddle with its cross-piece handle like a T was carried aboard, but a sail was also standard equipment. The smaller coulialas, as he saw them, did not as a rule have built-up sides and were never more than twenty feet long.

French, British, and Dutch adventurers proved somehow more acceptable to the Caribs than had the Spanish, and during the early seventeenth century these nations made their first tentative colonial developments on islands occupied by those Indians. In his journal of a

voyage to Puerto Rico in 1596, an English divine identified as Doctor Layfield wrote of a hospitable reception by Caribs at Dominica, their first landfall in the New World:

Their Canoes are of one Tree commonly in breadth, but containing one man, yet in some are seen two Yonkers sit shoulder to shoulder. . . . Besides their Merchandise for exchange, every one hath commonly his Bowe and Arrowes. . . . they have Wickers platted something like a broad shield to defend the raine. . . . they provide shelter against the raine because it washeth off[f] their red painting.

The use of some sort of shelter to protect the cosmetic artistry of the crew is a singular observation, but more significant is Layfield's report that in some canoes two paddlers sat side by side. Comfort considerations aside, two men sitting together could not paddle efficiently in a narrow dugout. These canoes evidently were of the pirogue type, spread wider than the simplest hollow-log craft.

Modifications in canoe construction came quickly. Metal cutting tools became the most desired trade items among the Indians, and the ax of iron had a revolutionary effect on their craftsmanship. Not only did it reduce the time and labor required to make a canoe but, as a tool that made greater control and precision possible, it opened the way to changes in the design of dugout hulls. The early adoption of such tools, and possibly also of some European techniques, makes it difficult to determine in retrospect where pure indigenous design left off and European-influenced modification began.

Seventeenth-century observers made it clear that Caribs used sail on canoes of all sizes but by that time they had had a century of intermittent contact with Europeans. The narrative of 1606 by John Stoneman, a British pilot en route to Virginia, bears specifically on the sail question. In passing the island of Dominica, his crew rescued a Spanish Franciscan, the lone survivor of a shipwreck sixteen months earlier. Two others who had got ashore had been killed by the Caribs but Friar Blasius had been spared, out of gratitude he explained, for he had shown them the great labor-saving benefit of making sails for their canoes. Abundant linen for sail-making had come from the cargo of another Spanish wreck.

According to Charles de Rochefort, whose French-language account was translated and published in English by John Davies in 1666, the distinction between canoe and pirogue was one of size. The French at the time were on good terms with the Caribs, and Rochefort stated that Carib canoes always came out to welcome French ships and to guide them to safe anchorage at Dominica.

The greater sort of *Piragas* are many times rais'd higher all about, especially towards the poop, with some planks: Sometimes they paint on them their *Maboya*; sometimes they represent Savages, or some other fantastick figures. These Shallops are so large as many times to carry fifty men with all their Arms. Before they had any acquaintance with the *Christians*, who furnish'd them with all sorts of Wedges, and other Carpenters and Joyners tools, they were put to a great deal of trouble to make their Vessels.

Rochefort understood that the *Maboya* figure represented an evil spirit or devil. He praised the Carib people, particularly their hospitality to strangers, and added a note concerning their discriminating palates: "They have heretofore tasted of all the Nations that frequented them, and affirm, That the *French* are the most delicate, and the *Spaniards* of hardest digestion; but now they do not feed on any Christians at all."

A Carib canoe raid was well organized. Rochefort explained that as well as village captains there was a captain for each pirogue, sometimes the owner, sometimes another whose job it was to command that vessel when at war. One of them also became the commander of the entire fleet. A woman was carried in each canoe and it was her function to apply the warriors' paint before an attack.

Arms and provisions were actually tied to the vessel sides or thwarts because upsets were frequent. Rochefort noted that they used sails of cotton or mats woven of palm leaves and that a raiding party even carried small canoes as tenders for the big pirogues. Carved and painted ornament was mentioned by a number of early travellers and in 1625 Thomas Gage, an English member of the Dominican order, noticed during a brief stop at the island of Guadeloupe that Indian canoes had each been painted with the coats of arms of the English, Dutch, or French.

The most satisfying canoe descriptions of all were left by Father Labat, one of those French priests who spent long mission years among the Caribs. He served on Martinique in the late years of the seventeenth century and the early years of the eighteenth, and his journal reveals that he was deeply interested in the temporal as well as the spiritual lives of those people:

Forty-seven Caribs came in two vessels. I thought that these were pirogues. I see, having descended to the edge of the sea, that I was mistaken. One of the two was, in fact, a pirogue, but the other was quite unknown to me. . . . One of the two vessels was much larger than the other and made in a completely different manner. On asking the name, I learned that it is called bacassa. I measured both of them. The pirogue was twenty-nine feet long and four and a half feet wide at its centre; it was pointed at both ends, which were higher than the middle by about fifteen to twenty inches. It was divided by nine planks or benches which appear to have been split, adzed smooth and not sawn. About eight inches behind each bench and somewhat higher there were sticks as thick as one's arm, with their ends fastened to the side of the pirogue; they served to support the sides of the vessel and to keep them always the same distance apart, as well as to provide support for the persons seated on the benches. The upper edge of the pirogue's sides were pierced with several holes strung through with cords of *mahot* which fastened down the baggage left there. . . .

19

A modern gommier made by Caribs of Dominica is ready for launching. The darker section inside is the original dugout, spread and braced, while the lighter wood above marks the closely fitted washstrakes. Bent cedar pieces brace and reinforce the finished vessel. The squared stern may later support a fisherman's outboard motor.

Traditional canoe-building is a continuing business for Dominica Caribs like the Valmond brothers. Primary shaping of the gommier or gumwood logs may be done in the high forest of this mountainous island, but the finer sculpting of the hulls is completed at a construction site near the windward Atlantic shore. A short-handled, finely honed ax is used to shave the partially finished outer surface to a smooth skin. The adze with a scoop blade is ideally suited to the final carving of the interior.

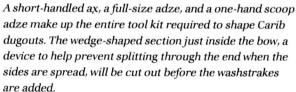

A short-handled ax, a full-size adze, and a one-hand scoop adze make up the entire tool kit required to shape Carib dugouts. The wedge-shaped section just inside the bow, a device to help prevent splitting through the end when the sides are spread, will be cut out before the washstrakes are added.

Logs are no longer burned into shape but fire retains its traditional role in the spreading operation. The completed dugout is propped upright and half filled with rocks and water. After some days of soaking, fires are kindled on the ground along each side and, under that heat and the pressure of the great weight inside, the sides of the softened hull are spread apart. The builder wedges cross-pieces called totes between the gunwales so that the now wider beam is retained as the hull dries.

Like the tree that provides its trunk for the basic dugout, the completed Carib canoe is called a gommier. A washstrake piece has been hewn to fit along each side of the spread dugout and rib-like braces called taquets have been fitted into the enlarged interior. The triangular noeud, to which the washstrake ends are fastened, is a stem post rising above the projecting ram-like bow. The Valmond brothers and other Carib builders supply gommiers to fishermen of their home island as well as Martinique, Guadeloupe, and St. Lucia.

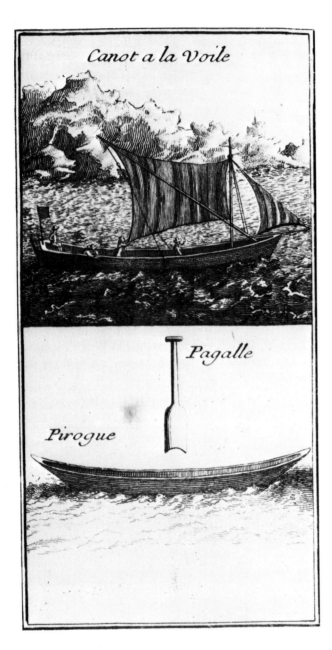

As reported by the earliest visitors from Europe, paddles were the familiar power source for Indian canoes in Caribbean waters. Whether or not the sail was known earlier to New World canoe people, its use was widely adopted in the sixteenth century. These sketches appeared in Father Labat's Voyages aux isles de l'Amérique. The pirogue, just as he described it in Martinique, has a distinctly rising bow and stern.

The bacassa was forty-two feet long and nearly seven feet wide in the centre. The bow was raised and pointed somewhat like that of a pirogue, but the rear was flat and cut like a poop deck. There was there the head of a grotesque figure, badly carved but well daubed in white, black and red, and also a man's arm *boucané*, that is dried and smoked over a slow fire, hanging beside the figure. They offered it to me very civilly saying that it was the arm of an Englishman who they had killed recently during a raid they had made on Barbuda, where they had massacred six people and carried off a woman and two children. I thanked them even more civilly for the gift they wanted to make to me and I offered them much brandy and to trade for merchandise if they wanted to bring their three prisoners....

The bacassa had benches like the pirogue. They were both made of *acajou*. It is a kind of cedar of which I will speak again. They were all of a piece, worked very neatly and smoothly. The sides of the bacassa had an *évuage*, that is to say an extending or raising of planks of the same wood adzed smooth, about fifteen inches high, that increased considerably the size of the boat. Neither had a rudder. The Carib who steers is seated or standing at the stern of the vessel and steers with a *pagalle* which is a good third longer than that used for paddling.

Like earlier Spanish observers, Father Labat found that the *pagalle* reminded him of a baker's peel. It was five to six feet long, the shaft three-quarters of that, and the blade about eight inches wide and an inch and a half thick at the center. The paddle blade was decorated with a pair of grooves and its lower end finished, he said, in a crescent-shaped curve.

Labat explained that a paddler occupied less space than a man with oars and hence the Carib canoe could carry at least twice as many paddlers as oarsmen and thus attain greater speed. The steering paddle was extralong because the stern of a pirogue or bacassa was raised and also because the steersman remained standing while the paddlers sat on thwarts, thus affording him a clear view over the heads of the paddlers. Labat added

that "one can turn a pirogue around a point with as much speed as one can turn a horse around a stake."

He recorded that the Carib pirogue usually had two masts and two square sails. The larger bacassa had three masts at this stage of development and sometimes carried topsails. He confirmed Rochefort's report that one or two women went with each war-canoe crew but sketched a quite different scene when the big boats set out for trade or pleasure trips. They took along their wives, their children, their arms "which they never forgot," their hammocks, and all their household utensils. Canoes were loaded with graters, sieves, earthenware pots, calabash vessels—all used in preparing cassava—not overlooking the *platine*, the stone slab on which the cassava cakes were cooked. It seems likely too that on long trips such cooking was sometimes done over a fire in the canoe.

Mahogany, *acajou* in French, was a familiar and useful timber tree in the West Indies but, as Father Labat's text makes clear, the French had applied that term also to the magnificent red cedar (*Cedrela odorata*) of the islands. While cedar was the favorite of the Caribs, both trees are well suited to dugout manufacture. Huge trees of both species were common before commercial exploitation by Europeans. Even early in the nineteenth century, observers in Jamaica reported that mahogany and cedar rose ninety feet from the ground before branching. Yet not every island provided timber of adequate size for making large canoes. Caribs of the Virgin Islands went to the Arawak island of Borinquen, now Puerto Rico, to fell great cedars for their *bacassas*. The most massive trunks were those of the *ceiba*, the wild cotton or silk-cotton tree, found throughout the islands. Its bulk, however, was the only factor recommending it to canoe-builders. In every other quality desirable for dugout-making it is inferior to cedar, mahogany, and gumwood, but it remained the standard canoe timber in Jamaica after the supply of other large trees was much reduced.

By the eighteenth century the *gommier* or gum tree (*Dacryodes hexandra*) was the familiar raw material for canoe-making where the Caribs yet held out. Thomas Atwood, preparing a history of Dominica published in 1791, was told by a carpenter there, "The gommier make for the big canoes—we shape and cut, and make a long hole to put hot stones which make the boat wide."

Dugouts made from trunks of the silk-cotton tree, in some areas the only remaining large timber, are still used by fishermen along Jamaica's south coast. The exterior is shaped with ax and adze before the hull is overturned and the interior cut out. The trough-like vessels do not have their sides spread or gunwales raised and the fish seiners and conch divers who paddle them are frequently half awash.

Canoes retaining some of the complex design characteristics of earlier Indian vessels are yet to be seen in the waters of Dominica and neighboring islands. Elsewhere in the West Indies the dugout survives as the basic hollowed log, like this battered veteran in the shallows off a Haitian beach.

(LEFT) The Martinique fishing boats purchased from Dominica's Carib craftsmen are fitted usually with one or two masts to carry sails of flour sacking, but hand-made oars and paddles are standard equipment, and the gommiers today increasingly are powered by outboard motors. The horizontal line where the original dugout joins the washstrake gunwale is obvious in the near canoe.

For everyday fishing, gommiers often carried sails of whatever nondescript material was readily and cheaply available, but for the keenly competitive races held on holidays in Martinique, boatmen raise the best the sailmakers can provide. Most gommiers carry two masts, each with a square lugsail and a diagonal yard.

Resting on a couple of logs on the beach while not in use, two Martinique fishing craft display the distinctive gommier bow, with its lower ram section painted blue, clearly demarcating the basic dugout. The washstrakes, which increase a gommier's freeboard, have been painted red.

Atwood's informant was, of course, describing the spreading process. Basic to advancing dugout technology was the ancient discovery that wood, when water-soaked and heated, could be bent and shaped more easily than when dry. Left on a beach under a hot sun, a simple dugout partially filled with rainwater or sea wash will open up somewhat without human effort. To observe and then improve upon the process by forcing sticks between the two sides of a dugout was a revolutionary advance in marine boat design.

Forcing the sides farther apart gives greater beam and thereby increases stability in rough water. Spreading, however, is accomplished by sacrificing freeboard; when gunwales are pushed apart the sides become lower. Restoring freeboard, and increasing it beyond that of the original hollowed log, was achieved by fastening planks along each side, as described by the French missionaries. One, sometimes two, planks, fitted and tapered to the newly spread gunwale line, were bound by fibrous vegetable cord through holes drilled in the planks and the log sides.

The French and the English were continuing rivals in the exploitation of the Lesser Antilles. Each wooed the Caribs as allies, the kind of friendship that proved, of course, disastrous for Indians. British and French together drove them from St. Kitts. On St. Vincent, Caribs had interbred with escaped Negro slaves and had become what the British termed a "truculent" problem. They solved it by rounding up the Indians like cattle and shipping them to the Bay Islands just off the mainland coast of Honduras. Although the Treaty of Aix-la-Chapelle in 1748 decreed that wild and mountainous Dominica be left entirely to the "native Indians," in a few years the British took control of that island. They pushed the remaining few hundred Caribs, the only significant group then surviving in the Antilles, into a reserve on the rocky and windward northeast coast, a piece of land of no interest to European planters.

When the ornithologist Frederick Ober visited Dominica near the end of the nineteenth century, he found that the Caribs used steel axes to fell gommiers that were eight feet in diameter. Once a tree was down, they used the traditional burning technique, while cutting away charred sections with steel rather than the ancient stone tools. Rough hollowing only was done at the felling site. Dragged from mountain jungle to seashore, the canoe was then smoothly finished without further burning.

Communal canoe-building ended when there was no further need for large inter-island vessels. Today one individual does most of the work on a canoe. After a tree of suitable size and regular form is located, it may take a lone axman a full day to bring it down. More than one modern observer has reported that a gommier is felled only when there is a new moon. Caribs explained that wood-boring grubs would attack the trunk if it was cut at any other time.

The most valuable modern study of the Caribs, including their canoe manufacture, was done by Douglas Taylor and published in 1938 by the Smithsonian Institution. Taylor noted that the builder might camp at the felling site while shaping the log roughly to canoe form and reducing the bulk by chopping and adzing out the inside. Depending on the size of the log and the industry of the craftsman, this took from four days to two weeks. When it was ready for "hauling" he gathered ten to twelve friends who used mahot or liana cords to drag it to the shore. According to Taylor, the men sang chanties traditionally reserved for this occasion as they worked the rough hulk through bush and jungle, over steep slopes, and through wild ravines, finally to the owner's home close by the sea.

Canoe-building remains the same today. Using an ax, a comparably sized adze, and, particularly for finishing, a small and short-handled scoop adze, the craftsman goes about smoothing the hull inside and out and shaping the unique cutwater that slopes from the "keel" upward and back so that the most forward bow point will be below water. A typical canoe at this stage is twenty-four feet long and has a maximum width of twenty inches.

Propped upright with sticks, it is then half filled with water and rocks and left to soak for some days. Bow and stern may be tightly bound up to prevent their splitting. A few feet back from the dugout shell a series of fires are kindled on the ground along each side. Water-soaked and now heated, the canoe opens up, as Taylor said, "like a flower in the sun."

When the spreading sides are stretched farther apart by rigid cross-pieces, the canoe may measure at the beam up to three and a half feet. Braces are fitted to strengthen the new interior hull lines. Planks to raise the sides are hewn along one edge to fit the now gently curving gunwales. The rise of the plank at center may be fifteen inches but at bow and stern only half that. Forward, these bulwarks fit into a triangular cedar block about ten inches high. Together with the ram-like projecting cutwater below, this *noeud* gives the Carib canoe bow a thoroughly distinct character.

More wooden braces are fitted inside the hull after the sides are raised, and caulking made of straw or cotton lint mixed with shark oil and tree gum is squeezed into every seam. Although increasingly canoes are powered by outboard motors, two masts with lugsails usually complete the modern Carib dugout. If work progresses steadily it can be ready for launching three weeks from the time the tree is cut.

The modern dugout, or *gommier* as it is called today, is a fisherman's boat. Caribs of the Dominica Reserve still rely heavily on their canoe fishery and they also sell great numbers of these vessels to fishermen of nearby Martinique, Guadeloupe, and St. Lucia. The *gommier*, it is said, also serves sometimes as a carrier for bottled goods in inter-island trade accomplished without the blessing of customs agents.

Wherever there was navigable water there were dugouts, but one Panama account in this period reported the making of bark canoes, probably of the "woodskin" type familiar in tropical South America. This is a craft of simple sheath construction, with minimal reinforcing and a bow and stern closed by pleating and sewing the single sheet of bark. Among the Chiriqui of the Pacific slope an English traveller, John Cockburn, was ferried in such a canoe thirty feet long. Paddlers remained standing. The women, he said, were responsible for portaging between streams: "I have seen a woman carry one on her head with two children in it besides a good deal of luggage."

Along much of the Caribbean coast below Mexico, the seagoing dugout has a rounded bottom and is called a *dory*, the same term later applied to small fishing boats in the cold waters from Newfoundland to Massachusetts. A dugout made from a single log, it is perhaps misleading that some ethnologists have called it a keeled canoe. On the other hand, the dory, as modified by Europeans and Africans, came to have a well defined "keel" ridge along its bottom, a feature that serves to stabilize the vessel in open water where wind and current provide problems that small boats do not encounter in sheltered river travel.

The larger latter-day dory may be reinforced with half-ribs or knees. When its sides are raised by adding planks, the fitting is so smoothly done that the join is not readily apparent after painting. On the coast and among the Bay Islands of Honduras, the large dory may be partially decked and have an enclosed cabin. It is steered with a tiller and is usually powered by an inboard gasoline engine. Whatever its size, the dory with rounded bottom is decidedly easier to handle and quicker to respond than a flat-bottomed dugout.

The *cayuca* is the small version, a round-bottomed dugout for one or two persons. It needs no ribs. The craft is pointed bow and stern, but while the bow has a rising line, the sharp stern may be cut vertically, particularly if it is to carry mast and sail. Cayucas have commonly been used on lagoons and river estuaries and the Cuna Indians use them among the San Blas Islands off the lower Panama coast. For steering under sail a single paddle, often with a lance blade, is used.

The *pirogua* or *piragua* of the Panama area differs from the cayuca in being truncated, with a platform bow and stern where the pole men stand. Probably the most common of dugouts is the *pitpan*, a flat-bottomed canoe used everywhere on inland waters. It is long and narrow and its thick, flat bottom makes it the indestructible workhorse on rock-strewn shallow rivers. The pitpan is usually tapered slightly towards each end, but bow and stern, as a rule, are cut almost square. A flat deck or platform area extends at bow and stern, each just large enough for one person to stand and wield his push pole. Paddles are carried for use in deep water. Pitpan is the regional English term, while *pipante* is the Spanish. Each derives from the Mosquito word *pitban*, whose original meaning suggests a plaited product. Tradition has it that the Mosquito people once made little boats of tightly plaited withes, covering them with a thin layer of clay.

Among the Spanish colonials the largest dugout used on lake or river was called a *panga*. The English turned the word into *bongo*. For their length they were generally wide in the beam, with a narrow deck at the stern for the steersman. Usually flat-bottomed, they were dugouts pure and simple or dugouts built up with planks to make a vessel capable of carrying up to ten tons of cargo. Either paddles or oars were used, as well as sails, and generally there was a shelter aft called a *chopa*, covered with palm thatch, boards, or hides. A regular *panga* route was the trip from the upper end of Lake Nicaragua, then down the San Juan River to the Caribbean coast. In the nineteenth century the round trip, about 350 miles, took twenty to thirty days.

Still another cargo dugout, used on the Mosquito coast rivers, was the *bateau*, built by cutting a large pitpan lengthwise into equal halves. Flat bottom boards were inserted, the two halves rejoined, and then further planks used to raise the sides. The average bateau had six paddlers and carried two and a half tons. Others, up to sixty feet in length, were capable of freight loads up to five tons.

In present-day Panama the shallow-draft, flat-bottomed piragua still requires push-pole power on the shoaling stretches of jungle rivers. In deeper water, and for those who can afford them, outboard motors are well suited to the unmodified traditional dugout. In the lower picture the cayuca, as modified for marine use by the Cuna people, is shorter in length, wider in the beam, and rounded in the hull, with a sharp cutwater and a rising and flaring bow and stern. Cuna women transport fresh water in calabashes from the Panama mainland to their San Blas Island homes.

In the Gulf of Honduras the smallest round-bottomed dugout is today called a paddle dory. The larger dories are used in trade service between the mainland and the Gulf Islands. They have cabins, are driven by gasoline engines of eight to twelve horsepower, and travel at six to eight knots. A *creer* is a dory with a sail, but with the introduction of gasoline engines it has all but disappeared.

The old tales of extremely large dugouts become entirely credible when one reads reports of the timber resources before major exploitation. Mahogany, for which this coast became so well known, was a popular and durable wood for dugout-making. Writing in 1855, an American traveller, R. G. Squier, reported mahogany timbers measuring five and a half feet "in the square." He saw cedar eighty feet high and seven feet thick. The ceiba or silk-cotton tree was used to make the largest river dugouts, and he assured readers that he had seen boats hollowed from single trunks that were seven feet across.

While Spanish communities were built looking out on the Pacific, British traders and travellers for many years found fortune and adventure on the humid eastern coast of Nicaragua and Honduras. British planters and mahogany-cutters adopted the Indian canoe, although their black slaves did the paddling. And Captain George Henderson noted in the early years of the nineteenth century that canoes figured in Christmas activities:

Hewn from the mainland hardwood called tibruce, *the finely shaped dory of the Belize coast is speedy and stable in practiced hands. In the beach shallows of Cay Caulker, Peter Young poles homeward with a load of conch, the region's most highly regarded shellfish. The moored dory will carry a greater load under pole, sail, or outboard-motor power, but, by contrast, it is more a trough than a boat.*

At this season water-sports are also common, and *Dory-racing* affords a very general amusement; and on these occasions large sums are freely betted both by owners and slaves. This species of diversion has no small share of utility attached to it, as it contributes to render the latter highly expert in a kind of exercise that is inseparably connected with the labour in which they are principally engaged.

To visit mahogany-cutting operations in the interior, Henderson was transported by pitpan, the only feasible vehicle, and was pleased at measures taken for passenger comfort: "They are commonly furnished with capacious awnings, hung round with curtains to defend the passenger from the sun by day and the dews by night."

A retired British soldier, George Byam was a tourist who travelled in a large dugout from the Spanish town of Granada, at the northern end of Lake Nicaragua, under sail across its shark-infested waters and thence under oar down the San Juan River to the Caribbean. The "piragua" was about forty feet long and eight feet across, and each side was raised by two planks. Seated on five thwarts, each of ten men pulled an oar, a blade more practicable than a paddle in a vessel whose sides probably rose high above water level. "A respectable-looking patron," wrote Byam, looked after the steering and the ten Indians at the oars were dressed all in white with red sashes. Out of sight of Granada they "stripped themselves perfectly naked, and remained so day and night until about a mile before our arrival at the sea-coast, when they again put on the trowsers and shirts."

Carrying such appealing exchange goods as fishhooks, glass beads, and small looking-glasses, Orlando Roberts first brought his trading brig to the lower Panama coast in 1816. What he most keenly wanted was fustic, and Indians from all along the coast began coming to his base with dugouts loaded with wood from this tree, greatly in demand in Europe as a yellow dye agent. Larger dugouts, he reported, carried as much as five tons.

The enterprising Roberts also fitted out two large dugouts to cruise the coastline, seeking tortoise shell and cocoa for the British market. He purchased three Indian canoes in Chiriqui Lagoon, near the present Costa Rica border, and loaded them with European goods for a tortuous upriver trading trip. His Indian paddlers travelled in the cool of the morning and again late in the day and reserved their clothing to don just before reaching a principal destination.

Trading with the Mosquito Indians of the Nicaragua coast, he learned that the Woolwa and Dongula tribes were canoe-manufacturers whose territory extended along the upper reaches of the Bluefields River. Roberts, who never did properly distinguish between different dugout forms, referred to "canoes, dories and pitpans, which these tribes bring down the river roughly formed or blocked out, and they are afterwards finished and decorated for sale." Coastal middlemen paid for the unfinished dugouts with old axes, adzes, beads, and other items acquired from traders like Roberts, who recorded his favorable impressions of the finished products: "I found that those of mahogany are best for working to windward under a press of sail; but that those of cedar are more buoyant, and do not sink even when full of water and partly loaded."

When a customer on the coast ordered a large canoe, the business arrangements between client and builder were meticulous: "The contract is made by giving the Indian with whom they agree, a piece of twine or packthread, on which is marked, by knots, the length, breadth, and depth of the vessel wanted: The Indian is at the same time furnished in advance, with two or three axes, adzes, and other articles, to the value of about one fourth of the price agreed upon." The client kept a duplicate of the dimensions record as well as another string with knots in it, corresponding to the number of days required to complete the canoe. He untied one each day and when the string was free of knots he could be certain the builder would that day deliver his canoe.

As a Spanish prisoner for a short time, Roberts travelled up the San Juan River to Lake Nicaragua. The vessel, a *bongo*, was similar to that described by Byam. Even on the San Juan, a river without major obstructions, such large vessels, carrying up to sixteen tons of cargo, encountered difficulties. The current occasionally was such that the full crew at their oars could scarce stem it, and in the treacherous mud of the river banks, with lurking alligators a constant danger, tracking the big dugout upstream with tow ropes was a disquieting experience.

Orlando Roberts' experience at dory sailing with a crew of Mosquito Indians left him with high regard both for the sailors and for their marine dugouts. They were caught in a wild gale among the Bay Islands, unable to hold a course, their rigging fouled. The mast down, they struggled to raise it again and then shipped such a sea as "must have sent any ordinary boat to the bottom." Most of the Indians went over the side to lighten the boat. The others were immediately bailing, using their hats, calabashes, whatever would serve. "We kept the boat before the swell, the men overboard held by the gunnels until we were ready to readmit them, and they again made sail with as much fearless alacrity as if nothing unusual had occurred."

When Samuel A. Bard, a footloose American painter, reached the Mosquito "capital" of Bluefields in midcentury, his first outing was to attend a funeral. Spanish travellers had observed that Indians in Honduras covered the dead with a canoe, and Bard found in Nicaragua that a pitpan had been cut in two and the body placed in one half. Mourning women circled the dugout bier in a "tread-mill step" until interrupted by the sudden appearance of four disguised, painted men. They rushed into the center of the group, fastened a rope to the half pitpan holding the corpse, and hurried into the heavy woods, dragging it like a sledge. Mourners, musicians, and the curious visitor followed.

33

In a small clearing the canoe coffin was placed in a shallow trench and the other half was placed over it. The grave was filled quickly by the four painted men and a tiny hut of sticks and palm branches as quickly put together above it. An earthen vessel of water was left in the hut, and the dead man's turtle spear thrust into the ground beside his grave. The funeral ceremony concluded, the painted men ran to the river to purify themselves.

With two Indian friends, Bard purchased a dugout and went exploring and camping among the cays and on the rivers of the coast. He joined the natives for night fishing with torch and spear and went aboard their larger canoes for a turtle hunt: "Although the sea was comparatively smooth, yet the boats all carried such an amount of sail as to keep me in a state of constant nervousness." Though alarmed, he had to concede that the Mosquito men rode the waves like gulls. "If upset, they right their boats in a moment, and with their broad paddle-blades clear them of water in an incredibly short space of time."

While visiting a Towka Indian village, Bard and his friends joined in the celebration to mark the coming of age and the marriage of a young tribesman. The author noted that the punch bowl was ready: "The event had been anticipated by the preparation of a canoe full of palm-wine, mixed with crushed plantains, and a little honey, which had been fermenting, to the utter disgust of my nostrils, from the day of my arrival." The canoe was dragged to the edge of the dance circle and the surface of the liquor was covered with small white calabashes the size of coffee cups. The queasy traveller never did raise a calabash to his lips but he made a sketch when the party was over. The brew was gone, the canoe was overturned, and the empty calabashes littered the circle where the dancers had swayed and shuffled.

In the eighteenth century, British adventurers considered the Honduran coast pretty much their own. In 1735, according to the traveller John Atkins, five hundred merchants and slaves worked at logwood-cutting on one river emptying into the Bay of Honduras, using "canoos" to carry the raw dye material to their base camp. Dugouts were the only means of transport when the same brash enterprisers, many of them buccaneers turned respectable, began to exploit the rich mahogany stands along those same rivers.

The complex, sinuous shaping evolved to adapt the hull to demanding marine conditions is displayed in these splendidly sculpted Cuna cayucas. The mast seating block and the gunwale blocks to support seats for passengers and paddlers are integral with the dugout.

34

On the San Blas Islands, just off Panama's Caribbean mainland, the Cuna people use log rollers to beach and launch the cayucas on which they depend for fishing, transportation, trade, and communication, and even for procuring their fresh-water supplies. A mainsail and jib are standard equipment for many of the vessels.

Some students speculate that Cuna sailors who worked aboard European ships came home with experience and ideas that helped to change the old dugout lines. Whatever the model or inspiration, the need for seaworthiness dictated specific changes. The dugout had to be made deeper and wider in the beam. Instead of truncated ends, the new canoe evolved with pointed, flaring bow and stern, each raised higher than the gunwale line to reduce the wash taken aboard in a brisk sea. The flattened poling platforms disappeared because poles are of no use in deep water. The present-day cayuca, as the Cuna dugout is known, suggests little of the old river-canoe character. It moves under paddle or wind power, often carrying a jib as well as a mainsail.

These island Indians bathe and swim frequently and their children are entirely at home in the water. Tiny canoes are among their first toys, and children of five and six are already capable paddlers. While visiting mainland Cuna in the seventeenth century, Lionel Wafer noted that immediately after birth a child and its mother were taken to be washed in a mountain stream. A clearly related purification ritual, one that may have developed with increasing dependence on the canoe, has often been reported among the island Cuna. In a maternity house, the mother gives birth in a hammock and the baby is lowered immediately to be bathed in a water-filled canoe set below the hammock. Most modern Cuna are island people, dependent on cayucas for inter-island transport and mainland trade. A minority remaining in the mainland interior still use a narrow dugout with a flattened "deck" platform at bow and stern. Even among the river dwellers, however, instead of being truncated like those of old, many of their dugouts have pointed ends like those of their offshore kin.

All over Central America there are people who yet depend for transport on the canoe. Fishermen on each salt coast continue to cast their lines and nets from log dugouts. The great long coastal runs made by Indian vessels before the Europeans came are forgotten, but some few merchants can still be found carrying present-day wares and produce upriver by canoe.

Among the San Blas Islands, just off Panama's Caribbean coast, there lives a group of people today who seem unlikely to relinquish the dugout canoe for a long time to come. The Cuna Indians are a federation of surviving tribes which, since the coming of the first Europeans, have resisted the intrusions of outsiders. In earlier times they lived on the mainland and travelled the rivers of the interior in canoes probably of the style that still survives there—long and narrow with undercut bow and stern. With the arrival of the Spaniards, the people from whom today's Cuna descend drifted towards the Caribbean shore. Salt-water experience, however, made apparent the shortcomings of the riverine canoe. If they were to paddle on the sea they would have to modify their dugout design to meet its challenges.

35

(OPPOSITE) *On the Cuban coast, Columbus reported seeing a large Arawakan canoe sheltered in a boathouse of palm thatching over a wooden frame. What he called a ramada has a modern counterpart in this cane-and-palm-leaf housing for Cuna canoes on a San Blas beach.*

(THIS PAGE) *Dories of about twenty feet, deep in the hull and with rounded bottoms, are used in great numbers by fishermen in the relatively shallow waters inside the reef that skirts the Belize shore. Tiny dories, nested on the decks of larger fishing boats, are carried as tenders, while among the Bay Islands off Honduras larger dories with inboard engines do all-purpose workhorse duty.*

38 *A stylized map of the city of Tenochtitlán accompanied letters sent by Hernan Cortés to Charles V, describing the wondrous Mexican lands he had won for the Spanish crown. The importance of the* acalli, *the dugout of the Aztec lake country, is emphasized by the numbers represented on the waters surrounding the city. In the upper section are waterfowl nets tended by canoe crews.*

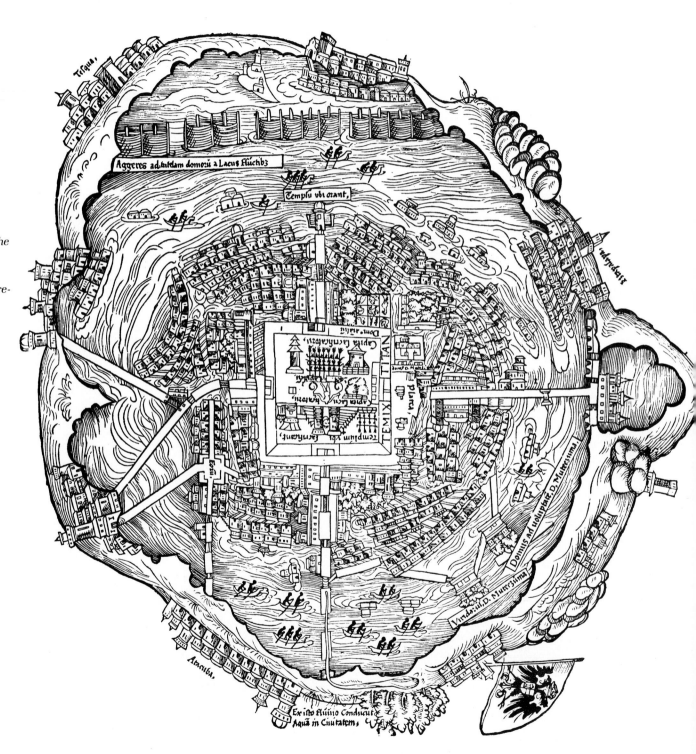

Mexico of the Aztecs

IN THE MILE-HIGH Valley of Mexico, protected by volcanic mountain ranges midway between oceans east and west, there flourished what may have been the world's most splendid city in the fifteenth century. Located in the center of today's sprawling Mexico City, Tenochtitlan was a proud city state, a community of gleaming carved-stone buildings set on an island in a lake and laced by a network of canals. Every citizen moved about by dugout canoe.

Just two hundred years before the arrival of the Spaniards in 1519, there had been no Tenochtitlan. Before that time a number of independent city states had developed along the shores of the valley lake system. The climate was moderate, the hillsides were heavily forested, and the surrounding fertile lands had been developed by valley farmers. When a band of poor relations arrived they were not warmly welcomed. Wanderers for many years, they had come from the northwest, from a homeland called Aztlan — Land of Herons — from which they were to take the name Aztec. It had been a home, according to legend, where a happy people tended their gardens in canoes.

Although the valley people shared with the Aztecs a culture and a language, they thought the latecomers a mob of rude barbarians. Despite a chilly reception, the uncouth arrivals, hardy and disciplined, were not to be put off. Their principal god had led them here; this valley was their promised land. In the largest of the lakes was a swampy bit of island that no other group thought worth claiming, and on this damp foothold the Aztecs began about 1325 to build a city.

A farming technique already familiar in this region was the means of establishing a town foundation. They built *chinampas*, floating gardens, by matting together dead trees, branches, and reeds into crude rafts and covering these with mud and decayed material dug from the lake bottom. Food crops planted in the rich soil of the securely moored rafts provided two harvests each year, and with repeated supplements of lake muck the rafts settled to become firm land. As the plots were extended, narrow channels for canoe passage were left to separate them and provide access for the farmers.

The boat of the valley was a dugout, in the Nahuatl language an *acalli*, "house on the water." It was the vehicle with which the Aztecs built their community, retrieving refuse and lake mud to extend the *chinampas*, carrying away any kind of land fill they could acquire from the mainland. The pattern of farm fields separated by canals became the pattern for the town as, rock by rock, rectangular plot by plot, firm land rose from the lake to become a camp, a village, and at length a city.

Its citizens hired out as mercenary soldiers to one or another of the neighboring cities involved in local disputes, but, as their city grew, so grew their own position and strength. Within an incredibly few years Tenochtitlan became the foremost city of the valley and its builders came to dominate an empire. By battle and by weight of fearsome reputation, its armies subdued peoples and regions far beyond the immediate valley, and while the Aztecs did not set out to actually govern their subjects, they did levy specified, periodic taxes.

From most communities in what is now central Mexico, the levy came in the form of agricultural produce, game and fish foods, timber, and all variety of mineral and manufactured goods. It was the steady flow of tribute, carried overland on the backs of porters and over water in dugout canoes, that made Tenochtitlan wealthy. Continuous warfare became basic to the support of a state religion which demanded a constantly increasing number of human captives to be sacrificed to its bloodthirsty gods. One of the few gods opposed to such sacrifices was Quetzalcoatl, who, among other attributes, was understood to have invented the canoe and taught his people to use it.

Tenochtitlan was connected to the mainland by three causeways, each several miles long, while throughways within the city consisted of canals bordered by footpaths. Thousands of homes were built along the canals, many having a special entry way for canoes. If a comparison is to be made, early descriptions of that city suggest that it is Europe's Venice that might be regarded as an Old World Tenochtitlán.

In a diversified economy, woodworking was highly developed, and distinct groups of workers pursued the separate trades of lumbering, carpentering, and sculpting. Timber and canoes came to the city by the tribute-payment system. At Xochimilco, today a Mexico City suburb where all sorts of small vessels still ply the canals, a single craftsman required a week to complete the average dugout. At the time of the Spanish conquest in 1521 there may have been as many as 50,000 canoes in the Aztec city and perhaps 200,000 altogether on the lakes and canals of the valley.

The spruce called *huiymetl* was the wood most frequently used for all kinds of construction, including canoe-making. Logs were hewed smooth after felling and then dragged by ropes down the mountain sides. Displacing stone-age tools, copper axes, hatchets, and adzes were the principal implements of the lumber trade and of canoe-manufacturing. Evidently the copper came from the mountains of Michoacán, the Tarascan country to the west, and copper axes were among the tribute payments made regularly by some towns. The outline of a copper adze is part of the glyph, the ancient picture symbol, which represents the little town of Tepotzlán in the mountains just south of the valley. The metal heads were bound to curved wooden handles and in old hieroglyphic tribute lists they were painted conventionally in yellow to indicate they were made of copper.

Among the old codices, the painted picture books of the Indians, canoes appear with slightly upturned ends. Their small scale suggests that one person, standing, could propel the craft with his shovel-shaped paddle. Conquest period records refer to dugouts up to fifty feet long being used by warriors in battle, for large cargo transport, and as gala canoes for royalty and nobility. In the *Lienzo de Tlaxcala*, an Indian document from the sixteenth century, there appears a ceremonial canoe with a raised bow carved to represent an eagle's head. While the utility canoe was the simplest of craft, about fourteen feet long, the canoe of the aristocrat was a distinguished vehicle. Moctezuma's canoe was in every respect a royal barge, for Cortés said that it was fitted with a throne and covered with a rich and decorative canopy.

40

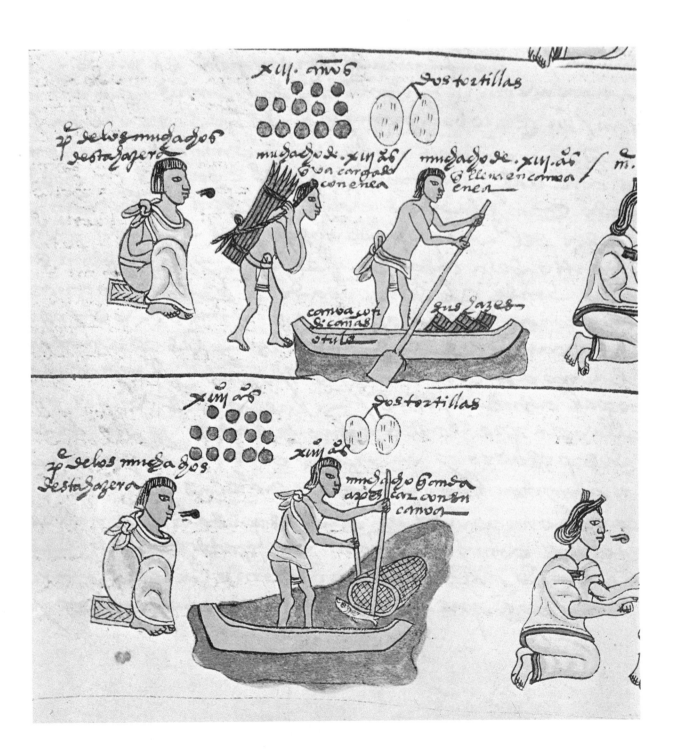

(LEFT & ABOVE) *In the* Lienzo de Tlaxcala, *a mid-sixteenth-century pictographic document, an Indian artist represented the Aztec capital by an encircled temple symbol, surrounded by canoe-borne warrior defenders. The Spanish invaders with their Indian allies are represented occupying mainland towns in the highland Valley of Mexico. From the same source, a canoe with a carved eagle-head bow is without doubt an aristocrat's vessel. It contains a paddle and what is probably an ax.*

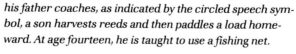

(OPPOSITE) *From what is now called the* Codex Mendoza, *a traditional painted book prepared by an Aztec artist for New Spain's first viceroy, early-sixteenth-century pictures illustrate the training of Indian boys in canoe use. The blue dots indicate the proper age for certain instruction. While*

his father coaches, as indicated by the circled speech symbol, a son harvests reeds and then paddles a load homeward. At age fourteen, he is taught to use a fishing net.

In the mid-sixteenth century, Indian artists prepared a rich variety of illustrations for Bernardino de Sahagún's descriptive work on the life-style of the Aztec people, Historia general de Nueva España. *Among them is a sketch of an* acalli *with two paddlers blowing conch horns, participating probably in some religious ceremony. In another of this series of pictures, now known as the Codex Florentino, a sculptor works with a copper chisel and a woodsman wields a tempered copper ax. These tools were also used in making dugout canoes. The highly stylized illustration at the left represents an attack by warriors in canoes on an island city. From the* Codex Nuttall, *it is a Mixtec pictograph from the period before the Spaniards arrived.*

The city could not have existed without a steady supply of foodstuffs from other parts of the valley. With its own grid system of canal streets, and water links to all the neighboring communities, the delivery by canoe of mountains of fresh produce was a simple matter. Great numbers of fishermen in canoes supplied the city markets. The duck hunters strung long nets just above the lake surface to trap waterfowl in flight. Ducks by the thousands descended on the marsh lands and many of them were sent quickly on, via canoe, to the cooking fires of the towns.

When in 1519 travel-worn Spanish soldiers were led by Hernan Cortés from the Gulf coast across rugged mountains to the lake-lapped Valley of Mexico, they found a gleaming and vigorous city, a wondrous island capital that they could scarcely credit. Lavish gifts of elaborate feather-work, brilliantly colored mantles, and exquisitely worked figures in gold had been sent to Cortés by Moctezuma, the Aztec ruler. Even so, they were stunned by the great size and splendor of the Aztec capital.

The Spanish were later shocked and repelled by the Aztecs' barbaric rituals, but they were reduced to wonderment by the many tall and richly carved pyramidal temples, the extensive flower gardens, the handsome stone-built palaces, the evidence everywhere of advanced engineering skill. Europeans had sailed westward initially to seek the riches of the Orient; when this ragged party of adventurers gazed upon the capital of the Mexican Indians, they could scarcely have been more impressed had they actually reached the palaces of Cathay. Cortes described the city they entered:

Its streets (I speak of the principal ones) are very broad and straight, some of these, and all the others, are one half land and the other half water on which they go about in canoes. All the streets have openings at regular intervals, to let the water flow from one to the other, and at all these openings, some of which are very broad, there are bridges, very large, strong, and well constructed, so that, over many, ten horsemen can ride abreast.

Vivid recollections that rank with the best of old soldiers' tales of any period were left by Bernal Díaz del Castillo, a veteran sergeant in the campaign. From atop the principal temple pyramid in the heart of the city, Díaz watched a multitude of canoes delivering food supplies and other merchandise. The city seemed to him built for amphibious living and he noted that residents went from house to house in their canoes. Canoe transport, according to Cortes, was regulated by taxation: "wherever the canoes are unloaded, which is where the greatest quantity of provisions enter the city, there are guards, in huts, to collect a *certum quid* of everything that comes in."

Cortes wrote of the twin masonry conduits built along one of the causeways to bring spring water from mainland Chapultepec to Tenochtitlan:

Conduits as large round as an ox's body bring the fresh water across the bridges...and everybody has water to drink. Canoes peddle the water through all the streets, and the way they take it from the conduits is this: the canoes stop under the bridges where the conduits cross, where men are stationed on the top who are paid to fill them.

The markets of the city were the greatest cause of amazement to the visitors. The Mexican capital had a population of about 300,000, making it a larger city than any in Europe at the time. Each quarter of the city had its own market, but the market of the Tlatelolco quarter was the greatest and most varied of all. Moctezuma himself led Cortes to inspect the wonders of this great plaza where every kind of produce and manufacture from the empire was offered. Most merchandise came directly to market by canoe, for one paddler in a dugout could transport appreciably more than several porters.

Bernal Díaz listed produce and merchandise that he recognized and guessed at other goods exotic to his experience. He persisted with his very thorough description, even to the least delicate, and concluded by reporting that human excrement could be purchased by the canoe-load. Díaz explained that it was used by leather-workers for tanning and that the loaded canoes were moored some little distance off from the marketplace. Urine too was recycled. Householders stored it in pottery jars until it was collected by canoe crews for eventual use as a dye mordant. Along canals and causeways public privies were built and the accumulated wastes were removed by canoe to be used as fertilizer. Compared to contemporary European cities, Tenochtitlan must have been the very model of an hygienic community.

For Cortes, diplomacy—even duplicity—was essential to his successful leadership in dealing with his own nine hundred men as well as with the Mexican Indian groups. Earlier he had won to his side the Aztecs' most bitter enemies and his key to success would continue to be the playing of one American people against another. During the protracted stay in Tenochtitlan, however, the balance between loot-hungry Spaniards and resentful Indian hosts became increasingly unstable. Taking Moctezuma hostage was a bold and desperate move by Cortés but the Aztecs immediately chose a new leader, one who had no illusions as to Cortés's intentions.

Moctezuma was a casualty of the first confrontation and the Spanish were forced to make a disastrous retreat from the city. Aztec forces destroyed bridges along the causeway route, and during floundering struggles in the water gaps Spanish prisoners were carried away by canoe for sacrifice at the war god's temple. Horrified survivors, on reaching the mainland, rallied with their Indian allies from Tlaxcala and together they moved off to the latter's stronghold, about a hundred miles to the east. It was midsummer, 1520.

The invaders did not return to the valley until the following spring but they came well prepared. Although the Spanish were numbered only in hundreds, their horses and guns gave them great advantage. The bulk of the attacking force, however, was the army of the Tlaxcalans, a people who refused to pay tribute tax to Tenochtitlan. Records left by Cortes, by Díaz del Castillo, and by Indians on each side in the struggle contribute to the story of a battle encounter that was surely the most significant ever fought between forces of the New World and the Old.

Some of the cities along the lake shores resisted; some joined the Spanish. But Tenochtitlán was an island citadel and Aztec warriors in battle canoes controlled the waters. They carried circular shields and their arms were barbed darts, lances, and awesome sword-clubs, mounted with sharp obsidian blades. Huge numbers of canoes gave the Aztec forces tremendous mobility; they could land troops for a lightning raid and withdraw them quickly. In the southeast of the lake system they used 2,000 canoes to land 20,000 fighters for a savage assault at the town of Chalco. When the Spanish cut the aqueduct that supplied Tenochtitlan, canoe carriers in the early phase of the siege were able to bring sufficient water, and food as well, from the mainland.

It was a standoff until the attackers brought, overland and in sections, thirteen brigantines that Cortés had had built during the recuperation in Tlaxcala. Rigged for sail and oar power and each just big enough to carry a small field gun, they were completed and launched for assault. When they sailed out on Lake Texcoco, some five hundred Aztec canoes came to meet them and waited just beyond effective gun range. When a favorable wind arose the brigantines flew to the attack, sails billowing, and in each of them twelve men straining at the oars. The Aztec navy couldn't match the speed and many canoes were crushed and others overturned when the forces met. Warriors were killed and drowned in great numbers and the brigantines pursued the survivors until they gained shelter and safety within the island city's canals. A simultaneous assault led by horsemen gained a foothold on one of the great causeways that led to the city, and with help from the brigantines, soldiers were able to struggle across those gaps where the defenders had destroyed the bridges. By night the fighters in canoes attacked furiously along each side of the causeway. By day the brigantines controlled the lake on one side of the causeway, but on the other the water could scarcely be seen for hostile canoes.

For a week there was one brutal encounter after another, but with the breaching of the first causeway the brigantines moved through to reduce the canoe navy threat over much of the main lake. The defenders fortified some areas by mounting sharpened stakes below the water surface, effectively denying the brigantines a close approach to long stretches of the causeways. Using provision canoes as bait in ambush, they badly mauled the crews of two Spanish boats and carried one of them off. When attackers floundered into pits dug in the water shallows they found Aztec canoes bearing down immediately upon them. The Aztec warriors defended their city with fury, asked no quarter for themselves, and sent a steady supply of prisoners to the priests wielding bloody sacrificial blades.

Brigantine attacks were pressed again and again so that the hostile paddlers had to flee more frequently into the city canals. In time the brigantine blockade cut off entirely their food and water supplies. The siege turned into a bitter house-to-house fight and the Spanish set about to destroy totally the once magnificent city. At the end of three months the stubborn defence collapsed. Cuauhtemoc, the Aztec leader who had replaced Moctezuma, was captured. A civilization lay in ruins. Over the shards and shambles a new but very different city was built. It was baroque and European and was the colonial headquarters for the conquerors. This Mexico City had dry paved streets and its citizens travelled in wheeled carriages rather than gala canoes. Even the lakes were gradually drained, although some canal passages continued in use.

Spanish settlers who flocked in came to dominate the city's commercial life, but Indians went on running the canoe transport system that carried the great bulk of the agricultural produce from the southern valley area around Chalco and Xochimilco into the city center. The route was preserved and used until the early years of the present century, a six- to eight-hour passage across the shallow southern lakes and then through the Viga Canal, to bring fresh produce directly to the main plaza and market of Mexico City. Dugouts of from fourteen to fifty feet in length moved silently along that canal by night and at dawn landed fresh tomatoes, melons, in fact every kind of fruit and vegetable, at the great marketplace.

As in pre-conquest times, a canal-watcher might have seen almost any portable goods delivered by canoe. Stone, lime, and brick for construction were familiar cargoes for dugouts, and great supplies of fresh flowers, lavishly displayed in the old Aztec and the modern Mexican markets, transformed the supply canoes into brilliant festival floats. One vessel could carry up to 70 *fanegas* of maize, and in the harvest season in the seventeenth century the dugout fleet moved about 5,000 *fanegas* each week from the Chalco docks to the city market. (The Spanish *fanega* is equal to about one and a half bushels.) In 1710 over 155,000 *fanegas* of corn were brought in, representing more than 3,400 canoe-loads. Canoe fishermen remained important food suppliers for a time, and in the early seventeenth century they were landing over a million fish each year from the southern lakes. The catch decreased as lake waters were lowered, but the waterfowl harvest was important to the market into the present century. The ancient bird-nets, tended by canoemen, were reported still in use by a few hunters as late as 1940.

45

Salen huyendo Guavtemoc
vltimo Rey de mexico. con la suyos
en canoas en que llauavan oro y
plata y demas Joyas. danles al=
canse los vergantines. y prenden=
lo a ora de visperas de S. Hypo=
lito. con que se conchuyo el Cerco
de Mexico en nombre de su
Mage[st]
Guavtemoc Reyde Mex.___ 1
Bergantin que te alcaço ___ 2
Canoas de oro yplata ____ 3
Carrisalar _____ 4
Indios que yban huyendo __ 5

47

The most momentous single struggle ever between native
Americans and invading Europeans was the siege of
Tenochtitlán in 1521, in which battle canoes played the
most vital defensive role. To match the Indian navy, the
Spaniards built brigantines, each carrying one small artil-
lery piece. Even so, it was only after three months of fighting, with the almost total destruction of their splendid city
and facing starvation, that the Aztecs submitted. The
painting of the capture of Cuauhtemoc, the Aztec leader,
by brigantine crews was done in Europe possibly a hundred years or more after the event; as a kind of formal
statement, like many paintings of the period, it is not
entirely unconvincing in its treatment, but the canoes in
the foreground suggest that the painter may have taken
some inspiration from the Caribbean illustrations published in histories by Oviedo and Benzoni.

In suburban Mexico City, the "floating gardens" district of Xochimilco has long been a popular Sunday resort. While weekend holidayers and tourists tour the canal network in the punts sometimes called canoas, *flower-sellers still dart about the waters in their tiny board canoes. In 1968 the canoeing events of the Olympic Games were staged on a specially built paddling course, close by the ancient* chinampa *canals.*

The dugout survived for many years as the familiar workhorse of the waterways, although it was later supplemented by the simple plank-built boat, a craft that confusingly was also called a *canoa.* The Spanish had brought the term from the Caribbean and applied it to the Aztec dugout and later to larger punt-like boats used in ferry service on the shrinking lakes. Today in the southern suburb of Xochimilco, utility craft like punts are called *trajineras*; they transport fruit, vegetables, hay, and even livestock on the canal system surviving there. But the real tradition of the old Aztec *acalli* lives on in the narrow, sharply pointed board canoes built to hold one person. On Sundays, when city people and tourists together flock to this park-like gardening quarter, they are taken on large canopy-covered punts to cruise for an hour or two along narrow *chinampa* canals like those of the former Aztec capital. Darting among them are floating flower stalls, each a tiny canoe holding a woman who is paddler and peddler too, offering for a few pesos nosegays of violets and gardenias.

Just two hundred miles west of the throbbing modern city that has replaced the Aztecs' Tenochtitlán, there remains an Indian people who preserve to a degree the way of life they once shared with the peoples of the Valley of Mexico. The Tarascans, who were never subjugated by the Aztecs, live, as they did then, in the region centered by Lake Pátzcuaro, in the state of Michoacán. Indian villages and the ancient capital of Tzintzuntzan — Place of the Hummingbirds, as well as the colonial town of Pátzcuaro, lie on the rim of the shallow, elbow-shaped lake which is little more than ten miles in length. In earlier times fishing was as important as maize culture. With greatly reduced catches in recent times, it is difficult to make a living from the green lake waters but, in a land where marginal living is normal for many, fishing with nets for the minnow-like *charales* and translucent whitefish goes on.

The fishing boats today are the same flat-bottomed canoes used before the Spaniards came. Hewn from pine trunks in nearby mountain villages, Tarascan canoes are angular, almost box-like, with sides that slope inwards as they rise so that the flat bottom is slightly wider than the span between the gunwales. Awkward though they appear, the Lake Pátzcuaro canoes move with surprising speed, propelled by distinctive Tarascan

The unmistakable Tarascan paddle is well suited to the shallow, weedy waters of Lake Pátzcuaro. The raised, projecting stern of the dugout reflects a feature familiar in earlier inland canoes in many parts of the continent.

paddles which resemble ping-pong bats with long handles. This dugout is as stable as a barge, an important quality whether in the one-man model, traditionally used for fishing with the wide *mariposa* net, or in the larger, longer canoe that carries an active crew to manage a net hundreds of feet long. The distinctive paddle is well suited to local conditions. The circular blade, a foot at most in diameter, is dipped only so far as to avoid entanglement with the heavy water-weed growth in the lake. Illustrations from the earliest surviving record of Tarascan life show that the modern carved canoe and its unique paddle are identical to those of the sixteenth century.

Tarascan villages lie on the mountain sides and all about the lake rim and on the islands that rise from its surface like smudged blue-green stepping-stones. Inhabitants from every village meet each week at the regular marketplaces, each of them carrying the products of their trades or crafts. Potters display fired clay kitchen wares. Farm women sit with heaps of corn and beans

and tomatoes. The woodworkers have furniture and guitars to sell. The fishermen bring their lake catch and mountain woodsmen bring bundles of firewood. And the metal-workers, descendants of those who once made copper axes for distant trade, show hammered-copper cooking pots. The Sunday market in the lakeside village of Erongarícuaro is one where the barter system is still familiar. Shore people and islanders crowd the landing place with their heavy dugouts. The wives of fishermen, from islands long since stripped of trees, exchange *charales* for firewood from the high sierra country. By noon the big canoes that came in at sunrise with cargoes of fish are reloaded with fuel for the week's cooking fires and their owners push off from muddy banks to paddle back to their island homes.

Elsewhere in Mexico canoes still see a great deal of service. The Seri people on the Sonora coast and the Island of Tiburón in the Gulf of California use dugouts in the quest for big sea turtles. On the Pacific side of the Tehuantepec Isthmus the Huave have become active fishermen along the coastal lagoons, but they have to buy their dugouts from inland people who have the suitable timber. Canoes are common on many rivers and they lie on the beaches of countless coastal fishing villages. The machine age has even spawned the dugout equipped with an inboard engine and called "canoa de motor."

On the Río San Pedro, just a few miles inland from where it meets the sea and a hundred miles north of the popular resort town of Puerto Vallarta, the island village of Mexcaltitán becomes for a few months each year a little Tenochtitlán. The village is entirely above water most of the year but the heavy rains from August to October turn all its streets into shallow canals. As the river rises, residents go nowhere except by canoe. Tending their weirs, local fishermen are in canoes the year round, but when the annual flood comes their families and neighbors go about their daily lives just as the Aztec citizens of Tenochtitlán did five hundred years ago.

The smaller of the present-day dugouts of Mexico's Pacific coast are suited only for use in sheltered lagoons and bays. Larger fishing dugouts, their gunwales raised by washstrake pieces, are built to withstand open-water conditions off Barra de Navidad.

50

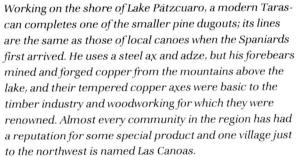

Working on the shore of Lake Pátzcuaro, a modern Taras-can completes one of the smaller pine dugouts; its lines are the same as those of local canoes when the Spaniards first arrived. He uses a steel ax and adze, but his forebears mined and forged copper from the mountains above the lake, and their tempered copper axes were basic to the timber industry and woodworking for which they were renowned. Almost every community in the region has had a reputation for some special product and one village just to the northwest is named Las Canoas.

In a larger canoe the Tarascans call a tepari, *a fishing crew on Lake Pátzcuaro retrieves a seining net that may be as much as a thousand feet long. Near the stern (right) two elbow-shaped* tortugos, *fastened to the farther gun-wale, serve as fulcra for long-shafted paddles. The outer surface of the hull may be protected with a coating of pitch.*

Lands of the Maya

EFORE THE ARRIVAL of the Europeans, the busiest trading route in all the Americas was the canoe passage skirting the mainland along the Caribbean Sea and the Gulf of Mexico. Merchant crews with paddles plied the entire sea course bordering Central America and most of present-day Mexico, but the passage where freight dugouts moved constantly back and forth was that around the Yucatan peninsula.

When Christopher Columbus sailed into the Bay of Honduras in 1502, he and his men came upon a boat and crew different from any that Europeans had yet seen in American waters. Among the Bay Islands they met a canoe "as long as a galley," according to young Ferdinand Columbus, and "eight feet wide." (To the Spanish, a galley was a single-decked warship propelled by oars and sail.) There were twenty-five men to paddle this canoe and, amidships, a palm-thatched shelter protecting the owner or captain and his family. In waters that would soon see Spanish galleons carrying away the gold and silver of the New World, Columbus had met an Amerindian treasure ship. It was a carrier of luxury goods in the most highly developed trade and transport system in the Americas. The explorers inspected the cargo and Columbus kept samples of whatever was valuable in his terms. The stock included finely woven cotton clothing in different styles and dyed in a variety of colors. He was intrigued by a selection of wooden swords, each with a deadly cutting edge of obsidian points, and Ferdinand

reported that they would be as effective against naked flesh as his own steel blade. They found copper bells and a supply of crucibles, evidently for smelting use, and, of special significance, copper hatchets suitable for cutting wood. These were the first metal tools that Europeans had found in American hands.

For provisioning, the canoe carried grain which the curious inspectors were later to learn was maize, and also a beverage brewed from that grain "like the beer of England." For the first time, too, Europeans were introduced to the cacao bean, widely used as currency in Middle America. "They had many of those kernels which serve as money," wrote Ferdinand, referring to the ripened seeds of the chocolate pod, a medium of exchange that persisted in some isolated parts of the mainland until the end of the nineteenth century. Only later did the Spanish learn that the beans were also used to prepare a luxury beverage. Cacao trees flourish in humid, low-lying tropical lands. Canoe merchants relied heavily on the supplies from growers in the rain-forest country at the head of the Bay of Honduras and the often sweltering lands at the bottom of the Gulf of Mexico. Their two most important shipping terminals were established at these locations.

The copper products probably originated in the Tarascan country of highland Mexico, west of today's Mexico City. An eagle's direct flight from that mining and manufacturing region to the islands off Honduras would be at least a thousand miles. The tortuous route travelled by overland porters and freighting sailors to link the two would have been at least twice as long.

Columbus did not identify for history the nationality of the crew or the home port of that mercantile dugout, but it has become clear since then that the sea-borne trade of the area and period was a virtual monopoly of that branch of the Maya people occupying the lowlands along the southern shore of the Gulf of Mexico. A great network of jungle rivers drains into the Gulf through this area and they had a tight grip as well on a fresh-water carrying trade that extended into what is now Guatemala.

The Maya developed a highly advanced, theocratic civilization at a time when much of western Europe was in a state of virtual savagery. Their arts and sciences flowered most brilliantly between about A.D. 200 and A.D. 800, a period in European history labelled the dark ages. They have left the monumental ruins of their civilization throughout present-day Guatemala, parts of Honduras, Belize, and El Salvador, all of Yucatan, and the most southeasterly parts of Mexico. They produced magnificent sculpture in stone and hardwood, and although archeologists have not yet reported old dugout fragments as proof, one suspects that craftsmen so given to ornament must have applied their decorative fancy on occasion to some of the thousands of canoes that carried trade goods, warriors, and other travellers.

52

Early canoe illustrations from the Maya region predate any done by European artists. In a mural (LEFT) from the Temple of the Warriors at Chichén Itzá, the high bows and sterns suggest canoes designed for marine conditions. Some scholars believe that the strange devices just left of center at the water's edge represent the coastal navigational aid reported in Diego de Landa's account. The spirited passengers and crew (ABOVE) in what seems to be a riverine canoe appear in a very small engraving on bone, recovered from a burial site at Tikal. Copied from one of the old painted books of the Maya, the god Itzamna (BELOW) paddles a craft resembling somewhat the warrior canoes in the mural.

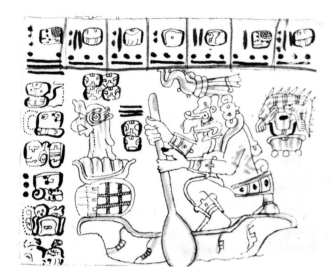

In the ruined city of Tikal in the heart of the Guatemala jungle, archeologists have recovered several small engravings on bone which date from about A.D. 700 and which depict canoes of a design far in advance of the crude burn-and-scrape technique. The archeological museum in Mérida, modern Yucatan's capital, displays a small ceramic canoe model that was a funerary object; the low-relief decorative device on its bow is an exotic marine creature. Dated about A.D. 1150, a reconstructed mural from the northern Yucatan city of Chichén Itzá illustrates a coastal village with warrior canoes in the foreground. The dugouts have dramatically upturned bows and sterns and, in each, a single paddler—surely a conventionalized rather than a realistic rendering— wields a long paddle with a pointed, leaf-shaped blade. These few period depictions provide the only pictorial evidence on which an image of the coastal trading canoe can be based.

A complex trade network had developed over a long period and had reached its busiest phase evidently in the few hundred years before Europeans arrived. The rapid development and flourishing in the fourteenth century of the Aztec community was a major factor in its growth and commercial stability. The Aztecs became major consumers and producers, and a goodly proportion of the wares carried in those canoe bottoms either came from or was destined for their markets. Diego de Landa, who was Bishop of Yucatan in the sixteenth century and whose writings are basic to whatever is known of the Maya of that time, reported that trading was their favorite occupation and that salt, cloth, and slaves comprised perhaps the most important stock-in-trade of the coasting canoes. In his *Relación de las cosas de Yucatán* he

referred to metal obtained in sheets through the canoe trade, metal from which hatchets and chisels were made. Certainly edge tools of hardened copper were used in the Mexican highlands for felling trees and shaping canoes and it is possible that some Maya boat-builders had adopted them before the European invasion.

When Spanish expeditions in 1517 and 1518 scouted the Yucatan coast they met the Maya everywhere in canoes. They were, as a rule, loaded with warriors who convinced the foreigners they were not welcome. The Hernández expedition, the first to report Indian cities with large masonry buildings, encountered dugouts that held forty persons. The following year, the Grijalva expedition, seeking anchorage in a river mouth where it met the Gulf of Mexico, was deterred by a force of fifty fighting canoes. This party did manage to do some trading at a Maya town; they bargained for six hundred brightly polished axes that they took to be gold, but by the time they got back to Cuba the ax heads were "rusty." They were, of course, copper and one of the crewmen remarked later that they were as worthless as the beads with which the Spanish had paid for them.

Canoe traffic was heaviest between Yucatan peninsula ports and the two great trading posts, one at the mouth of the Ulua River in the Bay of Honduras, the other on the far side of the peninsula at the western edge of Maya territory. Each of these centers was well served by rivers offering canoe routes into the interior. Traffic was lighter on the more extended routes along the Gulf coast

A small stylized canoe model of pottery is a treasure retrieved from the island of Jaina on Yucatan's northwest coast. Now displayed in the Museo de Arqueología e Historia in Mérida, it was found among the grave goods from a burial of some time between A.D. 700 and 1000.

54

farther north and the Caribbean coast farther south. Salt from Yucatan was shipped as far as present-day Tampico and other products on occasion were sent as far south as Panama. The full extent of the coastal passage by paddle may have been as much as three thousand miles.

Those ports of trade were pivotal to the stable functioning of the entire system. The long-distance merchants did business only in the trade enclaves, neutral centers where nothing was held more sacred than commerce. Such ports were located strategically throughout the range of the Maya merchants, and within these precincts traders from different nations maintained warehouses to store their goods. The greatest of them was Xicalango at the western end of the Laguna de Términos, a huge lagoon, protected from the open Gulf of Mexico and receiving the fresh waters of most of the important rivers of the region. Here, on neutral ground, was to be found the headquarters of all the leading traders, and also their palm-thatched depots, where merchandise from all parts of Middle America was stored, awaiting trans-shipment by canoe.

Another enclave, perhaps the principal center concerned with fresh-water commerce, was located in the lowland basin of the Candelaria and the Usumacinta rivers, no more than a hundred miles upstream from

Xicalango. It was known as Acallan, "the land of canoes" in the language of the Aztecs. To each of these centers came the important Aztec traders with their caravans of porters. From the Mexican capital and from the uplands tribute towns they came overland with trains of slaves who carried the merchandise, ready to do business with their Maya counterparts who controlled the canoe fleets. The principal town of Acallan was Itzamkanac, described by a Spaniard in 1529 as having a thousand stone-and-stucco buildings. It was a wealthy community, entirely dependent on the canoe freight traffic through its territory. After the disruption of native long-distance trade by the Spanish conquest, it dwindled within a few years to a ghost town.

Such trade was so important that not even war was allowed to disrupt it. So secure was neutrality within the boundaries of an enclave that merchants from two nations entirely hostile to each other could meet and trade freely there. In the Gulf of Honduras, Ulua was a comparably important trade center. There was another at the Bay of Chetumal, where modern Mexico borders on Belize, and for traders venturing farther south, probably a less busy port at the mouth of the San Juan River, which now forms Nicaragua's southern boundary. Canoe crews usually stopped at the island of Cozumel and at the Bay of Ascension, farther south on that coast. Merchants bound to or from Ulua beached their canoes and paused long enough to make sacrifices at shrines sacred to the god of commerce.

Lagoon passages and long stretches of water protected by offshore reefs made coastal canoe travel less hazardous than it might seem. Slipping behind sandbars and islands, threading through lagoons and straits and marsh mazes, the trade canoes moved along routes that heavier shipping could never follow. Along the Gulf coast, sailors relied on navigational aids, and Diego de Landa referred to a great lagoon where Indians placed signs on the trees along the shore to mark the canoe route.

Cedar was the favored wood of canoe-builders, and along the lower reaches of the Usumacinta and other rivers draining into the Gulf of Mexico there were huge trees to supply their needs. Several centers on the peninsula coast were known for canoe-manufacturing, one of them near Cape Catoche at the northeastern tip, the only part of Yucatan proper with sufficient rain to grow large trees. Canoes for the coast trade were also carved in the heavily forested area around Lake Bacalar and were floated down to the Bay of Chetumal on the eastern shore. The price of a canoe, according to a Spanish historian of the sixteenth century, was a hundred cacao beans.

A unique dugout found only on Lake Atitlán in highland Guatemala is built by the local Maya from guanacaste, the cedar that thrives on the mountain slopes up to 9,000 feet above the sea. No doubt because Atitlán's waters are subject to sudden squalls, most of their canoes are raised all about by washstrakes. Absolutely flat boards, nailed to an even higher bow, give the vessel a graceless character. Even though the men always stand, paddling can be difficult in the largest canoes, whose gunwale edges may be four feet above the bottom.

They shared a transient proprietorship of the ruins of Yaxchilán. While Charnay made molds from Maya sculpture, Maudslay directed workmen who were busy with chisels reducing the mass of a splendid carved stone lintel. Charnay's molds went to the coast by pack animals and canoes. Casts made from the molds were displayed later at the Trocadero Museum in Paris. Maudslay's lintel, its blank side pared until the weight was down to a quarter-ton, was packed in the bottom of the largest canoe. The heavy trophy went by paddle and pole very slowly upstream against the current of the Usumacinta and then its tributary, the Río de la Pasión. There followed an overland trek, but at the head of canoe navigation on the Belize River, the porters were relieved and the stone carving was packed carefully once more in the bottom of a large dugout. The bull work largely done, it was an easy passage to the river mouth and the little capital of the British settlement. The Maya trophy was shipped on to London and the British Museum.

The most tireless explorer among nineteenth-century Mayanists was a solitary soul whose passionate concern for the monuments of the dead was in contrast to his distrust of and distaste for living men. Austrian-born Teobert Maler travelled the Usumacinta and its meandering tributaries more extensively than any non-Maya before him. His reports to Harvard University's Peabody Museum describe those canoe explorations, including the experience of lining dugouts through hazardous stretches of that mighty river system:

It was a very difficult piece of work, because the cayuco, gliding along at the foot of the sheer rock, remained invisible to those handling the ropes....at this point the water dashed over the half-concealed boulders with such force that we could not think of towing the boat through with its load. The sight of the stupendous walls of rock, which we had just passed, the din of the water, forced between rocks and rushing along at the most frightful speed, caused my men utterly to lose their heads.

Maler discovered lost Maya cities but often it was the *chicleros*, the harvesters of the raw material for chewing-gum, who pointed the way. In the United States the growing passion for gum-chewing had set off a wide-ranging search through the jungle of the old Maya territory. The hunters, armed with machetes, went searching for sapodilla trees to tap for their sticky, latex-like sap. In this long-deserted area they frequently found previously uncharted ruins, nameless cities built in a distant past by their ancestors. For archeologists like Maler, it paid to keep in regular touch with the *chicleros*.

The sapodilla is found in that region marked on modern maps as southern Mexico and Yucatan, Guatemala, and Belize, a region where the dugout has never entirely gone out of style. So it was that when the gum market developed, some *chicleros* found the canoe route the only convenient way to get their harvest to a buyer. Bleeding the trees is a rainy-season occupation. In jungle camps the raw latex was boiled until thick, then poured into blocks. With the coming of the dry season the hard bricks were carried out sometimes by burro but as often as not in the bottom of a canoe. To this humble level the once mighty canoe-borne commerce of the Maya people had fallen.

61

62   *Below the volcano peaks that dominate Lake Atitlán, one of the shorter cedar dugouts displays its pleasing lines before square board washstrakes are nailed on. The handles projecting from the stern are integral with the dugout log and are used in launching and beaching the craft. A third such handle is sometimes to be seen projecting from a pointed bow.*

(OPPOSITE) In the shallow Everglades waters of southern Florida, poling is the usual means of moving the Seminole canoe. The traditional wood is cypress, highly resistant to decay, but today there remain very few trees of suitable size. There survive even fewer experienced builders.

Florida

PROBING FARTHER NORTH into the North American continent, the earliest European explorers nowhere found cities to compare with those of the Mayan and Mexican peoples. They encountered natives of widely varied cultural levels but seldom did they meet a people in these wide lands who did not build and use canoes. When Juan Ponce de Leon, the Spaniard who in 1513 was the first to land on the Florida peninsula, set out to search for the rejuvenating waters, he gave up after an attack by no fewer than eighty dugout canoes, carrying warriors armed with bows and protected by shields.

To the Spanish of the time, Florida was a name given broadly to all the land north of Mexico. The explorer who wandered most widely in that great region was Hernando de Soto, who arrived in 1539. He landed on the peninsula and for more than three years led his men on a fruitless search for gold. They hiked north, south, west, and east and saw a great deal of the present states of Georgia, Alabama, Mississippi, Arkansas, Texas, and, finally, Louisiana.

Each of the period accounts of the de Soto expedition contains references to native canoes. On the Savannah River, according to a Portuguese author identified only as "a gentleman of Elvas," the wanderers met a *cacica*, a woman chieftain, who travelled in her own very special state canoe. She reclined on cushions beneath a canopy that protected her from sun and rain. She was hospitable to the visitors and provided canoes so that they could cross the Savannah and continue their trek.

On a great swing to the northwest they reached the Mississippi River, probably near what is now the southern border of Tennessee. They crossed it, made a circuit through Arkansas country, and returned to the river. On the Mississippi itself and its tributaries they encountered fleets of military canoes and, while they were building brigantines to descend the great river, they were surprised by a flotilla of two hundred dugouts and a force of what probably were Chickasaw braves. The Elvas account described an impressive navy:

The Cacique came with two hundred canoes full of Indians with their bowes and arrowes, painted, and with great plumes of white feathers, and many other colours, with shields in their hands, wherewith they defended the rowers on both sides, and the men of warre stood from the head to the sterne, with their bowes and arrowes in their hands. The canoe wherein the Cacique was, had a tilt over the sterne, and hee sate under the tilt; and so were other canoes of the principall Indians. And from under the tilt where the chiefe man sat, hee governed and commanded the other people.

De Soto never made the trip downriver to the Gulf. He had been ill with fever, possibly typhus, and it was here, in this camp, that he died. His men attempted to conceal the leader's death from the Indians and, according to one account, placed his body in a weighted canoe and sank it at night in the Mississippi. The survivors, under a new leader, Luís Moscosco de Alvarado, were anxious to quit the country as quickly as possible. They were harried as they went by a well-disciplined Indian naval force.

It was the American-born Garcilaso de la Vega who interviewed veterans of this expedition and completed for publication in 1605 the most vividly descriptive account of the de Soto epic. In his report of the downriver retreat, each of the brigantines carried a canoe as a ship's boat. To transport horses they tied dugouts together in pairs and the mounts went downstream with their forefeet in one canoe and their hind in another. Garcilaso claimed that the Spanish were pursued by a "magnificent fleet," more than a thousand canoes, the largest and best canoes seen during the entire trip. He described "command ships" with twenty-five paddlers and thirty armed warriors. He wrote of paddles that were brightly polished like Spanish lances and he maintained that one of those battle canoes at full speed travelled as fast as a horse at full gallop.

Modern historians are cautious of accepting Garcilaso's every word as literal truth, for his romantic descriptions are not always confirmed by other early accounts. The prudent reader, therefore, must weigh for himself stories that were published almost four hundred years ago. In Garcilaso's book one reads that Indian canoe crews chanted songs in which they taunted their foes or praised their own chiefs. And while no other accounts made a comparable mention, Garcilaso described a color-coding system by which canoe crews and warriors could be recognized. Each group of canoes was painted a different color and the clothing, plumes, and war paint of the paddlers and warriors therein were painted the same color. Even their arms and paddles, he said, were painted the same. This mode of ready identification made it possible for units within a large canoe fleet to be maneuvered in disciplined formations over the surface of the wide Mississippi.

While the retiring Spaniards attempted to hold together their little group of brigantines, the Indian canoe fleet behind separated into three units along the right shore. The vanguard shortly moved out and past the Spanish on the right, cutting across their front in a strung-out formation and releasing a rain of arrows. Once ahead of the Spanish, they fell back to a position on the right bank. The second canoe unit followed the pattern, launched another fusillade of arrows on passing the Spanish front, and then also returned to the west bank. The third followed and when its assault was made, the brigantines had come level with the position of the first unit. This force, rested and re-armed, once again paddled quickly along and past the Spanish, let go a flurry of arrows, and moved to a new position along the right bank.

The capacity of native Americans to shape wood into complex forms using a burn-and-scrape technology is well illustrated in the drawings of Jacques Le Moyne de Morgues from the period 1562-5. In an engraving of Timuca Indians in what is now northern Florida, the dugout canoe and paddles are rendered more convincingly than in any earlier pictures by Europeans. Before acquiring metal tools, many Indians finished their vessels with squared or gently rounded rather than pointed ends.

In a 1910 photo, Wilson Cypress of the Mikasuki band maneuvers a canoe of the type that enabled about a thousand Seminole fighters to stand off United States military forces for six years. By the time the war in the Everglades ended in 1842, the United States Navy had also put some hundred and fifty "pirogues" into patrol service.

Although propelled by oars and carrying sails of animal hides, the brigantines were crudely built and no match for the fast, maneuverable native canoes. For ten days the attacks continued. Few horses survived. Few Spaniards escaped arrow wounds. Only when the drifting, one-sided skirmish approached the mouth of the Mississippi did the Indian navy give up the long chase and turn upstream and homeward. The badly mauled Spanish reached salt water and, hugging the Gulf coast, eventually arrived at the Mexican port of Panuco, known today as Tampico.

Two attempts were made by French Huguenots, in 1562 and 1564, to settle in greater Florida. The attempts failed but one of the colonists left to history the earliest European pictures of any indigenous canoes north of Mexico. The first colony was begun on the coast of what is now South Carolina, and the second, Fort Caroline, near the mouth of the St. Johns River on the northern coast of present-day Florida. Each was destroyed by the Spanish, who were determined to maintain full control of a strategic coast which flanked the homeward route of their treasure-laden galleons.

Jean Ribaut, who had led the first group of settlers, landed in England the following year and published the story of his experiences. The canoes of the Carolina Indians, he wrote, were worked hollow "so cunyngly and fyttely" that they could carry as many as thirty persons. Jacques Le Moyne de Morgues, who had been commissioned to chart the coasts and rivers and to portray the life and manners of the native people, was one of the few who escaped the butchery of French prisoners when the Spanish took Fort Caroline in 1565. When he escaped he took with him his completed paintings of the settlement people and of Timuca Indians, who then occupied much of the northern Florida peninsula. After Le Moyne's death, the forty-two pictures were acquired by the noted engraver Theodore de Bry, who published them in London in 1591. A comparison of the only original painting that now survives with its corresponding engraving shows that de Bry took no liberties, as print-makers often did, with the artist's work. This encourages modern students to hope that all the Le Moyne pictures were rendered with equal fidelity. The remaining views, of course, are known only through the engravings.

In the late nineteenth century this type of sail was still in frequent use on Seminole dugouts on lake and sheltered coastal waters. A stout paddle served for steering.

The canoes of the Timuca, as drawn by Le Moyne, are trough-like, as Ribaut described them, and are of the utmost simplicity in design. The bows and sterns are cut square across and slightly undercut. The ends of a dugout manned by French settlers are shown more gracefully shaped, an indication perhaps that even then the influence of the metal ax was apparent. The Timuca, as pictured, used paddles in deep water, poles in shallow.

The sixteenth-century historian Juan López de Velasco left an account of a Florida fishing technique which, because it was incorrectly translated into English, has suggested these many years something of a stunt man's circus performance. According to the older English version, Tequesta Indians in canoes went out into the waters of the Florida Keys after whales. Coming alongside an evidently unsuspecting whale, a hunter threw a rope around it and, even more boldly, thrust a pointed stake into one nostril to prevent it from diving. With some colorful license, López, of course, was describing the hunting of the manatee, a much smaller marine mammal common on the Florida coast. Whatever the virtues of the hunting procedure he told of, stalking the manatee by dugout in the lagoons and among the Keys was entirely practical and scarcely the hazardous exploit suggested above.

South of what is now Cape Canaveral, the use by the Ais Indians of dugouts to form the base of a kind of throne may have suggested, symbolically, the importance of canoes in their culture. Jonathan Dickinson, who was shipwrecked on this coast in 1696, described a state occasion at which the chief's two canoes were lashed together with poles, making a platform on which he, sitting cross-legged, was carried about.

Within recent years a considerable number of old dugouts have been recovered from lake and river beds in the state of Florida. Studies at the Florida State Museum indicate three recognizable types. The modern Seminole canoe, long and shallow, with a bow rising to a high vertical cutwater and an overhanging, rounded stern, is immediately identified by its unique design. The second is a heavy dugout pointed at each end and bearing the distinctive surface marks left by metal axes and adzes.

Canoes of this type may well have been the work of European settlers. Canoes of Indian manufacture, recovered in peninsular Florida, were made by the burn-and-scrape method and they are, for the most part, similar to the dugouts in Le Moyne's pictures. Carbon dating indicates that a number of them are from the pre-European period and that one of them, made about 1090 B.C., may be the oldest surviving American watercraft. The original canoe was about twenty feet long and its surface reveals no sharp tool marks whatsoever.

During the final quarter of the eighteenth century William Bartram, pioneer naturalist, made an extensive tour of the Carolinas, Georgia, and Florida. For part of the trip he used a small cypress dugout. The account of his tour, one of the first to deal reliably with the natural history of North America, was published in 1791. In it he recorded his visit to Indians in northern Florida, evidently along the Suwannee River, and described their trading exploits:

These Indians have large handsome canoes, which they form out of the trunks of Cypress trees (Cupressus disticha), some of them commodious enough to accommodate twenty or thirty warriors. In these large canoes they descend the river on trading and hunting expeditions to the sea coast, neighbouring islands and keys, quite to the point of Florida, and sometimes across the gulph, extending their navigations to the Bahama islands and even to Cuba: a crew of these adventurers had just arrived, having returned from Cuba but a few days before our arrival, with a cargo of spirituous liquors, Coffee, Sugar, and Tobacco.... They deal in the way of barter, carrying with them deer skins, furs, dry fish, bees-wax, honey, bear's oil, and some other articles.

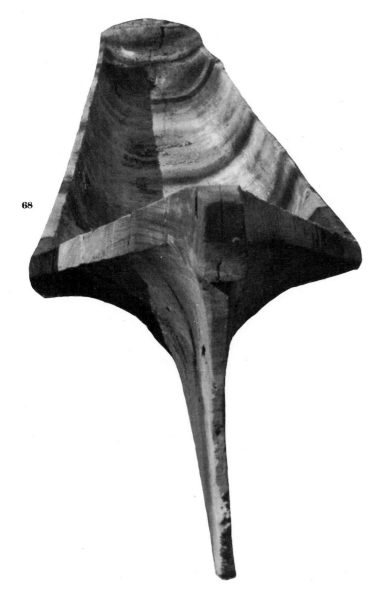

That route lies along the west coast, the Gulf side, of the Florida peninsula, much of it via lagoons and along the lee shores of island chains, but there is no sheltered passage from the Florida Keys to the Bahamas or the West Indies. The shallow river-type canoe that has survived to the present time among Florida Indians would be a risky vessel indeed for such marine adventures. Voyages in dugouts between the Florida peninsula and the Bahamas and Cuba had been reported from the time of the earliest Spanish landings in the Antilles. The Lucayans of the nearer islands had certainly made occasional trips to the mainland, and Spanish historians mentioned Cuban Indians who fled and crossed the strait in dugouts.

But the people of whom Bartram wrote late in the eighteenth century were newcomers to Florida. The Indians encountered by earlier explorers and colonists had dwindled to small groups or had disappeared. Once dominant in northern Florida, the Apalachee had been greatly reduced by European disease and entirely destroyed as a people when, in 1704, the survivors had been carried off as slaves to Carolina. When the pressure of expanding white settlement began to upset the established farming life-style among the Creek family of nations in what is now Georgia and Alabama, some bands began moving into what was then an unoccupied northern Florida. Those who chose to stay called the emigrants *Sim-in-oli*, the wild ones. The Spanish authorities in Florida did nothing to deter their move and so the Seminoles resumed there a prosperous farming life.

(LEFT) The sharp, high cutwater of the Seminole canoe was designed to open a passage through the sawgrass of the Everglades. The flared bow thrusts weed growth aside and prevents its bunching up beneath the shallow-draft vessel's flat bottom. Although poling was the norm, a paddler in the vessel would be protected from sawgrass cuts by that same action.

They raised corn, potatoes, and beans; they kept groves of orange trees and had savannah ranges for their cattle herds. Bartram recalled that during his visit the Indians brought him, as a hot-weather treat, a canoe loaded with watermelons.

Moving deeper into the peninsula, one group settled at Charlotte Harbor on the Gulf coast and the men were encouraged by the Spanish to become seamen and fishermen. The Americans later were to call these people the Spanish Indians. The fishermen used European-style boats as well as dugouts and there may have followed some merging of Old World and native boat-building ideas. It may have been at this time that Seminoles adopted a simple version of the gaff-rigged mainsail for their larger canoes.

The migrants brought with them the tradition of the Creek canoe, a simple dugout designed for river use. They brought also the white man's ax, and they used it, evidently, to make seagoing craft of some sophistication. One real possibility is that Seminole bands absorbed small surviving groups of such peoples as the Calusa and the Tequesta, each with a worthy marine tradition, and learned from them something of the advanced craft of making canoes for salt-water use. Kirk Munroe, an American author who in the 1890s wrote with sympathy and apparent integrity on the Seminoles, illustrated one of his pieces with an engraving of a dugout on the Miami River. It carries mast and sail and the skipper stands in the stern holding a push pole. Most significantly, however, this dugout appears to have had washstrakes added to each side, a modification that would have increased its depth and beam and made it suitable for use on the sea.

The difference between the marine dugouts and the riverine may have been essentially a matter of size. Prior to the ravages of nineteenth-century lumbering, Bartram had seen cypress trees with clear, straight trunks rising to ninety feet and with diameters up to twelve feet. Today it is seldom possible to acquire a straight trunk thick enough to make a shallow canoe with a twenty-inch beam.

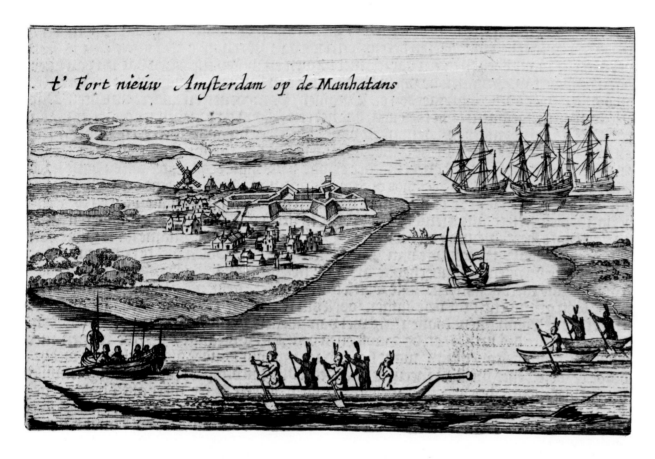

The earliest known view of New York City, published probably in 1651, incorporates a dugout canoe that at one time may have appeared a fanciful European concept. The Florida State Museum, however, now has in its collection an Indian-made dugout (RIGHT) with bow and stern platforms almost identical with those of the canoe in the engraving. This is a vessel of pre-European style, from an archeological site in Florida. Each platform is perfectly suited to support a person with a pole or a fishing spear. The dugout in the old engraving serves as a conventional ornament and probably had no association with the New York area; the smaller craft to the right represent bark canoes, evidently of the Micmac people hundreds of miles to the northeast.

The distinctive modern Seminole canoe may have evolved only when these people migrated into the great swamplands, the Everglades, that cover some five thousand square miles at the southern end of the peninsula. The farther south they were pushed by the whites, the more important, the more general, became the use of the dugout. Moving through the swamp regions required a shallow-draft vessel, and the Seminole canoe bow, sharply pointed and rising to a high vertical cutwater, appears to have been designed to open a passage through the tall sawgrass that grows so thickly there. In other respects its Creek heritage is evident: a long, shallow vessel, sometimes with several lateral bulwarks that are an integral part of the original log. They add strength and help reduce any tendency for the wood to twist as it dries. A gar-like creature of the swamp channels, it may be twenty-five to thirty feet long but only twenty inches wide. A canoe no more than eight inches deep has a vertical bow that rises to sixteen.

70

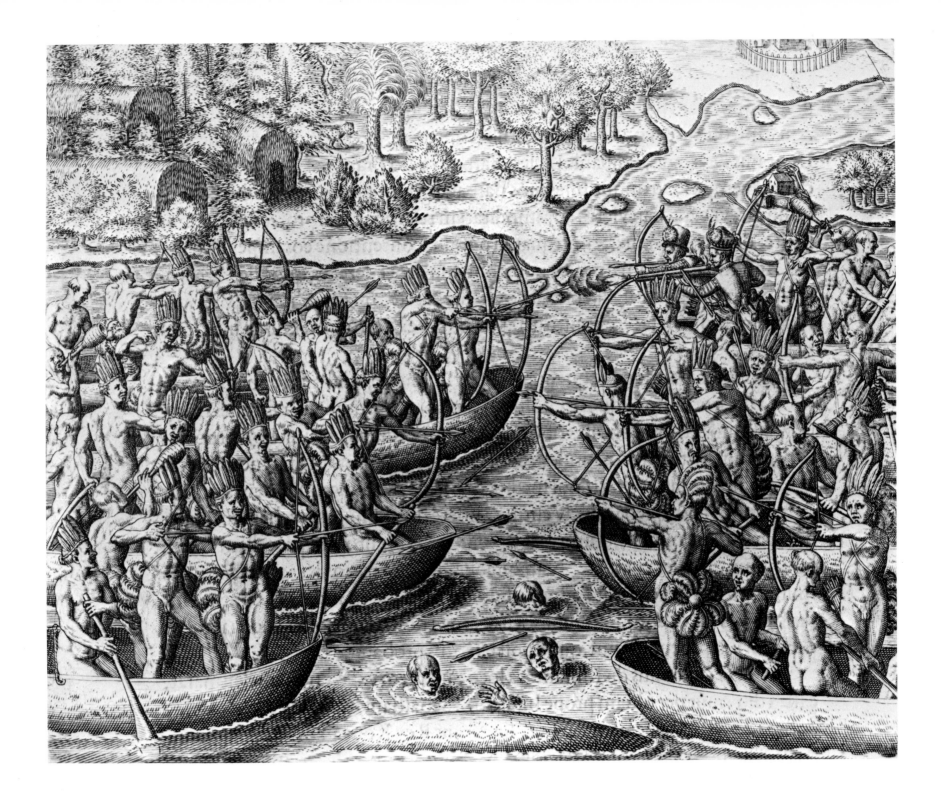

Paddles were not often used, but an oar, its shaft linked to one gunwale by a short loop of rope, was a familiar means of steering when under sail. A tribal elder once conceded to an interviewer that there was some risk in taking a canoe out on the Gulf of Mexico but that the Indian sailors carried native tobacco as "medicine" to protect them from danger. Hugh L. Willoughby, a writer who went canoe exploring in the Everglades in 1896, emphasized the importance of the push pole. Those he saw each had a triangular wooden bracket nailed close to the lower end to prevent the pole from sinking far into the mud of a soft bottom. The canoe's somewhat raised stern had a board platform for the pole man, giving him a clear view over tall grass ahead. Willoughby reported that in earlier days the Indian canoes had been much ornamented, primarily in red and white. At one time contrasting colors in striped or broken lines were painted on the inner surface of the dugouts, in patterns that identified the owners' families.

On behalf of publishers catering to a growing curiosity about the New World, European illustrators at the beginning of the seventeenth century did not hesitate to borrow elements from the accurate reporting of artists like Le Moyne and White. Their conjectural engravings were, however, romantic rather than realistic and their canoe pictures were often absurdly fanciful.

When the United States acquired East and West Florida from Spain in 1819, the Seminoles, displaced persons once before, migrated southward again. By 1827 the firmly established government policy was to transfer all native people to "Indian Territory" west of the Mississippi. A treaty in 1823 had provided for reservation land in Florida but pressure on the Seminoles continued to increase; the growing population of whites wanted the Indian lands and did not pretend otherwise. Under forced negotiation, many Seminoles were moved west; others refused to go. The struggle that followed involved, at the most, a thousand Indian warriors who for six years carried on a guerilla defense of their Everglades refuge. The war ran on from 1836 to 1842 and cost the United States between twenty and forty million dollars. In 1837 the Americans had nine thousand men in the campaign. The Seminoles made quick, short raids, then slipped away into the swamplands in their shallow dugouts. The canoe was vital to their defensive campaign, and the mobility it provided them prolonged the struggle between forces that were so unevenly matched.

There were no major battles. For the Americans, it was a war of searching, of destroying Indian campsites, crops, and, most importantly, canoes. In an effort to match the mobility of the Seminoles, the Navy in 1837 ordered fourteen pirogues from Charleston in South Carolina. Coastal blockade vessels, whose function was to prevent Cuban arms from reaching the Indians, began to carry canoes in order to launch attacks into the Seminole territory. The effective war became a canoe war. On the southwest coast, twenty-eight Seminole canoes crossed a thirty-mile open channel in a daring raid to completely surprise and overrun an American garrison in the Keys. Later in the same year, ninety Americans, dressed and painted like Indians, worked their way in sixteen canoes deep into the Everglades to reply in kind. The Indian leader was killed and the captured warriors were hanged.

In canoe patrols the Americans moved more confidently into Seminole territory but did not always apprehend or even locate Indians. On one patrol, two hundred sailors and marines spent four days paddling fifty miles up the course of the Shark River; it took about the same time to return through grassy lakes and mangrove swamps to the coast. For all their effort they sighted two Indians and, failing to overtake them, had to be content with destroying some crops and three dugouts.

In 1841 the Navy contracted for a further thirty-five canoes, most of them of a size for five men, some few large enough for ten. A Navy officer, on his return to Washington, reported later that his canoe-borne forces had paddled nearly five thousand miles "through swamps and morass." Patrolling rivers, inlets, and swamps, another party spent sixty days in canoes, each about thirty feet long and four feet wide. They used paddles as a rule but also carried small square sails.

The campaign of blockading and patrolling was increasingly effective. Towards the end the Seminoles were almost without powder. Their resistance was stubbornly protracted but the end result was never in doubt. Through defeat and capture, group after small group was transported to that Indian Territory in the west. For the United States it was an expensive war—nearly fifteen hundred men lost. After six years of struggle, some 3,800 Seminole people had been removed from Florida. The war petered out and the Indian farmlands were resettled by whites. Even then a few hundred Indians eluded the roundup and melted again into the Everglades. According to government records they didn't exist. They did, however, survive, living in secluded campsites, tending crops on little fields hidden in the swamps, getting about in their dugouts. Not only did they survive; they increased. Today a thousand or more of their descendants live in southern Florida.

The only United States naval flotilla ever engaged in an Indian campaign was disbanded when the war ended. An inventory of its equipment at the time included one hundred and forty dugout canoes.

71

72

Among the archeological treasures of the Florida State Museum at Gainesville is a carved wooden paddle from Key Marco. It is identical with those in the hands of Timuca boatmen drawn by Le Moyne before 1565 (see page 65), and it owes nothing to Old World technology. The hull, made from two logs faced together, is evidently the work of European settlers in Florida. With their metal axes, they would have had no real difficulty in hewing timbers to the snug, longitudinal seam required. This technique was later used to make craft from as many as seven logs.

The Eastern Seaboard

S IN THE FLORIDA PENINSULA, cypress was the favorite canoe tree among Indians throughout what is now the southeastern United States. Harder than most conifers, its wood is so resistant to decay that dugout fragments a thousand years old and more have been recovered by archeologists. The bald or swamp cypress (*Taxodium distichum*) can reach a height of one hundred and seventy feet with a base diameter of fifteen feet.

When Giovanni da Verrazzano, a Florentine in the French service, came ashore in 1524 on the North Carolina coast, he found the native canoes there were made from cypress. The largest, he recorded, held ten to twelve persons and they were built by the same laborious burn-and-scrape process as in the West Indies. When the English captain Arthur Barlowe landed in 1584 on the Virginia coast he was told that Europeans had already visited the area. The Indians recounted that the survivors of a shipwreck had fastened together two Indian dugouts and had fitted that twin-hulled vessel with a mast and had made a sail from pieces of their own clothing.

The record-keepers have left numerous accounts of canoe-making but to quote more than a few in the original form would be to succumb immoderately to the charm of archaic orthography. The classic account is that of Thomas Hariot, surveyor and historian, who came to this coast in 1585. He returned to England the following year, reputedly delivered to Sir Walter Raleigh the first potato and the first tobacco to be seen there, and published *A briefe and true report of the new found land of Virginia*:

The manner of makinge their boates in Virginia is verye wonderfull. For whereas they want Instruments of Yron, or others like vnto ours, yet they knowe howe to make them as handsomelye, to saile with whear they liste in their Rivers, and to fishe withall, as ours. First, they choose some longe, and thicke tree, according to the bignes of the boate which they would frame, and make a fyre on the grownd abowt the Roote thereof, kindlinge the same by little, and little with drie mosse of trees, and chipps of woode that the flame should not mounte opp to highe, and burne to muche of the lengthe of the tree. When yt is almost burnt through, and readye to fall they make a new fyre, which they suffer to burne vntill the tree fall of yts owne accord. Then burninge of the topp, and bowghs of the tree in such wyse that the bodie of the same may Retayne his iust lengthe, they raise yt vppon poles laid over cross wise vppon forked posts, at suche a reasonable heighte as they may handsomlye work vppon yt. Then take they of the barke with certayne shells.

With the bark removed and a further great expenditure of labor, "sometymes burninge and sometymes scrapinge," the timber on its platform was hollowed to become a boat.

John White was a settler, a colonial governor, and a painter who came first to this coast from England in 1585. The colony failed but his watercolors today provide a vivid insight into the life of the Indians of greater Virginia. Only Le Moyne's paintings can be compared to them, and any earlier illustrations of native boats by European artists are crude or inaccurate by contrast.

Captain John Smith, who is more frequently remembered as a prisoner redeemed by Pocahontas than as a colonial administrator and author, was among those who, in 1607, established the first successful English settlement on the seaboard. Like Hariot, he described for his readers the burn-and-scrape method of canoe manufacture but he reported also seeing larger canoes, some as much as forty to fifty feet in length.

When Robert Beverley published *The history and present state of Virginia* in 1705, his account of dugout-canoe making differed from that of Hariot, over a hundred years earlier, only in its less archaic language. The Indians, he said, used shell scrapers and fire to shape their canoes but other observers on the Atlantic coast had reported the Indians making canoes with metal tools obtained from the English and the Spanish.

While this entire region was truly dugout country, some Indians did make the occasional canoe from whatever bark they could peel in sheets of practicable size. The Nanticoke people of Virginia, wrote John Smith, used to travel north in the spring to obtain birch bark along the Susquehanna River. A pair of colonists, James Needham and Gabriel Arthur, in a sortie in 1674 westward in the Allegheny Mountains, made for themselves "perriaugers of bark" to navigate a stretch of what probably was the Savannah River system.

But the dugout clearly was the vessel found everywhere. Needham and Arthur had visited an Indian town where they saw a hundred and fifty dugouts, "made sharpe at both ends like a wherry for swiftness." Such shaping may suggest they had acquired metal trade axes. In his eighteenth-century memoirs, Lieutenant Henry T. Timberlake confirmed that the Cherokees of the southern Allegheny region had switched to metal tools and were then making poplar and pine canoes with flattened bottoms thirty to forty feet long. Powhatan Algonquins, descendants of those who had provided canoes for the earliest white settlers in Virginia, were still in the early twentieth century making and using dugouts of yellow pine and cypress for hunting and fishing in the Dismal Swamp, an expanse of marsh and tangled waterways where North Carolina borders on Virginia.

There were few, if any, boat-builders among the earliest colonists and they had to resort from the very beginning to Indian-made dugouts for transportation. Representative was the Virginia newcomer who in 1623 said, "The most evident hope from altogether starving is Oysters and for the easier getting of them I have agreed for a Canow...." He bought one from Indians for six pounds sterling.

For Virginia settlers the waterways provided natural and convenient channels for transport and communication. Most homes and plantations were located close to rivers or creeks and there are many archival references to the acquisition of Indian dugouts for use in keeping in touch with one another and in handling their shipping chores. The dugout in the early period was essential for the moving of plantation products, including the freighting of loads of pork and other farm produce along the seacoast. With the development of large-scale tobacco-growing there appeared craft like catamarans to transport the cured product in barrels; two dugouts, lashed side by side, could carry eight or nine hogsheads. According to John Lawson's *History of Carolina*, published in 1714, Indian "pereaugus" were used to ship lumber as well as plantation produce. Single-log dugouts, he wrote, could carry thirty barrels, but those split down the center, and enlarged by fitting another

timber between the two sections, could carry up to a hundred barrels. Such may well have been the five "Periaugers" in which many of James Oglethorpe's settlers sailed in 1733 up the river from the coast to found the city of Savannah.

The recovery in 1963 of the remains of an old dugout from a site not far from that of the earliest permanent white settlement provided archeological evidence to illustrate the meeting of Amerindian and European cultures in colonial times. Two sections of the craft, as first recovered, were found to bear the marks of metal-tool work. The scars were those of a two-inch gouge blade and a four-and-a-half-inch adze, and curators at Jamestown Festival Park decided that this evidence indicated it

Engravings based on John White's drawings of about 1585 were published in Frankfurt by Theodore de Bry only five years later. This view illustrates how Indians in Virginia used fire for felling trees, burning off the branches, and hollowing the logs to make canoes. One of them fans the blaze that he will soon quench so as to scrape away the charred wood with a sharp-edged shell. The bark has already been removed with shell tools.

74

had been made by white colonists. But the third and final section, retrieved somewhat later, revealed the charring of the old burn-and-scrape technique. It was, after all, an Indian-made dugout, probably acquired by colonists and worked over with steel tools to give it finer lines and to reduce its thickness and weight. The entire exterior of the hull had been adzed to remove all burn marks and to give it a decidedly flat bottom.

In eighteenth-century Carolina, dugouts were said to outlast plank-built boats, although some settlers remarked on a similarity between such craft and certain livestock feed receptacles. Ebenezer Cook, who arrived in Maryland in 1708, expressed the thought poetically:

Until the close of the nineteenth century, pine dugouts were made by the Powhatan descendants of the native people who had welcomed to Virginia its earliest immigrants from Europe. This late craft appears to differ very little from those illustrated by White. By the early years of the present century these Pamunkey Powhatans were making their canoes from boards. (ABOVE) In the earliest years, white settlers were entirely dependent for water transport on Indian-made canoes, which they later modified to suit their special needs. To carry heavy hogsheads of locally grown tobacco, colonists sometimes lashed a pair of dugouts securely together. This engraving was first published in 1800.

The Indians call this Watry Waggon
Cannoo, a Vessel none can brag on;
Cut from a Popular-tree or Pine
And fashion'd like a Trough for Swine;

Andrew Burnaby, a reverend English gentleman who visited Virginia in 1759, observed that there were innumerable coastal rivers that provided important shipping routes. The Potomac carried large vessels two hundred miles above its mouth and canoes made it a viable commercial route for a further two hundred.

The canoe itself was strange enough to white colonists and controlling it with the unfamiliar paddle must have seemed a needless additional challenge. Switching to oars no doubt made the dugout seem less outlandish. In the earliest period visitors and settlers often referred to oars and to the rowing of dugouts because their European vocabularies didn't yet include the word "paddle." By the eighteenth century, narrative descriptions and newspaper advertisements indicate that many colonists had turned their dugouts into rowing craft.

To identify clearly the African influence in modifying the dugout of this region is no easy task but the influence certainly was there. The first black slaves were landed in Virginia in 1620 and many of the canoes on which settlers depended were made and manned thereafter by Africans. Slaves provided the motive power for cargo-carrying canoes and for those plantation barges that were dugouts built along the lines of a ship's boat. Fishing from dugouts in coast waters, they supplied their masters' tables and the local markets too.

The slaves came from widely diverse backgrounds. Some had been hunters, some farmers. Some had lived in river-bank villages or on the African coast, and may virtually have been raised in canoes. When transported across the Atlantic, some who were set to canoe-building no doubt found it a familiar trade. The unanswered question concerns what of African tradition was incorporated, as a result, into the American canoe. Many white colonists found the basic dugout unstable, even treacherous, but it is important that their slaves, by and large, were quite at home in it. An observer in Virginia in 1736 described a log punt as "a very small and dangerous Sort of Canoa, liable to be overturn'd by the least Motion of the Sitters in it." Making it quite clear that the "Sitters" were white, he went on to explain, "The Negroes manage them very dextrously with a Paddle." An advertisement of the same period offered for sale a pair of slaves "that is capable to go in a Pettiauger." And when a Virginia slave-owner described a runaway as an African who had been a canoe man in his native Ibo country, he may have suggested the means whereby the fugitive had escaped.

By whites or blacks or both, the Indian dugout was modified. A popular hybrid model was one the Virginians called a punt; it was sharp at each end and, for greater stability and comfort, decidedly flat on the bottom and wider in the beam than the Indian craft. The type they called a boat canoe was similar but had a square-cut stern. On the older plantations such dugouts were often brightly painted inside and out. Punts, seldom more than fifteen feet long, were sometimes spread by using the Indians' hot-rock-and-water method to make the canoe body pliable.

The most notable dugout craft to be developed anywhere on the Atlantic coast was the Chesapeake log canoe, which has a hull made from two or more logs. The earliest of the type were made from only two logs, each shaped to form the half of a canoe and the two then joined by oak tenons. The two-log canoe has a narrow beam compared to European-style work boats but the three-log model is broad and heavy enough to make it

very clear it was not intended for paddling. Later there appeared canoes made of five and then seven logs. In documentary sources, the frequent reference to oars and the infrequent mention of sail may indicate that the broader vessels did not appear in great numbers until the second quarter of the eighteenth century. It was not until then that commercial oyster-fishing really began on Chesapeake Bay, a development that required the building of larger vessels.

(ABOVE & OPPOSITE) With the unit timbers in position, the next step in building the Poquoson multi-log canoe was cutting out the interior cavity with a scoop adze like that lying on the right side. Long days of carving went by before the graceful hull in the second photo emerged.

76

A sketch of a completed, fully rigged Poquoson canoe appeared in 1890 in the Report of the U.S. Fish Commission. The two-man crew is dredging for crabs.

On the Bay's lower shore the Virginia craftsmen made a canoe immediately recognizable as only a step or two removed from the process of shaping a usable boat from a single log. Their Poquoson canoes, taking the name of the river from whose banks so many were launched, were made without drawn plans or templates, and in choosing timbers, once the straight keel piece was selected, naturally curved logs were used to achieve the canoe shape. Except for the faces, where timber had to be tightly fitted against timber, there was little squaring of unit logs. When five logs did not quite complete the hull of a five-log canoe, the gaps were filled out by short sections. In the builder's yard the component pieces were blocked into position, the "garboard" logs one to each side of and raised a little higher than the keel log.

The "wing" logs which completed the five-log hull were supported in position slightly higher yet. It was this pair of outer logs that were chosen for their natural curve; the trick was to find two that matched.

Initial shaping of the canoe's interior was done with a scoop-blade adze. Then the logs were taken apart and the keel piece and those two forming one side of the vessel were fastened together temporarily with spikes. This unit was set on edge with the wing log uppermost while the boat-builder sliced away pine wood with his broadax. Then the spikes were pulled out, the keel log was turned over, the remaining two logs were positioned and spiked to it, and the other side was hewn to match. Its lines judged by eye rather than template, the finished hull was not absolutely symmetrical and, when under sail, could be held closer to the wind on one tack than on the other.

In a photo from the 1890s, one-man pine dugouts used by oystermen of the New Haven area move along the Quinnipiac River, which opens into that city's saltwater harbor on the Connecticut coast. The craft carrying two sails is a "sharpie," the vessel that by that period had almost entirely replaced the dugouts.

With all the logs blocked up again, further shaping was done both inside and out before the pieces were put permanently together, with pins of hard locust in the early days, and with iron bolts when they later became available. Large hulls were built up further with components that were really washstrake pieces, a latter-day illustration of the evolution of the complex wooden boat from the simple dugout canoe.

At the two principal centers for log-canoe construction in Maryland, the Pocomoke Sound shore to the south and the Tilghman Island area farther up the Bay, a more firmly rooted European tradition tended to obscure somewhat direct association with the indigenous dugout. While some were shaped by ax, adze, and the hewer's good eye, more often the Maryland canoe was made strictly to the proportions of a scaled half

model. If the lines were taken from an existing canoe instead, it was a matter of using a full-scale model.

The selected logs were usually squared by broadax before work was begun on the hull, as though builders found it proper to work with processed lumber rather than with irregular sections of tree. With the bottom completed, the Maryland procedure again diverged from the Virginian. Instead of the use of logs to build up the sides and gain freeboard, framing members were fastened to the completed inner hull and sawn planks added to raise the sides to the required height. Up the Bay the Tilghman canoes had smooth hulls with flush-fitted extra planking; the side planks of the Pocomoke canoes were overlapped, in clinker style.

The log canoe was fitted with a centerboard and rigged with a mainsail, more frequently perhaps a foresail and a mainsail, sometimes a jib as well. Masts were usually raked. The lateen may have been more familiar in the early days but the leg-of-mutton appears shortly to have become the standard sail. If becalmed, the fisherman could move his vessel by sculling with an oar of about ten feet in length.

These work boats, no more than twenty-five feet long, were the mainstay of the Chesapeake oyster fishery while hand-tonging remained the means of harvesting the shellfish. The later need for boats with greater capacity led to one forty feet long called a coasting canoe. The ultimate development was a hull shaped from five or more logs with plank-framed topsides and a fully completed deck above a commodious hull. This was the *bugeye*, which at first retained a sharp canoe stern as well as bow. Later, the stern was rounded and towards the end of the nineteenth century it was framed and completed entirely from sawn lumber.

Racing began early, possibly the day the second multiple-log canoe was launched on Chesapeake Bay, and a regular meet for rivals was organized as an annual event as early as 1840 at St. Michaels, Maryland. With competition came specially designed racing canoes, their log hulls shaved down to reduce weight, the beams made narrower, and the greatest possible amount of canvas crowded on. They weren't as stable as the work boats and only the weight of crewmen who "lay out" on "hiking" or "spring" boards prevented them from capsizing during a race.

The working fleets carried sail into the twentieth century but the advent of the gasoline engine put an end to the wind-powered oyster fishery. The making of log canoes was continued by only a few craftsmen, and the old craft still serviceable were converted to gas-burners. In 1880 there were more than six thousand log canoes at work on Chesapeake Bay. By 1900 they were in decline, and today among the oystermen they are little more than a memory.

In 1609, farther north along the Atlantic coast, Henry Hudson probed the mouth of the river that bears his name but only barely mentioned that when he went ashore he did so in an Indian canoe. In the Delaware River area that for a short time became New Sweden, an engineer named Peter Lindestrom made a visit in 1654 and observed admiringly that one Indian, equipped only with a hatchet and his flint to kindle fire, could go into the woods and complete a dugout canoe in a period of ten to twelve days.

In the Plymouth Colony, which had its beginning with the landing in 1620 of the *Mayflower*, governing officials determined that a ferry system was essential to link early trails and roads. Lesser streams were bridged by logs but for wider streams dugout-canoe ferries were decreed. A

A dugout provides ferry service for Cherokees in North Carolina in a 1908 photo. In the mid-eighteenth century, Lieutenant Henry Timberlake reported that Cherokees using European tools produced dugouts up to forty feet long.

later traveller from Boston to New York, a schoolteacher named Mrs. McKnight, was by no means happy when required to use such a ferry in 1704:

> The Cannoo was very small and shallow, which greatly terrify'd me and caused me to be very circumspect, sitting with my hands fast on each side, my eyes steady, not daring so much as to lodge my tongue a hair's breadth more on one side of my mouth than t'other. A very thought would have oversett our wherry.

By and large the indigenous dugout was used only as an interim means of transport in the primarily English-speaking settlements of the continent. But just as it did on Chesapeake Bay, the dugout for a long period became one of the standard dependable boats for oystermen on the Connecticut coast. In the wide reaches of New Haven harbor, providing extensive yet sheltered opportunity for fishing, the dugouts were familiar as late as 1900. The local Algonquin peoples had harvested the first oysters from coastal shallows and they provided the first boats for the Europeans who came to live and to fish there. The latter very quickly learned to make their own dugouts, modifying the log-round Indian boat to achieve a more stable flat-bottomed craft. Bow and stern were gracefully rounded, not sharply pointed. The bow was undercut so that it would ride over and break a passage through winter ice. Long hand tongs were used for shellfishing. The old-time oyster-fisher usually depended on a long sculling oar for power because he seldom had to cruise more than a few miles from his berth to make a day's catch. If he did raise a sail he used also a single leeboard, lifting and shifting it from gunwale to gunwale with each tack.

In the days of the young colony, white pine trunks cut within a few miles' distance were sufficient to supply the New Haven oystermen. Later they were supplied with dugouts hewn in Maine, others on the banks of the Connecticut River in Vermont and New Hampshire. According to a New Haven newspaper report of 1904, one builder in the nineteenth century took orders from the fishermen and then set up shop in the Finger Lakes area of New York State. Close to where they were felled, the pine logs were turned into dugouts, each about twenty-eight feet long. The finished canoes were towed, in raft formation, along the Erie Canal and south to New York by the Hudson River, and finally along the salt waters of Long Island Sound to New Haven. Each fisherman paid about thirty-five dollars for his new canoe and, to avoid any dispute over the choice in each lot delivered, individual ownership was determined by a lottery.

Although Chesapeake log canoes are no longer worked by oystermen of the bay, a few of the old-time craft still meet each year at St. Michaels, Maryland, for the sailing races that began there in 1840.

The Mississippi and Westward

HILE WHITE PINE was the favorite raw material in the northeast, for canoes in the Mississippi Valley many Indian groups used only poplar. After Hernando de Soto's party was harried out of the region, a hundred and thirty years elapsed before Europeans again came scouting the lower Mississippi waters, this time from the north, from New France. Louis Jolliet and Father Jacques Marquette came down from the Great Lakes country in bark canoes in 1673, past the mouths of the Missouri and the Ohio, as far as the Arkansas River. The river banks were heavily forested and Father Marquette wrote that "a species of cotton-tree" grew to such an extraordinary height and thickness that the Indians made from it canoes fifty feet long and three feet wide. He said they were big enough for thirty men and were more gracefully fashioned than those made by the settlers back in New France.

Seven years later, René Robert Cavelier, Sieur de La Salle, descended the Mississippi right to the Gulf of Mexico. Except for his own birch bark canoes, he saw only dugouts along the entire river route. A priest who accompanied the expedition, Father Zenobius Membre, left canoe notes similar to those of Marquette—he reported fleets of long dugouts made from massive cottonwoods at every village. He remarked also that alligators were a special hazard to canoe travel, there being places where no person could safely put a hand out of the vessel.

Later travellers confirmed that all the Mississippi Valley peoples were well supplied with dugout canoes. On the Ohio and the Mississippi itself the long dugouts were made of sycamore, cypress, and, most commonly, the cottonwood poplar. Black walnut canoes were reported on the Arkansas River. Large sycamore trees were sometimes hollow and such trunks could be used to improvise inferior canoes with comparatively little labor. But the river dugouts, as a rule, were well made, in contrast to those of the not far distant Texas coast people, the Karankawas. Their dugouts were graceless craft, of such minimal refinement that the tree bark was left clinging to their bottoms.

The settlement of French Louisiana began in 1699, and by the time author-colonist Antoine Le Page Du Pratz arrived in 1718, the Europeans had already adopted the dugout as their own. The native process for dugout-making, as Du Pratz saw it, required first the spreading of moist clay along the sides and each end of the log. A great fire, he said, was then built upon the log, the clay cover serving to prevent the fire from eating through what would become the vessel's sides and closed bow and stern. A constant watch, judicious fire-damping with mud or clay, and frequent scraping away of charred wood were the means of turning the log into a canoe.

Carpenters who had begun their trade in France learned quickly to shape huge cypress trunks into *pettyaugres* that carried cargoes of up to several tons. Du Pratz told of a carpenter who, from a single log, made two freighting dugouts, one of them capable of carrying fourteen produce barrels, the other sixteen. Early in the life of the settlement, Du Pratz observed that cypress had been so freely cut and imprudently used that it was

becoming hard to locate, and the price of cypress lumber had tripled. Du Pratz himself acquired one of the black walnut canoes from the Arkansas River country, and when he went off on a sporting river trip he was accompanied by two slaves who did the paddling.

The Louisiana community maintained from the outset a lifeline contact with New France; the Mississippi and the Great Lakes waterways provided a highway between them. The Louisiana people, going north, used pirogues and they paddled up the Mississippi River, the Ohio, and finally the Miami to its headwaters in the northwest part of what is now the state of Ohio. There they left the dugouts and hiked about two leagues to a stream that dropped down to Lake Erie. They switched to birch bark canoes for the down-current trip to Montreal or Quebec.

The letters of Jesuit missionaries suggest that dugout travel was not one of life's great pleasures. Paddling a pirogue upstream was heavy work and a day's paddling might take one no more than three or four leagues. Notes made on Mississippi travel concerning gnats, mosquitoes, midges, blackflies, heavy rains, excessive heat, and unbearable food make it clear that not every priest welcomed martyrdom. As a record of sheer misery in pirogue travel, few who committed their experiences to paper come close to matching the stories of distress that Father du Poisson contributed to the *Jesuit Relations*. This missionary to the Arkansas Indians, together with two other priests, left New Orleans in 1727 to go up the Mississippi in flood season. They had two pirogues and a crew of *engagés* to paddle. Their baggage was piled a foot above gunwale level and the churchmen were perched atop these chests and bales, quite unable to shift position for fear of upsetting.

Disaster threatened so frequently during the first few miles that they hauled up and sent back to New Orleans for a larger pirogue. While waiting, du Poisson fleshed out his official letter with details about the colony. Younger men who didn't find wet-land farming to their taste had hired themselves out to man pirogue ferry services. Others, he wrote, went up the Mississippi two to three hundred leagues to hunt buffalo. In spring they came down to a Louisiana market eager for the *plats côtés*, dried buffalo flanks, heaped in their dugouts. One Canadian, he added, had paddled to New Orleans in the preceding spring with a load of four hundred and eighty buffalo tongues.

The journey resumed, they travelled two leagues the first day, six the next. Seldom, said the priest, was upstream pirogue travel any faster. With the river forty feet above normal, it was all but impossible in that flooded lowland to find *cabanage*, some place to cook and sleep. When they did find a bit of muddy ground barely above flood level they covered it with piles of boughs to keep themselves above the quagmire. A simple framework of cane with a canvas covering made a stifling cocoon for sleeping; the alternative was to share the fresher night air with clouds of mosquitoes:

There are gnats, which are *brûlots*, except that they are still smaller; we hardly see them, and they especially attack the eyes. There are wasps, there are gad-flies, — in a word, there is *omne genus muscarum*; but we would not speak of the others, were it not for the mosquitoes. This little creature has caused more swearing since the French came to Mississippi, than had been done before that time in all the rest of the world.

They reached a point at which travellers sometimes cut their paddling distance by some ten leagues by hiking across an ox-bow to the spot where the river turned back on its own course. With the flood up, the portage was under water and they determined to paddle it. It was like going up a course of rapids through a forest of trees. The debris-laden water surged across the ox-bow, and to turn about would guarantee dashing a pirogue against a tree and breaking it to pieces. The desperate boatmen pulled their way from tree to tree and then, caught in a foaming rush between two trunks, they were suddenly half awash as the bow dipped in the muddy flood. Another moment and a pirogue was stalled on a mud ridge and all hands were over the sides to drag and shove the heavy dugout across the barrier. Then into the flood again, one man plunging ahead neck deep to hitch a line about a stout trunk and save the boat from runaway disaster.

When they reached the river channel proper, du Poisson could scarcely understand how they had survived: "This passage is well named *the passage of the Cross*; a Traveller who knows what it is, and does not shun it, deserves the Insane Asylum."

Much of the coast of Louisiana is a maze of marsh land. Along the Mississippi delta it is a widely indented shore, a country which, like the rocky muskeg and forest regions far to the north, offered to explorers, traders, and settlers only its waterways as practicable routes to travel. Just as in the woodland north the native birch bark canoe became the indispensable vehicle, so in Louisiana the dugout canoe was essential to travel and transport, essential to settlement and virtually to survival. The immigrant ships from France came only as far as the mouth of the Mississippi. Newly arrived colonists going up to New Orleans, which became the capital in 1722, made the hundred-mile journey by pirogue.

When a grandiose development scheme failed in 1720, German settlers, abandoned on Arkansas River lands, were relocated just above New Orleans. The industrious homesteaders created richly productive farms on the Mississippi bank and, lacking roads, used the familiar dugouts as water-borne farm vehicles. They loaded fresh produce in their pirogues and drifted downriver once a week to turn the village shoreline into a Sunday-morning market. It was the beginning, a German beginning properly speaking, of the "French Market," a New Orleans institution today.

Large pirogues remained the most important cargo carriers in Louisiana during the eighteenth century. Even after the steamboat came to dominate the Mississippi trade, some dugout vessels remained in service on the river. Throughout what is now the state of Louisiana smaller pirogues were used for local transport and for ferrying until the end of the nineteenth century. In the delta itself, the tradition lives on.

The sleek little Cajun pirogue, just big enough for one person, could, as tradition has it, "travel on a heavy dew." It was the craft of the trappers and fishermen who lived on the harvest of the bayou waters and their swampy shores. The uniquely shallow dugout was intended for personal transport and was used only on the protected, forest-canopied waters of the delta. Most were about twelve feet long, the longest fourteen, some as short as ten. Pointed at each end, they were eighteen to twenty-four inches in the beam and only ten inches deep, so shallow that each was made from only one-half of a cypress log. The timber was carefully chosen to be certain it was clear and firm and then it was split cleanly through the center with wedges. Each half, very much fined down, became a pirogue. The bottom was shaved to a thickness of an inch, the sides to even less.

Artfully shaped from a split section of cypress trunk, the pirogue of Mississippi delta waters and backwaters was a speedy and responsive craft, but it had very little freeboard. It was usually of diminutive size, perfectly suited to the requirements of a lone boatman like this bayou muskrat-trapper from Delacroix Island.

82

The long-handled adze, locally called *arminette*, was the principal tool for working the hull exterior to shape. The chopper, an adze with a very short handle and a curved blade, was used for the painstaking chore of hollowing the little shell, a carving and scraping process rather than a chopping action. A small plane, with convex wooden sole and blade, was used to smooth the entire pirogue, inside and out.

Although cypress is one of the most decay-resistant woods, pirogues may split if allowed to dry out in the sun. Owners took great care to moor or beach their craft in the shade, and to fill them with damp moss or cover them with palmetto leaves when not in use. Others left their little boats partially submerged. The best paddle, they used to say, was made from well-seasoned cypress, like a piece that had long served as a fence picket. The pirogue pole was called a *fourche* because it had a forked lower end, a means of preventing it from sinking deeply into the soft mud of a bayou bottom.

Some few dugout pirogues may yet be seen in delta country, but the making of them is a thing of the past. Their replacement is a pirogue made of cypress planks, its lines similar to those of its predecessor. A one-person craft, the modern Cajun canoe still serves the needs of fishermen and trappers. And on Lake Barataria, really a deep bay on the Gulf coast, and the place where the smuggler-pirates Jean and Pierre Laffite once used dugouts as courier vessels and for landing their contraband cargoes, these are the canoes to be seen in the annual Barataria Pirogue Races.

Much of the wealth of the Louisiana colony, in so far as it could be considered economically successful, came from the fur harvest of the upper Mississippi and its tributaries. Furs, skins, and hides from the heart of the continent were already moving by bark canoe to the great market and port of Montreal, but now there came a new flow of trade fur down the Mississippi in Indian dugouts and French pirogues. The firm of Maxent, Laclède and Company gained the Indian trade monopoly for the Missouri country, Upper Louisiana as the French called it, and in 1764 Pierre Laclède established a trading

83

An Oto man of the Siouan family beaches a cottonwood poplar dugout in the Missouri River country. Dated 1851, the drawing is by Rudolf Friedrich Kurz, who made many graphic sketches of Indian life in the American Middle West.

post at the junction of the Mississippi and Missouri rivers. It commanded for many years the fur business of the vast regions above and it thrives today as the city of St. Louis, a modern community that owes its beginning to a strategic location controlling thousands of miles of canoe routes.

A people calling themselves Missouris—people of the long canoes—gave their name to the tributary river that is longer even than its Mississippi parent. Fur traders travelled the Missouri into fresh country and by 1717 Etienne Véniard de Bourgmond had paddled as far as the

site of present-day Omaha. Early in 1803, before United States leaders had any idea that France was soon to propose to them an incredibly enormous real estate transaction, President Thomas Jefferson had received Congressional approval to explore the western territory along that Missouri River. In 1793 the Montreal-based trader and explorer Alexander Mackenzie had made his epic crossing of the Canadian Rockies and had reached and established British claim to the northwest Pacific coast. Jefferson, who was territorially ambitious for his own young nation, feared that Mackenzie, or some other Canadian explorer, might next complete a passage down the Columbia River to the Oregon coast. The fantastic proposal from Napoleon that the United States buy the vast territory of Louisiana, then the entire drainage area on the west side of the Mississippi, turned Jefferson's planned sortie towards the Pacific into a major exploration. What was to have been a quiet survey through nominally alien land became a military expedition to establish the American republican presence in newly acquired territory.

Appointed expedition leader, Captain Meriwether Lewis, friend and secretary to the president, was soon busy taking delivery of great quantities of equipment. One dugout canoe was ordered, and a keel boat, a barge-like vessel propelled by oars and sail, was built at Pittsburgh on the Ohio River. Lewis also spent considerable time at the government armory at Harpers Ferry, supervising the construction of his pet project, a portable, collapsible iron frame for a canoe about forty feet long. The keel boat had an eight-ton capacity, but when it was loaded with the expedition's equipment and supplies it grounded frequently in making its passage down the Ohio. It was only by transferring cargo to pirogues that her keel was floated clear of the river shoals. When they reached the Mississippi, Lewis and his crew were joined by the expedition's co-commander, Lieutenant William Clark, and they set up winter camp on the American shore, opposite St. Louis.

The Louisiana Purchase treaty was ratified by Congress in October of 1803. Late the following winter, Captain Lewis donned his lace-trimmed dress coat with silver epaulets, crossed the river to St. Louis, and was a formal witness to the signing at which the vast region became part of the United States. After carrying it for some three thousand miles over the trek that followed, Lewis was to trade that splendid officer's frock coat for an Indian's dugout canoe.

The exploring expedition began its long journey on May 14, 1804. The keel boat, the largest vessel yet seen on the Missouri, was fifty-five feet long, drew three feet of water, and moved ponderously under the power of twenty-two oars and a sail. Also heavily laden with gear were two pirogues, one with seven, the other with six oars. Just before the departure, Lewis sent a note to Clark, urging that "way-strips" be added to increase the freeboard of the smaller dugout.

Before cold weather sent the travellers into winter quarters sixteen hundred miles up the Missouri, they had experienced all the navigational hazards and idiosyncrasies of that treacherous, log- and driftwood-blocked river. In only a few days they had learned to reload the pirogues and the keel boat with the heaviest cargo forward so that their bows would give contact warning before entire vessels became thoroughly jammed on concealed timbers or shallow sandbars.

White men were no strangers in the territory they travelled that first summer. The country above was rich in furs and they passed traders and trappers in dugouts taking packs of furs down to the St. Louis market. A June entry in the journal recorded a meeting with French traders who had fastened together two dugouts with a platform to make a safer, more stable passage with their precious cargo.

Winter was spent in Mandan country near the site of what is now Bismarck. In March the men were busy making more dugouts from big cottonwood logs, and within days of the ice break-up a reduced party of thirty-two set off on the river again, now using the two pirogues from the first season and six newly completed canoes. The keel boat with the rest of the crew turned back to St. Louis. For the next thousand miles, into the shadows of the main peaks of the Rockies, the Lewis and Clark expedition was entirely dependent on dugouts. Making up the party with the two leaders were their soldiers and voyageurs, Clark's black slave, a couple of frontier interpreters, and the wife of one of them. This Shoshone woman, Sacajawea, carrying a newborn child, was to prove possibly the most valuable member of the entire expedition.

As they paddled westward into the Missouri current, Captain Lewis attended to his journal:

Frank B. Mayer was another of those mid-nineteenth-century artists who travelled west to sketch Indian subjects. His drawing of a Dakota Sioux dugout was made in 1851 on the Mississippi River near St. Paul. Two of the paddlers are Dakota women; the man in the bow is the son of one of them. Mayer is the relaxed passenger wearing a broad-brimmed hat.

Our vessels consisted of six small canoes, and two large perogues. This little fleet altho' not quite so respectable as those of Columbus or Capt. Cook, were still viewed by us with as much pleasure as those deservedly famed adventurers ever beheld theirs; and I dare say with quite as much anxiety for their safety and preservation.

On the Minnesota River, George Catlin in 1836 painted a Sioux hunting party in a poplar dugout pursuing a stag. While there he also sketched Sioux women harvesting wild rice in bark canoes purchased from the Chippewas, who were their immediate neighbors to the east. Catlin travelled comfortably in a Chippewa birch bark, but the narrow Sioux dugout he tried "required us and everything in it, to be exactly in the bottom—and then, to look straight forward, and speak from the middle of our mouths, or it was 't other side up' in an instant."

86

Northward, Coast to Coast

SOME THREE HUNDRED MILES north of the Ohio River another kind of trader, the far-ranging fur buyer, was a familiar transient at the outpost of Detroit, part of the French colonial empire until 1760. The fur dealers travelled in birch bark canoes but the natives of the immediate region, like those of the Ohio, more frequently built and used dugouts. French farming settlers about the fort bought dugouts from the local Indians, and the accounts of the Jesuit mission there include entries concerning the purchase of "pirogues" at a hundred livres each. Construction stone brought to the mission came under paddle power by "pirogue."

This was border country in terms of canoe-building material. The paper birch is a northern tree, its principal range extending as far south as central Minnesota, Wisconsin, and Michigan. North of that limit the bark canoe was the native boat most frequently seen, but below it and in a band across southern Ontario the dugout was the more familiar local product. The romantic image of the great bark canoe brigades, carrying traders right across the continent, has obscured the truth that dugout canoes were familiar craft even in areas where birch bark was readily available, including the old French colonies in Acadia and in the St. Lawrence Valley. When Baron de La Hontan, who spent the years from 1683 to 1690 in New France, described its forest trees and their uses, he remarked that *bois blanc*, probably white pine, was light in weight and used by the colonists for making small fishing canoes.

Acadian farms in that region where Nova Scotia now borders on New Brunswick exploited the high tides of the Bay of Fundy to maintain an adequate water level to float their home-made dugouts across the greater part of the Isthmus of Chignecto. With the construction of one small control dam, they turned existing creeks into a virtual canal early in the eighteenth century. It was a tow-path system and the farm vehicles loaded with produce on the route between the Bay of Fundy and Northumberland Strait were hollowed log canoes.

When Joseph Hadfield, an English merchant agent, came looking for business in Quebec in 1785, he mentioned that the French Canadians and the Indians both were "very dexterous in ye managing" of dugouts that were forty feet long and two feet wide. In the early nineteenth century in Huntingdon County on the south shore of the St. Lawrence, a craftsman named Eustache Dupuis was renowned for the large pine canoes he built; he called them *peeros*. On the Chateaugay River, just to the east, a dugout forwarding service was in operation by 1830. Going upriver, the vessels carried supplies, and sometimes new settlers and their baggage. On the down-river run the cargo was potash, two or three barrels in a canoe, bound for Montreal. Potash, derived from wood ashes, was often the only "crop" for which settlers could actually obtain cash.

An immigrant to the Chateaugay district in the 1860s, Robert Sellar likened the dugouts of that river to the boat that Defoe's Robinson Crusoe had built: "The largest available pine tree was sought out, felled, and had the top cut off, when the trunk was shaped and hollowed. The canoes averaged 3 feet wide by 30 long, and were generally managed by three men, two to row and one to hold the steering-paddle. When rapids were reached, the men jumped into the water, and thrusting a stick through holes at the bow and stern, worked the canoe up, half-lifting, half-pushing it zig-zag among the boulders where the water was deepest."

There was a charge of fifty cents per human passenger on the canoe ferry service crossing the St. Lawrence River between Huntingdon County, southwest of Montreal, and Glengarry County on the north shore. For livestock passengers the price was doubled: "Two canoes were lashed together, and the forelegs were in one and the hindlegs in the other. If it came on to blow, cattle would not balance themselves, but horses would."

A contributor to *Lippincott's Magazine* in 1882 reported that canoes made from pine trunks were much used by "French" lumbermen in the Ottawa Valley. They were just as quick to capsize as bark canoes, he wrote, but they were much in favor because they were never damaged by sharp rocks in the swift and shallow waterways the men had to travel. White settlers frequently

chose to use dugouts because they were more durable, because they thought them safer than bark canoes, or because they were easier to build. But when a group of Ojibwas, a tribe known for its well-designed bark canoes, moved into the Rice Lake district of south-central Ontario, the people adopted the dugout because there was no good-quality bark to be found in the region. Reginald Drayton, a settler and diary-keeper in the same district, watched them at work:

In 1871 the Indians all used dugout canoes which they made themselves out of basswood or pine or cedar logs about 15 feet long. These were hewn to as good a shape as they could and then the wood was dug out by means of axes and hollow adzes and the sides were made from an inch to rather less at the top where the gunwale was nailed on. The bottom was always left two inches thick; these canoes were not hard to paddle and on account of their weight did not stop the moment the paddle was taken from the water, as is the case with a birch bark or cedar built canoes.

The introduction of metal tools appears to have affected the choice of canoe type by some native peoples. The earliest records of visiting Europeans concerning the Indians of the Atlantic provinces of Canada mention only birch bark canoes, and yet, by the eighteenth century, with traders supplying metal axes, the Micmacs of the Restigouche River in New Brunswick were shap-

On the Nashwaak, a tributary of New Brunswick's St. John River, dugout canoes were used to transport provisions for logging crews working above the mill dam at Stanley. In a lithograph after an 1834 drawing by W. P. Kay, an empty craft with a truncated stern and a minimal bow decking lies on the rocky shore while a horse tows a supply-loaded canoe through the shallows. Some of the dugouts employed were thirty-six feet in length.

93

ing vessels from poplar logs. The Winnebago, a Siouan people on the Lake Michigan shore of what is now Wisconsin, were building only dugouts when Europeans made their first formal records in the region. The tribe's own tradition, however, has it that in earlier times the bark canoe was the norm and that the dugout did not replace it until the Winnebago had acquired sharp metal tools from a trade network that reached them even before they had seen a European.

Bark canoes were made where suitable sheet bark was available. Dugouts were made in that larger area where straight trees of adequate girth were found. Such territories overlap, and, while one type or the other was the more familiar in any given area, it was not unusual to find dugouts in the birch-tree range, although it was out of the ordinary to encounter bark vessels in primarily dugout country.

An Assiniboine man and his dugout were photographed on the Alexis Reserve north of Edmonton, Alberta, in 1926. The fine lines and distinctive bow and stern profile suggest the influence of a bark canoe model, possibly that of the Déné people in birch country farther north. Thwarts are unusual in a dugout but essential in a bark craft.

On Atlantic shores, in the woodlands, on the plains, dugout vessels were made from pine, poplar, basswood, whatever tree offered its trunk, and in the north even from driftwood retrieved from arctic waters. Some were crudely improvised troughs and some, fine serviceable boats; quality depended primarily on the raw material. When a people found a home among huge, superlative trees, as they did on the north Pacific coast, they designed and built some of the world's most splendid marine vessels.

94

(RIGHT, ABOVE) Indians in a nineteenth-century lithograph paddle bark canoes on Green Bay at Fort Howard, Wisconsin, but moored in the left foreground is what appears to be a dugout with a board shelter and some decking fore and aft.

(BELOW) In New Brunswick, Malecite birch barks were popular craft among white sportsmen, but dugouts, like that on the right, refined along the same lines as the bark canoe, were more durable.

(OPPOSITE) Lumbermen valued dugout canoes in their work because they stood up well to rugged usage on rocky waterways. In a photo by Alexander Henderson from about 1870, one of them paddles a small pine dugout during a log drive on the upper Ottawa River. The lines of the eastern woodlands birch bark canoe probably influenced the builder.

The North Pacific

A typical northern canoe of the north Pacific coast carries a Tlingit family. While the Haida traded hundreds of canoes to their Tlingit and Tsimshian neighbors who had less desirable timber to work with, this craft is almost certainly a Tlingit product. The picture was painted by Belmore Brown late in the nineteenth century and shows the mariners using oars, although traditionally these great dugouts were propelled by paddle.

FOR THOUSANDS OF unobstructed miles the long green swells of the north Pacific are driven eastward by wind and current to pound the shores of North America. Savage seas surge against tortured island rock, thrust deep into the fiords of the mainland, and batter millions of marine shells into beach sand. Winds and tides rip the coastal waters and turn them into churning confusion. Yet, from the state of Washington to Alaska there are channels screened by a thousand islands from the full power of the north Pacific. These were the familiar canoe ways for native peoples who voyaged for hundreds of miles up and down this coast as migrants, as traders, and as raiders. The boldest of them paddled out through the great combers of the open sea to hunt for whales beyond sight of land. The master mariners of the coast—the Haidas, the Kwakiutls and the Nootkas—met the challenge of this ocean by producing canoes unrivalled for their seaworthy qualities and by proving themselves seamen of extraordinary boldness and skill.

European sailors, scarcely lacking in daring themselves, were the first to tell the world of the mariners of this coast. An officer of the Spanish ship *Sutil* in 1792 reported that the Indians built canoes "so exactly proportioned that they are extremely light and strong and very well shaped. Men and women alike manage these canoes well in the sea; they are skilled in the use of oars, which they use also to steer the boats, since none of them have rudders." Captain James Cook was fascinated by the number of canoes in Nootka Sound in 1778.

"Many of them," he wrote, "are 40 feet long, 7 feet broad, and about 3 feet deep. Their breadth and flatness enables them to swim firmly without any outrigger, which none of them have. They have great dexterity in managing their paddles, but sails are no part of their navigation." Reaching the mouth of the Columbia River in 1805, Lewis and Clark were impressed by the standards of local seamanship: "When they embark, one Indian sits in the stern and steers with a paddle; the others kneel in pairs in the bottom of the canoe, and sitting on their heels paddle over the gunwale next to them. In this way they ride with perfect safety the highest waves, and venture without the least concern in seas where other boats or seamen could not live an instant."

It was the Canadian artist Paul Kane who, after crossing with an Indian crew the thirty-two miles from the mainland to Vancouver Island in 1856, left the most graphic description of native seamanship:

When we had been out for a couple of hours the wind increased to a perfect gale, and blowing against an ebb tide caused a heavy swell. We were obliged to keep one man constantly bailing to prevent our being swamped.

The Indians on board now commenced one of their wild chants, which increased to a perfect yell whenever a wave larger than the rest approached. . . . It was altogether a scene of the most wild and intense excitement: the mountainous waves roaming around our little canoe as if to engulph us every moment, the wind howling over our heads, and the yelling Indians, made it actually terrific. I was surprised at the dexterity with which they managed the canoe, all putting out their paddles on the windward side whenever a wave broke, thus breaking its force and guiding the spray over our heads to the other side of the boat.

A keen observer of Indian ways, Gilbert Malcolm Sproat, Commissioner of Indian Lands for British Columbia, admired the skill with which they handled a canoe in heavy seas. In 1868 he wrote:

If an angry breaker threatens to roll over the canoe, they weaken its effect quickly by a horizontal cut with their paddles through the upper part of the breaker when it is within a foot of the gunwale. Their mode of landing on a beach through a surf shows skill and coolness. Approaching warily, the steersman of the canoe decides when to dash for the shore; sometimes quickly countermanding the movement, by strenuous exertion the canoe is paddled back. Twenty minutes may thus pass while another chance is awaited. At length the time comes; the men give a strong stroke and rise to their feet as the canoe darts over the first roller; now there is no returning; the second roller is just passed when the bow-paddler leaps out and pulls the canoe through the broken water; but it is a question of moments: yet few accidents happen.

The Spanish explorer José Mariano Mozino remarked in 1792 that the fishermen most to be admired were those who went out after whale. "A small canoe," he wrote, "with a keel of scarcely fifteen feet and two-and-one-half foot beam, manned by three or four men, goes out to catch the most enormous animal that nature produces." Observing the life and especially the fisheries of the Nootkas, the Spaniard was shrewd in his analysis. "The inventive genius of man," he continued, "is always revealed in proportion to his needs, and that of the savages in the matter with which we are dealing is not inferior to that of the most civilized nations."

He was, in fact, commenting upon the most advanced maritime culture on the continent, one that had been developing since man settled on this coast at least eleven thousand years ago. The first migrants from the interior are believed to have come down the Fraser and other river valleys to the sea, mostly on foot, possibly making rafts for crossing rivers. But when they reached the coast they needed more sophisticated craft. Their first canoe may have been of cedar or spruce bark. Both were used for canoe manufacture into recent times, cedar towards the north and spruce bark by the Salish of the interior.

The earliest canoe, of course, might have been a naturally formed dugout, half of a hollow log found among the masses of beach driftwood. As did primitive boatbuilders elsewhere in the world, they may have plugged the ends of such natural troughs with clay before the predictable step of burning out a simple dugout. As they developed confidence in their seamanship they made larger, improved dugouts that carried them out of the tranquil waters of the deltas into the Strait of Georgia and along the coast and out to sea-girt islands. The development of a satisfactory marine canoe evidently came early; the Namu archeological site, in Kwakiutl country, dates back eight thousand years, and yet this camp is virtually inaccessible except by salt water.

Some anthropologists believe that migrants also approached this rich coast from the north, moving slowly south from Alaska in short sea trips. But in what sort of craft? In skin boats? The evidence suggests there were people on the Queen Charlotte Islands more than eight thousand years ago and yet the anthropologists believe the skin boat was devised only some four or five thousand years back. That they came in dugouts also seems unlikely, since sizeable trees were scarce in the regions they came from. The Haidas of the Queen Charlotte Islands have their own theory of their origin, as told to anthropologist Marius Barbeau: "Six canoeloads of people headed by Chief Githawn, Salmon-Eater, once sailed out of the foam. These seafolk beheld a new land to the north or to the east, set foot ashore, and established their first camp."

Whatever their origins, the newcomers to the coastal islands and mainland found a rich country. There were berries, camas, the roots of clover and fern and other foodstuffs, and in the forests and mountains such game as deer and elk, mountain sheep and goats, and several varieties of bears. The rivers yielded salmon and giant sturgeon. The coastal waters were, if anything, even richer in the promise of food—salmon and halibut and cod, herring and sculpin and the oily oolachan or candlefish. In tidal shallows there were clams and oysters, mussels, crabs, sea urchins, cuttlefish, flounder, and edible sea plants. Beyond the tidal line there were seals and sea lions, sea otters and porpoises, and the hunters' greatest challenge, the whales of deeper water. To harvest these abundant resources man had to take to the sea. Land travel along the coast was virtually impossible, for the mountains sloped steeply to the water and great fiords presented impossible barriers. Only with the canoe did those newcomers begin to make efficient use of the coastal riches, as archeologists are able to confirm. Near the mouth of the north branch of the Fraser, at the Salish village site of Musqueam, dating back about three thousand years, the finds include tools used for making dugouts, and harpoon heads and needles for net-making, suggesting that the inhabitants went hunting and fishing from canoes.

At Marpole, another site along that river, more sophisticated tools—the hand hammer, wedge, and adze—have been found. These are the tools needed for the construction of larger dugout canoes. The archeologists here have uncovered a greater variety of fishing gear, evidence of a more highly developed maritime capability. The prosperity resulting from improved technology gave these people more leisure for the development of fine carving and other arts, and the unearthing of copper which came from Alaska, obsidian from Oregon, and dentalium shells from the west coast of Vancouver Island suggests a far-ranging trade, conducted largely by canoes.

Whatever the character of the watercraft of the earliest people anywhere in the region, the archeological evidence makes it certain that advanced seagoing dugouts have been familiar in these waters for several thousand years. The great artistic and technological progress of an earlier age, spread, no doubt, by canoe, was led by the peaceful Salish of the Fraser delta, but they were later outstripped by the Haida and the Kwakiutl and the Tsimshian. These northern people, building increasingly larger canoes, began making long voyages to the south to prey upon the Salish and even to carry them off as slaves.

By the time the first Europeans arrived, late in the eighteenth century, the different Indian groups had claimed their respective territories and privileges in the best hunting and fishing areas. Although a disparate group of tribes, together no more than 100,000 people, speaking six languages and a variety of dialects, all looked primarily to the sea for their livelihood. When the Europeans came, there were on this coast enough canoes to put afloat at any one time the entire Indian population and much of its worldly goods as well.

Canoe-makers were revered for their craftsmanship and master mariners respected for their prowess. Central to their economy, a good canoe was a status symbol for its owner. They lavished their arts—sculpture and painting—on the canoe, and the vessel itself played a role in ceremonial life from infancy through initiation rites, marriage ceremonies, and funerals, and often served its owner as a tomb. Stories of supernatural canoes abound. They went to war in their canoes, and in all their elaborate finery they went in canoes to the great feasts, where they lavished gift canoes upon their neighbors or, to gain status in their eyes, made a prodigal display of wealth by burning canoes in ceremonial fires.

The giant red cedars of the coastal region, trees up to ten feet in diameter at the butt, provided a material unequalled for canoe-building. The wood is soft and easy to cut or split even with primitive implements, and it is relatively light and resistant to rot. Sound trees, large and small, brought down by storms or even the sea waves, were piled high on the beaches. Primitive man had only

When John Webber sailed into Nootka Sound with Captain James Cook in 1778 he had a whole new culture to record. Because he is accurate in all other details, his pictures of canoes are credible records. The canoes on the left lack the typical Nootkan truncated stern and the animal-like feature at the end of the bow is missing. The bow curve itself is much lower to the water than in later models. On the right, next to the ship's boat, is a sliver of a dugout which is identical to old Salish craft, and which is still being made today by Salish craftsmen. For comparison, see pages 259 and 274.

to burn off a length suited to his needs and then to shape it inside and out by controlled burning. As skill and ambition developed, they used longer logs to produce longer canoes. Three tools were developed for felling and working the wood: the splitting-wedge, the hand hammer, and the adze. All three have been found at the Salish Marpole site which flourished between 400 B.C. and A.D. 450. When the bone drill was added to these, the Indians completed the tool kit used in canoe-making.

As they became more discriminating in choosing materials, master canoe-builders came to prefer the timber of standing trees. But because the red cedar has a wide, flaring base, felling trees by fire was a formidable assignment. Early experience had taught them, too, the frustration that came when a fallen trunk remained hung up in the surrounding forest trees. Some Nootkans began, therefore, to cut out selected timber lengths from the upper trunk of living trees, first cutting a hole with stone or horn chisel and hammerstone, to ensure that the wood was sound. Then a huge notch was cut across the trunk to a depth slightly more than was needed for the dugout planned. High above the first notch another

was cut to the same depth, and wedges were used to begin a long downward split. As the seam opened, a pole was forced in at the top. Nature did the rest. As the tree flexed in winter winds, the pole dropped deeper and deeper into the lengthening split until the great piece of timber broke away and fell to the ground. It was floated to the village for shaping, but, if deep in the forest, it was roughed out first. When Europeans arrived, some canoe-makers still used the burn-and-scrape process, but the more advanced people worked largely with wedges and hammers, using stone and shell adzes for finishing.

A few more fortunate craftsmen were using locally made iron tools. Captain Cook's theory was that the coastal people had acquired iron by trading with other Indians who, at some steps removed, had contact with European settlements. The same, he thought, applied to their copper, extensively used on the coast for edge weapons and ceremonial decoration. The copper, in fact, was a native product, most of it traded from Alaskan sources, but iron was not recovered from nature by Indians. The mystery was partly solved in 1971 at Cape Alava on the Washington coast, when archeologists excavated a Makah village that had been buried and preserved by a mud slide between three and five hundred years before

(LEFT) Two Kwakiutl paddles, now in the Berlin Museum, were collected in 1881. They show the extraordinary artistry that was lavished on implements which might last no more than a season. The long blades suggest that they were used in canoes with a very deep freeboard. (ABOVE) The essential tools for dugout-making on the northwest coast were a hammerstone, a wedge of elkhorn or, in this case, yew, with the top bound with cedarbark rope to prevent splitting, an elbow adze, a hand adze, and a pair of palm drills. All had been developed before the arrival of Europeans and some already had iron cutting edges. (RIGHT) In 1786, this drawing of a Tlingit fishing camp was made by a member of the ill-fated French expedition under the command of La Pérouse. The craft is a small model of a head canoe, so called because of the huge fin projecting from the bow. A characteristic feature of these canoes was the trough just inside the gunwales which extended from bow to stern and acted as a sort of sponson, giving the craft lateral stability. By the middle of the nineteenth century this type of canoe had been supplanted by the northern-style canoe, such as that pictured on page 96.

102 *These Kwakiutl warriors appear to be in complete control of their craft and their domain. The picture was painted by Bill Holm, Curator of West Coast Indian Art at the Thomas Burke Memorial Washington State Museum, and is accurate in every detail. Holm has also made a full-size replica of a Kwakiutl canoe from archival Indian instructions and with traditional tools.*

the European arrived on the coast. Artifacts recovered included iron tools, but analysis revealed that it was not European metal; it was more like medieval Japanese iron. The current theory is that it was traded successively from Asia, through Eskimo groups and northern Tlingit, to the more southerly tribes.

The Indians of Nootka Sound knew about iron and sought it from the first white visitors with single-minded purpose. As they crowded in canoes around his ships, Captain Cook reported, "For the various articles which they brought they took in exchange knives, chisels, pieces of iron and tin, looking glasses, buttons or any kind of metal." When those Indians clambered aboard the *Resolution* and the *Discovery*, Cook was much concerned for the welfare of the vessels as their metal parts were rapidly traded off or stolen. "Nothing would go down with our visitors but metal," he wrote; "and brass had by this time supplanted iron, being so eagerly sought after that, before we left this place, hardly a bit of it was left in the ships except that which belonged to our necessary implements."

After Europeans began trading along the coast, the use of the steel ax became general, but even in the nineteenth century the building of a canoe remained a laborious business, a combination of carpentry and artistry, much influenced by tradition and superstition. Reading period descriptions, one can imagine a Kwakiutl builder rising from his solitary bed in the morning; had he slept with his wife at this time the canoe log certainly would have turned out to be hollow and useless. With chisel and hammerstone, he checks to see that the heart wood of the selected tree is sound. Satisfied, he swings a steel blade into the huge butt. He gathers a few of the chips and scatters them on the ground where he wants the tree to fall, urging it to follow the chips: "O friend, now you see your leader, who says that you shall turn your head and fall there also." Precise dropping of the tree was critical. The face that touched the earth was automatically the underside, the keel, so to speak, of the dugout. Most branches, the feller hoped, would be uppermost so that the knots they made within the trunk would be removed in the hollowing phase of the shaping work.

With a second cut through the prone upper trunk, he sets the length of the canoe and then, about six feet from each end, he chops two deep notches into the top of the log. The wood between them he splits away in slabs, reducing the basic form to what will be the gunwale level. Two humps of wood remain, one at each end, to give the canoe a rise at bow and stern. The butt end of the log will become the bow and with his ax he shapes it and the stern to points. He splits and chops away the outer sapwood until the sides are almost vertical, again and again checking by eye to see that the lines of each side are identical from end to end.

The shape of the canoe is an image in the carpenter's mind. He may measure with his outstretched arms, the span of his hand, or the thickness of a finger, but the form of the entire canoe is determined by his sculptor's eye. With the help of friends the canoe is then overturned to rest, bottom up, on a couple of short log supports. He splits away sapwood from the bottom to shape a cutwater bow and an upsweeping stern line that mark the canoe as unmistakably Kwakiutl. Turned upright again, the hull is ready to be hollowed. Using red-hot stones, his forefathers would have burned a series of holes along the flattened top surface. Instead, he simply cuts out trenches across the grain with hammerstone and chisel, splitting out blocks of wood between the holes with elk-horn wedges. His highly specialized tool kit contains some horn wedges that are curved to the desired inner curvature of the hull, as well as stone hammers designed for specific tasks, some that look like dumbbells, others oddly shaped like mushrooms.

If the work thus far has been done in the forest, this is the point at which the builder and his friends lash crossbars across the top of the roughly shaped form, then lift and tug against the bars to move the hull to water and tow it to the village. It is flat-sided, rough in form, and far from being a seaworthy vessel. The finishing work takes love and care as the carpenter goes to work on the outer surface with a hand adze of mussel shell or iron. It is a precise and rhythmic work of chipping. The people of the village listen to the tap, tap, tap of the adze and say that the woodpeckers are busy. In tribal tradition the pileated woodpecker has thus become the spiritual helper of the canoe-builder.

The carpenter measures the hull thickness from the outer surface. He drills lines of little holes along the length of the hull and slides a hemlock twig through them as a gauge, adzing the interior down to that variable thickness that long experience has proved ideal—one finger in breadth at gunwale level, one and a half fingers halfway down the sides, and two fingers thick at the bottom. When finished, he plugs the gauge holes with cedar splints.

For the weeks he has been at work the builder has not combed his hair; tradition says the great cedar hull might split if he did. Now that the sides of the dugout are ready to be spread, no one else is allowed to watch the process, for the presence of a witness might crack the bow and stern wood.

Slow fires are kindled along each side or, if the hull is raised, directly beneath it. He fills the canoe hollow with two parts fresh water and one of urine, heating the mixture with stones hot from the fire. As he splashes the liquid up along the sides the wood becomes soft, even flexible. Firmly but gently he forces crossbars between the gunwales, using successively longer sets of bars until the sides have assumed the curved spread he desires. The liquid is emptied and the canoe left to dry. When flat thwarts are sewn into position with spruce roots or softened cedar withes, the dugout's shape is set for its life.

The extraordinary dynamics of this process escaped early European observers. When the sides are forced apart, the ends, because they are closed, must rise slightly, and a keel line originally straight will curve upward from center to bow and stern. To produce a canoe with a straight keel line, for better sea performance, coastal people shaped the pre-spread hull with a hogged keel line. That is, the underside was cut in a gentle arc so that the bottom actually rose several inches higher in the center than at each end. When the cedar shell was spread, that bottom curve flattened out to a straight line. Equally important, the gunwale lines were hogged too, often rising towards the center in a more extreme curve. After spreading, the sides took a line of fairly constant height from bow to stern. As a result, washstrakes were seldom required.

Nor did Europeans at first understand why the Indians bothered with the spreading process. With such huge timbers at hand, why didn't they sculpt the wood into the desired form? The answer: for the sake of critical strength. To shape such a canoe with a wide beam would require considerable cutting across the grain, across the lengths of wood fiber, greatly reducing longitudinal strength. With the spread canoe, the long fibers of the wood are bent but unbroken. The gunwale is a continuous ribbon of wood with the grain running from bow to stern. Only at the ends of the boat was it really necessary to cut across the grain and these were the weakest parts of the canoe.

The highest skill was required in the fitting of rising bow and stern pieces, features that would help the canoe to rise and cut through oncoming waves, thrusting the waters to either side, and, with a following sea, would lift the vessel on the swells and part the combers that might flood it. These pieces were fastened to the basic hull, usually with dowels, sometimes with a post-and-socket joint. They were flush fitted, the joint made smooth with fine adzing and any cracks caulked with a mixture of gum and pulverized punk wood. In the finished canoe the joints were scarcely visible.

The extraordinary care in finishing the exterior began with "sanding" — grinding the chipped surface smooth with pieces of sandstone or sharkskin or an abrasive of hide to which grit had been glued. A smooth outer surface meant less water resistance and hence greater speed and easier paddling. Then a torch was used to scorch the outer surface to make it resistant to water and rot, and a blend of charcoal and fish-liver oil was the primer with which that surface was turned a flat black.

Decorating the Kwakiutl canoe was often a job for the recognized artists of the tribe. They arrived with stone mortars and pestles, pigments and oils, painting-sticks and patterns, to give the vessel an entirely individual character. The designs painted on its sides were adopted from the world of animals and spirits and might depict the totem of the owner or some great monster from their myths of the sea. The designs were bold and colorful, often flamboyant.

Compared to the typically northern canoes of the Kwakiutl, the Nootkan boats were spare and austere, almost flat in the bottom, broad at center, and silent in knifing through the waves. Flaring sides made them lift more quickly on a wave than the round-bottomed northern canoes. The uniquely shaped stern, curling out to sides and rear, gave lift on a following sea and threw the water back from the canoe sides. The bow piece was shaped to a single continuous curve from the boat's keel line up to a peak bearing a stylized wolf-head; coast people believed that when the killer whale came ashore he assumed the guise of a timber wolf. The *Haitlik*, the lightning snake, was sometimes painted on a Nootkan canoe, imparting to it magical powers. The decoration, however, was painted over with black; it was hidden and

(TOP) Two Kwakiutl canoes, on their way to a potlatch, give some idea of the flamboyance of this maritime culture and of the artistry that was lavished on the canoes by their owners or by artists of the tribe. The fabric sails are a post-European innovation, although crude sails of split cedar may have been used with a following wind before the first Spanish ship sailed into their territory.

(ABOVE) Two Kwakiutl paddles made of yew, the preferred paddle wood on the coast, are still tough and springy after more than one hundred years. Both surfaces of the black blades are scribed and painted in red with abstract images of the eagle, the dogfish, and the killer whale.

Some evidence suggests that some canoes of Salish origin may have been paddled at an early period, in tranquil weather necessarily, to the west coast of Vancouver Island, to what is considered Nootkan territory. An eighteenth-century engraving shows Captain Cook's men trading here with Nootka Indians, and yet all the canoes illustrated are small and some more Salishan than Nootkan in character. Cook himself described the canoes found there:

From the middle, toward each end, they become gradually narrower, the after-part, or stern, ending abruptly or perpendicularly, with a small knob on the top; but the forepart is lengthened out, stretching forward and upward, ending in a notched point or prow, considerably higher than the sides of the canoe, which run nearly in a straight line. For the most part they are without ornament, but some have a little carving, and are decorated by setting seal's teeth on the surface, like studs; as is the practice on their masks and weapons. A few have, likewise, a kind of additional head or prow, like a large cutwater, which is painted with the figure of some animal.

Accepting the artist's pictorial evidence along with Cook's written description is to assume that there were two types of canoe in Nootka Sound in 1778, small craft of the Salish tradition and larger seagoing dugouts of designs usually recognized as Nootkan.

113

To the three coastal canoe types—Salish, Northern (including Kwakiutl, Haida, Tsimshian, and Alaskan), and Nootkan—must be added the riverine vessel, long and narrow with squared, punt-like ends or bows and sterns rounded and curving slightly upward like the bowl of a spoon. The design is ideally suited to paddling or poling against a river current. Since it rarely has a distinctive cutwater, the current cannot bear strongly on one side of the bow; the water sweeps under the canoe, making it easier to control its course. The smooth, rounded bottom and narrow hull offer minimal resistance to rapid water, and yet large models of this dugout can carry enormous loads.

The sides of river canoes were seldom spread. They had virtually no sheer and often lacked thwarts. If a squared, punt-like bow became somewhat rounded, the canoe was called "shovel nosed," and a related craft among the Salish at the southern tip of Vancouver Island was identified as having a transom stern, with a piece of wood mortised into the canoe hull a few inches from the after end. Such a feature may first have been introduced to repair a canoe that had been split. The punt-style canoes of the Sanpail and Nespelem tribes in the state of Washington had identical ends, each with a small, squared platform, similar to some prehistoric canoes in the Florida peninsula. Bow and stern platforms provided firm footing for poling, for spearing fish, and for net-tending.

The Return of the War Party was painted by Paul Kane in 1847, but it is doubtful that he saw the event. In the lead is a head canoe, but Kane erred because he shows the Indians paddling it stern first; the great bow fin of the canoe is behind the crew of paddlers. The second canoe is a Munka, a Nootkan war canoe. In the foreground, in the shadow of a rock, is a perfect example of a Salish canoe.

The riverine canoe type of the northwest was to be found as far south as the northernmost part of California. The Yurok, living on the lower reaches of the Klamath and Trinity rivers, used the split half of a huge redwood log to make, in sculptural terms especially, the finest and most distinctive of the dugouts designed primarily for river or still-water use. The carvers relied primarily on controlled burning and the use of a mussel-shell adze to shape a heavy craft with rounded bottom and the familiar curve rising gently at bow and stern. Each end, essentially punt-like at water level, has above the gunwale level a rising feature tapering quickly to a point. An integral part was a seat in the stern with footrests like knobs left standing on the canoe bottom; the helmsman sat here and was the only crew member with a conventional paddle. The others stood and wielded poles six to eight feet long with blades that were narrow and heavy. In rock-strewn shallow rivers a great deal of poling was required for upstream progress while the helmsman, with his broad blade, could turn the round-bottomed hull quickly to avoid water hazards.

A unique feature of the Yurok canoe was the inward-rolling gunwale, apparently developed expressly to provide anywhere along its length a perfect handhold for crewmen who often had to manhandle the heavy craft through shallow rapids. The feature was equally useful for launching and landing. While canoe length varied considerably, the optimum was about eighteen feet. Such canoes appeared occasionally on sheltered stretches of the salt-water coast, but their features, ideal for shallow river use, made them poor and insecure seacraft. The Tolowa and Wiyot peoples of northern California followed the same design in canoe-making and, along with the Yurok, did a business in canoe sales with such neighbors as the Hupa and the Karok. Crude river dugouts were made by other peoples where timber was available, but the influence of northwest coast design persisted in California no farther south than Cape Mendocino.

The long, stable spoon canoes of the Bella Coola were truly riverine craft, ideal in rapids and fast river currents. Some idea of the capacity of these craft is conveyed by the enormous load of eulachon borne by the canoe on the right. The eulachon is a type of herring which was pressed for its oil, a highly prized food item for tribes that did not have rights or access to the eulachon run. The Haida accepted great quantities of the oil from the Nishka on the Nass River in exchange for their seagoing dugouts.

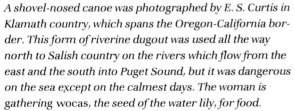

A shovel-nosed canoe was photographed by E. S. Curtis in Klamath country, which spans the Oregon-California border. This form of riverine dugout was used all the way north to Salish country on the rivers which flow from the east and the south into Puget Sound, but it was dangerous on the sea except on the calmest days. The woman is gathering wocas, the seed of the water lily, for food.

Trees became smaller in the north, but the Indians became cleverer in getting the biggest dugout from a given tree. By cutting a slot down the upper side of a poplar log and then undercutting the inner sides, they achieved a tubular form which, when the sides were softened with dry heat outside and hot water inside, could be spread into a boat considerably wider than the diameter of the original log. The Tlingit builder in the village of Klukwas has tied a rope around the near end so that it will not split during the spreading process.

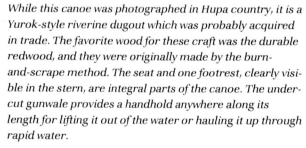

While this canoe was photographed in Hupa country, it is a Yurok-style riverine dugout which was probably acquired in trade. The favorite wood for these craft was the durable redwood, and they were originally made by the burn-and-scrape method. The seat and one footrest, clearly visible in the stern, are integral parts of the canoe. The undercut gunwale provides a handhold anywhere along its length for lifting it out of the water or hauling it up through rapid water.

From Alaska to California canoes played an important role in Indian ceremonial life. In their Yurok-style craft the Hupa Indians perform their boat dance on the Trinity River, California, as part of the White Deerskin Festival, held in late summer to renew the world and to assure abundance the following year. The festival was also a time to display wealth such as obsidian knives and prized albino deerskins. In the canoes they use both paddles and poles for propulsion.

It was for turbulent salt water that the largest northern canoes were developed by the skilled Haidas on the Queen Charlotte Islands. The dangerous surrounding waters protected them from rivals and enemies, and encouraged them to develop marine dugouts capable of carrying up to seventy people with equipment and supplies sufficient for voyages of hundreds of miles. Admired by neighboring tribes, these most seaworthy of canoes became the very basis of the Haida trading economy. The giant red cedars of the Queen Charlotte rain forests were the finest canoe-making material, superior to the yellow cedar, cottonwood, and Sitka spruce used by other tribes of the northern region. Combining the best raw material with excellent craft and design, the Haidas became canoe suppliers to the Tlingit of the north and the Tsimshian of the mainland to their east, occasionally trading as far south as Vancouver Island.

Winter, with its storms and rain and ever-present fog, was the season for arts and crafts activity among the Haida — weaving baskets and blankets and cedar-bark clothing, tailoring furs into garments, carpentering and decorating storage boxes, sculpting cooking vessels and ceremonial masks, and building the great canoes. By spring as many as thirty new canoes might be ready to launch in a large village such as Massett. They came in many sizes, and the biggest reported was the "Chief" canoe at Massett, said to have been ninety feet long. It was a vanity product, a vessel so huge that it was impossible to manage efficiently. But practical canoes of from thirty-five to sixty feet were common. A freighting dugout of sixty feet, with a beam up to seven feet, could carry forty men and two tons of cargo. The old war canoes, in the same size range, were relatively slim and therefore faster than the beamy freight carriers. Many war canoes were as long as the European vessels in those waters, and it is not difficult to imagine the apprehension of a trader captain meeting in mid-nineteenth century the ten-canoe squadron led by Chief Skidgate, each vessel manned by twenty to twenty-five Haida fighters. Anti-boarding nets were frequently rigged when the canoes of the native people approached.

Paul Kane sketched these northwest canoes in the middle of the nineteenth century. The side view at the bottom is a head canoe with its deep, plumb bow pointing to the left. A three-quarter view of the same canoe is on the upper left. The canoe on the upper right has the form of an ancient Kwakiutl war canoe, or munka. Judging by the foreshortened forms, Kane probably sketched them from models; both types had virtually disappeared by the time he visited the coast.

(OPPOSITE) In a culture that lavished its arts of sculpture and painting on just about all items of everyday life, it is not surprising that the northern peoples, who spent so much of their time in canoes, should extend their artistry to their watercraft. The sketch was made by Rudolph Cronau in 1883.

118

(TOP LEFT) *One of several figureheads that were photographed in the Tlingit village of Klukwan in the 1890s during a potlatch. Such adornments to the canoes were often detachable and reserved for ceremonial occasions. The winged figure with its black beard could represent a Russian; its chest is inlaid with a pattern of iridescent abalone shell.* (BELOW) *In this shaman's charm is tangible evidence of how the canoe crept into the Indians' spiritual and supernatural beliefs. Exquisitely carved from bone, the canoe is formed by the abstract shapes of an octopus and a sea lion, and standing in it are seven spirit figures.*

(ABOVE) *A superb sculpture of what is described as a northern diver is likely the owner's family or clan crest. It was photographed in the Kwakiutl village in Alert Bay on the northeast shore of Vancouver Island in 1913. The family clan or honor takes precedence over the clean lines of the canoe; although the cutwater is just below the diver's claws, the sculptural addition would have reduced the effectiveness of the bow curve in anything but the calmest seas.*

(TOP) *An old model of a Haida canoe displays the fine lines of a bow designed to lift on a wave and throw the water away from the hull. The paddles of the Haida men were often pointed and used for close fighting. The extra point on the near paddle made it an even more effective weapon, and it was also credited with a more silent stroke in the water for stalking sleeping seals and sea otters. (ABOVE) Most west coast tribes made models of their canoes, at first as toys for their children and later as curios for white traders. The models were not exact in their proportions;*

most were shorter and wider than the real canoes and are therefore not useful in providing a true scale of the originals. The little sculptured figure on this archaic Haida head canoe is not looking ahead to where the canoe is going, but astern to where it has been. The decorative painting is beautifully done but is so abstract that it is a problem to identify the creatures it represents. (RIGHT) On the upper Skeena River, north of Hazelton, in the Gitskan village of Kispiox, this totem pole, with its Tsimshian-style

canoe, no doubt had some very specific meaning for those who erected it. The canoe, as both a vehicle and a symbol, threads its way constantly through tribal mythology, the traditions of individual rights and titles, clan privileges, family honors, and even the Indian concepts of life after death.

A French artist with the La Pérouse expedition drew this Tlingit canoe in 1779. Although it has enormous fins at bow and stern, it is very different from the early Haida head canoes and was certainly a local product. For their big canoes — up to forty-five feet long — the Tlingit preferred red cedar, but in their northern region they often had to settle for Sitka spruce, which wasn't too onerous, since they already had iron tools when the first Europeans arrived. A Russian captain, F. D. Lutke, reported that the walls of their canoes were extended with side planking, a rare feature on the west coast. He also said that each canoe had a name such as Shaman, Otter, Eagle, or Raven, with figures on the bow and stern to carry out the theme.

122

When Europeans first arrived, a widely used dugout on the coast was one called a head canoe, distinguished by raised bow and stern projections that resembled great vertical fins. The action of wind and water made this canoe difficult to steer and, to reduce surface area and resistance, the Haidas cut a large circular hole in each of the fins. Ultimately they did away with the fin design altogether, replacing it with the great rising bow and upsweeping stern that characterized the northern canoe in the nineteenth century.

The family canoe of the north ranged in length from eighteen to thirty-five feet and served much like the all-purpose station wagon of the prosperous modern-day North American. They were seen coming and going constantly; a Hudson's Bay Company trader in one month counted more than eight hundred that passed his post.

Fast canoes for two or three persons were essential for hunting sea otter, seal, and dolphin. The same size model was used by women for fishing, berry-picking, and bark-harvesting. But it was the family model that was most in demand in the regional canoe market. The new dugouts were loaded with dried halibut and other such foods for trading to neighboring groups, but the canoes themselves were the most important stock-in-trade. The Haidas took in exchange for trade canoes superior furs from the mountains, copper, and jadeite from Alaska. Fish oil, pressed from the oolachan of the Nass River, was a dietary staple high on the shopping list. Canoes were also traded for slave children, brought from the interior.

A trade-in, an old canoe, was always part of the deal. It was the only means, and a hazardous one if it was a derelict, whereby the Haida merchants could paddle home.

That return trip in an inferior dugout through the unforgiving waters of Queen Charlotte Sound was often a nightmare. Travel on open ocean was hazardous enough in their most seaworthy craft, and even when they landed on a beach a high surf could pound the best canoe to matchwood. Landings were generally made stern first so that the bow remained pointing into the threatening waves, ready if necessary to be re-launched.

In the nineteenth century voyaging often was done under sails, the Haidas rigging them like the wings of a bird, angled out from each side of the canoe. Although the earliest visitors made no mention of sail use among the west coast people, it seems almost incomprehensible that they could have lived so much upon the water and not have used a following wind to help them on their way. When moving quarters — at least in latter times — and with canoes loaded with house planks, they often raised one of those large boards to catch the wind. The Kwakiutl canoemen improved upon this with a true sail of thin planks sewn together and held against a mast. To the south, the Makah wove square sails of cedar bark.

Whether carrying celebrants to a potlatch feast or emissaries to a peace-making mission, a Haida fleet on a ceremonial visit made an impressive show. The great black hulls were painted from end to end with the flamboyant designs that spoke of history, myth, and magic. The crews paddled with military precision, often to the beat of a cedar-box drum. The visitors wore formal finery, fur cloaks and sculpted head-dresses, set with iridescent abalone shell. As the soaring black prows neared the beach a chief scattered swan's down on the water, a sign that they came in peace. The crew members chanted of their prowess while some danced with rattles on the wide forward thwarts and another blew a single note on a seashell horn.

A young man's wedding party often arrived by canoe to claim the bride. Among the Makah the wedding ceremony included a pantomime performance of paddling the canoe, killing a whale, and heaving a harpoon at the bride's house. To reach the land of the dead, the soul of an Indian crossed a great river in a spirit canoe, and among some tribes the canoe he paddled in life became his sepulcher. Surrounded by the goods that would serve him during that last voyage, the canoe coffin was lodged in the branches of a tree or left above high water on some sacred island. Infants among these tribes sometimes slept in wooden cradles that were miniature canoes and their parents sometimes ate from wooden vessels carved in canoe form and decorated with family crests. Beyond daily utility, the canoe as an idea and symbol pervaded their entire life.

It is a tragic irony that the canoe, which for thousands of years brought such prosperity, should become for them a vehicle of destruction, transporting the dread diseases of Europeans to every part of the coast. Like natives throughout the New World, they had no immunity or resistance to diseases from the Old, and smallpox introduced by the Spanish in the eighteenth century wiped out entire villages. Other plagues arrived with seamen and miners, and influenza swept through in 1830. When the worldwide influenza epidemic of 1918 reached them, the coast tribes were devastated. The canoe, particularly the trading craft, carried diseases to the smallest and most remote community.

With the virtual destruction of one of the continent's richest cultures, the canoe was largely supplanted by European-style boats. A great social structure was wiped out and maritime traditions of incredible complexity passed into memory. The Haida today build no war canoes and the Nootkans build no whaling dugouts. Some of the coastal people, however, will recall the traditional story that their ancestors first came to this country in a copper canoe driven by copper paddles. Some will remember tales of a spirit canoe that could pass through mountains or speed over the water without the need of paddles or paddlers; some of the old people may dwell upon the irony of the ancient story-teller's tradition that pestilence always travelled in a great winged canoe.

The canoe grave of an Indian chief on the Cowlitz River was painted by H. J. Warre in 1845. Grave goods in these cedar sepulchers were generally broken so that they were dead things for the use of the dead. Even the canoes had holes cut in their bottoms. From a practical standpoint, the practice also discouraged marauders from pillaging. On the Columbia River, on one site just downstream from the mouth of the Cowlitz River, Commodore Charles Wilkes's expedition in 1837 counted some three thousand of these canoe graves.

Killisnoo Indians arrive at Sitka, Alaska, for a potlatch about 1900. The fine northern canoes they are paddling persisted into this century in part because the Indians were supplying salmon to canneries on the northwest coast and literally needed fleets of the familiar vessels.

124

European explorers, particularly on river surveys, used native craft and boatmen as the surest means of transport into the rugged mountainous country. This is a view of the Skeena River, near Hazelton, during the search for a rail route to the Yukon in 1899. The commodious craft is a northern canoe of the period.

California

THE FIRST MAN, so goes a tradition of the Chumash people of California, once said that all the world is a canoe and, whether paddlers or passengers, we are all one people together in that vessel. He made the first canoe, it is said, and the generations that came after went on making canoes in the same way. The old message is a humanist statement; it also makes clear the important role of the canoe in the life of the Chumash.

They lived on the Pacific coast, mainly in villages along the seventy-five-mile stretch of the Santa Barbara Channel. There are no navigable rivers in the region but, like neighbors to north, south, and east, they built tule balsas or reed boats, as well as some dugouts, and used them on sheltered coastal water. But they, and they alone on all the continent, made for bold use on the sea a graceful and sturdy craft constructed entirely of wooden planks. It was the only planked vessel produced by the indigenous people of North America. Along with a plank boat originated by Indians on the coast of Chile, it is the American craft that bridges the developmental gap between the simplest of dugouts and the advanced wooden boats and ships first brought to the New World by European adventurers.

Whether rowing craft or great cargo carrier, the wooden boats of the world have evolved from the simple and once universally familiar vessel that was made from a hollowed tree trunk. The addition of a single washstrake to each side of a dugout, raising it and increasing its beam and freeboard, pointed the way to the making of a boat entirely of washstrake pieces. The boat's keel represents the original dugout, and the side planks, the washstrakes fastened to it. With the fitting of stem and stern pieces and some lateral supports, familiar in many canoes, the evolution of dugout to ship was accomplished.

The plank canoe of the California Chumash makes the process immediately clear. The flat bottom board, the keel so to speak, was a single piece, very slightly scooped out, a practice that recalls the building of the earlier dugout. The sides were built up of carefully shaped and fitted boards, each cemented and sewed to all abutting boards. A post was fitted into the stem and another in the stern, and a single central thwart was installed. The completed vessel was technologically in a class with all the plank-made vessels of the world.

Only fifty years after Columbus reached the New World, a Spanish captain, Juan Rodríguez Cabrillo, anchored off the Chumash coast and reported that the Indians came off in canoes to barter fish. In 1602, Sebastián Vizcaíno gave the Santa Barbara Channel its modern name and noted in his diary that two men in a canoe came out "rowing so swiftly they seemed to fly."

The paddlers circled the Spanish ship "with such speed that it seemed impossible." The first white man to examine the Chumash craft appears to have been a member of a later expedition. His name is Miguel Costanso and his diary is dated 1769-70:

The expertness and skill of these Indians is unsurpassed in the construction of their canoes of pine boards. . . . they fasten the boards firmly together, making holes at equal distances apart, one inch from the edge, matching each other in the upper and lower boards, and through these holes they pass stout thongs of deer sinews. They pitch and caulk the seams, and paint the whole with bright colors. They handle them with equal skill, and three or four men go out to sea to fish in them. . . . They use long double-bladed oars, and row with indescribable agility and swiftness.

Only a few years later, Father Pedro Font, who also came overland from Mexico to Upper California, declared that their canoes were their greatest achievement, but he was confounded that the tools they used were in his eyes no more than bits of shell and flint. He reported that the canoe had no ribs, that one vessel he measured was thirty-six palms long, about twenty-five feet, and had been built by sewing together twenty or so boards of varying lengths and widths. Font noted as well that all canoes were painted red with hematite and some of them decorated with inlaid shell designs. The fishermen, usually only two to a canoe, sailed out even in rough seas.

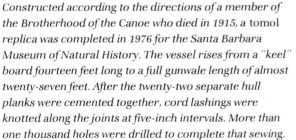

Constructed according to the directions of a member of the Brotherhood of the Canoe who died in 1915, a tomol replica was completed in 1976 for the Santa Barbara Museum of Natural History. The vessel rises from a "keel" board fourteen feet long to a full gunwale length of almost twenty-seven feet. After the twenty-two separate hull planks were cemented together, cord lashings were knotted along the joints at five-inch intervals. More than one thousand holes were drilled to complete that sewing.

Travis Hudson, the museum's curator of anthropology (left), and Peter Howorth, the construction chief, repair a split board by the same process. The Helek, sea hawk in Chumash, was finished in traditional red and has proven herself a seaworthy vessel on the Santa Barbara Channel.

Just as the birch woodlands people launched their bark vessels with great care, the modern Chumash crew carries the new plank canoe into the water before loading or boarding. Under way, the men wield double-bladed, eight-foot paddles; the blades conform in style to one now in the British Museum, collected on this coast in 1793 by Captain James Cook.

The Chumash name for their canoe is *tomol*, which also means "red" pine, one of the regional woods suitable for its construction, although redwood was always the preferred material. Pine grows in the mountains but, without rivers to float them coastward, moving logs down to the beaches was arduous. The building material actually used was driftwood from ocean beaches, much of it trunk sections of the redwood from farther north, delivered to the Chumash coast by the southbound current. While driftwood logs were seldom of a size suited to dugout-making, the Chumash had learned to split out boards from this material, using wedges made from the rib bones of whales.

The other natural product, without which the tomol would never have become a thoroughly practicable boat, is asphaltum. The Spanish reported swamps of bitumen and the native people spoke of *wogo*, the hard, tar-like material they mined from deposits along the beaches. They used it as an adhesive and a waterproofing in many ways but particularly in canoe-building. They melted the wogo with pine pitch to make a softer and stickier product called *yop*, used both as a glue in putting together the board canoe and as a sealer for its joints.

The tomol was designed for deep-water fishing and it became essential to the active trade the Chumash conducted, particularly that with the people of the islands of the Santa Barbara Channel. The shortest distance between the mainland and any island—Santa Cruz, Santa Rosa, and San Miguel—is twenty miles. Chumash captains loaded their plank canoes with home produce, including acorns and other seeds, as well as bows and arrows. Returning from the islands, they carried manufactured stone tools, baskets, and beads of shell and fish bone. Split planks were important in trade, as were cakes of wogo.

As a cargo vessel, the tomol could carry as much as two tons, as a ferry, ten or more passengers, but its normal complement was a working crew of two. The job of a third man was bailing; even though lavishly coated with pitch, the tomol was not the driest of boats. When it was lightly loaded, its crew carried rocks for ballast. The double-bladed paddle had a shaft about eight feet in length with a blade, shaped from a plank, mortised and lashed to each end. The tomol, up to twenty-five feet long, had a beam from three to four feet; greater width, of course, would have made it awkward to use a double-bladed paddle.

The prosperity of the Chumash economy depended heavily on the work of the canoe crews who fished, hunted, and traded offshore. Ownership of a tomol indicated that a man was indeed wealthy. Just accumulating the drift logs for planking was time-consuming, but commissioning the construction of a canoe meant putting to work a group of specialized craftsmen for a period of up to six months.

All manufacturing was in the hands of the Brotherhood of the Canoe, which combined the functions of a professional guild and a fraternal order. Veteran builders and apprentices worked together, perhaps six men on one canoe job, so that the skills and traditions of design and construction detail were preserved. Each craftsman, perhaps an expert at only one aspect of the construction process, kept his own kit of highly specialized tools in a sack of netting.

The channel shore community still known as Carpinteria came by that Hispanicized name because it was a busy canoe-building center of the Chumash. When the Franciscans built their missions in upper California in the late eighteenth century, the ownership and control of plank canoes, and hence economic control of the sea fishery, often came into the hands of the mission fathers. Then, with the near extinction of the coastal Indians that followed the movement of the military and of Spanish settlers into the region, the splendid tradition of the tomol was all but lost.

Patient efforts have recently brought to light in comprehensible form the remarkable notes of an anthropologist who interviewed the last surviving member of the Brotherhood of the Canoe. Fernando Librado, Kitsepawit to give him his Chumash name, was born about 1804 and lived until 1915. He remembered his fellow canoe-builders and the art they practiced in the period from about 1820 to 1850. The anthropologist was John Peabody Harrington, a man devoted to detail but not to order. His chaotic records have been painstakingly organized by researchers at the Santa Barbara Museum of Natural History. A remarkably full description of canoe-making and the tools and materials required is now available in the words of a man who actually built them. The aging Kitsepawit explained that the canoe-maker had his own helpers from the Brotherhood but that he allowed no other persons to stand around and watch.

The tools that he recalled include the hand adze with a heavy Pismo clam shell blade, one chisel with a flint or shell blade for working the planks, another with a tapered wooden edge for pressing the caulking material, tule pith, into cracks and seams. A piece of red ocher was used for chalking lines prior to cutting the boards and a stick tied in bowed form was the guide that determined the curve of the hull. With a hammerstone on a flat anvil stone, the hard tar was pounded into pieces and then combined with pine pitch in a stone pot and melted to make yop. A brush to apply it was contrived from pounded bark fiber bound to the end of a stick. The auger for starting the hundreds of paired holes, through which all component pieces were sewn together, was a pointed and sharpened flint or bone piece. Smoothing the planks was accomplished with a large scraper made from hard abalone shell. Like other coast people, they found that dried sharkskin made an excellent abrasive for fine finishing.

Only the flat bottom of the tomol required a full single board. The sides were built up from knot-free planks of varying length; Kitsepawit recalled that six to eight pieces usually went into the first full round or tier of boards fastened to the bottom piece. They were worked down to a constant one-finger thickness, the builders being careful to make such measurements always by the same finger of the same man. Boards were bent to the desired hull curve after being soaked in hot water. Cementing the side boards to one another and to the bottom was done quickly since the yop set rapidly as it cooled. Scarf joints were made where the board ends butted. The job was left for several days and then the holes were drilled for binding the side boards to the bottom with *tok* string, made from fibers of the red milkweed. A groove was cut between each pair of holes and the string laced through and knotted on the inside. It was recessed in the groove on the hull exterior and then covered with yop.

The painstaking fitting, cementing, and sewing of boards went on for weeks or even months. Some tapering of boards provided for a rising bow and stern. Depending on the width of the pieces available, as many as five or six tiers were needed to complete a canoe. The single center crossbeam was mortised into the sides just before the gunwale round was added. This last circuit was left without joining at either end, leaving a distinctive bow and stern notch, a feature probably once required for the passage of harpoon lines. The resulting structural weakness was compensated for by a rope bound tightly around the hull at the bow and stern. Rounded board "ears" were added to each side at bow and stern, their function best explained by Kitsepawit, who said simply that a tomol would not look right without them.

In part to please the Chumash eye, in part to prevent it from becoming quickly waterlogged, the tomol was painted with red ocher mixed with bitumen and pitch or animal fat. Inlaid shell designs were sometimes used to heighten the decorative appeal, and the old canoe-builder recalled particularly the tomol of a tribal princess, a vessel that had been given a spangled finish by spattering finely ground abalone shell across its hull before the red paint was quite dry.

The plank canoe of the Chumash was a vessel developed in response to the need for marine transport, despite the seemingly inadequate building materials available. The challenge of the waters of the Santa Barbara coast was answered by the imaginative application of technology to devise a boat form distinct from any other on the continent. Other peoples facing different challenges in quite different environments answered them by evolving entirely different vessels.

The Skin Boat

132 *(PREVIOUS PAGE) Some of the excitement of a day of furious trading was captured by Lieutenant Robert Hood in 1819 when the Hudson's Bay Company ships* Prince of Wales *and* Eddystone *appeared off the Upper Savage Islands at the south tip of Baffin Island. There are at least nineteen Labrador-style kayaks clustered around the ships, as well as a boxy eastern Arctic umiak, no doubt loaded with furs and ivory for barter. On the nearest kayak the hunter has his harpoon on the foredeck, while on the afterdeck are the sealskin bladders used to mark a kill and to keep a carcass afloat. The two posts behind the paddler are used as bollards for towing home animals too heavy for deck cargo.*

During Parry's second voyage to the eastern Arctic, Captain G. F. Lyon sketched the people in the area of the Melville Peninsula during a caribou hunt. Easy prey when they were swimming lakes and rivers, the caribou were killed with a special spear called an ippoo. *The kayaks of these people were round-bottomed and built for speed.*

They were measured at twenty-five feet long including a projection three feet long at each end which turned up a little. Because they spent so much time inland in summer, these people did not use umiaks.

Kayak and Umiak

OWHERE ON THE CONTINENT is there an environment less generous than that of the far north. The hunter's job of providing food and the means of shelter for his family was scarcely easy in any region, but in the Arctic it was a responsibility made specially difficult by a harsh and unforgiving climate. Long, sub-zero winters made hunting a hazardous occupation and a precarious means of support. In those dark months, the waters of the Arctic become a rigid seascape of crushing ice; only along parts of the Alaska coast and at the southern tip of Greenland does the ocean remain unfrozen.

But when the sun comes back and the days grow warm and the sea ice melts, then the walruses, fur seals, and sea lions return to coastal waters. Whales swim again along the shores. Lakes and rivers and sea offer an abundance of fish, and the air is alive with migratory birds. Caribou herds move north to browse the barren lands through the brief warm season. Summer is all too short, but for the well-prepared hunter it was a time of plenty, a time to stockpile oil and flesh, hides and furs, to carry his family through the lean cold months that returned so soon.

The hunter needed a boat to carry him close enough to kill sea mammals with short-range weapons. He needed a craft to attack migrating caribou in the water, for they were most vulnerable when swimming across rivers and lakes. As much as, even more than, most natives of North America, the Arctic hunter needed a boat, but of all regions, his surely was the most discouraging to the boat-builder. Wood was essential to most native craft construction, but the few spruce growing north of the tree line are dwarfed and even the willows in that harsh environment are scrubby and stunted. Indians living to the south were hostile to the Inuit, and so the Arctic natives were denied access to better timber there. The best they had was driftwood carried north by rivers and driven by wind and current to arctic beaches.

Every scrap of the sparse harvest was carefully hoarded, and from this driftwood they learned to build their boat frames. Every other bit of material used to complete them came from the bodies of land and sea mammals. These animals provided the greater part of the Inuit diet but also supplied by-products—bone and ivory, horn and antler, teeth and claws, hides, gut and sinew, and the flexible whalebone called baleen. The hunter preserved fish and animal oils and heavy grease and raw blubber and knew the waterproofing qualities of each. Choosing from these materials, the Arctic people built two distinct boats excellently suited to their difficult environment. The *umiak* is a large, open craft which carries a number of people. The *kayak*, decked completely except for a cockpit, is narrow, pointed at each end, and carries one person. Each consists of a wooden frame covered with skin.

Archeological evidence from sites in western Alaska suggests that some such watercraft were used there between four and five thousand years ago. As the Eskimoan migrants travelled east and north, following the game, they spread the basic skin-boat idea throughout the Arctic. By 2000 B.C. some had moved as far east as Greenland, and a long period of adaptation to the eastern Arctic environment culminated in what is called the Dorset culture. Skin boats were often the vehicles for migration, and in new settlements the boats assumed regional distinctions as they were modified to meet different water conditions and to serve for hunting different varieties of game.

The Dorset people spread south to the mainland, along each shore of Hudson Bay, and into Labrador as far as the Gulf of St. Lawrence. They were the people, no doubt, encountered by the Vikings, who gave the name Vinland to some part of the northeast coast. When Thorvald, son of Jarl Eric of Greenland, came ashore here in A.D. 1004 to repair his vessel, his crewmen found three overturned skin boats on the beach. There were three men sheltered beneath each, and the Vikings killed all but one. The escapee soon came back with a veritable fleet of skin boats, and Thorvald himself died with a native arrow in his ribs.

The Norse called the people Skraelings, and the skin boats on the shore almost certainly were umiaks, turned upside down to dry since the hide covering rots if left constantly wet. The boats carrying the avenging attackers could scarcely have been other than speedy hunting kayaks.

When later Europeans began probing the eastern Arctic, some seeking a northwest sea passage, others looking to native trade, they began sending home descriptions of what they saw. Master Dionise Settle, the chronicler of Martin Frobisher's voyage in 1577, recorded that the natives of Davis Strait had two kinds of leather boats: "The great sort are not unlike our wherries, wherein sixteene or twenty men may sit: they have for a sayle drest the guts of such beasts as they kill very fine and thinne, which they sew together: the other boate is but for one man to sit and row in with one oare."

Frobisher met large numbers of kayaks, from ten to a hundred at a time, made from "the skins of red Deare and Seal Skins," and "flat in the bottome, and sharpe at both ends." Early in the trading game, English seamen gave up trying to chase the Inuit boatmen they encountered; one kayaker with his double paddle could outstrip a ship's boat with twenty oarsmen. Frobisher's men were intrigued by the speedy little boats and on one occasion bought five kayaks to take home to England.

Late in the sixteenth century John White recorded a skirmish between members of Sir Martin Frobisher's crew and the native people, likely near the shore of Baffin Island. It is one of the earliest European pictures of a kayak, and although it is not drawn with sufficient accuracy to identify it as a typically Baffin Island or Labrador type, the picture does show that the Inuit were, in their skin craft, very much masters of the sea.

134

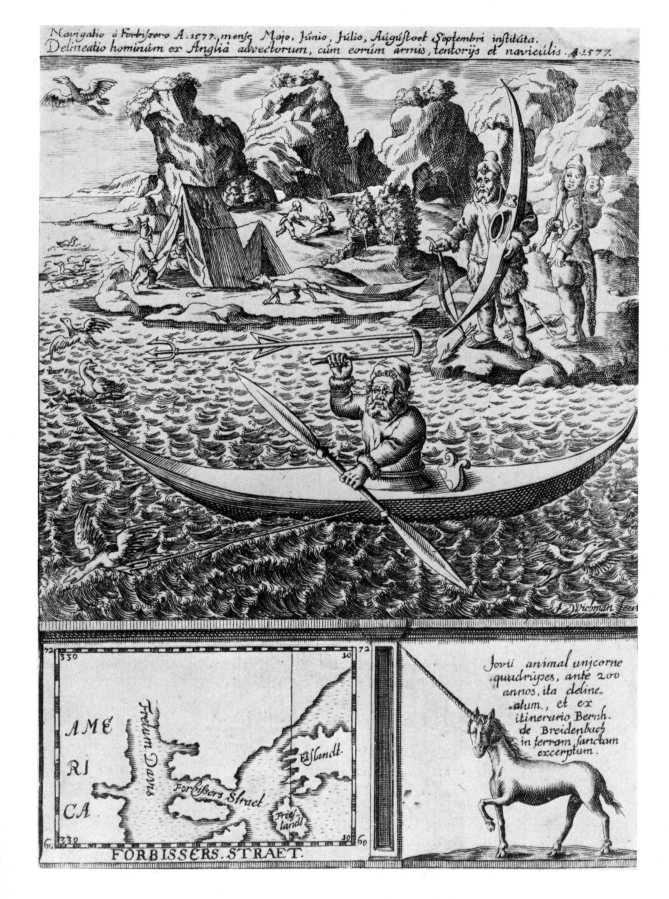

In the English rendering of Charles de Rochefort's account of the Caribbean, a trading captain who had seen kayaks in Davis Strait in 1656 is quoted:

> They consist of little thin pieces of wood, whereof most are cleft like Hoops: These pieces of wood are fasten'd one to another with strong cords made of the guts of fishes which keep them together.... They are cover'd on the out-side with the skins of Sea-Dogs, which are so neatly sewn together, and so artificially done over with Rozin about the seams, that the water cannot make the least entrance into them.

He went on to explain that the boats averaged about fifteen or sixteen feet in length, and that at the middle they had a circumference of about five feet, tapering to the ends in sharp points, which were "plated...with a white bone, or a piece of the Unicorn's horn." The leather decks were flat while the hull was "fashion'd like the belly of a great fish; so that they are very swift upon the water." The cockpit he described as raised with a small ledge of whalebone and just large enough for the waist of one man.

In the frontispiece to the 1675 edition of Martin Frobisher's Historia navigationis, *reality has been distorted a bit by artistic license. But the Inuit did use the trident bird spear with extra barbs on the shaft and they did use the spear thrower. The ferrules around the shaft of the double paddle served to help keep the paddler's hands dry, and the little device on the deck behind him was used to tie seals to the deck or to tow them home. The quaint little unicorn below was inspired by the ivory narwhal tusks the sailors found in the Arctic.*

In Captain James Cook's reports these two kayaks are labelled "Canoes of Oonalashka." The top one is a two-man Aleut baidarka, although the curved and forked bow had its origin on the Alaska Peninsula. This strange feature was the result of the framing and was a nuisance because seaweed got caught in the slot. In the lower picture the Aleut, in his sunshade hat decorated with walrus whiskers, is paddling a kayak which likely had its origin among the Asiatic people of the Chukotski Peninsula, just across the Bering Strait from Alaska. In the two-man baidarka the hunters are using single paddles, while the lower hunter is using a double paddle with a reserve single paddle on the foredeck.

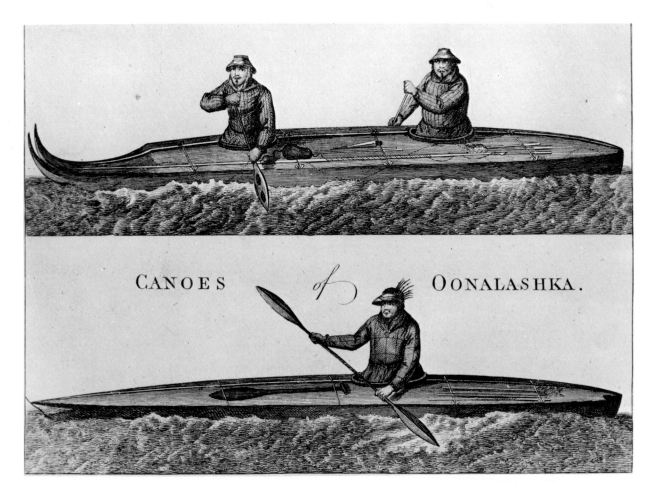

CANOES *of* OONALASHKA.

When he went to sea the Inuit hunter donned a short coat of dressed skin, covered with gum, which reached from the waist to the top of the head and closed tight around the face. The sleeve wrists were tied tight, and the lower end of the coat was fastened to the ledge of the cockpit so that no water could get into the coat or the kayak. Man and kayak became one, as the captain saw in Davis Strait:

> They are so confident in them, and so vers'd in the guiding of them, that they shew a thousand tricks in them . . . diving and rouling themselves in the Sea three or four times together; so that they may be taken for perfect *Amphibia.* . . .
>
> The Women have not the use of these little Boats; but that they may also sometimes divert themselves on the water, their husbands . . . bring them aboard in other vessels which are about the bigness of our Shallop or Long-boats, and such as may carry fifty persons: They are made of poles ty'd together, and cover'd with Sea-Dogs skins. . . . When it is calm they go with Oars, when there is any wind they fasten the Mast to certain Sails of Leather.

In 1814 a young lieutenant aboard H.M.S. *Rosamund* leapt from his bed and raced up to the deck when he heard that Eskimos, the foreigners' name for these people, had been sighted as the ship was passing the Ungava Peninsula. Later he described the scene:

> Alongside the ship, were paddling a large assemblage of canoes, of the most curious construction: these were built of a wooden frame-work of the lightest materials, covered with oiled seal-skin, with the hair scraped off; the skin being sewed over the frame with the most astonishing exactness, and as tight as parchment on the head of a drum. But the most surprising peculiarity of the canoes was their

being *twenty-two* feet long, and only two feet wide. These canoes are only capable of containing one person, for any useful purpose; the slightest inclination of the body, on either side, will inevitably overturn them; yet in these frail barks will the *Esquimaux* smile at the roughest sea.

On the north Pacific shores, where Russian, Spanish, British, and American ships explored and vied for the trade of the native people, essentially the same skin boats were used by the Koryak and Chukchi of the Asiatic mainland, the Aleuts on that chain of islands stretching

The Alaskan umiak still retains the fast lines of a hunting boat. At the same time it can carry the whole family, with tents, food, game, and even dogs, to and from summer fishing and hunting camps. In dangerous drift ice its split walrus-hide cover absorbs the hard knocks and its frame flexes under stress. It can be paddled, sailed, rowed, tracked along the shore with a dog team, or driven by an outboard motor. It can be carried over sea ice on sleds to open leads and it is still used for hunting sea mammals, including whales. In the Canadian Arctic, the umiak has been supplanted by the square-ended canvas canoe with an outboard motor.

westward from the Alaska Peninsula, and the mainland people of the northernmost American coasts. The first strangers to see Aleut kayaks, or, as the Russians called them, *baidarkas*, were the men of Vitus Bering's exploring expeditions to northeastern Siberia and the surrounding waters. During the second trip, in 1741, Georg Steller, a young German scientist, examined the native craft in some detail:

The boats of these Aleuts are about two fathoms long, two feet high and two feet wide from above; in the front, at the prow, they are pointed, at the stern the sides form an angle. Evidently the frame consists of two longitudinal poles which are joined at the ends and kept apart by cross bars. The frame is covered outside, as it seems, with seal-skins and painted a dark brown colour. . . . About two arshins [four feet, eight inches] from the stern there is a round opening with a skirt of whale's guts. By means of a cord, put through a hem, the lower border of the skirt may be tightly bound around the edge of the hatch while down in the hatch and stretching out his legs the American draws the upper hem of the skirt around his body under the armpits and ties it with a noose; thus the water cannot penetrate into the boat.

Bering's men had no idea that the strange craft they were inspecting was to become the key to the Russian fur trade, soon to develop on the northwest American coast. As it happened, one of Bering's ships was wrecked; survivors built a small boat and sailed back to Petropavlovsk, carrying with them a few lustrous skins of the sea otter. These furs, it was learned, commanded fabulous prices in China. Soon the rush was on.

Lured by the promise of fortunes, Siberian freebooters, known as *promyshlenniki*, systematically enslaved the Aleuts. They terrorized the people of the islands, burning villages whose people would not cooperate, killing, and violating Aleut women and making of them hostages to force the men into hunting the otter for them. By 1784 one of the traders, Gregory Ivanovich, had planted the first permanent Russian colony on Kodiak Island, just south of the Alaska Peninsula. In 1791 he installed as manager there Alexander Baranov, who was to make of himself a legend and who began his term by arriving in the settlement in a kayak. He had built it himself and covered it with sea-lion skins, after the fashion of the Aleuts.

When Catherine the Great sent a scientific exploring expedition to inspect her Alaskan holdings, its English commander, Captain Joseph Billings, found that the Shelikov-Golikov Company, by keeping wives hostage, could call out all the men between eighteen and fifty for otter-hunting sweeps. Up to a thousand men would appear in waterproof jackets made from the intestines of sea lions. The company owned six hundred baidarkas which, unlike the one-man kayaks of the eastern Arctic, each had cockpits for two or three hunters. Ranging for hundreds of miles through the Aleutian Islands and south along the mainland, the skin-boat fleets were usually accompanied by an eighty-ton galliot, a boat that carried provisions and stored the fur catch. The baidarkas were hauled aboard from time to time to be dried and waterproofed.

Martin Sauer, secretary of the Czarina's fact-finding expedition, was thoroughly impressed by Aleut seamanship. "The natives," he wrote, "observing our astonishment at their agility and skill, paddled in among the breakers, which reached to their breasts, and carried the baidarkas quite under water; sporting about more like amphibious animals than human beings."

In the center cockpits of three-man baidarkas, Russian fur traders accompanied their fleets of Aleut hunters on voyages of hundreds of miles in search of sea otter. By holding the wives of the hunters hostage, the Russians could call up as many as a thousand Aleut hunters at a time for great sweeps along the Pacific coast. The curious framing at the bow is clear in the uncovered baidarka.

138

Despite the kayakers' extraordinary ability in rough seas, the ocean took its toll of them, and once, when moving southward along the coast, Baranov lost thirty kayaks with their two-man crews when a giant wave engulfed them all. Yet the fleets of Aleut paddlers covered untold sea miles in the hunt for otter. Baranov on one occasion made a deal with a Bostonian, Joseph O'Cain, mate of the *Enterprise*, lending the Yankee trader sixty Aleut hunters with their baidarkas and hunting gear for a poaching venture into the otter-rich waters off the coast of Spanish California. Baranov received urgently needed supplies and a share of the furs. The Spanish were furious, but they had no craft that could match and intercept the swift kayaks.

On the hunt baidarka fleets were often strung out for miles. When an animal was sighted the boatmen paddled as stealthily as possible until one of the hunters was close enough to let loose an arrow. When the otter dived, the hunter gave a shout and raced in closer. As many as eight baidarka crews surrounded the area and waited for the animal to surface. The tiring otter was driven under again and again until dispatched, and then the skin boats strung out once more in a long, sea-sweeping line.

Sauer was enchanted by the grace of the little craft, in particular that of the Unalaska kayaks:

If perfect symmetry, smoothness, and proportion, constitute beauty, they are beautiful; to me they appeared so beyond anything that I ever beheld. I have seen some of them as transparent as oiled paper, through which you could trace every formation of the inside, and the manner of the native's sitting in it; whose light dress, painted and plumed bonnet, together with his perfect ease and activity, added infinitely to its elegance.

The kayak was a hunting tool, designed to carry the hunter to within striking distance of his prey. The hunting techniques for different creatures dictated different characteristics for the craft. To match a swimming caribou, the Inuit hunter needed a fast kayak, long and narrow and round-bottomed as well to present the least surface to the water, reducing skin drag to the minimum. Slain caribou floated and could be retrieved after the killing had been done.

Hunting sea mammals, however, demanded more stealth than speed. The hunter moved cautiously to get gradually within harpoon range of wary prey. He often had to put to sea in foul weather and to face wickedly dangerous water. Often, when a kill was made, he had to carry the carcass within the kayak or on its deck. Or he might tow the animal home, first blowing air beneath its skin to increase its buoyancy and plugging holes in the skin with ivory pegs. Needing, therefore, greater stability, his craft had more beam, a flatter bottom, and more carrying capacity than that of the caribou-hunter. Sea hunters of the Canadian Arctic and northern Alaska had a cockpit coaming tilted up at the front to keep out water that broke over the foredeck.

Of all the variety of flat-bottomed kayaks, there were two broad categories: those of the Canadian eastern Arctic and those of Greenland. Hunters in Greenland developed a small, narrow vessel with a flat, or almost flat, bottom to guarantee stability. It was scarcely possible to carry game home on this kayak, and the hunter normally towed a kill to shore. Being smaller and sitting lower, the boat tended to ship more water, and so the hunter sealed himself in with an apron and drawstring or a complete hood tied around the cockpit coaming.

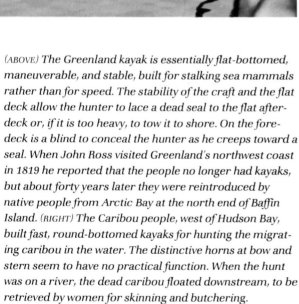

(ABOVE) *The Greenland kayak is essentially flat-bottomed, maneuverable, and stable, built for stalking sea mammals rather than for speed. The stability of the craft and the flat deck allow the hunter to lace a dead seal to the flat after-deck or, if it is too heavy, to tow it to shore. On the fore-deck is a blind to conceal the hunter as he creeps toward a seal. When John Ross visited Greenland's northwest coast in 1819 he reported that the people no longer had kayaks, but about forty years later they were reintroduced by native people from Arctic Bay at the north end of Baffin Island. (RIGHT) The Caribou people, west of Hudson Bay, built fast, round-bottomed kayaks for hunting the migrating caribou in the water. The distinctive horns at bow and stern seem to have no practical function. When the hunt was on a river, the dead caribou floated downstream, to be retrieved by women for skinning and butchering.*

This did away with the need for a high coaming to withstand deck wash. The man and his kayak were capable of weathering heavy seas, and if capsized by a breaking wave the hunter could right himself with a deft sweep of the paddle. In fact, to avoid a big, breaking wave that could damage the vessel, the hunter would purposely capsize, take the great force of the water on the kayak bottom, and right himself when the wave had passed.

In much the same way, the umiak was adapted to specialized local use. In Alaska, when it was used for hunting sea mammals of varying size and habit, it was small and built for speed under the thrust of a few single-blade paddles. Some Alaska umiaks were larger, carrying six to eight paddlers and a harpooner, and intended for whale-hunting.

Ancient taboos prevented women from using the hunting boats, and so other large umiaks were built just for transport and travel. Women paddled along with their men and often made up the entire crew. With overhunting of the greatest of sea mammals, the whale hunt slowly died out in the eastern waters, and the umiak became a woman's boat. Umiaks on the northwest coast of Greenland, where whale-hunting persisted to a more recent date, retained finer lines than those of the south.

And the umiaks of Hudson Strait were so box-like that one suspects the builders there had long since lost interest in fine boat crafting.

The construction of a kayak or an umiak was a communal affair, both men and women contributing essential talents to the end product. In every instance, local preferences, traditions, supplies of materials, available tools, and the water and hunting conditions influenced the builders and shaped the character of the craft.

The making of a kayak was supervised by an experienced builder. He had the form of the boat in his mind and could calculate the various measurements with his hands and arms. As he walked or paddled along the beaches, looking for driftwood, he assessed just how each piece might fit into his plan. There were gunwales to split out and stringers and ribs as well, and so he collected more material than was actually required, making a clear allowance for errors and unexpected fractures in the precious and very limited wood supply. The job might take a year.

(OPPOSITE) *The eastern Greenland kayak does not seem to have changed since the 1850s when a native artist, Aron of Kangek, turned to painting to depict the legends of his people. In his watercolor the kayaks appear to be identical with those used today. Like modern sporting kayakers, the hunters in the foreground are leaning on their paddles for balance.*

(ABOVE) *With trade ranging for hundreds of miles up and down the northwest coast of America, Indian ideas and products were often adopted by Arctic people, and Arctic products by the Indians. While some people in Prince William Sound in Alaska made dugouts, just to their south some Tlingit Indians bought Aleut baidarkas for hunting sea otters. The crew of the antique model umiak from Kodiak Island are wearing Tlingit-style woven hats, and the pattern of their paddles is more Indian than Arctic.*

The first step was shaping and smoothing the two gunwale pieces that gave the kayak frame its strength. The ends were fastened together and the gunwales were then sprung apart to establish the actual shape of the craft. This form the builder made permanent by mortising deck beams between the gunwale strips—straight across if a flat deck was intended, or slightly curved to give the deck a camber that would drain any wash. Towards the center of the kayak, a humped deck beam was inserted to support the cockpit coaming, and behind it an open space was left for the cockpit itself.

The deck frame was turned over and rested on a couple of supports. Shaping the ribs was next, and then mortising their ends into holes drilled or cut into the underside of the gunwale pieces. These ribs were of split cedar or spruce, softened in hot water to ease their bending, or of green willow withes that needed no soaking. The rib curve chosen gave the kayak a round bottom for speed or a flat bottom for stability or a gentle V profile as a compromise. With all the ribs in position, a keelson was laced to each of them inside the frame, curving from bow to stern, the profile varying from region to region. Further stringers were laced outside the ribs to fill out the kayak's particular local form and to increase its longitudinal strength.

There was enormous variety in the shaping of bow and stern, design distinctions that affected the behavior of the craft in the water and that gave each boat type a recognizable local character. In some kayaks the keelson simply curved upward to join the gunwale ends in a sharp point. In others the gunwales, keelson, and stringers were mortised at each end into a naturally curved root piece or a carefully shaped board or block which formed stem and stern pieces. The regional procedure established the regional profile.

With the now rigid kayak frame righted once more, the cockpit hoop was tied into position. This framing might be circular or oval, D-shaped, or essentially triangular with corners rounded. It might be cocked up at front to shed water coming over the foredeck or lie level with the deck if the hunter was to use an apron to keep water out.

141

1

2

A two-man kayak is a rare boat in the eastern Arctic, but the way it is built differs little from the normal one-man hunting craft. The construction of a kayak in the Belcher Islands of Hudson Bay is a joint venture of the men and women of the community. It starts with the collection of essential materials: driftwood carefully selected from the beaches, caribou sinew procured from the mainland, and seals killed off their shores for skins.

1. The strength of the kayak lies in its heavy gunwales, split from a driftwood log, sculpted to form a rounded stern, and carpentered to a long, pointed, slightly upturned bow. The gunwales are held to their boat shape by deck braces which are laced in position. A special humped deck brace is inserted just in front of each cockpit opening to support the leading edge of the D-shaped cockpit coaming. A single deck stringer is lashed from bow to stern to the center of the deck braces, broken only at the cockpit openings. The frame is held together by lashing and lacing with sealskin thongs.

2 & 3. With the deck frame turned upside down, holes are drilled in the gunwales from bow to stern. Round ribs are fashioned from split driftwood, softened in hot water, and bent to shape using mouth and hands; then their ends are seated in the holes in the gunwales.

4. A long, flat stringer is lashed to the center line of the ribs, and two curved stringers are fitted close to the curve of the ribs as they diminish in width toward bow and stern, giving the kayak a flat bottom. Two more stringers are fastened to the sides of the ribs and the whole frame is secured with time-proven lashing and knots.

5 & 6. Meanwhile, the women have skinned sixteen to eighteen seals, scraped the fat from one side and the hair from the other, and then "ripened" the skins in a bag to make them rubbery for stretching over the kayak frame. Trimmed to shape and scraped thin at the edges, the skins are sewn with blind, waterproof stitches into a long cover for the kayak bottom. The thread for sewing the cover is a combination of fine cotton twine and split caribou sinew. When the deck cover is sewn to the bottom skins and the cockpit coaming is lashed into position, the cover is allowed to dry, during which time the skin becomes drum tight. The craft is then ready for the water.

As the wooden framework of the kayak neared completion, the women began to prepare the sealskins that would cover it, scraping and curing the skins, removing every scrap of fat, keeping them naturally moist by storing them in a leather sack, then scraping again as the hair became loose. They matched the skins, trimmed them to size, and chewed the edges where they would be sewn with threads of animal sinew, of which the caribou supplied the longest and most durable. Then, working in a group around the wet rawhide pieces, the women sewed them into one long sheet with overlapping seams and blind stitching. This was draped along the overturned kayak frame and stretched out by many hands, drawn tight across the stringers, pulled taut around the gunwales, and sewn at bow and stern; then the long edges were pulled together over fore and after decks with a cross-thonging. Nimble fingers with bone needles worked quickly to complete the sewing before the skins began to dry. With the drying, the hide covering became drum-tight and hard within a few hours.

This sealskin sheath seldom lasted more than one season. When ice locked the waters, many kayaks were stripped, and the old covering and its lashings were dispatched by the often ravenous sled dogs. Whether with its skin cover or stripped to bare frame, the kayak was stored for the winter on a stone or wooden scaffolding, securely out of the reach of dogs and wild animals.

In winter the people worked on the accessories for their kayaks, carving double-bladed paddles, trimming the blade edges with bone to withstand chipping by ice, and making ferrules, usually of leather and mounted one to each side of the paddle grips, to prevent icy drip water from reaching the hunter's hands. Paddles were decorated with bone and ivory inlay work and colored with paint compounded of red ocher and fish oils. There were ivory plugs to be carved for emergency use should a kayak develop holes in its skin while at sea. There were toggles of bone to be made to hold the hunting weapons securely to the deck in front of the paddler.

The framework for an Alaskan umiak starts with a heavy keel and strong gunwales held in position by temporary supports. The split driftwood ribs are lashed in place and stringers are lashed to them from bow to stern to support the skin cover. The technique has changed little in two hundred years, since these Arctic people already had Asian iron cutting tools when the Europeans arrived.

144

The toughest covering for a western Arctic umiak was split walrus hide, which could withstand a buffeting from ice that would grind a European whaleboat to matchwood. Because the frame was lashed together, it too flexed under the pounding of waves or ice pack, and broken ribs or stringers could easily be spliced, or replaced when a new cover was made. A boat of this kind was ideal for whale-hunting or for transporting tons of meat back to a winter settlement.

Then there were hunting tools to make: harpoons and lances, throwing sticks and bolos, nets and other fishing gear, bows and arrows. Many of the old implements and accessories reveal an exquisite artistry in utilitarian forms, work which, with stone-age tools, often took months to complete. The long, severe winters provided the months for such work, and as the craftsmen sat comfortably among their furs in their sod houses or igloos, they sang and they talked and they retold stories that had been told a hundred times before.

The kayak was a source of pride to the hunter who owned it; it proved that he was capable of acquiring the necessary raw materials and of mustering community help for its construction. To the family it was an economic necessity, the means of obtaining their food and clothing. For the craftsman it was an important project on which he could lavish his skill and creative imagination. To the band, as to the family, it was a vital asset, for the successful hunter shared with those who were hungry.

The traditional skin kayak has all but disappeared from the Arctic. Commercially made canoes with outboard motors have long since supplanted it as the chief transport for hunters. The old skin-covered kayaks today are more often to be seen in museum exhibits than in arctic waters. Among the Inuit people, who conceived and developed it as the perfect boat for their needs of yesterday, it is becoming a memory. A recent newspaper story has reported, not without some appreciation of the irony, that a British firm which manufactures kayak kits has been seeking to establish a market for its products among the Inuit of the Canadian North.

145

(OPPOSITE) *When European whalers converged on the eastern Arctic, they soon depleted the whale population, so that the natives virtually gave up the hunt for the huge mammals. As a consequence, their umiaks lost their fast lines and degenerated into heavy transport boats used by women. Even at that, the woodworking that went into their framework impressed Europeans. Unlike the bent ribs common in Alaskan umiaks, the frames in the eastern Arctic were square and carpentered, giving the craft a flat bottom. Only on the northwest shore of Greenland, where the natives still hunted whales, did the umiak retain its fast lines for speed and maneuverability. (LEFT) The kayak of the Nunivak delta at the mouth of the Yukon River had a distinctive hole in the bow, and its ridged deck ended in a spur at the stern, both good handholds for lifting the craft in and out of the water. For a short trip the kayaker is carrying a passenger. In the eastern Arctic, passengers were sometimes carried prone inside a kayak. (BELOW) In all the cultures that used kayaks, children were encouraged and taught to use them at an early age. In Greenland, special tiny kayaks were built to give young boys a sense of balance and to teach them the techniques of hunting. The* First Lesson in Canoeing *was painted by the Danish artist J. E. C. Rasmussen and printed in the* Illustrated London News *in 1876.*

The Bull Boat Family

THE MOST SUPERB BOATS of animal skin were made by the people of the Arctic, but, although natives elsewhere on the continent never approached the Inuit level of achievement, many were familiar with hide-covered craft. For some groups the skin boat was a makeshift, for short-term use, but for others, like the people of the central grassy plains, a leather-covered basket was their only vessel. There, the readily available materials were the springy green branches of riverside willow, from which a rigid circular frame was made, and one or more buffalo skins, sewn together with sinews, were fastened securely over it. Because that plains coracle was sheathed in buffalo hide, it was called a *bull boat*.

With two friends, the painter George Catlin made a river crossing in such a craft in upper Missouri River country in 1833. An Indian woman carried it on her head to the river's edge. The three passengers climbed in, and the ferry woman waded into the water, pulling the boat behind her. When the water rose above her waist, she

Close by Fort Clark, just north of present-day Bismarck, North Dakota, Mandan women cross the Missouri River. They use willow-framed bull boats in the endless task of ferrying firewood and other necessities to homes in their village of Mih-Tutta-Hang-Kush. As in the nearest craft, the buffalo's tail remains part of the hide to serve as a towing rope. The engraving is after an 1833 watercolor by Karl Bodmer.

drew her dress over her head, threw it ashore, and set off, swimming with one arm, towing the bull boat with the other:

In this manner we were conveyed to the middle of the stream, where we were soon surrounded by a dozen or more beautiful girls, from twelve to fifteen and eighteen years of age, who were at that time bathing. . . . we found ourselves suddenly in the delightful dilemma of floating down the current in the middle of the river; and being turned round and round to the excessive amusement of the villagers, who were laughing at us from the shore, as well as these little tyros, whose delicate hands were besetting our tub on all sides.

Like these Mandan of the Missouri, the Sioux, Assiniboine, Arikara, Cherokee, Hidatsa, Omaha, Kansa — in short, most of the plains people — used the same basic leather boat. The Blackfoot, when migrating, improvised ferries from frames of green boughs covered with their tipi skins. With few exceptions among prairie tribes, the bull boat was a woman's boat; it was her job to tow or paddle it and her job to backpack it over land.

The economies of these people depended on the plentiful herds of shaggy bison, and since they always had hides on hand, they could make a boat in a few hours. The circular form was the most familiar, but the Omahas made one with a distinct bow and stern, a slightly elongated craft covered with dried hides, the seams so tightly sewn as to be waterproof. This *mandeha* was framed with red willow branches, serving as bowed ribs, and two saplings formed gunwale strips.

Paddlers sat towards the bow and a steersman in the stern.

According to Catlin,

the skin canoes of the Mandans . . . are made almost round like a tub, by straining a buffalo's skin over a frame of wicker work. . . . The woman in paddling these awkward tubs, stands in the bow, and makes the stroke with the paddle, by reaching it forward in the water and drawing it to her, by which means she pulls the canoe along with some considerable speed.

John D. Hunter, who spent his boyhood years as an adoptee among the Kickapoo, the Kansa, and the Osage tribes of the American Middle West, became familiar with their boat-building methods in the early years of the nineteenth century:

The skeletons or frames are made of osier or flexible poles, lashed together with bark or some other materials, and are covered generally with the skins of the buffalo sewed together, and to the frame, with the sinews of the deer. They vary in size considerably according to the service for which they are wanted: sometimes a single skin covers one, at others, a half dozen are required. The hair is left on the outside: it, however, soon wears off, when the boat moves rapidly in the water, and is easily managed.

150

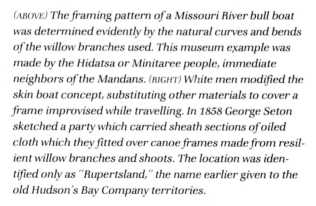

(ABOVE) *The framing pattern of a Missouri River bull boat was determined evidently by the natural curves and bends of the willow branches used. This museum example was made by the Hidatsa or Minitaree people, immediate neighbors of the Mandans.* (RIGHT) *White men modified the skin boat concept, substituting other materials to cover a frame improvised while travelling. In 1858 George Seton sketched a party which carried sheath sections of oiled cloth which they fitted over canoe frames made from resilient willow branches and shoots. The location was identified only as "Rupertsland," the name earlier given to the old Hudson's Bay Company territories.*

The Indians smoke, oil, and preserve them with great care, which makes them very durable. When travelling, they often remove them to the land, invert and use them for shelters against the rain; and being exceeding light, they are carried without inconvenience over the longest portages.

Moose skin was sometimes the covering for rough-and-ready boats among people of the woodlands region; in the seventeenth century, north of Lake Superior, Pierre-Esprit Radisson fell in with a party of Cree that was using such vessels. Lahontan some few years later described in eastern Canada Indian canoes of elk skin used after the spring breakup. The young John Gyles, captured in 1689 by Malecites, lived with these Indians in the upper Saint John River Valley of New Brunswick. When the rivers froze, the bark canoes were stored away and he went with a hunting party into the bush for the winter: "When the spring came and the rivers broke up we moved back to the head of the St. John's River and there made canoes of moose hides, sewing three or four together and pitching the seams with balsam mixed with charcoal. Then we went down the river to a place called Madawecok."

While almost everywhere the rigid frame was the norm, New Brunswick Malecites sometimes made a moose-skin craft in the same way they made birch bark canoes. A sheet of rawhide was stretched over the chosen building bed in place of bark. The sides were raised to form a skin trough and stakes were pounded into the ground outside to support that trough in familiar canoe form. The builder then cut gores along the sides, sewed the gunwale frame into it, inserted long stringers of dressed wood, added bow and stern frame pieces, and finally forced into the interior the pre-bent cedar ribs.

Indians of the north and of Labrador shared to some extent the environment and the culture of the Inuit, and so they sometimes produced boats of similar form. While the Arctic people used seal and walrus hide for covering, some Indians followed much the same construction procedure with moose skin. The Loucheux of Alaska and northern Yukon did so in making freight vessels very much resembling the umiaks of waters just to the north. In recent times they have substituted canvas as a covering over scow-like frames made from spruce saplings.

A moose-skin boat with immense cargo capacity was photographed on the Mackenzie River in 1927. John Gyles, an English captive of Malecites in New Brunswick in 1689, described moose-hide boats that they used when spring ice still clogged the rivers; and Nahanni Indians of the Mackenzie district formerly carried their furs to the trading post in moose-skin vessels, usually stripping off and bartering the canoe sheath as well.

151

Such boats, and some canoes that took on characteristics of the kayak, were probably familiar to most of the Déné, the northern Athapaskan people. Like the Micmacs of Nova Scotia, thousands of miles to the east and south, Slave Indians improvised moose-skin boats to carry their furs to market. Where Alaska borders on British Columbia, near Skagway, the coastal Chilkat Tlingit traded with the Déné from the interior. They kept skin boats for this use at the head of Lake Bennett, beyond Chilkoot Pass, using them season after season and storing the skin coverings each winter.

Just as they adopted native bark and dugout canoes, white men learned to use bull boats on rivers of the plains. It was in coracles of buffalo skin that men of the Lewis and Clark team conducted in 1806 the earliest recorded exploration of the Yellowstone River. According to Captain Benjamin Bonneville, whose explorations of western plains and mountains in the 1830s were first romantically told by author Washington Irving, bull boats were used by the first whites to explore Great Salt Lake.

The longest bull-boat voyage recorded by frontier travellers was made by Captain Nathaniel Wyeth and five companions, who set off in 1833 from the uppermost navigable water of the Bighorn River, at the very foot of the eastern slope of the Rockies. Their craft was eighteen feet long, five and a half feet wide, pointed at each end, and round in the bottom, and it drew a foot and a half of water. Three buffalo skins were stitched together for the covering, and the seams were coated with a mixture of elk tallow and wood ashes.

Although it was not the familiar tub-like craft of the plains, the crew certainly called it a bull boat. It withstood well the rough river passage, but the travellers soon learned they had to haul it from the water from time to time to dry the skin covering. Under steady use such boats had a short life because water-sodden leather rotted and fell to pieces. A daily drying at each campsite became the practice, sometimes before a roaring fire.

Down the rapids of the Bighorn and into the Yellowstone River and northward, the crew found the greatest hazards were sandbars, snags, and sunken trees. From Fort Cass on the Yellowstone, navigation became easier, and whenever they were favored by a following wind, they skimmed downriver under a sail that did normal duty as a tent. They floated out onto the wider Missouri

River, paddled to nearby Fort Union, distribution post for the American Fur Company, and then continued downstream in a cottonwood dugout which had been obtained from local Blackfoot Indians and was better suited to the larger river. Their leather boat had carried them some five hundred miles in about ten days.

Just as Blackfoot on the move once used the buffalo-skin coverings of their tipis to improvise simple boats, so traders and settlers did the same with their wagon canopies. An English writer described the procedure about 1860 when his party prepared to cross a river in the Lake of the Woods region where Ontario meets Manitoba:

The guides constructed, as usual, a sort of boat, by drawing up with a cord the edges of the water-proof covering of the baggage cart, purposely prepared for such an exigence, and then stretching it by laying the two wheels inside. The body of the cart was laden and floated over, and the horses were driven into the stream and forced to swim. The whole process often occupied several hours, but no accident of consequence occurred.

Writing in 1737, John Tobler, leader of a German-Swiss group of immigrants to the Carolina country, reported that a local merchant had purchased from the Indians—probably Chickasaws—buffalo, deer, and bear hides and also a folding leather boat large enough to carry four or five persons. About the same time, James Adair, trader and author, living in the same region among the Catawba, Cherokee, and Chickasaw peoples, described a similar boat:

152

When we expect high rivers, each company of traders carry a canoe, made of tanned leather, the sides over-lapped about three fingers breadth, and well sewed with three seams. Around the gunnels, which are made of saplings, are strong loop-holes, for large deer-skin strings to hang down both the sides: with two of these, is securely tied to the stem and stern, a well-shaped sapling, for a keel, and in like manner the ribs. Thus, they usually rig out a canoe, fit to carry over ten horse loads at once, in the space of half an hour; the apparatus is after-wards commonly hidden with great care, on the opposite shore. Few take the trouble to paddle the canoe; for, as they are commonly hardy, and also of an amphibious nature, they usually jump into the river, with their leathern barge a-head of them, and thrust it through the deep part of the water, to the opposite shore.

In the eighteenth and nineteenth centuries, the Seminoles, who moved into the Florida peninsula, from time to time used makeshift skin boats, and when the pioneer American botanist William Bartram toured that region, he carried a folding leather boat. He used it in 1778 to cross the Ocmulgee River:

We immediately sat about rigging our portable leather boat, about eight feet long, which was of thick soal leather, folded up and carried on the top

of a pack of deer-skins. The people soon got her rigged, which was effected after the following manner. We, in the first place, cut down a White-Oak sapling, and by knotching this at each end, bent it up, which formed the keel, stem and stern post of one piece; this was placed in the bottom of the boat...which being fastened by thongs to two other poles bent round, the outside of the rim formed the gunwhales: thus in an hour's time our bark was rigged, to which afterwards we added two little oars or sculls.

A woman of the plains region demonstrates the effective paddle stroke to be used in a circular vessel. She reaches out to dip the blade, then pulls it toward her leather ferry boat. The photograph, from about 1900, is by Edward S. Curtis.

The need to make do with whatever resources were available in any given place was demonstrated to Caleb Swan, a United States Indian agent, who in 1790 was travelling south with a party of Creeks. Day upon day of steady rain had raised every stream to flood level. When they reached the banks of the Alapaha River, in southern Georgia, Swan suggested they make a dugout, but their one small hatchet seemed a futile tool for such a job. The Indians took on the problem. They scouted the immediate woods and encountered a stray cow, which they killed and skinned. Returning to the swollen river, they cut saplings, made hoops, and stretched the green hide over the very simplest frame to make a bowl-shaped craft. Swan reported the ferrying of the Alapaha: "the Indians commenced the business by swimming and towing the skin boat by a string, which they held in their teeth, getting up a general war-hoop, to frighten away the voracious alligators that inhabit this river in vast numbers. By uncommon and hazardous exertion, we were, with all our baggage safely towed over."

On the plains, where other building material was often difficult to acquire, the leather bull boat for some peoples became their principal watercraft. Except for the arctic rim, other parts of the continent provided alternative materials, and the favored vessels were the dugout, the bark canoe, or some form of float. But when the familiar was not immediately at hand, skin-covered craft were improvised almost everywhere to serve immediate needs.

Since the bull boat of the plains was a working transport and not a travel vessel, it was almost exclusively a woman's craft. In the Missouri River country of what is now North Dakota, Rudolf Kurz in 1851 sketched Hidatsa women carrying their boats to or from the river. To help preserve the skin covering the boats were removed from the water when not in use.

The Bark Canoe

The Woodland Indians

The range of the paper birch (Betula papyrifera)—better known in the canoe fraternity as the canoe birch—extended from Maine to central Alaska. The quality of the bark varied greatly, as did the size of the trees; while one thick sheet of birch bark might serve for a large Huron canoe in the south, some very small Déné canoes in the northwest were patched together with ten or twelve pieces of thin bark.

(PREVIOUS PAGE) In 1845, Paul Kane painted a night fishing scene on the Fox River, which flows into Green Bay, Wisconsin. The fishermen are probably Sauk or Fox Indians who used very small bark hunting canoes. This method of night fishing was used almost universally by the Indians before the arrival of Europeans; the iron fire basket was only a refinement on native torches of resinous wood, or of birch bark clamped in the split end of a green pole.

WHILE INUIT OF THE ARCTIC made outstanding watercraft from the skins of animals, over much of the temperate region of the continent, Indians used the skin of a tree to produce a vessel that was a unique engineering achievement. Wherever a sheet of bark could be peeled from a trunk, serviceable boats were built with it, but one tree species (*Betula papyrifera*) supplied such superior bark that it is commonly called the canoe birch. From sixty to eighty feet high, it is the most widely spread geographically and grows as far north as any other deciduous tree. Except for the west coast proper and the central plains, it thrives from Alaska to Labrador and Newfoundland, south to New York, northern Pennsylvania, central Michigan, and Minnesota, and across to northern Montana and northwestern Washington.

Throughout this territory native peoples evolved many different styles but the typical birch bark canoe is probably that made by the Ojibwas of the upper Great Lakes region. For them, as for all woodlands people, spring was a very busy season. It was the time to grease the webbing of the snowshoes and to cache them, safe from dogs and bears. It was time to sew the bark containers to catch maple sap. Most importantly perhaps, it was time to make new canoes.

As the sun grew warmer one might see men from one band go off to the woods together to select birch bark. There was some urgency because winter and spring

bark were the strongest; bark taken in summer tended to bubble and separate into thin sheets, better suited for making their wigwams. They wanted pieces about eighteen feet long and sought trees with clean trunks rising to some height before branching. The lower bark, saturated by late winter snow and made spongy and weak, was of no use to them. They would take bark samples, weighing them in the hand, looking for trees that would give sheets about three-sixteenths of an inch thick.

The selection made, one young man climbed the birch and, perhaps twenty feet from the ground, made a single girdling cut through the trunk bark, using a stone ax. Below him a friend made a similar cut just above the snow line. Then they made one continuous vertical slash between and, using flat moose-rib spudders, rounded and smooth at the working ends, they very carefully began separating the corky bark from the red cambium layer beneath. Anxious faces peered upward as the bark came free in a curled sheet and gentle hands lowered it to the ground. It was rolled up and tied with spruce root and the men turned to another tree. When they came home laden with rolls of bark they submerged them in the water of a stream and weighted them with flat rocks; kept wet, the bark would remain soft.

Another group came into camp carrying lengths of split white cedar. These men had been in the woods several days, felling by fire the trees they had girdled the year before, and splitting the trunks with bone and stone wedges. The master canoe-builder checked the straight white grain and nodded his approval. He had already reminded the women to collect *watape*, spruce roots for sewing and lashing, and spruce gum for sealing the canoe seams.

The men discussed plans around the fire. How many canoes should they make? For summer travel the band needed ten, and only five from the previous season were still serviceable. So they would build five for their own use and six more to trade with the Iroquois for maize. The women chatted quietly among themselves. Eleven bark canoes; they would need a great deal of gum and watape.

In the morning the master builder selected several level plots on the beach. The children cleared away stones and then spread sand over each of these building beds. The old man spent most of the morning splitting and smoothing cedar to make two thin strips about seventeen feet long and two inches wide. Along each strip, using the chisel-sharp teeth of a beaver or a fine flint blade, he cut five tiny holes. Then he tied the matched lengths together at each end and spread them apart at the middle. Using his worn memory stick with key dimensions notched into it, he measured off shorter lengths and fitted them into the prepared holes to preserve the boat form. He had completed the frame that would determine the canoe shape.

(ABOVE LEFT) Ojibwa canoe construction starts with the careful selection of birch bark in later winter or early spring. Bark blackened by snow at the base of the tree is spongy, and rejected.

(ABOVE) The second major material is cedar or black spruce, split and carved into long gunwales, ribs, and thin sheathing. The men use the traditional crooked knife to shape the wood. Thwarts are made of a hardwood that splits readily, such as hard maple or ash.

The bark is laid, white side up, on a building bed that is slightly raised at the ends. The long gunwale strips have been lashed together at both ends and spread apart into a boat form with the thwarts. This boat-shaped form has been laid on the bark, weighed down with stones, and the bark is being staked up along the sides.

Meanwhile, the women are collecting long spruce roots, peeling off the bark, and splitting them into half-round thongs for sewing the bark seams and lashing the bark to the gunwales and frames.

158

(OPPOSITE TOP) The ribs have been softened in hot water, bent to shape, and left to dry in the heat of the sun and the fire. The bow frame has been made and it too is drying on the right. (BELOW) Additional panels of bark have been added along the sides and secured by temporary slats behind the stakes. The building frame is being raised inside to the level of the gunwale.

That afternoon the women arrived with coils of spruce roots and bark boxes full of gum. All day they had been scraping sticky accumulations of gum from spruce trees and nicking the bark to make the resin flow into little birch bark cones which they could gather in the days ahead. They had been grubbing up long strands of root from the black earth, and their stained clothes and skin were proof of their labor.

In camp the dirty lumps of gum went into bark packages with holes punched in them, and these were dropped into a larger sealed birch bark box filled with water. With red-hot stones dropped in, the water heated, and the gum melted and seeped through the holes. The bits of bark and dirt remained in the packets and the gum floated on the water surface. Still liquid, it was skimmed off into clay pots and bits of hard moose fat were blended in so that it would be less brittle when it set.

When canoe-building was resumed the next day everyone had a job. The young boys were told to build two big fires. Girls were slithering the bark from coils of spruce roots while the women separated each clean, bare length into two half-round strands. There was little conversation because, after she started the split with a fingernail, a woman held one strand in her teeth while with sure fingers she controlled the split down the length of the root.

The canoe-maker showed the young men how to split and smooth cedar pieces for ribs. With his greatly prized copper knife, which had come from upper Lake Superior country, he was adding to the pile of laths at his side. Each was about five feet long, two inches wide and a quarter-inch thick. The old man nodded towards the fires, one burning fiercely over a pile of round stones and the other in a bowl-like hollow in the rock. The youths raked the fire out of the depression and filled it with water, then immersed the cedar laths, keeping the water near to boiling with stones from the other fire.

From time to time they hooked out a couple of laths and took them to the old man for bending. He flexed the first two together against his knee, shifting the pressure up and down their length until they were bowed into a flat U shape. Then he tied their ends together to hold the curve. As he worked, the ribs diminished in size to conform to the narrowing shape of the canoe, and he sprang each new rib inside the previous one so that they nested together tightly. In the sun or beside the fire they would dry in a permanent bow.

The following few days were chilly and everyone worked at gathering more bark and cedar, more watape and gum. Then the weather changed. A hot sun warmed the sheltered camp, and they started the first canoe. They laid the building frame on the sandy bed and piled more sand at each end. This would make the bottom of the canoe rise up a little at bow and stern. Around the frame they pounded stakes into the ground about an inch from its edge, and positioned in pairs. At the ends the stakes were placed very close together for about eighteen inches because the bow and stern pieces, when they were added later, would increase the overall length of the canoe. The shape of the canoe was now outlined in upright stakes, about three feet high at the middle and four feet at the ends. The building frame was lifted from its position. The stakes were pulled gently from the soil and laid beside the holes. Then the long sheet of birch bark, its white outer surface up, was laid in place, covering the canoe bed from end to end. The old man came over to supervise; he wanted the building frame replaced on the bark exactly over its original position. Once satisfied, he weighted the frame down with rocks so that it wouldn't shift.

With a sureness of hand that told she had done the job many times before, one woman with a flint blade made a series of gore cuts about two feet apart, from the outer edge of the bark nearly to the edge of the frame. As she lifted up each flap of bark, the men replaced the stakes in their holes to hold the bark in its trough form, while another woman looped a strand of basswood bark around each pair of stakes to hold them upright. The men turned to the next canoe bed. There was nothing they could tell their wives about working birch bark or sewing with spruce roots. Five or six women made themselves comfortable around the shell and got to work. Each had her own bark box of spruce roots in warm water, each her own flint knife and a new awl for punching holes. It was a fine social time as they trimmed and sewed and chatted. Along the center, where the canoe was wider, the bark didn't rise as high as the ends, so they laced another panel of bark to each side to bring it up to gunwale level. As the sun dropped, the bark grew cooler and more difficult to work. They splashed hot water on it to keep it supple while they finished the sewing.

Next morning the building frame, lying inside the bark trough, was raised and held just within the upper rim of the sewn bark shell. The two long sides of the frame would become the inner gunwale strips. When they added another long cedar strip to each outer edge, the bark was sandwiched between two pieces of wood. The craftsman was busy again with his memory stick, measuring the depth of the canoe, and eyeing its length to see that it had no twist. When he was satisfied, the women punched holes just below the gunwales, lacing spruce roots through and around the wood to complete groups of bindings, about four inches apart, from end to end on both sides.

The shell was now rigid enough to be turned bottom up, resting on a couple of logs. The old man brought the stem pieces he had made for the bow and stern, curved frames which would give the canoe its distinctive profile. He had made the tight bends in the wood by splitting it into laminations and soaking it in hot water. The women now slipped the stem pieces between the folded bark at each end, trimmed the bark to conform to the curve of the frames, and sewed them into position.

The women have taken over, to sew the long seams at the sides, trim the excess bark at the top and ends, and lash the bark to the gunwales. The bow and stern frames have been slipped into place at the ends of the bark cover and these will be sewn in position. It begins to look like a canoe.

(RIGHT) The dependence of the Ojibwas on the bark canoe is evident in this camp, where there are at least seven three-fathom canoes to serve their needs for hunting, fishing, and travel. The canoes have the old-style bows, since the scene was painted by T. Mower Martin in 1880.

160

The canoe was turned upright and the ends of the gunwale strips were lashed into notches in the stem frames. The bark shell was complete, but it was as yet a graceless and angular structure. That would change when the ribs were forced into it. But the women had one last job before the men took over; they poured hot gum over the seams inside and covered any weak spots with bark patches.

While they waited for a hot day to guarantee supple bark, the men split long, flat pieces of cedar for the inner sheathing, rounding the ends of each. When the day came, they started at the inside bottom of the canoe, at the bow and stern, pushing the feather-thin wood pieces between the bark skin and the stem pieces. Working up the sides, they added sheathing until the whole interior was covered with very thin cedar, held in place by a few temporary ribs. The job of fitting the permanent ribs was reserved for the master builder. Trimming each to length, he pushed them gently into place with their ends wedged under each gunwale. Then, as he hammered them into their final position, they stretched the soft bark into its ultimate rounded form.

The final task was to make the canoe watertight and the Ojibwa women, who often sat on the canoe bottom while paddling, had every reason to seal the seams with care. They poured the hot liquid gum over every seam and lace hole, licking their thumbs and squeezing it into every crevice. If the gum set before they were satisfied, they used a glowing stick from the fire to soften it, then pressed it flat so the canoe would present a smooth hull to the water.

(LEFT) The men are back at work, laying thin, horizontal strips of cedar inside the bark shell and wedging them in position with temporary ribs. The inner sheathing gives the canoe more longitudinal strength. (ABOVE) The canoe is now a bark shell with gunwales, thwarts, end frames, and inner sheathing. The men are stretching this shell by forcing the ribs into position and so stretching the bark. Each rib is cut to exact size, its ends forced under the gunwales, and it is hammered into place with a wooden maul. The tension of the bark cover holds the whole canoe together. (OPPOSITE TOP) Using hot spruce gum mixed with a little tallow, the women waterproof the seams they have sewn and the joins at bow and stern. If the gum on the seams gets too hard to work in with a wet thumb, they soften it with the heat of a glowing forked stick. To help the gum set, ground charcoal is sometimes mixed with it, making the seams black. (RIGHT) The gunwale caps are pegged or nailed to the top of the gunwales to protect the bark from the rub of paddles, and the canoe is ready for the water.

The master builder watched as the first completed canoe was launched. He waded into the water, placed one foot in her center, shifted his weight aboard, and pushed off with the other foot. He settled on his knees, then raised and dipped a paddle. The tight bark vessel darted and cut the water evenly. He shifted his stroke and she turned instantly to the shore, and the old man proved he was yet agile enough to step out into the shallows before the birch skin touched the sand. It was a good canoe; he was satisfied.

In the Mohawk Valley of what is now New York State, heart of the Iroquois country, there was little birch to be found and the Indians here resorted to elm bark. It made serviceable but slow and comparatively crude canoes. The heavy bark was shaved thin towards each end and actually pleated to raise bow and stern. Where the bark sides met at each end they were lashed together between two vertical flat sticks. A couple of lengths split from a sapling and lashed along each side served as gunwale strips. The bark was stiff and held its trough form without ribs; a couple of thwarts between the gunwales preserved the whole structure in canoe form.

Outside the birch tree range, the canoe of spruce bark, with a sticky surface that never dried, was probably one of the most disagreeable of vessels. Elsewhere canoes were made occasionally from the skin of a chestnut or cherry tree but, like those of elm, sometimes they were made to serve only briefly, then to be discarded. As well as a trade carrier among tribal peoples, the birch canoe itself became a trade item, and in marginal country the Indian who could afford to buy one of those fine Ojibwa vessels could forgo the local products. When the white man arrived, he too came to value the bark boat of the woodlands.

164

(LEFT) Wherever wild rice grew, and particularly south and west of Lake Superior, it was a staple of the Indian diet and an important trade item. At harvest time in early September the women lined their canoes with thin birch bark and paddled them into the standing rice. The stalks were bent over the gunwales and the ears of rice were beaten with short paddles so that the grains fell into the bottom of the craft. Industrious harvesters, like the Ojibwa women sketched by Seth Eastman, could fill a canoe three times in a day.

For a people who depended for their living on hunting, fishing, and gathering their food from the wild, the bark canoe was the perfect vehicle. It could be made from the forest around them, and used for gathering wild rice one day, for fishing the next, and for moving camp when the spirit moved them. This sketch by William Armstrong shows an Ojibwa canoe with the bowman spearing sturgeon on Lake Huron.

166

Spruce bark was often used as a poor substitute for birch bark in canoe-making, from the Interior Salish of British Columbia to the Malecite of New Brunswick and far to the north among the Indians near the Mackenzie River. Some native people, such as the Interior Salish, built a great many of their canoes of spruce bark, although it could not be sewn together like sheets of birch bark and had to be used when it was fresh and flexible. On the Nelson River in 1914, this Salish builder is starting a canoe of the uncompromising material.

A four-foot model of an elm bark canoe was collected by an army officer before 1825, probably from the community of refugee Hurons who had settled near Detroit, beyond the range of birch bark. Well preserved in the Peabody Museum of Salem, it shows a wealth of accurate construction detail, including the pleating of the elm bark near the bow and stern, quick lashing techniques, and simple framing. A reflector of bark and a torch of splintered fat pine are mounted at the bow for night fishing.

The French Period

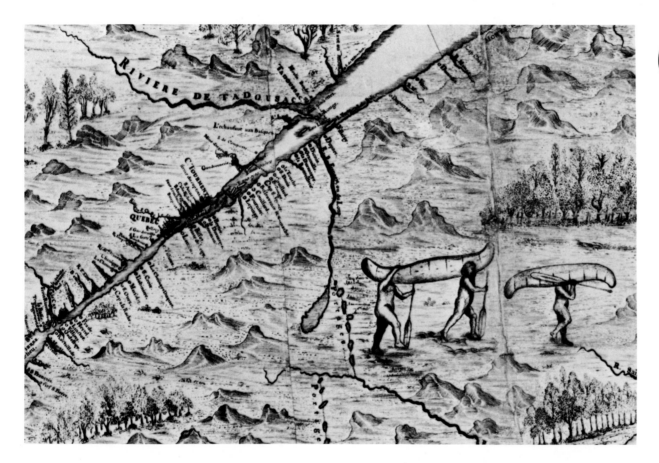

A manuscript map of New France was produced by Joannes Ludovicus Franquelin in 1676 outlining the known features of the St. Lawrence River and its tributaries.

Among its illustrations is a trio of Indians (detail) portaging their Micmac-style canoes. In fact, the sketch shows how a canoeman could paddle up the Rivière du Loup, portage over the height of land, thread through a chain of ponds, and catch a downstream current to the Bay of Fundy.

OF THE EUROPEANS who came to stay in North America, it was the French who first landed in birch country. It was French explorers who travelled most extensively through the great range of that tree and who not only saw the bark canoe used widely by the native peoples but understood that it would be the vehicle essential to so much of their own travelling. The French came into the Gulf of St. Lawrence and were led in their ships up the wide St. Lawrence River eight hundred miles into the continent. A labyrinth of connecting waterways beyond offered the adventurous newcomers passage by canoe for thousands of miles. Light enough to be carried over any obstacle, the Indian's bark craft was the key that opened to them the vast expanse between the oceans.

Initially, however, it was an item of curiosity. Jacques Cartier, the French sailor who cruised along the north shore of Newfoundland in 1534, reported to his king that the strange people he saw there painted themselves and that they went out in birch bark canoes to catch seals. His notes on the vessels of these ill-fated Beothuks were scant but the English, who followed to exploit and colonize Newfoundland, left vivid descriptions. John Guy, exploring the island shore in 1612, took a mariner's view of them:

Their canoes are about twenty-foote long, and foure foot and a half broad in the middle aloft, and for their keel and timbers, they have thin light peeces of dry firre, rended as it were lathes: and instead of boards, they use the outer burch bark, which is thin and hath many folds, sowed together with a thred made of a small root quartered. They carry four persons well, and weigh not one hundred weight: They are made in the form of a new moon, stem and sterne alike, and equally distant from the greatest breadth. . . .

Distinct from any other canoe, that of the Beothuk had gunwales which curved from bow and stern to rise in a sharp peak amidship, the gunwales held apart at that point by a long thwart. The hull was deep and V-shaped and it was the only canoe in North America to have a keelson, which gave it longitudinal strength to withstand the waves of the sea. Ballasted with stone, it was almost exclusively a marine vessel and well suited to the lifting of heavy loads, like seals, over the gunwales.

Captain George Cartwright, who made hunting and trapping expeditions in the eighteenth century, thought it incredible that Indians should venture in such boats as far as Funk's Island, forty miles east from the Newfoundland coast. In nesting season each year Beothuks made the eighty-mile round trip to load their canoes with sea birds' eggs. Earlier, Cartier had made two stops at Funk Island to replenish his ship's supplies. When on land the clumsy auks, which Cartier reported "as large as geese . . . marvellously fat," were easy to catch, so easy that before 1844 they had been clubbed to extinction. The Beothuks of Newfoundland, however, had been annihilated even before this date in what can only be described as a brutal genocide by Europeans. Nor does there survive a single full-size specimen of what clearly was the finest bark canoe designed for salt-water use.

Off the mainland coast of present-day New Brunswick, other Indians came boldly out to meet Jacques Cartier. Almost certainly these were Micmacs, another eastern people who travelled in open canoes suitable for seacoast use. As Cartier recalled, there were forty to fifty canoes, eighteen to twenty-four feet long, with low, rounded ends and a humped look caused by gunwales rising in the center. The confident welcome they offered suggested they were already familiar with visiting Europeans and had done some trading with them.

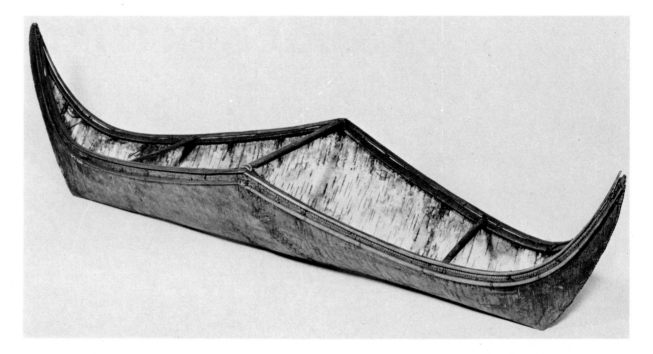

Just to the north, while sheltered in Gaspé Bay, the French met another band with a different language. There were more than three hundred in forty canoes. "They came to the sides of our ships," said Cartier, "and we gave them combs, beads, knives, and other gewgaws, at which they showed signs of joy, lifting up their hands to heaven and singing and dancing in the canoes." This explorer, however, was not impressed: "They go quite naked, except for a small skin with which they cover their genitals, and for a few old furs which they throw over their shoulders." Cartier underrated what he saw. The "few old furs" were probably what the French traders later called "castor gras d'hiver," beaver with only the fine soft fur remaining after the guard hairs had been worn off. Nor did he suspect that the bark canoes would become the vital transport for French explorers who followed him. All he could see was a people "who have no other dwelling but their canoes, which they turn upside down and sleep on the ground underneath."

No full-scale Beothuk canoe has survived to demonstrate the ingenuity of the original mariners of Newfoundland who were annihilated by Europeans. Only a small model of Beothuk origin remains, in the Royal Scottish Museum, and it lacks framing details. The seagoing Beothuks made the only bark canoe with a keel. It was V-shaped in cross-section and its gunwales rose to a high point amidships. In them they travelled out of sight of land to offshore islands and, perhaps, to Labrador.

(OPPOSITE) A quaint picture by an unknown artist gives a wealth of visual detail on Micmac life about 1820. The unmistakable shape of their seagoing bark canoes shows how they closed them in at bow and stern to cope with waves, and how they raised the gunwales amidships with lots of tumblehome to allow heavy game or fish to be lifted from the sea. The use of sail by the Micmacs was reported in very early French narratives, although it was very likely a borrowed idea.

168

170

The following summer Cartier was back, moving farther along the St. Lawrence, with a route to the Far East always on his mind. At the Ile d'Orléans, a few miles below what is today the city of Quebec, the French met Indians who welcomed them and brought out gifts of food. The next day there was a ceremonial welcome when the chief himself, accompanied by a party that filled twelve canoes, came out to the ships. As his craft approached Cartier's *Emérillon*, Donnacona stood to make his formal speech, an address accompanied by such vigorous theatrical gestures that the French almost certainly gained some respect for the sturdy stability of what seemed so frail and insecure a vessel. The speech completed, Cartier then stepped down into the canoe of the Iroquois chief and ordered food and drink to be brought for the welcoming natives.

Although Cartier was welcomed, Donnacona did not want him to continue any deeper into the country. To deter the French, his medicine men sent emissaries from the god Cudougny; the visitors were astonished by the arrival of a canoe with a crew of devils, dressed in dog skins and wearing long horns. The demons exhorted them to go no farther or they would freeze to death. Cartier, who felt the mummery covered self-interest, persisted in his upriver exploration.

At a village called Hochelaga, about one hundred and fifty miles to the west, at the limit for navigation by large ships and a site now built over by the city of Montreal, the French were given a tumultuous welcome by the Huron population, a people who were relatives but firm adversaries to Donnacona's Iroquois. It was another canoe welcome, the French in their longboats escorted by an honor guard in the native birch bark boats.

European fishing fleets had begun exploiting the rich banks off Newfoundland, but Cartier and his contemporaries were not caught up in the fur commerce. In Europe the beaver demand was yet to come. Marc Lescarbot, the historian who later accompanied Champlain, explained, " . . . in the time of Jacques Cartier, beavers were held in no esteem; the hats made thereof are in use only since that time." When the hatters discovered the superb felting properties of beaver fur and made the beaver hat high style, the chunky rodent would become the economic mainstay of a French colony here. In Cartier's time the French were obsessed by the idea of a western route to the Orient. This St. Lawrence might lead on to the treasures of Cathay and the Spice Islands. The canoeloads of fur would wait. The first efforts to establish a colony were plagued by the problems of Indian hostility, starvation, scurvy, altogether more factors than need cataloguing, and the idea was abandoned by the middle of Cartier's century.

Some English captains who touched on the coast took bark canoes home as curios. In 1603 Martin Pring acquired one at the mouth of the Piscataqua River, where Maine meets New Hampshire:

Their boats, whereof we brought one to Bristoll, were seventeene foot long and foure foot broad, made of the Barke of a Birch-tree, far exceeding in bignesse those of England: it was sowed together with strong and tough Oziers or twigs, and the seames covered over with Rozen or Turpentine little inferiour in sweetnesse to Frankincense. . . . it was sharpe at both ends, saving the beake was a little bending roundly upward. And though it carried nine men standing upright, yet it weighed not at the most above sixtie pounds in weight, a thing almost incredible in regard of the largenesse and capacitie thereof. Their Oares were flat at the end like an Oven peele, made of Ash or Maple very light and strong, about two yards long, wherewith they row very swiftly.

In the manuscript book of about 1700 now known as the Codex Canadensis, *considerable space is devoted to Indian life by the Abbé Nicholas, who drew from his experience in New France after 1667. The naive illustrations include "La Pesche des Sauvages," a sort of composite which includes a canoe, painted paddlers, fish, and various fishing implements. The curious canoe has gunwales which rise to a low peak amidships, which may suggest the craft he saw in Micmac camps; the bow and stern, however, are not Micmac, and the canoe, too, may be a composite.*

It was Samuel de Champlain who recognized the advantages of adopting the native boat for travel in North America. In 1603 he was invited to accompany François Du Pont-Gravé on an expedition to the New World. A seasoned soldier, navigator, and seaman, Champlain had already travelled to the West Indies and was eager to join the enterprise. While the expedition leaders traded for furs with Indians on the St. Lawrence, Champlain asked them about routes leading west. He was told about the rivers and lakes of the interior and learned how they were navigated. He made a few sorties above the site of Montreal, but in heavy ship's boats he was frustrated by the rapids. He tried to force his way up the fast current in a skiff but very soon he and his crew had to take to the water to free the craft. Meanwhile, "The savages' canoe passed easily."

At the Lachine Rapids, a three-mile stretch of violent St. Lawrence water, the Frenchman was appalled. Champlain reported that he had never seen a torrent of water pour through with such force. Travel by foot through the dense bush seemed a quite impracticable means of probing the continent and the wild waters he saw just above the Island of Montreal convinced him he could go no farther in a European ship's boat or pinnace:

We went by land . . . to see the end of the rapid, which is a league away, and there we saw no more rocks or falls, but the water runs with the utmost possible swiftness; and this current extends for three or four leagues, so that it is vain to imagine that any boats could be conveyed past the same rapids. But he who would pass them must provide himself with the canoes of the savages, which a man can easily carry. . . .

And besides this first rapid, there are ten more, for the most part difficult to pass; so that it would be a matter of great toil and labour to be able to see and do by boat. . . . But with the canoes of the savages one may travel freely and quickly throughout the country, as well up the little rivers as up the large ones.

Earlier that spring, Champlain had admired the bark canoes of a large trading party of Malecites, Penobscots, Algonquins, and Montagnais which met the French ship at the mouth of the Saguenay River. He saw them launch

well nigh two hundred canoes, which go extraordinarily well; for though our shallop was well manned, yet they went more swiftly than we. There are but two that paddle, the man and the wife. Their canoes . . . are so light a man can carry one easily; and every canoe can carry the weight of a pipe [about 1,000 pounds]. When they wish to go overland to get to some river where they have business, they carry them with them.

On the Saguenay, the Montagnais gave him a detailed description of the route to the north—rivers, rapids, portages, and lakes—to their rendezvous on the far side of Lake St. John with other bands with whom they traded European goods for more furs. Averaging twelve to fifteen leagues a day, the Indians made this trip in ten days. On the lower St. Lawrence Champlain was able to try the Indian craft himself, and the next summer, when charting the salt-water coastline from Cape Breton to Long Island, he kept a bark canoe aboard and took every opportunity to investigate the rivers. Entering Penobscot Bay, he dropped anchor not far from the site of the city of Bangor, Maine, and with Indian guides continued up the Penobscot River by canoe. From local Abenakis he learned one could go up that river, across Chesuncook Lake, portage north to the headwaters of the Chaudière River, and so drop by canoe down to the St. Lawrence. Farther south on the coast they saw no more bark canoes but met Massachusetts Indians who had "canoes built of a single piece [dugouts] and very liable to upset unless one is skilled in managing them."

When bark canoes did appear this far south they were likely to have been carrying a party of raiders. Champlain was much impressed with the eastern canoe's seaworthy qualities when he learned that four hundred Micmac and Malecite allies had paddled about one hundred and sixty leagues to the south, to attack the Armouchiquois in present-day Massachusetts. The historian Marc Lescarbot frequently saw Micmac Indians fishing and travelling on the sea. It appeared to him that they carried with them so many possessions that they needed "horses":

These horses are canoes and small boats made of bark, which go as swiftly as may be without sails; when they move they put all they have into them, wives, children, dogs, kettles, hatchets, matachias, bows, arrows, quivers, skins, and the covering of their houses. They are made in such sort that one must not stir nor stand up in them, but must crouch or sit in the bottom, otherwise the merchandise would overturn. They are four feet broad, or thereabouts, in the centre, and grow narrower toward the ends, with a high prow, in order to pass easily over the waves. I have said that they make them of bark, to keep which in shape they garnish them with semicircles of cedar, a wood very supple and pliable, whereof Noah's ark was made; and to the end that they leak not, they coat with the gum of fir-trees the seams where the said pieces of bark are joined together, which is done with roots.

After a colony was established at Quebec in 1608, Champlain decided that he must support the Hurons, Algonquins, and Montagnais in their war with the Iroquois, a confederacy of tribes based in what is now upper New York State. The new colony was to live on the proceeds of the annual fur harvest, acquired by trade with the friendly tribes of the St. Lawrence watershed, but that trade was threatened by frequent harassing from those Iroquois just to the south. Because he was eager to go exploring in their territory to the north and west, Champlain was anxious to bolster the existing friendship and so in early summer the next year he went to war alongside his Indian allies—and he went in their bark canoes.

On the return trip Champlain went down the St. Lawrence at twenty-five to thirty leagues a day, "their usual rate," he commented. At Tadoussac, at the mouth of the Saguenay, he was fascinated by the ceremonies that greeted the victorious warriors: "Approaching the shore each took a stick, on the end of which they hung the scalps of their slain enemies with some beads, singing meanwhile all together. And when all were ready, the women stripped themselves quite naked, and jumped into the water, swimming to the canoes to receive the scalps of their enemies...."

In 1611 Champlain was on Montreal Island when his Huron friends arrived from up the Ottawa River. They trusted this man but had no confidence in other French traders who operated in the area, and so set up camp above the Lachine Rapids and sent a messenger by night to guide Champlain to their fires. Returning from the council the next day, Champlain came down those rapids which had so awed him when he first saw them. He wrote:

To do this, they made ready eight canoes, with which to run the rapids, and they stripped naked, but left me in my shirt; for it often happens that some are lost in running the rapids. Consequently they kept close to one another, in order to give prompt help, if a canoe should happen to capsize. . . . I assure you that even the bravest people in the world who have not seen nor passed this place in small boats such as theirs, could not do so without great apprehension. But these tribes are so clever at shooting rapids, that this is easy for them.

Algonquins in little fleets of canoes also arrived to trade, further firing Champlain's desire to travel westward by their tales of the vast interior. But he was to wait two years more, much of the time in France, before he stood again at the foot of the Lachine Rapids, planning with Algonquin friends his first sortie on the waterways that led west, he knew not how far.

(ABOVE) While Samuel de Champlain quickly developed an appreciation for the virtues of the various canoe types in the New World, the engravers who interpreted his sketches were less discriminating. When Champlain went to war against the Iroquois with his Huron, Algonquin, and Montagnais allies in 1609, he travelled in birch bark canoes. The Iroquois war party he met was afloat in heavier and slower elm bark canoes. Drawing from his limited knowledge, the engraver has depicted all the canoes at the encounter as square-chined boats.

(LEFT) A number of British officers, trained to observe, draw, and paint as part of their military education, left fine pictorial records of Canada for later historians. Among the best was Thomas Davies, who painted A View near Point Levy opposite Quebec *late in the eighteenth century. The clothing and lodges suggest that it is a Micmac camp, but the canoes, with their pointed bows and strong rocker, look Montagnais. The people could have been a party of traders from southern Labrador or the interior of Quebec bringing their harvest of furs south to the St. Lawrence for trade.*

Travelling south on the Richelieu River, there were twenty-four canoes with sixty men, including Champlain and two other Frenchmen. The latter had their first experience of portaging on that upstream route, although Champlain noted that the Indians went up through some rapids by making the load lighter by having one man from each canoe go round by land. Each night the Indians built semicircular barricades and pulled the canoes up on the beach, ready for instant launching. The French saw reconnaissance canoes being sent ahead in the dark to guard against surprise attack. Closer to the enemy's country they travelled stealthily and only by night; they gave up hunting and lived on field rations of baked Indian meal. About ten o'clock one evening, on Lake George, they met the Iroquois. The northern allies drew out into the lake while the Iroquois went to shore in their elm bark canoes.

The raiders remained afloat during the night, keeping their canoes close together. In the morning the two war parties took up battle positions on the shore and Champlain fired a shot that felled three chiefs and made the Iroquois uncompromising enemies of the French. A volley from his French companions, and the Iroquois were routed. The battle was over except for the scalping.

174

They provided two small canoes, sufficient to carry Champlain, four other Frenchmen, and one Indian guide—three persons in each craft. It was the first time that Champlain had set out as a working paddler and not as passenger, and he learned quickly that canoe travel can be hard work. In his journal the leader wrote, "On the twenty-ninth we passed a rapid partly by portage, partly by tracking, and were forced to carry our canoes, clothes, provisions, and arms on our shoulders, which is no small labour for those who are not used to it." At the Long Sault and other rapids on the Ottawa River they had to drag the canoes along the shoreline by rope. He remarked that "dexterity" was required to get a vessel through rapids this way but added that the Indians did so with the greatest skill, "seeking by-ways and safe places which they recognize at a glance."

The skills of paddling, poling, portaging, and tracking came slowly to the novice canoemen. Moving up the Ottawa, against the surge of spring floodwaters, past the site that was to become Canada's capital, the Frenchmen learned canoe management under the tuition of their guide, and they learned it the hard but practical way. These many years later the Ottawa River remains no light challenge to those who would travel against her current, and, for those who would confide to latter-day diaries their tribulations on the water or on the portage, there is nothing new to be written of mosquito and blackfly plagues, of pack-weary backs, bruised limbs, and taxed muscles. Champlain described all succinctly in his journal in 1613.

The adventurers pushed on to a point just short of what is now Pembroke, Ontario, where they met and were entertained by the canny chief of a little band which operated a river-traffic toll system. Canoe crews, principally those going downriver to sell furs to the French, were charged a tariff on the portage trails that skirted the rapids on either side of the band's island stronghold.

They went no farther. The French youth who maintained that he had been taken on this route as far as a salt sea, just the season before, confessed his fraud when challenged by the Indians. Champlain was disappointed when he turned downriver but he was no doubt confident that, given canoes to paddle, the French themselves could travel and survive in this land.

Always a practical man, he induced a large Indian party to go downriver with furs to trade. Forty canoes set out, but the bark flotilla grew en route and by the time they reached the St. Lawrence there were eighty canoes packed with furs for bartering. Some of them were larger vessels that carried four or five men, together with their arms, food, and trade goods; Champlain could scarcely have failed to note that this size would be well suited to the travel needs of the French.

In the years 1615 and 1616 the French enthusiastically adopted canoe travel; Champlain himself, the earliest of the church missionaries, and the first of those who came to be known as the *coureurs de bois* threaded their way up the Ottawa River to the Huron country and

beyond. When Champlain arrived in his ship, the *Saint-Etienne*, in May of 1615, he brought with him three Récollet priests and a lay brother. So eager was Joseph Le Caron, one of the priests, that he set out with a Huron party even before the master explorer. But by early July, Champlain, Etienne Brûlé, and one other Frenchman crowded into two bark canoes along with ten Indians to follow the Ottawa route. A discreet Champlain scarcely mentioned in his journal the discomfort of travelling at a forced pace in those overloaded craft. They took the paddle path that became a vital Canadian highway for two hundred and fifty years, the Ottawa River to the Mattawa, westward along that stream, across Lake Nipissing and down the French River to Georgian Bay, itself a fresh-water sea and yet a part only of the larger expanse that the Hurons called Lake Attigouantan. On today's maps it is Lake Huron.

In so many words on paper, it sounds a simple course, but the forty-mile link from the mouth of the Mattawa to Lake Nipissing alone included eleven portages and they covered that distance in one day. The farm-supported towns of the Huron country lay between Georgian Bay and present-day Lake Simcoe, and the first community they reached was Otouacha. The Hurons were keen to cement the alliance with the French and to make that alliance their bulwark against the Iroquois raiders. When Champlain stepped out of his tightly packed canoe onto Huron territory he had already promised the Indians to join them in war against the tribes which were threatening to close the Ottawa route to them. Assembling the forces took much of the summer, but in early September a Huron army with Champlain and his companions, along with ten Frenchman from Father Le Caron's group, launched their canoes and headed southeasterly towards Iroquois country.

Champlain was always keenly interested in native provisioning and by now he was familiar with the dry meal made from maize on which paddle travellers relied so heavily. He watched the army on the hunt, with five hundred men moving in a line, shouting to frighten and drive animals before them. The deer took to water, where other hunters waited in canoes to kill them.

The battle fleet crossed southern Ontario via Lake Simcoe to the Kawartha Lakes and then the Trent River system to the Lake of the Onondagas, now Lake Ontario, at the Bay of Quinte. The French no doubt gave up counting the portages. By now they realized that canoe travel involved certain footwork and backwork. The fleet's guides apparently knew the route well, for they went across the end of Lake Ontario by a series of five islands and were never more than seven miles from a landing. They put ashore just south of what is now Sackett's Harbor, New York, hid their canoes in the woods, and marched south towards the villages of the Onondagas, one of the Iroquois tribes.

The attack on an Onondaga stronghold was repulsed; the Iroquois defenders proved a much better organized force than the attackers and, having heard about Champlain's earlier assault on their Mohawk neighbors, they were not overawed by French firearms. When the Huron group gave up the siege Champlain and his party had no choice but to return to Huronia and to spend the winter there. While en route he was reminded that it was all but impossible to travel in this land without canoes. He wandered from the portage trail and became thoroughly lost for two days. Only the familiar marks left by canoe carriers led him eventually to his friends. The expedition had been frustrating and he greatly resented being forced back to Huronia for the winter, but the lessons under paddle and on the portages were sound experience for the French, who were now no longer aliens in a land where to travel at all was to travel by water.

The fourteen Frenchmen with Champlain became accomplished paddlers, for the Indians would not have tolerated such a number of non-working passengers. Men like these were the forerunners of the *coureurs de bois*, a new breed of men emerging from the French colony to whom adventure and the freedoms of life in the forest held more appeal than did living in a tiny settlement under the restraints of a European civilization. They learned to handle canoes as well as the natives and they took to the Indian life-style and languages and very quickly formed blood kinships with their wilderness hosts.

175

(OPPOSITE) *Voyageurs in the service of the fur trade were always glad to avoid the tedious labor of a portage, and "tracking" a canoe up a rapid generally saved hard work. The two men in the canoe are holding the fragile craft off the rocks with setting poles, and in a stiff current could help the crew on the line by poling. The sketch was made on the Ottawa River by Philip Bainbrigge in 1838.*

Philip Bainbrigge was a British Army officer and about 1840 he painted this busy scene during his travels in eastern Canada. The bark canoe being poled up the rapids has the lines of a river canoe of the Malecite Indians who lived in eastern New Brunswick and the adjoining area in Quebec. The freight canoe being portaged around the rapid is a small one, likely about twenty-five feet, and designed for travel on smaller rivers.

Etienne Brûlé, on a mission to contact other Indian allies, travelled south and was the first European to go down the Susquehanna River. Two seasons later, with another young man named Grenalle, he paddled north on Georgian Bay, then west along the shore of Lake Huron to reach what is today the St. Mary's River. Brûlé was no keeper of records but adventure led him on in his canoe, and other chroniclers of the period have left descriptions that suggest that he and his companion may have paddled into Lake Superior and possibly through the Straits of Mackinac into Lake Michigan.

The first missionary to Huronia had meanwhile survived wintering in that country. Le Caron's example was to be followed by many other priests in the years following. Churchmen, merchants, and explorers had learned to travel by bark canoe, each of them motivated by particular goals. It was impossible, however, to separate their functions entirely. Explorers may have been seeking a route to the Orient and they certainly were concerned with learning on behalf of the French king the extent of this domain and what it might contribute to the royal coffers. But at the same time they were expected to make their voyaging turn a profit in furs. The businessmen who went to the new frontier to acquire furs were also explorers, ever seeking new sources of trade, looking for richer fur harvests. The priests who went by canoe to save souls were often the first of their color to visit a region, and some appear at times to have been contributing more to the map than to the mission. They were tied to the larger fur trade as well and the colonial managers expected priests in the forest to see that the fur harvests from their wild parishes went into the holds of French ships. The Indians, for their part, expected the priests to help negotiate better deals for them with the traders. The three functions were very much intertwined in the early years, and priests, explorers, and merchants often shared the same canoe, the same pot of greasy stew, and the same back-break on the portage.

Champlain never went far afield again by canoe; he was too busy fighting in the New World for the survival of his fledgling colony or all but begging for its support in

France. He died at Quebec in 1635. But the year before, still dreaming of the Orient, he had sent a trusted interpreter, Jean Nicolet, west from Huronia, prepared for the courts of the Ming emperors with a "grand robe of china damask." Nicolet set off by canoe with seven Indians, coasted the north shore of Lake Huron, then paddled south to the Straits of Mackinac, along the north shore of Lake Michigan to Green Bay. He didn't locate the Ming court, but his flowing robe and noisy pistols made him an impressive ambassador among the Winnebago Indians, and he succeeded in negotiating peace between that tribe and the Hurons. He travelled about fifteen hundred miles on the round trip by canoe, put Lake Michigan on the French maps, and opened the way for traders to another lucrative source of furs.

It was a Jesuit priest, Father Jacques Buteux, who in 1651 explored the St. Maurice River country, north from Trois Rivières. He left with thirty-five Indian canoes and could scarcely believe that he was expected to live on just a few ounces of fish each day. He later recalled the experience:

On the day after embarking we encountered horrible waterfalls—among others, one in a place where the river, after rolling over many rocky levels, falls suddenly into an abyss, like a stone trough or cradle, hundreds of feet long.... To avoid these falls, we carried our canoes and our baggage over high mountains, by a narrow path on the edge of a precipice; and at every moment there was but a step between us and death.

But the important activity was in the western Great Lakes area, and the impetus for change lay in Indian trade patterns. The Iroquois wanted access to more furs to sustain a new way of life that depended on the acquisition of European goods. They traded south to the Dutch settlement and coveted the position of the Hurons and Ottawas who acted as middlemen between the French and the more western and northern tribes. The fur demand caused notable depletion of the beaver in the Iroquois country and so raiders from the south began to infiltrate the territory of the Hurons and the Algonquins.

Coming in their elm bark craft or in birch bark canoes acquired by trade or in war, they mounted a campaign to blockade the Ottawa River by ambushing fur-laden canoes coming down to French settlements on the St. Lawrence. In 1645 they negotiated a treaty with the Hurons and the French in order to become active participants in the lucrative trade, but when the Hurons failed to deliver any part of the bounty in the following year, the Iroquois decided to take over the trade by conquest.

In 1648 the tiny community of Trois Rivières was besieged by Iroquois and a party of two hundred and fifty Hurons came to its aid. In the absence of these warriors from their homes, the Iroquois struck in Huronia with savage force, slaughtering men, women, and children and destroying their winter stores of food. In early spring, a thousand-man army of Senecas and Mohawks struck there again and finished the job. The Huron nation was scattered, some as prisoners of the Iroquois, some to Manitoulin Island in Georgian Bay, some seeking refuge among tribes on Lake Superior, others among old allies on the Susquehanna River, and some few seeking asylum with the French near Quebec. As a result of the disaster suffered by their allies, the French fur traders were forced to go farther and farther west to reach tribes that had supplied furs to the Hurons. And the Jesuits, the mission force which replaced the Récollets, had to go too.

In the rugged country to the northwest of Lake Superior two voyageurs were painted by William Armstrong in 1871. They are carrying their north canoe right side up, balanced by the man at the bow with a line over the gunwales.

The Ottawas, great traders and fine canoemen, were another casualty of the Iroquois invasion. Many of them retreated to Green Bay on the western shore of Lake Michigan or to Lake Superior. The Saulteurs, the Ojibwa group occupying the strategic trading-route river between Lake Superior and Lake Huron, were pushed west for a time and some resettled on the south shore of Lake Superior around Chequamegon Bay. But they resumed, as did the Ottawas, their traditional roles as middlemen, trading between westerly peoples and the French. As the distance for some was now nearly doubled, the Indians were far less inclined to make the long canoe trip to the markets on the St. Lawrence, and French peddlers increasingly had to load their canoes with trade goods and go up the lakes for the fur harvest.

The *coureurs de bois* took cheerfully to this business and men who chafed at the restrictions of life in the colony became as skilled as the Indians at surviving in the bush. They lived with Indian friends and most adopted Indian dress. Sometimes they feasted and on occasion they starved; life along the canoe routes was sometimes easy and at others it was nothing but killing toil. In the villages of the Indians they enjoyed the favors of women and their licentious abandon horrified the mission priests. Colonial officials depended on their work in the fur trade but insisted that their uninhibited behavior and independent attitude threatened the morals of the French community. When there was a guilder or a pound to be made, instead of a pistole, their loyalty to the French crown often proved to be tenuous. When the English captain David Kirke sailed up the St. Lawrence in 1629 to capture Quebec, his pilot was none other than that first *coureur de bois*, Etienne Brûlé. When the trading partners Pierre Esprit Radisson and Médard Chouart Des Groseilliers gained no support among French officials for their proposal to trade south from Hudson Bay, they took the plan to the English; the result was the Hudson's Bay Company. Other French woodsmen served English colonists as canoe guides into the fur country, while the governor of New France complained bitterly of their perfidy. And it was by no means unknown for *coureurs de bois* to send fur-loaded canoes to English traders at Albany; the latter offered trade goods that were superior and cheaper.

(LEFT) An illustration from Joseph-François Lafitau's 1724 book on his travels in North America draws together canoes from many regions at Niagara Falls. On the left is a copy of John White's dugout-making in Virginia, flanked by two Micmac canoes from Nova Scotia and a crooked canoe of the Montagnais. In the foreground two Indians are paddling a Micmac-style canoe past another which could be Malecite. The small buildings were taken from Le Moyne's Florida illustrations.

Newcomers to French Canada were, without exception, fascinated by the mobility of the bark canoe, which could carry huge loads and still be carried with ease past rapids. The demonstration is from Lafitau's account of adventures among the Indians.

It was a hazardous life. Some died in quarrels with Indians, some in quarrels among themselves. Brûlé at length so incensed his Huron companions that they boiled and ate him. Canoe upsets in treacherous rapids sent others to their deaths, but the lure of the wilderness woods was such that few returned for long to a quiet home in the colony. Once they stepped into the canoe they were free agents in every respect. And when they stepped out of that canoe again on their return to the French community, officialdom regarded them increasingly as a serious social problem.

Baron La Hontan wrote of them in the English version of his book, which appeared in 1703, the same year as the original French edition:

> You would be amaz'd if you saw how lewd these Pedlers are when they return, how they Feast and Game, and how prodigal they are, not only in their Cloathes, but upon Women. Such of 'em are married, have the wisdom to retire to their own Houses; but the Batchelors act just as our *East-India-Men*, and Pirates are wont to do; for they Lavish, Eat, Drink, and Play all away as long as the Goods hold out; and when these are gone, they e'en sell their embroidery, their Lace and their Cloaths. This done, they are forced to go upon a new Voyage for Subsistance.

Reaching farther for the fur resources of the west, the northwest, and the southwest, two classes of French traders began to emerge. In a letter he received from the colony in 1681, the Marquis de Seignelay, then dealing with the affairs of New France at the court of Louix XIV, was told:

> The first go to the original haunts of the Beaver, among the Indian tribes of the Assinibouets, Nadoussieux, Miamis, Illinois and others. These cannot make the trip in less than two or three years. The second, who are not so numerous, merely go so far as the Long Sault, *Petit Nation* and sometimes to Michilimackinac, to meet the Indians and French who come down, in order to obtain, exclusively, their peltries, for which they carry goods to them....

179

This changing pattern in the fur trade was the direct result of the incredible voyages of exploration made by the French in the thirty years after 1655. Using the canoe to maximum advantage, they fanned out across the continent and then moved south to contain the English colonists on the Atlantic seaboard.

While the *coureurs de bois* who paddled in Champlain's wake were largely unlettered men and so left few written records, the French priests, most of them Jesuits, more than made up the literary gap. Revealing a fine sense of the historical value of their missions in the wilderness, the personal narratives of the black-robed priests comprise a great archives of a mission revealing so much of the troubles and the triumphs of paddling for a cause.

For most of these men of the cloth, travel by canoe was tedious indeed. Some endured it as a mortification of the flesh but it appears seldom to have exalted the spirit. Those who were in no way averse to hideous martyrdom under torture at Iroquois hands had already recorded for distant superiors the arduous conditions of day-to-day living in Huronia and the onerous experience of journeying to that remote province in a frail bark vessel. Among the Indians they travelled in every season, often in the most appalling weather, subsisting on a native diet that was frequently meager and rarely appetizing. One starving blackrobe told of sharing with fellow travellers the flesh of a decomposing deer and how that acrid flavor remained in his mouth. The mosquitoes, blackflies, and no-see-ums came in torturing clouds and the party travelled without repellents and fly-proof tents.

About once every hour the voyageurs in the great freight canoes were allowed time out from paddling to pack and light their short clay pipes. For the French canoemen the breaks became known as "pipes" and they were so regular that distances were recalled as "trois pipes" or "sept pipes." The tranquil scene is a retrospective painting by Arthur Heming, who travelled with the last of the fur brigades in the early years of this century.

Nights were restless hours in a flea-infested blanket or crouched over a suffocating smudge to escape the worst attacks of the insects. The priests travelled frequently with trading parties and these went at a furious pace, a relentless routine of paddling, lining, dragging, and portaging the heavily loaded canoes.

Family travel among the Indians was more relaxed. In 1616 Father Biard reported,

> our foresters start off to their different places with as much pleasure as if they were going on a stroll or an excursion; they do this easily through the skillful use and great convenience of canoes. . . . a single one of them will hold an entire household of five or six persons, with all their dogs, sacks, skins, kettles and . . . the most heavily-loaded canoe can draw only half a foot of water, and unloaded it is so light that you can easily pick it up and carry it away with your left hand; so rapidly sculled that, without any effort, in good weather you can make thirty or forty leagues a day.

On the St. Lawrence in early April, Father Le Jeune explained that the ice which still formed during the night was a special hazard:

> either it was too sharp, or the bark of our gondola too thin; for it made an opening which let the water into our canoe and fear into our hearts. So behold us all three in action, my two Savages paddling, and I bailing out the water. We drew with all the strength of our paddles to an Island which we fortunately encountered. When we set foot upon shore, the Savages seized the canoe, drew it out of the water, turned it upside down; lighted their tinder, made a fire, sewed up the slit in the bark; applied to it their resin, a kind of gum that runs out of trees; placed the canoe again in the water, and we reembarked and continued our journey.

When they encountered the massed ice from the spring breakup, the danger was even more acute:

> We were a little frightened, but my people approached it nevertheless, as they had noticed a small opening in it; they glided into this, turning our little gondola first to one side and then to the other; in order to always make some headway. At last we found these masses of ice so firmly wedged together, that it was impossible either to advance or recede, for the movement of the water closed us in on all sides. In the midst of this ice, if a sharp wind had arisen, we would have been crushed and broken to pieces, we and our canoe, like the grains of wheat between two millstones. . . . My savages, seeing our predicament, leapt from one piece of ice to another, like squirrels from tree to tree; and, pushing it away with their paddles, made a passage for the canoe. . . .

For those members of the Society of Jesus who were to follow him on the Ottawa River route to the mission at Huronia, Father Le Jeune drew on his own experience to set down the "ten commandments" of canoe travel:

> You must have sincere affection for the Savages. . . .
> To conciliate the Savages, you must be careful never to make them wait for you in embarking.
> You must provide yourself with a tinder box or with a burning mirror, or with both, to furnish them fire in the daytime to light their pipes, and in the evening when they have to encamp; these little services win their hearts.
> You should try to eat their sagamité or salmagundi in the way they prepare it, although it may be dirty, half-cooked and very tasteless. As to the other numerous things which may be unpleasant, they must be endured for the love of God, without saying anything or appearing to notice them. [For example, the priest had seen Hurons urinate in their cooking vessels while travelling by canoe.]
> It is well at first to take everything they offer, although you may not be able to eat it all; for, when one becomes accustomed to it, there is not too much.

Accompanying a survey party in Labrador in 1861, the artist William G. R. Hind sketched one of their Montagnais or Naskapi canoemen carrying baggage, paddles, and personal hunting gear over a rugged portage trail.

You must try to eat at daybreak unless you can take your meal with you in the canoe; for the day is very long, if you have to pass it without eating. The Barbarians eat only at Sunrise and Sunset, when they are on their journeys.

You must be prompt in embarking and disembarking; and tuck up your gowns so that they will not get wet, and so that you will not carry either water or sand into the canoe. To be properly dressed, you must have your feet and legs bare; while crossing the rapids, you can wear your shoes, and, in the long portages, even your leggings.

You must so conduct yourself as not to be at all troublesome to even one of these Barbarians.

It is not well to ask many questions.... Silence is good equipment at such a time.

You must bear with their imperfections without saying a word, even without seeming to notice them.... In short, you must try to be, and to appear, always cheerful.

Each one should be provided with half a gross of awls, two or three dozen little knives called *jambettes* [pocket-knives], a hundred fishhooks, with some beads of plain or coloured glass with which to buy fish or other articles when the tribes meet each other, so as to feast the Savages.... Each one will try, at the portages, to carry some little thing, according to his strength; however little one carries, it greatly pleases the Savages, if it be only a kettle.

You must not be ceremonious with the Savages, but accept the comforts they offer you, such as a good place in the cabin....

Be careful not to annoy any one in the canoe with your wide brimmed hat; it would be better to take your nightcap. There is no impropriety among the Savages.

Do not undertake anything unless you desire to continue it; for example do not begin to paddle unless you are inclined to continue paddling. Take from the start the place in the canoe that you wish to keep....

Finally, understand that the Savages will retain the same opinion of you in their own country that they will have formed on the way....

Le Jeune took a thoroughly practical approach to canoe travel and, in another letter, summed up what other priests should expect: "Be with whom you like, you must expect to be, at least, three or four weeks on the way, to have as companions persons you have never seen before, to be cramped in a bark Canoe in an uncomfortable position, not being free to turn yourself to one side or the other; in danger fifty times a day of being upset or of being dashed upon the rocks."

Accidents were frequent. A young seminarist travelling with a band of Algonquins on the Ottawa had not gone far before the canoe capsized. "In doubling a point," wrote Le Jeune, "the surging of the water, as of a heavy tide, dashed against the canoe and overturned it with all that was in it, so that they thought all was lost....Behold the chest, the chalice, the alb, and the chasuble, and all his outfit engulfed on the one hand, and he on the other...."

When a flotilla of twenty or thirty family canoes arrived at a portage at the same time, the scene could become chaotic. George Catlin made a quick sketch of this Chippewa band carrying canoes, baggage, children, and old people around the "Fall of St. Anthony," on the Mississippi where St. Paul stands today. The Indians were returning home after making a pact with the Sioux in the 1830s.

An Italian Jesuit who was working among the Hurons in 1653 expressed his fear of "shipwreck" when travelling in a little bark craft on one of those vast lakes where storms can rage no less severely than on the sea. And yet Father Bressani concluded that river travel was the more hazardous. Rather than portage, he and his companions dragged their canoes upstream when possible, often up to their necks in rushing, icy water. Carrying the canoes and baggage, he thought, was just about as bad, pushing through brush, scrambling over sharp rocks in bare feet, fording swamps and torrents.

After a season in the mission field a priest became accustomed to the regimen of hardships and there were some who took to life on the canoe routes without real difficulty. Father Jacques Buteux was a tyro when he set off on a journey up the St. Maurice River, a tributary of the St. Lawrence, but he was a secure initiate when he returned:

We passed almost continually by torrents, by precipices, and by places that were horrible in every way. In less than five days, we made more than thirty-five portages, some of which were a league and a half long. This means that on these occasions one has to carry on his shoulders his canoe and all his baggage, and with so little food that we were constantly hungry, and almost without strength and vigour. But... these fatigues and difficulties—the mere recital whereof would have frightened me—did not injure my health.

Certainly the priests were expected to pull their weight. Father Claude Allouez travelled nearly two thousand leagues in bark canoes and he recalled the occasion when his Indian host put a paddle in his hand and urged him to use it, "assuring me it was an honourable employment, and one worthy of a great Captain. I willingly took the paddle and, offering up to God this labour in atonement for my sins, and to hasten the poor Savages' conversion, I imagined myself a malefactor sentenced to the Galleys; and, although I became entirely exhausted, yet God gave me sufficient strength to paddle all day long, and often a good part of the night. But this application did not prevent my being commonly the butt of their jokes; for, however much I exerted myself, I accomplished nothing in comparison with them, their bodies being large and strong, and perfectly adapted to such labours."

According to Father Le Jeune,

183

he who would sail with them must know how to handle the paddle; and, as it is hard work, especially at first, when one is not accustomed to it, we give to every Canoe in which any of our Fathers embark a large sheet which serves as sail, to relieve them of this work; but, although these Barbarians may be told that this sail is the Fathers' paddle, that they do not wield any others, they do not fail sometimes to make them take one of wood, which has to be well worked to satisfy them.

Priests learned respect, even reverence, for canoes. Selecting a specimen of Huron language to send home, one chose a prayer by a Huron Christian, Joseph Chihwatenhwa, which read in part, "Just as we are masters of the canoe, which we have made a canoe, and of the cabin, which we have made a cabin, so thou art master...." And Father Jacques Buteux introduced into the wilderness the old French custom of blessing the fishing fleet: "On Saint Mark's day, after the Procession and Mass, we blessed the lake, and gave it the name of Saint Thomas; we also blessed the canoes, and gave to each one the name of some Saint which was inscribed upon it with red paint."

An Indian canoe became a funeral vehicle for Father Jacques Marquette, a priest much respected by the Indians with whom he had worked. He died, on the trail, in 1675 and a hunting party on Lake Michigan in the spring went ashore where he had been buried. The Indians opened the grave, cleaned and dried his bones, then laid them carefully in a box of birch bark and set out for the mission of St. Ignace, in what is now northern Michigan. One of the mission fathers described the arrival of that cortege under paddle:

There were nearly 30 Canoes which formed, in excellent order, that funeral procession. . . . When they drew near our house father nouvel, who is its superior, with father piercon, went out to meet them, accompanied by the frenchmen and savages who were there; and . . . before conveying it to land, they intoned the *de profundis* in the presence of the 30 canoes, which were still on the water. . . .

The relative advantages of different tribal canoes became apparent, particularly the superiority of birch bark vessels in general over those of the Iroquois made of elm bark. Father Le Jeune mentioned a fierce battle on the water between Algonquin and Iroquois warriors, making it clear that the light-weight birch craft of the former was a deciding factor in their victory.

When the fathers built their fortified mission of Ste. Marie in Huronia, it was obvious that they fully appreciated the role that the canoe filled in their life in the wilderness. For greater security they provided an underground passage at river level so that canoes could be floated right into the fort interior. Three locks were installed to raise the craft to that inner level.

The uncounted miles of canoe-journeying narrated in the *Jesuit Relations*, the accumulated annual reports of the missionary priests, reveal that some of those experiences on the water were enough to terrify the boldest spirits. In 1654 a mission had been founded in the Iroquois heartland south of Lake Ontario, but the peaceful relationship between these Indians and the French was not a lasting one and the latter had soon to flee, fifty-three of them in small boats and both birch bark and elm bark canoes. The initial retreat to Lake Ontario was successful but two days later their little fleet was nearly swallowed up in icy rapids of the upper St. Lawrence. Father Paul Ragueneau's report was a narrative of terror:

For, having entered unawares a rapid of considerable extent, we found ourselves in the midst of its billows, which, meeting with many large rocks, raised mountains of water, and hurled us into an abyss at every stroke of our paddles. . . . Yet we were forced to go on, the violence of the current bearing us along, in spite of ourselves, through extensive rapids and by ways never navigated before. Our fears were redoubled at seeing one of our canoes swallowed up by a breaker which extended across the entire width of the rapids, and which, nevertheless, afforded the only route by which all the rest were to go. Three Frenchmen were drowned here, a fourth luckily escaping by clinging to the canoe, and being rescued at the foot of the falls, when he was on the point of relinquishing his hold, strength and life nearly failing him at the same time.

Its light weight, which made the canoe portable, was the key to travel on these lake and river systems but the portage trail itself could be at times a detour of special danger. In time of war it was the perfect place for a hostile force to ambush a canoe party. At many river hazards the travellers had no choice but to go ashore at a specific landing and to follow the one existing route to calm water beyond. Heavily laden with canoes and packs, they were easy victims to an attack. So it was that after 1650 the portage trails on the vital Ottawa River route often became death traps as Iroquois raiding parties lay in wait for the trading canoes coming downstream with their bounty of furs. Montagnais, Algonquin, and Huron groups were more and more reluctant to risk the trading trip to the French on the St. Lawrence, and the little settlement of Ville Marie on Montreal Island felt its very life blood cut off.

Without furs to buy, the people of this fledgling community could not survive. In 1657 the Indians did not bring them a single beaver pelt and in 1658 only nine canoes of the Ottawa arrived with furs. By the following season their economic plight was desperate, and out of that desperation came a bold proposal by the young commander of the garrison, Sieur Dollard des Ormeaux. He reasoned that if the Iroquois could successfully ambush the canoe brigades of the Ottawas and Algonquins, then a well-armed French party might successfully ambush the Iroquois parties as they paddled homeward down the Ottawa.

Dollard and sixteen companions from the settlement paddled cautiously through spring ice along the Ottawa and chose their ambush site at the Long Sault Rapids, about forty miles up from the St. Lawrence. With a few Algonquins and forty Hurons who joined them there, they made their base at a derelict palisade and sent scouts up the river. When two canoes of Onondagas arrived at that portage, only two warriors escaped the French trap. But this had been the scouting party for an army of Iroquois men. The following day two hundred of these warriors swept down the river in their canoes, a gun at every bow. Dollard's French and their Indian allies retreated to their inadequate defences and began a desperate battle to survive. The Onondagas attacked and used the French birch bark canoes as torches in an effort to breach their palisade with fire.

The battle was a standoff for seven days. Then the French were astonished to see the river suddenly covered by canoes as five hundred Mohawks and Oneidas of the Iroquois confederacy came paddling in to reinforce the Onondaga attackers. The odds were overwhelming and it wasn't long before Dollard's allies began deserting the hopeless defence. Dollard and his dwindling band fought with that fanaticism for which the Iroquois themselves were known. Three more days passed, and when the Iroquois finally overran the palisade there were only five survivors for them to kill.

The real thrust of that huge battle fleet of Iroquois had been aimed at the destruction of Ville Marie. But they lost more than eighty warriors beside the Long Sault and soberly abandoned the planned attack on the French community. When they seeded their little plots that spring the settlers knew that the Ottawa route was once again open to the fur traffic.

While Dollard's group was making its heroic stand, a pair of *coureurs de bois*, Radisson and Des Groseilliers, had been assembling a huge fleet of canoes among the upriver Ottawas, to carry down to Ville Marie the accumulated furs of several years of trapping. A jubilant Radisson, perhaps a little careless with absolute truth, claimed a total of three hundred and sixty loaded canoes, some carrying up to seven men. As they prepared to set out, according to his story, the Indian women pushed off from shore and stood naked in their canoes, "to encourage us to come and lodge with them again."

Despite the large size of their party, these middlemen of the fur trade were cautious as they moved down the Ottawa, but there were no enemies lurking about the portage trails. Approaching the silent site of Dollard's siege, they were apprehensive when they came across abandoned Iroquois canoes and totally alarmed when they found headless bodies slumped at the torture stakes. The victims had lain there for six weeks. Under the urging of Radisson and Des Groseilliers, the paddlers made the Long Sault carry and moved warily onward. When they reached the St. Lawrence they left 50,000 pounds of skins with the French of Ville Marie and took a further 150,000 pounds to the fur merchants at Trois Rivières.

If the Iroquois forces had not been deterred at the Long Sault, almost certainly they would have ambushed and scattered this caravan, then transported the precious beaver pelts to the Dutch base at what is now New York City. Furs would have been traded for muskets and powder, possibly to mount more devastating attacks on the French outposts. Dollard's stand had saved Ville Marie from direct assault; the arrival of the huge fur shipment saved its very economy.

Inveterate travellers, Radisson and Des Groseilliers were the first Europeans to see many of the water routes of the upper Great Lakes and the rivers that led on to north, west, and southwest. Although their records are inexact and confusing as to geography, they left no doubt that, except for winter marches on snowshoes, they went by canoe. While a captive among the Iroquois early in his New World career, Radisson had admired the skill of Mohawk hunters who in less than two hours stripped the bark from an elm tree and completed a usable canoe. He learned soon that, when necessary, canoes were improvised from whatever bark would serve the purpose. When travelling on foot with an Indian party in the Susquehanna Valley he told of spending ten to twelve days making four canoes from walnut bark. Craft such as these were made often for ferrying, soon to be discarded.

It is more than likely that he saw dugouts in the Susquehanna country. He learned to make elm bark canoes for his own needs, and during his later travels he described frequent stops to make "boats." In the spring, probably in Wisconsin or northern Michigan, he told how a group of one hundred and fifty Indians discarded their snowshoes and spent three weeks building birch bark canoes before continuing their journey. Radisson at one point made a rendezvous with Des Groseilliers, whom he found with a company of Crees using boats made of moose skin. The pair of *coureurs de bois* evidently had some experience with each of the three basic varieties of native canoe.

Singly and together, the two men paddled thousands of miles with Indian companions. Des Groseilliers coasted along Lake Huron into Lake St. Clair. The pair may have done a full circuit of Lake Superior and they explored rivers reaching into Minnesota. One of them travelled from south to north on Lake Michigan, and together, in that forested land of the northwest, they spent four months on a trip, as they described it, just going from one river to another. They met people of many different tribes and somewhere they listened while a wilderness friend pointed downstream and southerly and spoke of bearded men with iron knives. It was an echo of Spanish explorers; the two adventurers from New France almost certainly had reached the headwaters of the Mississippi.

In a larger area, where different types and varieties of canoes were known, there was bound to be variation from time to time in the character of the vessels of some particular band or tribe. The recurrent wars among the native peoples, disputes which were affected by the economic influences of the encroaching Europeans, were factors which most obviously influenced such change. Under the inexorable pressure of Iroquois hostility, many tribes were displaced from what had been their traditional community and hunting regions. In the mid-seventeenth century, the refugees from Huronia were scattered, some of them to disappear within other tribes. Similarly, one of the Ojibwa groups moved west to displace the Fox in northern Wisconsin and a Sioux band in the area was pushed west of the Mississippi waters.

A forced move usually meant a change in environment, a change in the materials and resources by which they lived. The metal tools that French and Dutch traders brought them made a distinct technological change that can be understood if not accurately measured by history. And the activity of the fur trade itself demanded changes in the capacity of the canoes that were the freight carriers of this commerce.

So it was that some people who had once made bark canoes settled in a new country and built dugouts, possibly with the aid of metal axes. Some found that neighbors in a new region had somehow evolved a superior design or building process and, by adopting these ideas, they were able to make a bark canoe superior to their old models. Iroquois people, spending time in birch-growing country, learned to make birch bark canoes, and northern prisoners, adopted into Iroquois bands south of Lake Ontario, adjusted to the limitations of the elm bark vessel. The unmistakable lines of the elm bark canoe were recognized everywhere, and about the end of the seventeenth century, Bacqueville de la Potherie told of the panic at the post of Michilimackinac when a fleet of Iroquois canoes was sighted. They were elm bark, of course, but manned by Ottawas who had built them, probably just for this one trip, to visit the French traders on the island in the straits between Lakes Michigan and Huron.

185

From his travels in New Brunswick in 1791, the Scottish author and traveller Patrick Campbell left this sketch of river travel. The old-style Malecite canoe, with its distinctive bow and stern, is being forced up a rapid, probably in the St. John River, with paddle and pole.

The French demand for beaver pelts pushed the search for greater supplies north and west so that traders and middlemen found the trips between source and market increasing in length and duration. At least until the middle of the seventeenth century, those Huron and Algonquin canoes of twenty to twenty-two feet had been considered adequate to carry two or three Frenchmen with their trade goods into the wilderness. But as the length of the trips increased, as traders had to go to Michilimackinac and beyond to seek the furs, they needed vessels that would carry more trade goods the one way and more furs back the other. Safety was another factor. Explorers might go almost anywhere in tiny craft, but merchants carrying a valuable cargo on the open water of any of the Great Lakes needed larger and more seaworthy canoes. When French colonial officials licensed for the fur trade only a limited number of

canoes, it was inevitable for this reason alone that individual canoe size would increase. The Indians who supplied the traders were asked to increase both length and beam in the mercantile bark canoe.

They grew to thirty feet and more. The paddling crew increased to handle the larger vessel, both on the water and on the portage, and, as a larger force, was less vulnerable to attack while on the trail. The big canoes became military transports in New France, capable of carrying troops into hostile Iroquois country or of moving garrison forces and supplies to and from the forts being built at strategic locations on the Great Lakes.

The Sulpician priest René de Galinée, who by 1670 had already paddled from Montreal to the upper Lakes and back, made a clear distinction between the traditional Algonquin canoe and those used for freight and war. The former he described as

about twenty feet long and two feet wide, and could be carried with ease by one man. A canoe of such dimensions was capable of carrying four men and eight or nine hundred pounds of baggage. . . . Some there are which carry ten or twelve men with their outfit, but it requires two or three men to carry them. . . . the canoes used in war or trade were much larger, being from thirty to thirty-five feet in length and from five to six feet in width. Including the weight of the canoe, they could carry a load of from four to five tons.

Baron de La Hontan, who came as an officer to New France in 1683, described the canoes he saw arriving at and leaving Montreal:

I saw but now above an hundred Canows some great and some little; but considering that the former are only proper for Martial Expeditions, and long Voyages, I shall confine my Description to that sort. Even the great ones are of different sizes; for they run from ten to twenty eight Foot long. For those of a larger size will easily afford stowage for fourteen Persons; though they are commonly mann'd only with three Men, when they are employ'd in transporting Provisions and Merchandize; and even then they'll carry twenty hundred weight.

Later, when travelling with Indians, he said that their canoes were "so light, that two Men carry 'em upon their shoulders with ease," but he warned that such craft "are of no use for the Navigation of Lakes; for the Waves would swallow 'em up, if they could not reach shoar when a wind arises."

Scarcely any one of the French put in more canoe miles than the Récollet Father Louis Hennepin. A more trustworthy reporter than La Hontan, he wrote that

some . . . are much bigger than others. They carry generally about a Thousand pound Weight, some Twelve hundred, and the biggest not above Fifteen hundred pounds. The least . . . can carry Three or four hundred pound weight, together with two Men or Women to steer them along. But the Greater must have Three or Four Men to manage them, and sometimes when Business requires Expedition, Seven or Eight to quicken their pace.

In 1670 there were two developments which were to increase the dependence of the French on the canoe as a vehicle of commerce and defense. To the south, the English, who had replaced the Dutch at New York, were pressing their Iroquois allies to supply more furs; the Iroquois chose at this time to switch from warfare to diplomacy in the continuing effort to gain access to northern furs. They sent ambassadors to the Ottawas, the middlemen, to convince them that by shifting their business south they would receive trade goods of better quality and lower price. The campaign of persuasion did not result in the wholesale change the Iroquois had anticipated — they envisioned a major trading rendez-vous on the shores of Lake Ontario — but the French were sufficiently upset to learn that one band of Ottawas had actually paddled south from the upper country to try the advertised English goods.

The bow profile of birch bark canoes varied enormously and depended primarily on what water conditions they were designed for, how the bow frame was made, and how the gunwales were attached to the bow frame. In many cases the tribal identity of a canoe could be recognized from a long distance simply by the bow shape, but even tribal types evolved and changed over the years. (UPPER LEFT) Malecite, from New Brunswick; (UPPER RIGHT) very old-style Algonquin, used in 1900s in Manitoba for survey work; (LOWER LEFT) old-style Algonquin made by Patrick Miranda, Lac Rapide, Quebec; (LOWER RIGHT) family-style Algonquin canoe from the 1920s, from Lac Poisson Blanc, Quebec.

It was the year, too, that the English trade squeeze closed in on the French from the north, from Hudson Bay. It was, ironically, the hard-working Radisson and Des Groseilliers, the pair whose big fur fleet had brought an economic transfusion to New France, who engineered this second threat. When they arrived in the spring of 1660 they were reopening a long-blockaded trade but, even so, to the governor of the colony they had been trading without his license. Instead of being rewarded they were fined and Des Groseilliers was for a time imprisoned. When there was no restitution to be gained in France, the two bitter and disillusioned men turned to the English.

The plan they offered to France's rival was that of sailing directly into Hudson Bay to trade for the furs of the northern Indians. Des Groseilliers was aboard the first ship that made a successful venture in 1669 and the following year the charter was issued for the Governor and Company of Adventurers of England trading into Hudson's Bay. That firm, although suffering some little interruption as a result of hostilities in its earliest period, has been trading for furs in the north from that year to this.

The near monopoly of the fur commerce hitherto held by the French was now most seriously challenged, but those who traded from the St. Lawrence yet held one major advantage. They had canoes and they had men who knew how to use them. The English established a base within Hudson Bay but their main holding was the Atlantic seaboard from New England south. The French, with the bark canoe to carry them, had penetrated deeply into the continent. Even the new English base to the north could be vulnerable to sudden attack by canoe-borne forces.

The push to control the fur resources of the west did, of course, stretch to the ultimate the limited capacities of the colony of New France, and its lines of communication were extended beyond belief. It was the return, also in that fateful year of 1670, of the popular Jean Talon that firmly bolstered an expansionist policy. With one term already behind him, he was again named Intendant, second only to the governor of New France and

functionally the supreme business manager of the colony. Under his direction the active search for greater fur supplies, and for mineral resources, was promoted. The explorer in his birch canoe was unquestionably the paramount figure under the new management. In the years immediately following, the French added phenomenally to the recorded map detail of the continent.

Even a couple of years prior to these developments, the Jesuit Father Claude Allouez, following the scattered remnants of his flock after the devastation of Huronia, paddled west on Lake Superior and reported fresh river routes into unknown country. He went north on the Nipigon River and explored the lake of the same name. This later would be the fur merchants' access to a tributary of the Albany River, a great and vital highway running northeast to the salt water of James Bay. In 1670 that mission traveller paddled southwest from Green Bay on Lake Michigan up the Fox River and met there Indians of the Sauk tribe. "We passed," he wrote, "the portage called by the natives Kekaling [today's Kaukauna], our sailors dragging the canoe among rapids, while I walked

Some early French artists drew canoes that looked silly, like half-moons. Yet they had good grounds for their drawings in the crooked canoes of the Montagnais and the Eastern Cree. These river craft, designed to turn on a sou, had so much rocker that when they were afloat their bows and sterns stuck up high above the water. The bow-to-stern curve on the bottom of this Eastern Cree canoe is gentle compared with some models.

on the river-bank, where I found apple-trees and vine-stocks in great numbers." Progress continued with difficulty the following day as "our sailors ascended the rapids for two leagues by use of poles, and I went by land as far as the other portage, which they call Ooukocitiming. . . ." He was not far from Lake Winnebago.

There were many canoe travellers like Father Allouez, men who probed strange country and left valuable records, but best remembered are the names of a few who, dependent on the preliminary work of such explorers, made trips that popular history has dramatized. Picking up three years later where the one Jesuit had left off, another, Father Jacques Marquette, and the fur merchant Louis Jolliet, paddled the Fox River route, went over the portage watershed to the Wisconsin River, and came very soon to a larger stream that Marquette identified on his map as "la Rivière de la Conception." They were afloat on the Mississippi proper.

Talon had chosen this pair for the expedition to bring more Indian groups under French influence because they were experienced wilderness travellers and men of proven tact. Their journal from the Mississippi was a recital of marvels: fertile land, prolific game, monster catfish, strange paintings on rock faces, and herds of shaggy buffalo. They paddled south, out of the land where the birch thrived, and about two hundred miles downstream they met a band of Illinois Indians, people who used only dugouts. The visitors noted for posterity that these people admired their bark canoes and had never before seen anything like them.

The big river they found was for the most part smooth and placid after the experience of rock-strewn rapids and torrents in Canada, but there were some hazards. As they approached the junction with the Missouri, Marquette heard the sound of rapid water. "I have seen nothing more dreadful," he wrote. "An accumulation of large and entire trees, branches and floating islands, was issuing from the Mouth of The river *pekistanoui*, with such impetuosity that we could not without great danger risk passing through it." Nor were they joking when they mentioned dangers provided by monstrous fish, "one of which struck our Canoe with such violence that I thought that it was a great tree, about to break the Canoe to pieces. . . ."

Not only the main Mississippi but the Missouri and Ohio rivers were faithfully drawn on Marquette's map during the trip, and they probably went as far south as the Arkansas River. It was clear that the Mississippi must flow into the Gulf of Mexico but, anxious to avoid any encounter with the Spanish or with more southerly Indians they thought might be hostile, they turned back about four hundred miles from the Gulf. At the suggestion of the Indians who gave it its name, the Illinois River was the connecting route they took from the Mississippi to the Great Lakes, so that they added to the map the important Chicago portage to Lake Michigan.

Although described by some historians as a key to the continent, the Chicago portage has not always been an easy passage. In a wet season, the portage was sometimes no more than a mile long but in late summer the carry could become a nine-mile struggle over a poor trail. In very dry weather it appears to have extended from the south branch of the Chicago River to the junction of the Vermillion and the Des Plaines rivers; in other words, the upper stretch of the Des Plaines was not usable in drought time. As a short-cut route to the Mississippi and the heart of the continent, however, the Chicago portage was often of vital importance to French travellers.

The bow shape of a tribal group can vary considerably, as can be seen in these Cree canoes beached at Oxford House, Manitoba, in 1880. As a characteristic, almost all the small Cree canoes have a fat look compared with the slim Malecite or Algonquin models.

The man who was later to lead the first canoe expedition all the way to the mouth of the Mississippi had by this date begun his first explorations from the Montreal base. René-Robert Cavelier de La Salle spoke so often of finding a route to China that his property on Montreal Island had been dubbed La Chine, a name which survives today as that of one of the municipalities of metropolitan Montreal. He sold his land to finance his travels and he began by joining a pair of Sulpician priests who planned missions among the Indians of the Ohio.

Birch bark canoes were carried into and out of the water to protect their covering and to avoid wracking the inner woodwork, and they were loaded and unloaded while they were afloat. For lake travel when the canoe might be bridging waves, long poles were laid along the bottom of the canoe to distribute the weight of the cargo. In the watercolor by Alice Killaly from the 1860s, the fur traders are loading their small canoe in the approved fashion.

190   Of the two, it was François Dollier de Casson who for his *Histoire du Montréal* is remembered today as an author, but it was the other priest, René Bréhant de Galinée, who left the more vivid descriptions of canoe travel. He recorded that the preparations for their trip — buying canoes, enlisting crewmen, choosing trade goods, hiring Indian guides — were done hurriedly and on short notice. As interpreter, they hired a Dutchman who spoke Iroquois perfectly but scarcely any French. There were seven canoes and three men in each and Galinée, like other chroniclers before him, told how vital was the bark canoe to such expeditions:

> The convenience of these canoes is great in these streams, full of cataracts or waterfalls, and rapids through which it is impossible to take any boat. When you reach them, you load canoe and baggage upon your shoulders and go overland until the navigation is good; and then you put your canoe back into the water, and embark again.

Since travellers expected for the most part to live off the land, their provisioning was fairly simple. The supplement they carried in their canoes was maize, ground to a coarse meal. This could be the survival ration if a party was travelling fast. It was usually boiled to a gruel called *sagamité* and, if there was time for hunting or fishing, the catch was added. Hoarded fat, other Indian vegetables like squash, or berries picked on the trail went into the stew. French travellers, particularly those new to the canoe routes, left no doubt as to their opinions of Indian cookery. Cuisine was scarcely a word they employed.

Cleanliness and flavor distinction were of no concern; fish went in whole, scales, guts, and all. If the hunters brought back fowl, then feathers might float to the bubbling surface. Father Hennepin told of Iroquois who fished for frogs, "which they take, and put them whole into their Caldrons without skinning them, to season their *Sagamite*, which is a sort of Pottage made of Indian Corn."

By this period the French were familiar with most of the natural food resources of the country and they took full advantage of them while travelling, often buying supplies from the Indians. Maize was the main staple but, in addition, Indians planted their own beans and squash and the peas whose seed came from the French. There was wild rice, nuts, fresh and dried berries, wild grapes, and other fruits. The native maple sugar was about the only sweetener, while subsistence food included such things as the soft inner bark of slippery elm and the lichens called rock tripe. Except for the last-resort items, most such foods were kept for winter use as well.

The techniques for preserving fresh meat that had been developed by the native peoples were vitally important to white travellers for about three hundred years. Father Galinée recalled the difficulty of keeping meat in the hot season and explained:

the mode of curing it in the woods, where there is no salt, is to cut it in very thin slices and spread it on a gridiron raised three feet from the ground, covered with small wooden switches on which you spread your meat. Then a fire is made underneath the gridiron, and the meat is dried in the fire and smoke until there is no longer any moisture in it and it is as dry as a piece of wood. It is put in packages of thirty to forty, rolled up in pieces of bark, and thus wrapped up it will keep five or six years without spoiling. When you wish to eat it you reduce it to a powder between two stones and make a broth by boiling with Indian corn.

English-speaking woodsmen later called the process "jerking" and the product "jerk" or "jerky." As the French moved westward into prairie country, they encountered another preserved food made of dried buffalo meat, pounded fine, and mixed with the same animal's fat, sometimes with dried berries melded to add flavor. This was the *pemmican* that became the staple of the fur trade in the far west.

When it came to accommodation on the trail, the French learned that the tree that provided the canoe material frequently gave its bark for a roof. Father Galinée explained:

The inns and shelter for the night are as extraordinary as the vehicles, for after paddling or portaging the entire day you find towards evening the fair earth all ready to receive your tired body. When the weather is fine, after unloading your canoe, you make a fire and go to bed without otherwise housing yourself, but when it is wet, it is necessary to go and strip some trees, the bark of which you arrange upon four small forks, with which you make a cabin to save you from the rain. The Algonkins carry with them pieces of birch-bark, split thin and sewed together so that they are four fathoms in length and three feet wide. These roll up into very small compass, and under three of these pieces of bark hung upon poles eight or nine men can easily be sheltered. Even winter cabins are made with them that are warmer than our houses.

The French learned to rely on materials from the bush to repair a damaged canoe. Travelling light was the policy, and if sharp rocks put a hole in the craft there was always at hand, not far from shore, spruce roots for sewing, birch bark for patching, and spruce gum for sealing the seams. If they secured no food en route, then the basic ground-maize ration did not last long. Battling high winds on the west shore of Lake Michigan, Father Hennepin recalled that "the Wind forc'd us toward Night on a Rock cover'd with thick Bushes, where we remained three Days, and there made an end of all our Provisions which consisted of Gourds and *Indian* corn we had brought from the Poutouatami's."

The waters of the country offered not only travel routes but great catches of fish which, for some native groups, were their primary sustenance. Galinée estimated that the Indians on the river "by which Lake Superior falls into the Lake of the Hurons" could catch enough whitefish to feed 10,000 men. These were the people of an Ojibwa band called Saulteaux or Saulteurs who, as the historian La Potherie said,

take their name from the fall of water which forms the discharge of Lake Superior into Lake Huron, through extensive rapids of which the ebullitions are extremely violent. . . . The savages surmount all those terrible cascades, into which they cast a net which resembles a bag. . .attached to a wooden fork about fifteen feet long. They cast their nets headlong into the boiling waters, in which they maintain their position, letting their canoes drift while sliding backward. The tumult of the waters in which they are floating seems to them only a diversion. . . .

When La Salle and his two Sulpician friends reached Lake Ontario they paddled west to Burlington Bay, at what is today Hamilton, and portaged to the Grand River in order to go down to Lake Erie. When they met Louis Jolliet, then returning from a copper-prospecting trip to Lake Superior, he offered them a canoe he had cached.

The priests accepted and decided to concentrate their mission efforts in the Great Lakes region rather than the Ohio. La Salle went south with the Iroquois guides and paddled the Ohio River well on towards the spot where it empties into the Mississippi. Before he parted from the priests, Dollier de Casson said mass, "on a little altar prepared with paddles on forked sticks and surrounded with sails from our canoes."

The Sulpicians found the water level on the Grand so low that it would scarcely float their canoes. A stretch that under paddle might be covered in one day required eight days of dragging their loaded craft. They surveyed Lake Erie, then proceeded up through Lake St. Clair to Lake Huron. Somewhere en route they demonstrated their religious ardor when they came upon some sort of natural stone idol to which Indians paid homage. According to Galinée, "I consecrated one of my axes to break this god of stone, and then having yoked our canoes together we carried the largest pieces to the middle of the river, and threw all the rest in the water, in order that it might never be heard of again. God rewarded us immediately for this good action, for we killed a roebuck and a bear that very day."

Each year French explorers probed fresh territory and added ever more detail to the maps of the continent. In 1672 Father Charles Abanel took his canoe from Lake Mistassini in northern Quebec, through the labyrinth of lakes and streams to the Rupert River, which carried him at length to the salt water of James Bay. Only a few years later a *coureur de bois* named Daniel Greysolon Dulhut was paddling west on Lake Superior near the community which now, as Duluth, memorializes his name in slightly modified form. Because Indian wars were bad for the fur trade, his mission was to bring peace between the Sioux farther west and the natives about western Lake Superior.

191

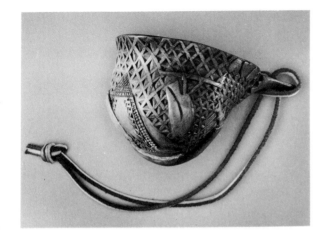

(LEFT) Wooden canoe cups were personal utensils of the voyageurs for scooping a quick drink of water over the gunwale or for ladling sagamité from the communal cauldron. Whittled by their owners on stormy days or at night around the campfire, some of the canoe cups became works of folk art with birds, animals, fish, and maps carved into their surfaces. (RIGHT) Fire baskets for night fishing were common items of equipment in canoes. Filled with resinous wood or birch bark, they burned bright at night to attract the fish, as shown in the scene on pages 154-5.

As it was with others, the Mississippi route was much on his mind. In 1679 he had built the first Fort Kaministikwia on the site of what is now the city of Thunder Bay, Ontario, then headed south. In early 1680, with four other Frenchmen and an Indian interpreter in two canoes, he entered the Brule River, not far east from present-day Duluth, "where after having cut down some trees and broken through about one hundred beaver dams, I went up the said river and then made a carry of half a league to reach a lake, which emptied into a fine river [the St. Croix], which brought me to the Mississippi. . . ." It was here he learned that Father Hennepin, who had been travelling on the Illinois River and later discovered St. Anthony's Falls on the Mississippi, was a captive of Sioux Indians. The bold Dulhut turned north, met the captors, and secured the priest's release, and together they paddled back to Michilimackinac. The modern telling is done in a few sentences, but Dulhut's travel that season was a canoeing epic. Among the French who went by paddle to the wilderness, however, the epic voyage was the everyday norm.

La Salle, who, ever since his arrival in New France, had been contending with delay, diversion, frustration, and disaster, at long length in the fall of 1681 had an expedition ready for the Mississippi. Compared to the modest and minimal preparations made by Marquette and Jolliet eight years earlier, La Salle had gathered a small armada at Green Bay. French and Indian together, there were over fifty persons in twelve canoes when they moved south on Lake Michigan towards the Chicago portage. Down the Illinois to its mouth they went, then south on the Mississippi until, in April of the following year, the bark skins of those northern canoes tasted the salt of the Gulf of Mexico. The Louisiana which he claimed in the name of Louis XIV was in reality the entire Mississippi Valley, at least a third of all the land area of the United States of today. Almost entirely as a result of exploration in bark canoes, the French now claimed the great arc of territory from the mouth of the St. Lawrence in the northeast to the mouth of the Mississippi in the south.

West of the Great Lakes the French were faced with a skein of riverways yet unknown and lakes and ponds which appeared to promise beaver in abundance. A few years after La Salle went down the Mississippi a trader named Jacques de Noyon struck out to establish the next link in the canoe highway to the west. He paddled from the head of Lake Superior up the Kaministikwia River, portaged over the height of land, and threaded his way through a maze of water passages to Rainy Lake, down Rainy River to Lake of the Woods, where Ontario now borders on Manitoba and Minnesota. Noyon's report was given little attention for nearly thirty years. It wasn't until after the Treaty of Utrecht in 1713, ending the War of the Spanish Succession — Queen Anne's War in American terms — that the French again turned serious attention to consolidating their interests in the Lake Superior country.

By 1727 a veteran military officer, Pierre Gaultier de Varennes, Sieur de La Vérendrye, was appointed to command the post on Lake Nipigon; two years later he was in charge at Kaministikwia and was given the fur monopoly of the northern trading posts. By that time his conversations with Indians of the region had convinced him that the long-sought western sea was just beyond the Lake of the Woods. The colonial officials authorized further exploration as long as La Vérendrye paid the costs with the revenues from his own dealings in fur.

It was a family effort with stout aid from four sons and a nephew, two of whom died on the canoe trails, but the La Vérendrye name was immortalized as that of the last of the great explorers of the French regime. From the lakehead, working in the 1730s and 1740s, they pushed their canoe crews beyond Lake of the Woods and broke out of the rocky river and lake country of the Laurentian Shield. They became familiar with Lake Winnipeg and the Red River, built trading forts, and paid the French imperial way with beaver skins. They went west on the Assiniboine River and finally son Pierre found the mouth of the Saskatchewan River where it empties into Lake Winnipeg. Upstream he established a post at Cedar Lake. Elsewhere, of course, the family La Vérendrye went overland on the plains, dipped into the Dakotas, and continued west to come within sight of the Rocky Mountains.

The mighty Saskatchewan River was their special contribution to the canoeing chart of the French. This system, which drains as much land as the Great Lakes, became the route to the west and north, linking the St. Lawrence base with the lands of the western mountains. But a Hudson's Bay Company man had actually found the Saskatchewan earlier than La Vérendrye. By the Treaty of Utrecht, France had recognized the British firm's right to trade in the north, and La Vérendrye's campaign of exploration was conducted always with this bitter rivalry in mind.

Son Louis-Joseph took his canoe as far as the forks of the Saskatchewan River, close to what is now Prince Albert, but history was already closing in on the French colony and the traders from New France were not to win the great profits promised from this seemingly limitless land. French and British were warring again while these men were paddling the Saskatchewan River in 1748. There was a respite of six years and then came the final major dispute between the old rivals who had shifted their major quarrel from Europe to North America. When this round of fighting was done, New France itself and its canoe-borne fur commerce were in British hands.

Traditional canoes were frequently of considerable value to the French soldiery, but they did not have the same significance for the British. The bark canoe did not serve dramatic roles that made it vividly remembered as the factor that swung the odds in any of the major battles of the war for the continent. But for the raiders from New France crossing the border in quick sorties, the canoe was sometimes there in the background.

The canoe is better remembered as the vehicle that gave French forces extraordinary mobility in earlier disputes with some of the native peoples. By far the most impressive was the expedition of Count Frontenac, governor of the colony in 1673, when he led a force of four hundred men up the St. Lawrence to the fort La Salle had established at Cataraqui, where Kingston now stands. Strictly to overawe the Iroquois, whose territory lay immediately to the south, he arranged his battle fleet of two flat boats and one hundred and twenty canoes on Lake Ontario. He had four divisions in canoes in a lead line, then his flat boats, and behind them the Governor himself with his guards, followed by militia in trading canoes on one flank and his Indian allies in their canoes on the other. The businesslike fleet advanced over the lake waters in a disciplined show like any modern navy. The effect was everything that Frontenac planned; Iroquois emissaries came out to meet them in one of their canoes to announce that their chiefs were waiting to talk peace at the trading fort.

The crooked knife was the standard tool of bark-canoe builders. It was held in the hand with knuckles up, and drawn toward the carver. It is thought to have had its origin in the Indian cutting tools made of beavers' teeth, which were hafted and held in the same way.

The canoe, swift and silent, was well suited to quick surprise attacks. In one successful effort to deter their rivals on Hudson Bay, Frontenac chose Le Moyne d'Iberville to lead a canoe assault. This stout woodsman, whom Frontenac described as "a born canoeist and hardened to the water like a fish," took a hundred Frenchmen and some Indians by snowshoe and toboggan along the Ottawa route, then overland to Lake Abitibi. There they switched to bark canoes for the dash down the Abitibi River. The 1686 attack on the English was like a sudden assault from nowhere. They took not only Fort Rupert but the Governor of the Company and his ship as well.

Ceremony was a normal part of the Indians' canoe-borne war parties. About the same period a party of Ottawas was described as they painted themselves and donned their wildest finery as they prepared to embark on a raid:

Their canoes are of various colours and are ornamented with figures or with the arms of the leader on the front of the canoes; you see there depicted the war bundle, the raven, the bear, or some other animal . . . the spirit which is to guide the enterprise.

As soon as they embark they push their canoes fifteen or twenty yards out and range in line, very close together, the end of one not projecting beyond the other, in which matter they are very exact. . . . they give a great shout altogether and start off at the same moment in the direction in which they are to go, as if they saw the enemy before them, and it may be said that their boats are like arrows.

When they have reached the enemy's country, they go warily; they keep silence, observe everything, and never shoot firearms.

An anecdote told by Ojibwas of the Lake Superior country revealed what happened to a raiding party of Fox Indians which violated the rule of stealth in hostile territory. The Fox warriors had come in small river canoes to reach Lake Superior. They lay in wait through the night and in the morning mist they captured four young Ojibwa women who were gathering firewood. They prevented any outcry and, satisfied that the raid had been a success, they returned to their canoes and paddled away with the Ojibwa captives. One brave, however, couldn't restrain his elation and let out a whoop of derision and defiance which alerted the Ojibwa village. The Fox warriors were away in the mists but the Ojibwas quickly manned their own canoes, larger craft designed for lake use, and set off on the chase. The bigger canoes were faster and it was simply a matter of time until the villagers came up upon the smaller vessels. The big canoes were also more stable and the riverine canoes were easy victims when they were overtaken. The little craft were overturned by the larger and the raiding party perished almost to a man.

Fast bark canoes provided for French forces a mobility in the wilderness that the British never achieved. They could move troops and supplies a thousand miles in a month and this capacity made possible raid and ambush tactics that allowed a few men to keep larger forces in a state of frequent alarm. The French did not win the struggle in the long run, but without the canoe and the kind of wilderness raiders that canoe life developed they might well have lost it rather earlier. An excerpt from the Jesuit *Relations* some years before the ultimate battle decision reflects on the effectiveness of their guerilla war:

Monsieur de Corbiere, a French officer serving in the Colonial troops, had been commanded, the previous night, to go to cruise on Lake Saint Sacrament. His company numbered about fifty Frenchmen, and a little more than three hundred Ottawas. At the first peep of day he discovered a body of three hundred

English, who had also been detached to cruise, in about fifteen barges. . . . The enemy no sooner saw themselves pursued than fear made them drop their arms. It was no longer a contest. . . . Whatever be the speed which the increased efforts of rowers can give to boats that science and skill of the workmen have made capable of swiftness, it does not approach, by a great deal, the fleetness of a bark canoe; this glides — or rather it flies — over the water with the rapidity of an arrow. Therefore the English were soon overtaken. In the first heat of the combat all were massacred without mercy. . . .

Although the British military was for the most part unfamiliar with canoes, the Dutch and then the British traders involved in the fur business came to know their importance in transporting the stock that made them rich. And a pair of Dutch churchmen, J. Dankers and Peter Schuyter, on a trip in 1680 up the Hudson River as far as Albany, came back to tell about the Indian craft:

There was a canoe made of the bark of trees, and the Indians have many of them for making their journeys. . . . They come in such canoes from Canada, and from places so distant we know not where. Four or five of them stepped into this one and rowed lustily through the water at great speed, and when they came back with the current they seemed to fly.

With his books on outdoor life and his dramatic paintings, Arthur Heming did much to dramatize the Canadian canoe heritage. Though some of the rapids he painted would chill the heart of the most avid white-water paddlers, they stirred the imagination of a generation of young readers.

In 1684 the Governor of New York, Thomas Dongan, began issuing passes to traders to authorize them to do business with western Indians. An Albany trader, Joannes Rosebloom, the next year led a canoe party to Michilimackinac and did very profitable business, but when he tried again the season that followed he was captured by the French.

The northern harvest frequently came to the British through smugglers. In 1699 an Iroquois told the New York Indian Commissioner, "there is an open road from this place to Canada of late, yea, a beaten path knee deep. . . ." Even some French officials invested in the lucrative business of sending fur by canoe to their enemies to the south. They hired Indians to man the canoes because it was illegal for the French themselves to trade south. About 1750 the mayor of Albany boasted to his London factor, "I do assure you Sir, that you have not a beaver skin from me last year but what I had from Canada." After the conquest, a Quebec merchant wrote from Albany in 1768, "In this place are severall Dutch people of Considerable Estates, before the Reduction of Canada many of them made a great deal of money in Contraband Trade with that country in furrs."

Two of the most inveterate smugglers in this trade were the Misses Desauniers, who for twenty-five years ran a store among the Caughnawaga Mohawks living on the south shore across from Montreal. In 1741 officials of the French West India Company complained that "these ladies have not brought in a single Beaver to the Company's office in fifteen years." Despite the efforts of officialdom, the sisters continued in business a further ten years, buying furs from the west, marshalling their Mohawk canoemen to slip the fur-loaded craft out through the patrols at night and down to the Hudson River and Albany.

When New France fell, British and American merchants were quick to grasp for full control of the great French fur trade. The officials of colonial New France went home to Europe and left the upper half of the continent to their rivals. But the men who had been paddling the canoes to sustain the fur trade remained. And the canoe itself remained indispensable to that trade. In the world of the wilderness men, it was only the management that changed; the life of the French and Indian canoemen who did the real work of bringing the fur to market went on as before. In the years ahead they would take their canoes across the continent to the Pacific and to the Arctic.

While the Cree Indians had their own distinctive style of small canoe, they were never above adopting a better model. The Cree family is paddling a medium-sized Ojibwa-style canoe on the Abitibi River in 1907, and they are reported to have made this style of craft for the Hudson's Bay Company along with Chippewan builders.

196

The British Period

WITH THE FALL OF MONTREAL in 1760, the war between the French and the British in North America came to an end. The conquerors found themselves lords of a vast wilderness that was rich in the furs that found a ready market in Europe—a wilderness, too, in which exploration had really only begun. Most of the newly claimed territory was accessible, as it had been for many years, only by bark canoe. For the British, this was a demanding and novel means of transport, and they needed help to put it effectively to work. They needed reliable people to build canoes and they needed experienced hands who could man them and guides who knew the principal waterways. If they were to re-establish the fur trade that the French had managed, they needed agents who understood the business of trading with the Indians and they needed interpreters who could communicate with the peoples of the various tribes.

They learned soon that there had been thousands of birch bark canoes in the service of the French colonial government, the military, the traders, and the clergy. Among the spoils of war they discovered in one government storehouse six thousand cords of birch bark, stockpiled raw material for the construction of the big freight canoes so vital to the functioning of the colony.

The newcomers learned that for over a hundred years the town of Trois Rivieres on the St. Lawrence River had been a principal supply depot for the fur trade and that the construction of trade canoes there was an old-established industry. Just ten years before the fall of New France, Colonel Louis Franquet, the French inspector of fortifications, had reported that the best canoes in the colony were made there: "They were thirty-three feet long, five in width, two and a half in height, and priced at three hundred francs. They are made to order and sent to Montreal. They are destined for the voyages to *des pays d'en haut*, the high country." The term was familiarly used to indicate the region north and west of Lake Superior. Among the artisans there were evidently some trade secrets, for Franquet observed that a builder would not reveal how he made the bow and stern frames which gave his canoes their distinctive profile. And he noted that one builder there made for the French king each year canoes to the value of six thousand francs, suggesting an output of twenty canoes.

Recognizing the urgent need to guarantee the means of transport into the interior, the British encouraged the established canoe-makers, and in a few years many of the newcomers developed an eye for well-made craft. John Long, trader and interpreter, observed in 1777 that the canoes of Trois Rivieres were superior to those built elsewhere and that they were sent in large numbers for sale at Lachine, the eastern terminus of the Montreal-based fur trade.

As late as 1808 John Lambert said that most of the big canoes for the North West Company were still made at Trois Rivieres. Among the builders there, he wrote, was a family named Le maître, "who built canoes which carried from 12 to 20 men, apart from baggage and merchandize." This craft, which became known as a *canot du maître*, was the big model used in the trade between Lachine and Grand Portage at the head of Lake Superior.

William Tomison wrote to the London Committee of the Hudson's Bay Company from York Factory in 1786 that canoe-building in that St. Lawrence town "for many years back has been a sort of monopoly from father to son. I am informed that they build about 100 canoes every year." In a later report another Bay man, Philippe Burns, suggested that Indian as well as French craftsmen were at work in the Trois Rivieres factories. Burns recalled that children played around the canoe shed amid a crowd of "Sauvages," picking up a vocabulary of Indian words which they used in conversation among themselves. They played among the big canoes with their high painted bows; they sniffed at the pots of bubbling resin used to gum the bark seams; and they watched the skilled Iroquois, under whose deft hands birch bark and cedar wood were turned into freight vessels. The canoe-building tradition went on generation after generation at Trois Rivieres, and there appears to have been only a few years of slowdown in the industry when the colony changed from French to British authority.

This factory operation ensured standards of size, design, and promptness in delivery, but it was not just here that canoes were built. Wherever good bark and cedar were found, the Indians made canoes for the fur trade. On all the tributaries of the Great Lakes and to the west of Grand Portage, smaller canoes of about twenty-five feet were better suited to the shallower waterways and the more frequent portaging on rapid rivers. Canoes of this size had most often been made for the French by Indians. It was a size that came to be known as the *canot du nord*, the "north canoe." Nicholas Perrot reported from Detroit early in the eighteenth century that a great deal of canoe-building was done there

198

by *Hurons*, *poux*, *outaouacs* and *misisaguez*. All these nations make a great many bark canoes, which are very profitable for Them. The women sew these canoes with Roots; The men cut and shape the bark and make the gunwales, cross-pieces, and ribs; the women gum Them. It is no small labour to make a canoe, in which there is much symmetry and measurement.

Similarly, the French historian Bacqueville de la Potherie, reporting on Michilimackinac in 1753, wrote, "The savages who dwell there do not need to go hunting in order to obtain all the comforts of life. When they choose to work, they make canoes of birch-bark, which they sell for two or three hundred livres each."

That hint of doubt over the capacity of Indians to deliver canoes when required was a worry to the new breed of fur traders, and they soon came to consider experienced French artisans a major asset. When the British set up a canoe factory at Grand Portage, where bark was in good supply, they made sure of quality standards and prompt delivery by retaining a staff of French builders.

In 1779 Philip Turnor of the Hudson's Bay Company described the north canoes of the rival North West Company and reported that when the traders arrived at Grand Portage they could always count on a supply of new craft made there. He emphasized that, no matter how well made, a canoe would not last two years in that demanding service.

The British newcomers found their experienced canoe crews chiefly among the French, men who had their roots in Canada and who remained in the land of their birth after the conquest. These men were the heart and muscle of the business, the men who had fought through raging rivers in spring flood and across tempestuous inland seas, who had slogged through mosquito- and fly-ridden swamps and had dipped their paddles in ten thousand nameless creeks and ponds.

An unusual feature in the painting by an unknown artist is the canopy over the lead freight canoe, as though it is sheltering a very important person from sun and rain. It was a rare contrivance in the north because it was an impediment to speed, but it was used at another time when American officials temporarily adopted canoe transport on the Great Lakes (see page 218). The canoe in the foreground is being lined or tracked up the rapids in the normal way.

In addition to the veteran professionals, many ordinary *habitants* had made a few voyages into the wilderness. At Trois Rivières in 1785, the English traveller Joseph Hadfield observed:

the people here and in the vicinity of it are engaged in tilling the land and other objects of agriculture. Some, particularly the young men, are accustomed to make voyages to the upper country and it is held disgraceful not to have been to Mackinac or the Grand Portage. The girls will not even receive the addresses of a man without he has been on one or more of these expeditions.

The men with the toughest, most venturesome reputation were *les hommes du nord*, who spent years in the interior, living with the Indians, setting up rude trading forts, hunting and fishing in order to eat, and forever pushing the bows of their small canoes into new and fresh territory in the continuing search for more Indians with whom to trade and for further rich fur-producing grounds. *Les hommes du nord* often took Indian wives, and many voyageurs were born of these unions. However, one of this tough breed, Jean Baptiste Lagimondiere, paddled from the distant west back to his home town of Trois Rivières to be married in 1807. He then bundled his Marie Anne into his canoe and paddled the fifteen hundred return miles to his remote Lake Winnipeg base.

The Indians continued to supply canoemen for the traders and became increasingly important to them as time passed. On the south shore of the St. Lawrence, opposite Lachine, the Caughnawaga community for years had provided the carriers for the illicit fur trade between Canada and Albany. These transplanted Iroquois had long since abandoned the traditional elm bark canoe for the light, fast birch model of the Algonquin. Expert paddlers and guides, the Mohawks of Caughnawaga became regular crewmen in the trade from Montreal to Grand Portage, and later right across the continent. It was said of the guide Jock Sakarontikitato that he hadn't missed the round trip from Lachine to Norway House on Lake Winnipeg for thirty years.

199

Concerning the voyageurs, Thomas L. McKenney, an Indian agent of the United States government, wrote in 1826:

They are short, thick set, and active and never tire. A Canadian, if born to be a labourer, deems himself unfortunate if he should chance to grow over five feet five, or six inches. . . . if he should chance to grow over five feet ten or eleven, it forever excludes him from the privilege of becoming a voyageur. There is no room for the legs of such people, in these canoes. But if he shall stop growing at about five feet four inches, and be gifted with a good voice, and lungs that never tire, he is considered as having been born under a most favourable star.

The near-exhaustion after a long portage was caught in a sketch by William G. R. Hind during his brother's 1861 geological survey of Labrador. In the fur trade, long and well-known portages on the east-west route of the fur brigades were broken up by established "poses" or resting places. There were sixteen "poses" on the nine-mile Grand Portage over the height of land between Lake Superior and the waters flowing north and west.

The voyageur needed muscle in the leg as well as in the chest and the shoulder. A *pièce* in the trade was a package of furs or merchandise weighing ninety pounds, and two of these were the normal load for a man to carry over the rough and often steep portage trail. With a tumpline around his forehead, many a voyageur carried more than his two *pièces*, sometimes earning a bonus for each extra pack carried above his contract total of six to eight packs. While two *pièces* made the normal load, explorer Alexander Mackenzie wrote, "There have been examples of men taking seven packages of ninety pounds each, at one end of a portage of half a league, and putting them down at the other without stopping." What is more, most of the men went over the portage at a stooped dog-trot.

At thirty-six feet, the *canot du maître* was an awkward burden when removed from the water. Weighing some five to six hundred pounds, it was generally overturned at the portage and carried by two men at the bow and two at the stern, each one supporting the gunwale on one shoulder. The *canot du nord*, twenty-five feet long and weighing three hundred pounds, was carried right side up by two men; one with a shoulder under the bow, the other with a shoulder under the stern, they each balanced the load with a rope over the gunwales above their heads.

The hierarchy among the voyageurs was relative to their skill, the least of the crew being the *milieu*, the middleman, who provided paddle power while under way, hauling power for dragging or lining the canoe through rapids, and carrying power on the portage. The guide was the most senior member of the crew and was responsible not only for choosing the route but also for paying the men's wages and maintaining discipline. The stern paddler, the *gouvernail*, and the bowman, the *avant*, were paid double the base rate for the greater skill and responsibility that went with their positions.

200

They were worth every penny they were paid. On a trip down the Coppermine River to the Arctic Ocean in 1819, the explorer John Franklin recognized that the entire expedition depended upon their skills:

We were carried along with extraordinary rapidity, shooting over large stones, upon which a single stroke would have been destructive to the canoes; and we were also in danger of breaking them, from want of the long poles which lie along their bottoms and equalize their cargoes, as they plunged very much, and on one occasion the first canoe was almost filled with the waves. But there was no receding after we had once launched into the stream, and our safety depended on the skill and dexterity of the bowman and the steersman.

201

By all accounts they were a special breed of men. Daniel Harmon, a fur trader of long experience in the northwest, tried to sum up their familiar characteristics:

The Canadian Voyageurs possess lively and fickle dispositions; and they are rarely subject to depression of spirits, of long continuance, even when in circumstances the most adverse. . . . they are obedient, but not faithful servants. By flattering their vanity, of which they have not a little, they may be persuaded to undertake the most difficult enterprises.

Despite the hard life, the voyageurs have left to history the image of a happy and carefree fraternity, always singing to the rhythm of their paddles, cock-proud of the finery they donned just before arriving at the trading fort, feasting like gluttons when there was food to spare, pushing on stoically when the pot was empty.

(LEFT) *Although H. A. Ogden's view is late 1870, the bustle of activity at a Hudson's Bay Company trading post was probably just the same a hundred years earlier. The canoe crew is loading the ninety-pound bales of fur for the annual spring trip from its Saskatchewan River base to the head of the Great Lakes. At the western end of Lake Superior, these wintering crews met the Montreal-based crews and exchanged a year's catch of furs for the supplies and trade goods they needed for the season ahead.*

The life was hard, but the voyageurs took pride in their ability to endure the long, laborious voyages. Their day started at first light and they paddled until about eight in the morning, when they stopped for a brief breakfast. They stopped paddling about eight at night. They slept under their overturned freight canoes and cooked their own rations: sea biscuit, dried peas, and salt pork between Montreal and Grand Portage; wild rice and pemmican between the Grand Portage and the Saskatchewan. The watercolor by Frances Ann Hopkins has a timeless quality; it could almost have been painted any time between 1600 and 1900.

Fine singers among the voyageurs were evidently sometimes paid a little more, but it was the vigor of the singing of the crews that was remarked by every passenger who went adventuring in the big freight canoes. Even the cultured Anna Jameson, travelling on Georgian Bay in the 1830s, was taken by their music: "This particular singing...is very animated on the water and in the open air, but not very harmonious. They all sing in unison, raising their voices and marking time with their paddles." After dinner the men sang her favorite ditty:

202

Si mon moine voulait danser,
Un beau cheval lui donnerai!

Fine canoes and lusty men to paddle them: with this legacy from the French regime, the newly arrived English and Scotch merchants would carry their trade and their influence from the St. Lawrence basin eventually to the shores of both the Arctic and the Pacific oceans. There were, in fact, four groups of businessmen keen on getting the fur trade operating again after the British takeover in 1760. Longest on the scene were the French free-traders who had remained in Canada after the conquest, tough individualists who knew every facet of the fur trade and many of whom had ventured as far west as the Saskatchewan River. Then there were the traders of Albany and Philadelphia, who had a firm grip on the fur business in the colonies to the south and who had always wanted access to the high-quality furs of the north and the northwest. A third group were colonial businessmen, who had supplied the British army during the recent conflict, and others who were already arriving in Canada, bringing their capital and influence and seeking lucrative opportunity. Finally, there was the Hudson's Bay Company with its royal charter giving it the exclusive right to trade in all the lands that drained into Hudson Bay, an area totalling forty-three per cent of what is today Canada.

With these competitive interests at work, the scene was set for the great commercial battle in which the bark canoe would reach the zenith of its importance in the commerce of the continent. It was a trade war in which the initial advantage lay in Montreal, since that was where there was to be found all the essential elements of canoe-borne trade from the French period: a supply of freight canoes, paddlers, guides, interpreters, good port facilities for supply ships, and a new source of good, cheap trade goods from Britain. Restoring the business from a Montreal base was only a matter of putting together again the old French organization for getting trade goods into the wilderness and the furs back out.

The new Montreal merchants, who were to force the Bay men to move out from their northern salt-water forts and posts to compete for Indian furs in the interior, set out on the old French route to travel and trade in the old French way. In the spring of 1761 the first English-speaking merchant went up the Ottawa River with a couple of five-and-a-half-fathom canoes, each about thirty-three feet long. He was Alexander Henry the elder, and he had come from New Jersey. Long friendly to the French, the Indians upriver and to the west considered the British their enemies, and they plundered Henry's canoes and goods, while he barely escaped with his life. In immediate returns his trip was a commercial disaster, but he learned much about the fur trade in the field, and before he returned to Montreal he was familiar with every aspect of canoe travel.

He was quickly convinced that the bark canoe was the only vessel suited to the fast-running rivers and the portages encountered on the long western trip. He was at first alarmed by the "billows of Lake Huron" but soon realized that a heavily laden canoe "rose on the water with the ease of a sea-bird." He learned what foods were required for the crews and how and when to acquire stocks of wild rice, corn, whitefish, and even maple sugar. He lived for a period with a friendly tribe and "became as expert in the Indian pursuits as the Indians themselves." On the Lake Ontario shore he watched with keen interest as his hosts in very quick time made two elm bark canoes to carry their party of seventeen across to Niagara.

The voyageurs were proud of their bark craft, gave them names, and painted their bows with Indian designs and European motifs. In the watercolor (detail), William Armstrong has caught the excitement of white water, and perhaps the reason the bowman was paid high wages.

Henry's experience was exceptional. Hostile Indians in the region, rallied by Pontiac, the great Ottawa chief, for several years more kept English-speaking merchants out of the western fur country. During the Pontiac uprising, centered in the territory south and west of Lake Erie, the only traders to travel in the area with any security were Canadians: François, "the French pedlar," Blondeau, Le Blancell, Etienne Campion. But with the end of Pontiac's war, the new masters moved immediately into the field. By 1775, Alexander Henry was again on Lake Superior, leading a band of fifty-two men in a brigade of twelve small and four larger canoes, loaded with British trade goods worth three thousand pounds sterling.

The competition was vicious, and at Grand Portage Henry found all the traders "in a state of extreme reciprocal hostility, each pursuing his interests in such a manner as might injure his neighbour." The Indians were quick to recognize the intense rivalry and to shop about among the traders for the best prices for their furs. To cool business heads it was clear that the interests of the merchants would be better served by some form of cooperation than by chaotic rivalry, and by September Henry's men were paddling amicably alongside the canoes of Joseph and Thomas Frobisher and a Mr. Patterson, making up a total fleet of thirty canoes with a hundred and thirty paddlers.

There were, according to Henry, four major Montreal interests struggling that year for the trade of the Indians as far west as the Saskatchewan River. The following year they agreed to merge their trading stock and, at the end of the season, to share the proceeds from a combined business operation. The benefits to all were soon apparent, and in 1779, Alexander Henry, the Frobisher brothers, Peter Pond, James and John McGill, and Simon McTavish formed one firm with its interests divided into sixteen shares. The North West Company had been born.

Joined in a significantly larger enterprise, initially to avoid price-cutting of goods traded to the Indians, the merchants soon enjoyed other benefits. The bulk buying of trade goods from England reduced their cost prices.

203

The increased size of the canoe brigades meant they enjoyed greater security wherever they travelled. They built improved facilities for the partners at the Grand Portage as well as permanent trading forts in the interior and food depots west of Lake Superior. The basic food supply they relied upon in that region was pemmican, dried buffalo meat pounded fine and mixed with one-third fat and sewn into ninety-pound rawhide packs; this highly nutritious concentrate was the fuel for voyageurs in the west. The cooperation also meant that the partners could set up a factory at the head of the lakes to ensure a reliable supply of the canoes required for travel beyond Grand Portage.

The curious humped look of these canoes, with their rounded bows, makes recognition immediate: they are Micmac. The little fleet of bark craft, paddled in ceremonial formation with flags flying, was painted by topographer William Hickman about 1800 at Bathurst, New Brunswick.

Over the years there were many changes in the partners of the North West Company, but the continuing strength of the company lay in the fact that shareholders and partners travelled each year into the fur country, some wintering there as well. At the western tip of Lake Superior, at the Grand Portage, they set up their staging depot and they gathered there for the firm's annual meeting, at which the coming season's operations were planned. With partners on the site, right in the fur country, there was never any delay in making decisions or acting upon them.

Meanwhile, their agents in Montreal looked after the ordering of trade goods and their repacking for canoe transport, the stocking of food, the ordering of freight canoes from Trois Rivières, and the buying of huge quantities of paddles. Joseph Hubert *dit* Lacroix, a Montreal fur merchant, contracted in 1780 with an habitant, Amable Delorme, for the making of two thousand paddles. In 1781 another merchant, Richard Dobie, let a contract to Joseph Perrault of the village of Champlain for one thousand. Many such contracts are to be found among the old records of Quebec notaries.

In the Montreal warehouses the trade goods were done up in packs of ninety pounds—blankets, woolen goods for clothing, printed cottons, shawls and gartering, nets and twine, brass and copper kettles, muskets, pistols, powder, shot and ball, flints, tobacco, vermilion, and many iron tools. Crews were hired for the new season. Corn and grease were packed to feed the men, and rum was decanted into small kegs for their regular ration. With the spring break-up the canoes were ready to be pushed off into the swollen waters at Lachine, each carrying some eight thousand pounds in freight and crew and riding low with only six inches of freeboard. The departure of the fur brigades in early May was a social highlight in the Montreal year, and hundreds of friends turned out to wish good fortune to the partners

and their men. Just a few miles up the Ottawa, whose flood current still carried random ice pans, the canoes stopped at the riverside shrine of Ste. Anne and the paddlers whispered quick prayers to their patron saint.

As the birch bows pointed again upriver, the crew fell into the old routine, the narrow red blades of their paddles flashing at forty strokes per minute. The traditional songs rang again across the water as the voyageurs drove cargo-heavy canoes in a test of strength against the heavy flow of the Ottawa. There was a pause now and then while they lit their stubby clay pipes; this was a breather for all the crew, and they measured their day as so many *pipes*. At each portage Alexander Henry's crew of eight

La Chasse Galerie is the French-Canadian legend of the young voyageur who, longing for his true love, accepts a quick trip home in the Devil's canoe which flies in the night skies. The price of his ride is his soul. The story echoes the French legend of Monsieur Galerie, who, as a punishment for hunting on Sunday instead of going to mass, is condemned to hunt through the night skies until the end of the world. The artist is Octave Henri Julien, who died in 1908.

204

men carried sixty pieces weighing ninety pounds, as well as the heavy canoe, up to the head of the rapids. They paddled usually till after dark, slept under the overturned canoe or a tarpaulin shelter, and, wakened by shouts of "Lève! Lève!," set out again at two or three in the morning. Breakfast wasn't scheduled until about eight.

In swift water a man might exchange his paddle for a *perche* for poling against the rapids. If the current became stronger, the canoe might be paddled or poled slowly and cautiously upstream — half loaded, *demi-chargé*, or entirely unloaded, *déchargé* — up through a surging, dangerous water passage, while the cargo was carried by land. With a following wind, the voyageurs gratefully raised a tarpaulin as a sail, but soon again they might be chest deep in the chilling flood as they dragged the canoe by hand through a stretch of treacherous water.

When they neared Grand Portage the men changed into the finery reserved for such occasions. Then, with a flourish of brightly colored costumes and with flashing blades they arrived at the North West Company's depot like kings of the forest. The Pigeon River was the access to the west, but for nine miles above its mouth it was impossible to navigate. The crew that had paddled from Lachine, as Alexander Mackenzie explained, had to carry the trade goods and provisions destined for the interior across the tortuous trail for which the company's fort had been named. With that labor done, the voyageurs spent a few days eating and carousing, singing, dancing, and wenching, before they turned east and homeward, the big canoes loaded with the bales of precious furs gathered in from across the northwest country. Some few of *les hommes du nord* might join them for the return trip to Montreal, while any men from the original crew who had signed on to winter in the *pays d'en haut* joined the westbound crews of the smaller *canots du nord*, now loaded with packs of trade goods. Everyone now was eager to be moving; there was little enough time for the lighter canoes to return to posts on the Saskatchewan or beyond and for the big craft to get back to their Lachine base before freeze-up again blocked the waterways.

The canoes stood up to thousands of miles of rough treatment and they were kept travel-worthy only because the crews carried rolls of birch bark, *watape* for sewing it, and kegs of gum, all for the frequent repairs required. Gumming the canoes was a daily process for paddlers who wanted to keep their moccasins dry. With the constant twisting and flexing of the canoe in rough water, it was often necessary to take the vessel out of the water and gum the seams several times in one day.

Simon Fraser, travelling west on the Peace River system in 1806, described an all-too-familiar experience at a difficult stretch of rapids. "The canoes," he wrote, "were towed up with the line but one of them struck upon a stem which broke a small hole in the bottom and it took us nearly an hour to repair it. Afterwards we gummed the three canoes which operation took upwards of two hours." In camp later that day the men gummed all the canoes once again. Fraser later commented that the canoes were in such bad shape and required such frequent gumming that the full keg provided for the trip was exhausted; they had no choice but to sacrifice precious travelling time each day while they gathered from the forest enough spruce gum to seal the seams of the three canoes.

An artist and writer who travelled extensively in the Canadian bush just before the end of the freight-canoe period, Arthur Heming, described the gumming process. "Whittling handles to dry pinesticks," he explained, "they split the butts half way down and placed that end in the fire. After a little burning, the stick opened like a fork; and, placing it over the broken seam, the voyageur blew upon the crotch, thus melting the hardened 'gum'; then, spitting upon his palm, he rounded it off and smoothed it down."

Sometimes a poorly made canoe caused untold trouble. Midway through one trip, Simon Fraser complained, "It is the worst made that I ever saw and is more like a trough than a canoe, and I am surprised how Mr. McDougall, who was present, would allow such a one to be made. It would be more easy to make a new one than to arrange it." But arrange it he did. He had his men take all the "wood" out of the canoe, gum it thoroughly inside, make new and longer thwarts, cut and bend new ribs to give the craft a flatter bottom, and then place the old interior splints back in position and spring in the new ribs. All this was accomplished between early morning and nine in the evening, whereupon they pushed off and paddled seven miles before making camp for the night.

When sand or dirt got between the interior woodwork and the bark skin, it often rubbed holes through the bark. But the ribs and that inner sheathing could be removed and the entire interior cleaned. Alexander Mackenzie recalled on one occasion sending five of his crew to carry the baggage across a portage, "while the sixth and myself took the canoe asunder, to cleanse her of dirt, and expose her lining and timbers to the air, which would render her much lighter."

There were many times when the voyageurs themselves built canoes while on a trip, or made smaller canoes from the remains of damaged larger ones, or made major renovations to their bark vessels just to keep themselves afloat and moving onward towards the objective. This kind of skill and enterprise, noticeably lacking at times among the employees of the Hudson's Bay Company, gave the Nor'Westers a distinct edge over their rivals in the fur-trading game.

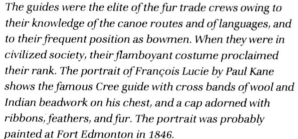

The guides were the elite of the fur trade crews owing to their knowledge of the canoe routes and of languages, and to their frequent position as bowmen. When they were in civilized society, their flamboyant costume proclaimed their rank. The portrait of François Lucie by Paul Kane shows the famous Cree guide with cross bands of wool and Indian beadwork on his chest, and a cap adorned with ribbons, feathers, and fur. The portrait was probably painted at Fort Edmonton in 1846.

In 1819 Captain John Franklin of the Royal Navy embarked on an overland trip for exploration of the Arctic. Heavily supported by the fur trade logistics, he and his party of seamen and French-Canadian voyageurs thrust north down the Coppermine River in two freight canoes, and in a few months mapped some 550 miles of Arctic coastline. The watercolor by Basil Hall shows three of the voyageurs who helped to make the incredible journey possible.

(RIGHT) On his trip to the Arctic seas as a midshipman with the Franklin overland expedition, Robert Hood sketched their little flotilla as it moved under paddle and sail across Lake Prosperous on the Yellowknife River in 1821. The large canoe is an Athabascan freighter and it is accompanied by several Copper Indians in their kayak-form canoes built of birch bark.

A bush traveller resets the ribs in his simple little Tête de Boule canoe at the foot of a timber slide in the region of the Saguenay River. Working alone, an experienced builder could put a rough-and-ready canoe of this size together in two or three weeks using only an ax and a crooked knife.

As these tough and self-reliant men pushed farther and farther west and north into lands which drained into Hudson Bay, it was inevitable that their interests would conflict with those of the Hudson's Bay Company. And just as the French had done before them, intruders from Montreal began intercepting furs which had been bound for Bay trading posts. For nearly a century that Company's policy had been to build forts and posts on the seacoast of Hudson and James bays, encouraging the Indians to bring their furs to the traders by canoe, by sled, or by backpack.

At the outset, in 1670, the Company did have the services of Radisson and Des Groseilliers, two of the ablest *coureurs de bois* in the business, to advise, to teach, and to manage, but their long experience with canoes was not exploited at all. Although the materials for canoe-building were readily available close to the shores of James Bay, and although among the Indian groups of the region were men and women long expert at their making, the Company saw no need to adopt the canoe and to move inland. In their own ships they were able to bring their trade goods directly to the trading posts, and they were doing very well by conducting business right there at the river mouths. The need to fortify its operations against earlier French attacks had channelled much of the energy of Hudson's Bay personnel into the work at such major fixed installations as Fort Albany on James Bay, a base that required bricks and mortar from England, as well as sheet lead for the flat roof, on which were mounted sixteen guns. The French traders, of course, had begun to intercept the inland fur supply before the middle of the eighteenth century, and now the Nor'Westers were doing the same.

Some of the Hudson's Bay men evidently did not think highly of the canoe. Factor Alexander Graham, who in 1771 wrote *Observations on Hudsons Bay*, treated it as a novelty and not a safe one. Of the Indians, he wrote, "their Vessels indeed are not of strength or Bulk to Venture fair out of Rivers into the ocean, being but very weak & thin and made of the Rhine of Berch." He was, however, fascinated as he watched the Indians building them:

They put between the Ribs and Rhyne of the Cannoes being: 10, 12 and 14 foot long and not thicker than paist board, having 20, or 30 of these in a Cannoe which makes itt stiff. . . . I once or twice see them fitting, and making one of these Vessels, they making a frame of the bigness the Vessel is to be, which Done they fix the Rhyne, having a good fire on Each side, for to make the Rhyn pliant, — they then take 2 pieces of the full Length and fix fast on each side for the Gunnels, they then Lay 3 Lath's or thin pieces on the Bottom, three or 4 Double, then fix the Ribs upon them, and with the heat of the fire turn the Rhyn to the side or gunnel, making them all fast, Building them to a sharpe at Each end, which turn's up, and round bottom'd., — the women then comes and sowes the Rhyn to the Gunnels or sides, the Ribs closing in between, having 4 thaw'ts one at Each End 2 almost in the middle, Leaving Vacancy for one to Sitt between each thaw't, when the women has Done Sowing; they Launch her out of the Dock or frame, turn her up and pitch the Seam's, which occationed. by cutting slits in the Rhyn to round itt, — this pitch is turpentine, they gett from the trees; which They style (peque) which some mixes up with fatt, others chaw's itt in their mouth's to make itt pliant, and this is the method I see, they making them mostly in Land, not being Berch within 60 or 8 [*sic*] miles of the Sea Shore.

The policies of the Hudson's Bay Company did not encourage independent decisions by men in the field. The unique circumstances in the St. Lawrence basin had spawned free spirits and free agents among the French, but the servants of the Company were bound about by regulations, handicapped by a rigid class structure, and very much controlled by management decisions made in London. Any enthusiastic spirit or spontaneous enterprise that might have led men at the posts to a fuller use of the native canoe was scarcely encouraged.

This is not to say that they did not use the canoe at all. The first of the Company's men to venture inland by canoe was Henry Kelsey, who set off in 1690 with some Indians from York Fort, which was situated on a point jutting into Hudson Bay between the mouths of the Nelson and the Hayes rivers. His instructions were "to call, encourage and invite, the remoter Indians to trade with us." Kelsey that year reached the Saskatchewan River, more than fifty years before Pierre Gaultier de La Verendrye, and reported in his rhyming journal that he found ample supplies of birch. At the time, however, his report was shelved and his exploration work went unexploited.

It was the lack of birch bark and cedar on the Hudson Bay shores that made canoe procurement so difficult when the Company later needed them to compete in the interior with those whom their men called contemptuously the Montreal peddlers. The Indians who came down the rivers to trade would not sell the canoes they needed for the return trip. Besides, most of these were small vessels and uneconomic for traders' use. The Chipewayans usually came on foot with their fur packs; they made kayak-like bark craft but used them usually for river crossing rather than for river travel.

The posts on James Bay were in a better position because they had access to birch and cedar, and traders there made much greater use of canoes. In the British Parliamentary Report of 1749, Matthew Sergent stated that Europeans could master the management of these craft "very expertly with a Year's Practice." In the same year John Hayter described how Henley House, one hundred and fifty miles up the Albany River from James Bay, was supplied with locally made canoes "24 or 28 Feet long, and 4 Feet wide" and drawing "about 8 Inches Water."

As competition with the Montreal interests increased late in the eighteenth century, the Bay men considered alternative craft for moving goods into the interior, where their rivals were buying their furs at source. Some idea of the quality of Indian freight canoes offered them at the time is to be had from Samuel Hearne's words. He described them as "long, narrow noways burthensome, and . . . only fit to Row wagers in." Philip Turnor observed in 1779 that "five of the Pedlar's men with one canoe will carry as much goods as ten of the Honourable Companys Servants can with 5 Canoes." When it was suggested that light skiffs built in England might solve the transport problem, experienced hands were cool to the idea. The skiffs were expensive, too, and when a few arrived in 1778, the men refused to use them, complaining that they were too fragile for the hard knocks of river travel and also impossible to repair while in the bush.

Humphrey Martin, who commanded at York in 1775, urged that large canoes be built at the forts on James Bay "where the Birch tree abounds," and then be sent by a company sloop to Severn House, farther north on the shore of Hudson Bay. He felt that men at the more southerly posts should be encouraged to become "Masters of Canoe-building." Any Company man who produced a good canoe was to be given a ten-shilling bonus above his wages. It proved a fruitful incentive, and in the Cumberland House Journal of 1776, Robert Longmoor reported that he was busily "making woodwork for a canoe." By the following spring he had completed two big canoes, "built after the Pedlars manner," in which to send his winter's trade fur downstream to York Factory. In 1778 he produced another, yet another in 1779, two in 1780, and three in 1781. Longmoor began teaching others his acquired skill, and more and more the Company men became reasonably competent at producing bark canoes.

William Armstrong's painting has caught a moment in the daily routine of the voyageurs. A long day of paddling is over and the portaging is nearly finished for the day. Under the tumplines of the canoemen, the last pieces of freight are coming into camp, and a small canoe is arriving in the background. The great freight canoe is propped on its high bow and stern to shelter tired bodies, and the inevitable stewpot is slung over the fire to cook the peas and salt pork, or the wild rice and pemmican, depending on the locality.

(RIGHT) The freight canoe running the rapids was painted by Frances Ann Hopkins in July 1863. It has the look of a six-fathom Hudson's Bay Company canoe, traditionally built at Trois Rivières. With the deep freeboard showing, it is evident that it is not loaded with freight, and the sixteen paddlers form an abnormally large crew. It has been suggested that the painting depicts a tourist outing, taking important guests through the Lachine Rapids for a thrill, with the highly experienced crew of a Montreal canoe, better known as a canot du maître.

By 1780 the posts were much better supplied with canoes, partly through the industry of their own men, partly through buying Indian craft. It was in that year that William Tomison wrote, "Longmoor and the men and Indians Arrived with the Birchrinde for Canoes....I gave them Seven gallons of Brandy which I was obliged to promise before any would consent to build one, or Else we must go without I has seven built by the Indians, and Two myself one as large as the Canadian canoes that will carry a Tone and a half for this River the Saskatchewan."

In 1775 Samuel Hearne had sounded the alarm over the great number of Montreal peddlers who had invaded the territory. He urged that the only way to win back the trade thus lost was to go inland as the Canadians did, "which cannot be Perform'd to any degree or Extent without a great Number of Cannoes and Men." When Longmoor wrote to the London Committee in 1779, he insisted that with seventy or eighty additional men in the field the Company could reclaim the business then going to the Canadians.

But even with canoes in better supply, there was yet a shortage of experienced crewmen. The "servants" of the Hudson's Bay Company came from England and Scotland and knew nothing about paddling; even the seabred men of the Orkney Islands, who made up a large part of the labor force, found the canoe entirely strange to their experience. No matter how willing the men might be, the factors could not entrust valuable cargoes to inexperienced crews. When Humphrey Martin sent a party of five men with an urgent cargo from York to an interior post in 1776, he reported: "as not one of these persons except Longmoor knows how to Steer a Canoe; I was obliged to engage two home Indians...for that Service."

While the Orkneymen were learning basic skills as canoemen, a totally new approach to the transport problem saw the introduction of double-ended, planked boats of a type familiar to those islanders. In 1779 such boats were used, with Orkney rowers, to supply Henley House on the Albany River. These first were called Albany boats and were the forerunners of the York boats that by 1810 had supplanted the canoe as the main river and lake transport vessel for the Hudson's Bay Company. The crew of a York boat could carry three times the amount of cargo transported by the same number of men in canoes. The bark, and later the canvas, canoe persisted in Company service on those routes with long portages or on shoaling rivers unsuited to the plank boats, as well as for exploration work, right into the early years of the twentieth century. But on major water routes of the northwest in the nineteenth century the canoe's job was taken over by the York boat, driven by oars as a rule, mounting great square sails under a following breeze, and crewed by men from the Orkneys.

Aided by the iron tools, muskets, and, later on, steel traps—all trade goods supplied by the two rival factions—the tribal hunters of the northwest steadily depleted the supply of fur-bearing animals. Finding new sources of fur was essential to guaranteeing continued profits, and both the Hudson's Bay Company and the North West Company were forced into what might best be called commercial exploration. In 1754 the former had sent Anthony Henday probing along the Saskatchewan River to induce more Indians to bring their furs to the Company's posts. He found French merchants from Montreal already trading from forts near the Lake Winnipeg mouth of that river, effectively intercepting groups of Indians who might otherwise have travelled with their furs to the northern posts.

"Thin Birch rind canoes," he reported, "will carry as much as an India Ships Longboat and draws little water; and so light that two men can carry one several miles with ease. . . . The French talk several Languages to perfection; they have the advantage of us in every shape; and if they had Brazil tobacco, which they have not, would entirely cut off our trade."

From 1769 to 1772 Samuel Hearne made three expeditions for the Hudson's Bay Company in search of copper sources in what is now Canada's Northwest Territories. He travelled west to Great Slave Lake and north to the Coppermine River. Trekking partly overland, resorting to canoes from time to time, Hearne was the first European to reach the Arctic Ocean by land. Although the Company made little immediate gain from his northern exploration, it did see fur profits increase after Hearne built its first inland post in 1774. This was Cumberland House, strategically situated on an island in the Saskatchewan River, just west of what is today the Saskatchewan-Manitoba border. From this trading post there was canoe access to both branches of the Saskatchewan River going west, to Lake Winnipeg on the southeast, to York Factory on Hudson Bay via the Nelson River, and, with extra portaging, to the Athabasca country by the best northwest route. During that year when he was building, Hearne recorded in his journal that about sixty canoes of the Montreal merchants came up from Grand Portage and then went in different directions above Lake Winnipeg. The Canadian-based traders had not at this date combined their interests, and Hearne explained, "The reason of their separating so wide from each other is on account of getting the furs cheaper and at the same time enables them to provide provisions for the men at less expense and with greater certainty."

Peter Pond, born in Connecticut, began his fur trade experience at Detroit and then on the Mississippi River, but by 1775 he was doing business on the Saskatchewan. He kept moving west and north over several seasons, paddling steadily along unmapped waters, always questioning the Indians about the country on ahead. It was he who found the Methye Portage which made a link between the Churchill River system, flowing to Hudson Bay, and the rich beaver country of the Athabasca. Like Superior and Winnipeg, Lake Athabasca became a hub for canoe travel with favorable routes leading in all directions. Pond's map of the region was invaluable to the traders who followed him there.

One of Pond's wintering partners was a young Scot named Alexander Mackenzie, and the two spent cold winter nights discussing the geography of the country, the need for further exploration, and the possibility of finding a route to the Pacific coast. In the earliest years of the new United States, Pond had spent time in Philadelphia seeking sponsorship for a Pacific-route expedition from Congress. While there he had learned about the great voyage of Captain James Cook. He was intrigued particularly by Cook's discovery of a major river mouth emptying into the Pacific; the next step, it seemed to Pond, was to locate the source of that river in the interior and follow it to the sea. Could that river be the one that flowed out from Lake Athabasca? It was the young Mackenzie who would answer this question and many others concerning the waterways of the north and west.

In early June of 1789, by then in charge of the Athabasca district for the North West Company, Alexander Mackenzie set out in a *canot du nord* with four trusted Canadian paddlers and a German. Two smaller canoes carried English Chief, two of his followers, and his two wives. The men were hunters and interpreters, while the women were expected to look after the party's food and clothing. The northern lakes were still icebound and progress was desperately difficult. Slowly they worked the bark canoe northwest to the huge expanse of Great Slave Lake. The river that drained it, the party was happy to find, headed west.

212

But the river swung later to the northwest, and Mackenzie's doubts about this route's being the passage to the Pacific increased as the weeks of paddling passed. It was five weeks after leaving Fort Chipewyan on Lake Athabasca that the little group reached salt water. Mackenzie knew this water could not be the Pacific; it was July and the sea was still clogged with ice, while the sun remained day and night above the horizon. They were standing on the Arctic shore.

The young explorer revealed how he felt when he called that long canoe route the River of Disappointment. Officially named later to honor his epic trip, the Mackenzie River is second only in length to the Mississippi system on this continent.

Returning home was a wearying upstream struggle. For mile upon mile the crew tracked along rocky shores, lining the canoe behind, and the two Indian women were almost constantly at work making moccasins to replace those torn to shreds. Cold, poor food, and unceasing toil sapped their strength. Finally, one hundred and two days after their departure they arrived back at Fort Chipewyan. Mackenzie felt it was a failed enterprise.

But Mackenzie's disappointment faded, and four years later he set out with a party of ten from Fort Chipewyan to seek again a route to the Pacific. From Lake Athabasca they turned the canoe west, then later south to the Peace River, a major tributary of the Mackenzie. On the Parsnip River they continued south in mountain country, and they fought their way up the difficult passage of the Crooked River to Summit Lake. That name tells the story: Mackenzie's party had paddled almost to the highest ridge of the continent. Surrounded by peaks of the Rockies, the men portaged their canoe and heavy supplies over the "Divide."

Moving up the slope, and trapped in a river canyon, they had pushed ahead only after cutting steps in the comparatively soft rock and hoisting themselves, their bark canoe, and their gear right up the all-but-vertical wall. Moving down the western slope of the mountains, they found and faced even greater difficulties and hazards. The west-running river they launched upon is now familiar as the Fraser, named for a later Nor'Wester who thoroughly traced its route. What began as a small mountain stream changed as the paddling days passed into a frequently roaring flood. The river volume grew and the current rose faster and faster; the canoe with its concerned crew often seemed to be a cork at the mercy of the torrent.

The upper Fraser flows northwest, then swings directly south for hundreds of miles, and the river and its valley dictated their route. In the treacherous waters the explorers again and again felt the sudden conviction that the voyage was about to end in disaster. Mackenzie's narrative is full of close escapes, including the wrecking of the canoe itself.

The trouble began when the bow struck a rock and the relentless current swung the stern about so that they were swept broadside down the rapids. It was impossible to avoid the looming rocks, and the canoe was suddenly crushed near the bow. In moments all hands were out and into the shallow, surging water; the current held the canoe in its grip and, again in deep water, they clambered back into the crippled vessel. They had scarcely regained their paddles when the stern was crushed as it swung against yet another rock. Held together now only by its gunwale strips, the canoe faced further punishment. The next impact crushed the bow entirely. The bowman grabbed an overhanging branch to slow the vessel, but he was whipped right out and landed on shore. The canoe raced on with the rest of the crew and shot over the brink of a small waterfall.

Suddenly there were large holes in the bark bottom, the thwarts came loose from the gunwales, and the expedition vessel simply unfolded. Mackenzie, reporting simply but graphically, wrote, "The wreck becoming flat on the water, we all jumped out."

The cargo and the floating fragments of the canoe were salvaged; the wreck was rebuilt sufficiently to get them afloat again, but a few days later they abandoned the canoe they had, by turn, paddled and carried from Lake Athabasca. Cutting fresh birch bark, they built a new canoe on the river bank and then resumed the down-current run, constantly dodging the hazards of the cruel stream, pushing on till that raging flow made travel on foot appear more appealing. The canoe, with rations for the homeward trip, was carefully cached, and from a point on the Fraser, probably not far from present-day Quesnel, they began to hike almost due west.

The backpacking phase of the epic trip presented its own hardships, but it had been the bark canoe that had brought them this great distance, now so close to the sea they sought. On the lower Bella Coola River they fell in days later with a party of Indians and were carried downstream as dugout passengers. There was salt water at the river's mouth, and on a rock facing the Pacific the young explorer, using a stick of vermilion paint carried as trade goods, wrote, "Alexander Mackenzie, from Canada, by land, the twenty-second of July, one thousand seven hundred and ninety-three."

Mackenzie had reached the Pacific, but he had found neither the Columbia River, whose mouth Cook had reported, nor indeed a safe canoe route to salt water. Partners in the North West Company, however, still thought the river Mackenzie had dared might be the Columbia, and some years later two of them took up the exploring challenge.

(PREVIOUS PAGE) The three-and-a-half-fathom express canoe was a beautiful craft, built for carrying important officials of the Hudson's Bay Company and important dispatches. The canoe is riding high in the water, since it carries no freight. The passengers are the artist, Frances Ann Hopkins, and her husband, Edward Martin Hopkins, private secretary to Governor George Simpson of the Hudson's Bay Company. Mrs. Hopkins' keen powers of observation gave her paintings a rare accuracy in every detail.

216

One was Simon Fraser, born in Vermont to a Loyalist family that moved to Upper Canada when the American colonies claimed their independence. He was a clerk with the North West Company at sixteen and a partner at twenty-five. In 1805 he was the partner selected to establish new posts on the headwaters of the Peace River, part of the firm's expansion to seek fresh fur supplies in the mountain country and across into the Columbia region, as well as south into the Missouri Valley. He was an experienced canoe traveller and knew the hazards to be encountered among the mountains.

The second man was David Thompson, a North West partner, who in 1807 crossed the Rockies to establish Kootenae House on what later was confirmed to be the Columbia River. As a boy, Thompson had been brought to the New World as a clerk by the Hudson's Bay Company. In a very few years he became a highly proficient surveyor and map-maker, but by 1797 he was so disenchanted by what he regarded as short-sighted policies and the failure to encourage exploration that he left that firm to join the Nor'Westers. Given what amounted to a roving commission to map the west, Thompson proved so effective that he was made a partner in 1804.

The pressure was mounting to move quickly and to establish claims in the western mountain country. As mentioned earlier, Thomas Jefferson, the president of the United States, was an expansionist, and with the opening of the nineteenth century he planned to send an expedition westward and through French territory. With the Louisiana Purchase in 1803, France sold its mainland colony west of the Mississippi and the United States doubled its area, pushing its western boundary to the Rocky Mountains and the undefined territory called Oregon.

The name was applied generally to the almost entirely unexplored region that lay between Spanish California to the south and Russian Alaska to the north. The Lewis and Clark party, sent by Jefferson to explore from the Mississippi to the Pacific coast, set out from St. Louis in 1804, and the North West partners knew that there would soon follow a flood of American traders pouring west to the mountains. The American explorers reached the mouth of the Columbia the following year, but the Montreal peddlers still planned to make a trader's claim to the Columbia Valley.

(OPPOSITE) *As the explorers pushed west into the mountains of British Columbia and northern Washington they passed through Kootenay country, where they found a new canoe form. The Kootenay Indians built unfamiliar canoes with ram bows and they used any bark that was handy: birch, spruce, pine, or balsam. It is possible that in the distant past the stiffer and less manageable barks actually dictated the form of their canoes. These sturgeon-nosed canoes had a curved bottom so that very little of the joins at bow and stern were under water. (LEFT) On the Yukon River, the birch bark canoes were built in kayak shape with flat bottoms, sloping sides, and long, pointed bows and sterns. The tension was put on the bark cover by forcing a rigid bottom frame against the wooden bow and stern posts, after which the ribs were added to hold the bottom frame in position.(BELOW) The canoes of the Slave Indians, southwest of Great Slave Lake, reflect the inferior birch bark in their region. The canoes are small, with covers that are patched together with little pieces of bark. The dimple on the top of the bow frame gives the canoe a unique profile.*

With nineteen voyageurs, two clerks, and two Indians, Simon Fraser set out in the spring of 1808 to dare the river that was to bear his name. The four canoes were either poorly built or old and beyond repair, and it wasn't long before the party stopped to build new bark craft. When they pushed off they faced five hundred miles of unknown river of what must rank as possibly the most dangerous canoe passage ever attempted on the continent.

(ABOVE) In 1826, Thomas L. McKenney, U.S. Superintendent of Indian Affairs, and Governor Lewis Cass of the Michigan Territory left Detroit by freight canoe to negotiate a treaty with the Chippewa nation at Fond du Lac, at the west end of Lake Superior. En route, McKenney enjoyed a canopy-covered canoe manned by ten voyageurs and equipped "with every appendage to render the trip convenient and agreeable." The artist, who formed part of McKenney's entourage, was James Otto Lewis.

(ABOVE RIGHT) While such historic events were taking place, the Indians continued to build and paddle canoes suitable to their particular needs. If the canoe sketched by William Napier at Fort William in 1857 looks a little peculiar, it is because it is a Cree crooked canoe with extreme rocker for maneuvering in the fast water of treacherous rivers.

It started placidly enough. Just below Soda Creek, in the heartland of what is now the province of British Columbia, the river course became broken and wild with a rapid of "awful and forbidding appearance." The canoes were committed; there was no way to turn back; the almost vertical banks rising above each side of the river seemed to deny the possibility of portaging. Fraser sent five of his most dependable men down the torrent in a lightly loaded canoe. Caught in a whirlpool, the boat was flung about like a bit of flotsam, then dashed against a projecting rock. Fraser and six others went to the rescue by lining themselves down the all-but-perpendicular bank. Their lives "hung, as it were, upon a thread." When they had dragged the broken canoe from the torrent, they crept back along the hazardous way and, like Mackenzie's men before them, made a desperate, clambering, vertical portage out of that canyon and past the wicked rapids.

As spring suns melted mountain snow, the river level one night rose eight feet to intensify the power of the flood. Fraser recorded next that a canoe "was sucked into a whirlpool whose force twisted off the stern."

When the party stopped on the bank to assess the hazards of the next raging river barrier, they saw a series of threatening cascades; but to look back was to realize there was no way to portage at this site. In Fraser's words, "all hands without hesitation embarked upon the mercy of this awful tide." Voyageur skill got them through this test, but it was the last by bark vessel. Fraser decided to cache the canoes and to follow the river course on foot. Scrambling along rugged canyon rims and narrow river edges, worn, hungry, discouraged, travelling short stretches in the dugouts of friendly Indians, defending themselves against the hostility of Cowichans in the lower valley, they pushed themselves along and came at length to the river's mouth. With his sextant, Fraser took an observation for latitude, and recorded it was "49° nearly, while the entrance to the Columbia is 46° 20'. This River, therefore, is not the Columbia." It was a weary and discouraged party that retraced its steps into the interior.

David Thompson, meanwhile, after establishing the post called Kootenae House, continued to explore and survey the upper reaches of the Columbia. In 1810 he learned that the astute John Jacob Astor was determined to dominate the Oregon fur business for his Pacific Fur Company. Astor, who later came to virtually monopolize the fur trade in the United States, dispatched a party in his ship, the Tonquin, to establish Fort Astoria at the mouth of the Columbia. Another strong party went westward along the Missouri River route to join and strengthen that enterprise. In this arena time was running out for the North West Company.

In the spring of 1811 Thompson built a canoe of split cedar planks and began his downriver exploration of the Columbia. At Kettle Falls he built another canoe and started off with an Indian and seven voyageurs "to open out a passage for the interior trade with the Pacific," but when he reached the mouth of the Columbia, he found Astor's Americans already in control.

The bark canoe by now had reached a limit in its usefulness. The trip from Grand Portage to the coast was just too long. Sea transport was taking over. When North West Company ships from England reached the Oregon shore, the crews found Astor's post in difficulty. Fur returns from the interior had been slim, and its seaborne supplies were cut off by the War of 1812-14. In desperation the Pacific Fur Company sold Fort Astoria, with its furs and stocks, to the Nor'Westers.

While the *canot du nord* was still popular with voyageurs on the coast, birch bark was hard to come by there. Although supplies of bark were shipped the long route by sea, the bark vessel gradually gave way to the dugouts of the northwest Indians and to larger coast vessels.

With men now entrenched on that west coast, the North West partners back in Montreal commissioned David Thompson to prepare one great map of what they considered their own domain — something of a greater *pays d'en haut.* He completed it in two years, and the enormous chart was hung in the great hall of the Nor'Westers at Grand Portage. It covered all the lands from Hudson Bay and Lake Superior to Lake Athabasca in the north and the Pacific shore on the west. Almost without exception, the territory encompassed had been surveyed from a bark canoe.

Even in the interior the importance of the bark craft as a prime carrier was decreasing. The North West Company and the Hudson's Bay Company were fighting a bitter battle for total control of the north and west. When amalgamation finally came in 1821 it was the Hudson's Bay interests that dominated the new firm, and their factors were not strong proponents of canoe transport. The bark canoe survived as a freighter primarily in remote regions unsuited to York boats. In 1821 Nicholas Garry, a Bay man and a member of the committee concerned with the union of the companies, reported, "The whole country may now be supplied with Boats except the Columbia, Athapascan and Mackenzie's River and Peace River between Athapascan Lake and Rocky Mountains."

219

As George Jehoshaphat Mountain was paddled west in 1844, from his Anglican Bishopric in Quebec to "Rupert's Land," he penned some pensive poems in his notebook about the toils of the voyageur. A sample reads:

    See that light skiff of bark whose paddles red
    Flash with each wave they break, beneath the sun;
    Six are on either side; one at the head
    Wields the stout guide; the practised steersman one.

In his 1869 book, Travel and Adventure in the Territory of Alaska, *Frederick Whymper wrote much on Indian hunting. He saw many moose, often driven into the water by persistent flies. The natives maneuvered their canoes around a swimming animal to fatigue it and then approached stealthily to stab it in the heart, often with just a knife. The bark canoes they used were built in the kayak form, generally with a deck at bow and stern.*

The canoe, however, remained essential for rapid communication, and one of its chief proponents was George Simpson, who became governor-in-chief of the Hudson's Bay Company. With company interests spread from Labrador to Vancouver Island, he had to move quickly on his tours of inspection. When he first arrived from Britain to manage the company's Athabaska district, just before the merging of the two big firms, he was disgusted with the Bay's canoes, which were "old, crazy and patched up, built originally of bad materials without symmetry and neither adopted [*sic*] for storage nor expedition, manned chiefly by old infirm creatures or Porkeaters unfit for the arduous duty they have to perform." By contrast, the Nor'Westers he met en route had fine canoes, new and well built, and the crews stowed baggage in an expert way and acted with precision. He took their example immediately and acted upon it. For the rest of his life he travelled first class for the company in specially built, narrow express canoes, manned by picked crews. He revelled in establishing speed records, and after a dash of four and a half days from York Factory to some remote point in the interior, he wrote, "I believe there is nothing in the annals of Ruperts' Land traveling equal to our journey." In one season he travelled seven thousand miles by express canoe, and during one trip to the Pacific coast he ran the Fraser River, which had so daunted earlier explorers. Simpson's crew took him down in the autumn, when the water was in its least troublesome mood, but even then the falls and rapids terrified those expert paddlers and convinced the governor that the Fraser was really no canoe route.

He was called "the little emperor" and his entourage was fit for one. One trader recalled that the lines of his canoe were unmatched for beauty, its bow "a magnificent curve of bark gaudily but tastefully painted that would have made a Roman rostrum of old hide its diminished head." His canoes were crewed by the company's best paddlers, mostly Iroquois, wielding matched paddles with vermilion blades. The skirling of his own

piper heralded the approach of the governor's fleet vessel, and with paddles flashing brightly and the company flag flying from the stern, Simpson's arrival never failed to impress the firm's employees and the Indians.

Until the railway was built the bark canoe remained the most certain and the most rapid means of travel from the Great Lakes to the Pacific coast. Like the Nor'Westers before him, Simpson frequently provided passage for official travellers, and particularly for visitors of some rank. It was such a canoe that carried Captain John Franklin of the Royal Navy northward on the Coppermine River to the Arctic Ocean. After one day's pounding by high arctic seas, Franklin found that "fifteen timbers of the first canoe were broken, some of them in two places, and that the second canoe was so loose in the frame that...there was danger of its bark separating from the gunwales if exposed to a heavy sea." Yet with only these fragile vessels Franklin on that first expedition of 1819-22 mapped more than five hundred and fifty miles of the arctic coast.

Some eminent Americans were introduced to canoe travel at about the same time. In 1820 Lewis Cass, governor of the Michigan Territory, left Detroit with a party of forty to explore the country north and west of Lake Superior and the routes between the lakes and the Mississippi. They travelled in three bark canoes purchased from Chippewas (Ojibwas) of Lake Huron. More accustomed to the dugouts "by which the savages formerly navigated the Hudson, Connecticut and Delaware," Henry Schoolcraft, the expedition's mineralogist, was pleased by the bark craft and agreed "that its slender and elegant form, its rapid movement, its capacity to bear burdens, and to resist the rage of the billows and torrents, excited no small degree of admiration for the skill by which it was constructed."

The flat, sloping sides of this kayak-form Alaskan bark canoe are established by the slope of the stakes. At the bow on the left is a row of pegs holding the bark cover to the bow post until it can be sewn in place. The long seam in the thin bark has been strengthened with a half-round spruce root which lies under the stitching. The women are lashing the gunwale to the upper edge of the bark shell.

In 1844 four nursing sisters from the order commonly known as the Grey Nuns made the long, tough trip from Montreal to Fort Garry to establish a nursing station there. When their canoe arrived they were met and welcomed by the company governor, Sir George Simpson. Anyone, in fact, who travelled west in Canada from Lake Superior did so in a canoe. Surveyors, geologists, soldiers, government agents of every kind, artists, clergymen, adventurers, and, in time, tourists—all found that for passage to the west they must rely on a boat made from bark. And many of them have left written records of their travels. The canoe that survives in the present day, both as a recreational and as a working boat, preserves the tradition of the bark vessel that until recent times was required for any travel through much of what is now Canada. Those many travellers of yesterday wrote much about their adventures under paddle and recorded in great detail the routes by which they went. What became clear only later is that it was in large part those records of countless miles of canoe travel that really established Canada's sovereign claim to the greater part of her territory.

221

Another American who had never seen a bark canoe before he arrived at Detroit in 1826 was Thomas L. McKenney, who headed the commissioners setting out to negotiate a treaty with the Chippewas at the west end of Lake Superior. He and his party treated the canoes pretty much as royal barges, but he certainly became very quickly an enthusiastic advocate of canoe travel. Embarking after a storm on Lake Superior, he wrote, "though the swells were high, the canoe rode them like a duck."

With similar pomp and ceremony, Sir Francis Bond Head, who became governor of Upper Canada in 1836, adopted a bark canoe as his vice-regal barge to carry him and his party cross Georgian Bay to distribute presents at a council of Indians on Manitoulin Island. "We embarked," he wrote, "in two canoes, each manned by eight Lower Canadians; and when we got a mile from the shore, nothing could be more beautiful than the sudden chorus of their voices, as, with their faces toward the prow, and with a paddle in their hands, keeping time with their song, they joyfully pushed us along."

The widespread use of the native bark canoe by other than Indians is confirmed by the frequent appearance of the craft in the work of both amateur and professional artists of the past. In A View of the Bridge on the River La Puce near Quebec, *Thomas Davies recorded in 1788 in watercolor the portaging of a birch bark canoe on a horse-drawn farm cart. Just downriver from the city of Quebec, the site today is officially Rivière du Sault-à-la-Puce.*

Tourists and Sportsmen

THE DISCOVERY BY MEN of a first means of moving confidently over water was an exhilarating occasion. Freeing themselves a little from the restraints of firm land was not just a matter of solving a transport problem; it was also the discovery of a stimulating and pleasureful experience. Canoes served hundreds of specialized needs in transportation and communication but they were also sporting and recreational vessels.

Wherever watercraft have become important to people, there has been boat-racing. The painter George Catlin, working before 1840 at his chosen task of recording the vanishing life-style of the Indians, found them racing with blanket sails in the upper Mississippi country. On the St. Mary's River, which drains Lake Superior, he watched paddle races among Ojibwas in bark canoes and saw that excited spectators wagered heavily on the outcome.

In the summer of 1837, on Manitoulin Island in Lake Huron, the writer Anna Jameson was a fascinated spectator at the gathering when nearly four thousand Ottawas, Chippewas, Potawatomis, Winnebagos, and Menominies met there with representatives of the government of Upper Canada. The Indian agent announced a special canoe race for women and offered as prizes twenty-five pairs of silver earrings:

Thirty canoes started, each containing twelve women, and a man to steer.... They darted off together with a sudden velocity, like that of an arrow from the bow. The Indians on the shore ran backwards and forwards on the beach, exciting them to exertion by loud cries, leaping into the air, whooping and clapping their hands; and when at length the first canoe dashed up to the landing place, it was as if all had gone at once distracted and stark mad.

Every journal-keeper who ever went journeying in the fur-trade canoes remarked that the Indian, Métis, and Canadian crews were always ready for fun and sport. They might paddle from dark till dark; they might bend themselves double carrying packs over the portage; still, they were always ready for a race with another crew.

In the late years of the eighteenth century, a North West Company partner, Duncan McGillivray, told of a race between rival brigades on Lake Winnipeg. It was a marathon event, an epic contest even for voyageurs. The paddlers dipped and pulled and dipped again, on and on, forty-eight hours without stopping. The men held their places, stroke after mechanical stroke. Guides fed them as they paddled, stuffing chunks of pemmican into hungry mouths. Then a steersman, drowsing in his exhaustion, leaned to dip his paddle, toppled over the gunwale, and disappeared into the icy water. Was the crew relieved that the contest was over? Relieved? There was a howl of dismay because they had to drop back and retrieve him.

For the voyageurs there was often a sprint for the best landing-place at a portage. As rival canoes surged forward, the novice on his first trip was certain that disaster was unavoidable. The strongest crew pulled gradually ahead and fairly shot through shallowing waters towards the shore. Then, just as the tyro expected to hear the rending of bark against jagged rock, at the bowman's sudden signal every paddler leaned instantly to backwater and the hurtling canoe was halted in a cloud of spray. Moments later the men were wading in the shallows, trotting off with the ninety-pound packs while the vessel was yet afloat.

There was in this adventurous life of the native peoples and voyageurs an appeal that drew early canoeing tourists to wilderness travel. The desire to flee for a little while the restrictions of one's own familiar society and to revel in the rough freedoms of frontier living is no recent phenomenon. The tourists who came in the wake of explorers and traders did so to experience a disappearing life-style. Some came early enough to experience the real thing, when the bark canoe was yet the only practicable means of travel in parts of North America.

Paddling birch bark canoes somewhere in Labrador, members of a Canadian government exploring crew cross an aptly named Mosquito Lake. In the wake of the fur traders, official surveyors in the nineteenth century relied frequently on Indian canoes for transport. This watercolor by William G. R. Hind was painted in 1861.

On the way to the border the Italian catalogued the indignities to which he was subjected—sharing fur traders' fleas, occasional wetting because he had to sleep at the outer edge of the tent to which he was assigned, and Major Long's refusal to allow him to eject from shared lodging an Indian member of the party.

Quite too much for an aristocrat if he was to maintain any self-respect. The Count would quit this expedition and head his own party of exploration, and he would head it then and there. Equipped with much self-confidence and such essential travel supplies as a large red umbrella, Beltrami set off with a couple of Chippewa men and announced that he would locate the ultimate source of the Mississippi River.

Entirely innocent of canoe management, he persevered—or had his guides persevere—until he and the two Indians looked out upon a little lake that he decided must be the true source of the great Mississippi. He also learned about Indian propitiation rites, so necessary, evidently, to safe travel. He became aware, however, that the offering of provisions and tobacco to the "Manitou of Waters" was decidedly more generous than normal because it was coming out of his supplies. Following some heated discussion, Beltrami found himself deserted on a river bank, alone with his birch bark vessel:

One who made up in flamboyance what he lacked in canoeing skill was an Italian aristocrat whose wanderings took him in 1823 to the upper Mississippi. At Fort Snelling, where St. Paul and Minneapolis have since grown up, he attached himself to a U.S. Army topographical expedition under Major Stephen Long. On a survey of the Red River, half the party set out towards the Canadian border in five Indian canoes. As they worked up the current, Major Long recorded in his diary that he began the trip with thirty-two men and "one amateur traveller," Count Giacomo Constantino Beltrami.

I jumped into my canoe and began rowing. But I was totally unacquainted with the almost magical art by which a single person guides a canoe, and particularly a canoe formed of bark, the lightness of which is overpowered by the current, and the conduct of which requires extreme dexterity. Frequently, instead of proceeding up the river, I descended; a circumstance which by no means shortened my voyage. Renewed efforts made me lose my equilibrium, the canoe upset, and admitted a considerable quantity of water. My whole cargo was wetted.

It is unlikely that Count Beltrami ever achieved great solo canoe proficiency, but of necessity he did learn to paddle well enough that he could move upstream or downstream by choice rather than by chance. As a one-man expedition he went on his way and, with that great red umbrella, caused considerable astonishment among the Indians he met along his river route.

As appearances seemed to threaten rain, I covered my effects with my umbrella, stuck into the bottom of my canoe. It was singular enough to see them conveyed thus in the stately style and manner of China, while I was myself condemned to travel in that of a galley slave.

In 1837 a French aristocrat, Count Francesco Arese, toured in the prairie and upper Mississippi Valley region. After firsthand experience with canoes of the area, he was able to compare the qualities of dugouts and birch bark vessels. Leaving Fort Snelling, where the Minnesota River joins the Mississippi, Count Arese went down the latter some two hundred miles, to Prairie du Chien, in a dugout that was thirty to thirty-five feet long and only two feet wide. He had a snug, hip-fitting position amidships between two Canadian paddlers, and at the beginning he scarcely dared move at all for fear of upsetting. He was a somewhat more relaxed sailor at journey's end, but he remembered that dugout as a teetering, cranky vessel that took water over the gunwale from every slight river wave.

Through Minnesota, Wisconsin, and Michigan, across northern New York, and as far as Maine, wherever the bark craft had been traditional in the United States, the white hunter on holiday in the late nineteenth century was often taken back to the near-wilderness by a guide who provided an Indian birch canoe. This thoroughly pleased hunter was photographed about 1900 in central Wisconsin.

By 1850 the Adirondack region of New York State was an increasingly popular wilderness resort area. Spending many summers there, the artist Arthur Fitzwilliam Tait was a keen outdoorsman and an accurate recorder of the adventures of privileged city folk in the "North Woods." In his view of the well-provisioned camp site, entitled A Good Time Coming, the party's bark canoes are drawn up on the lake shore below. In the second oil painting, Going Out: Deer Hunting in the Adirondacks, Tait's thorough familiarity with birch bark canoes is immediately evident. Both scenes were reproduced in 1863 and widely distributed as popular colored lithographs by the firm of Currier and Ives.

The Earl of Dunraven, an Irish politician and keen sportsman, travelled extensively in Canada and the United States, beginning in 1879, and published books full of advice for would-be tourists. He praised the American government for setting aside Yellowstone Park, the first of a great network of national parks, and he offered readers a number of routes to visit this land of geysers and hot springs. Yellowstone is located where Wyoming meets Idaho and Montana, but for British visitors he recommended the approach through Canada, beginning with the comfortable steamer service along the St. Lawrence and through the Great Lakes system. Then, he explained, the visitor could proceed westward with entire security by the new railway from Duluth to Bismarck, but, for those who shared his own adventurous spirit, he urged the far more exciting canoe alternative from Fort William to Fort Garry. Canoe travel, Dunraven reported, was "somewhat expensive" but well worth it:

At Prairie du Chien he switched to a bark canoe and travelled, as a passenger, across Wisconsin eastward to Green Bay on Lake Michigan. He paid his fare—four woolen blankets, two pounds of gunpowder, and four pounds of shot—and set out with a Menominie family. After the dugout experience this was travel in first-class style and comfort. Arese declared the birch bark craft superior in every way; it was wider and more comfortable, far more stable, higher in the water, and, therefore, dry, and faster than the dugout.

What was more, the Indians travelled in comfort and made sure that their guest was given the best food, the snuggest, dry sleeping facilities. He admired immensely their efficiency. They made good time on the river, and when they put up their paddles for the day the Menominies were ashore immediately and cutting poles, building a secure shelter for the night. Scarcely was the shelter enclosed when a fire was kindled in the center and the kettle was hung to cook their supper—fish or ducks or other game. Count Arese relaxed by the fireside and recalled his travels in Europe, during which he stayed always at the finest inns, leaving all arrangements in the hands of efficient servants. His tour with Indians, he made clear, was no less a form of first-class journeying.

228

While Malecite guides with white spruce poles bucked the brisk current of New Brunswick's Tobique River, the author Charles G. D. Roberts reported that his fly-casting party took all the trout they needed to guarantee fine dining en route. The outing was about 1880, and when they turned about for the downstream run, the guides exchanged their poles for paddles.

Among all the modes of progression hitherto invented by restless man, there is not one that can compare in respect of comfort and luxury with travelling in a birch-bark canoe. It is the poetry of progression. Along the bottom of the boat are laid blankets and bedding; a sort of wicker-work screen is sloped against the middle thwart, affording a delicious support to the back; and indolently, in your shirt sleeves if the day be warm, or well covered with a blanket if it is chilly, you sit or lie on this most luxurious of couches, and are propelled at a rapid rate over the smooth surface of a lake or down the swift current of some stream. . . .

Dreamily you lie side by side—you and your friend—lazily gazing at the pine-covered shores and wooded islands of some unknown lake, the open book unheeded on your knee; the half-smoked pipe drops into your lap; your head sinks gently back; and you wander into dreamland, to wake presently and find yourself sweeping around the curve of some majestic river, whose shores are blazing with the rich crimson, brown, and gold of the maple and other hard-wood trees in their autumn dress.

Presently the current quickens. The best man shifts from the stern to the bow, and stands ready with his long-handled paddle to twist the frail boat out of reach of hidden rocks. The men's faces glow with excitement. Quicker and quicker flows the stream, breaking into little rapids, foaming round rocks, and rising in tumbling waves over the shallows. At a word from the bowman the crew redouble their efforts, the paddle shafts crash against the gunwale, the spray flies beneath the bending blades. The canoe shakes and quivers through all its fibres, leaping boldly at every stroke.

To tempt the appetites of far-off readers, Dunraven told of a trailside meal at sunset, a savory stew compounded of fat pork and partridges, potatoes, onions, and fish with dumplings. Ballasted with this fare, the traveller, he suggested, was ready for "the digestive pipe, sleep on sweet pine-tops till you're levéed by the steersman in the morning."

As one leg of a transcontinental tour in 1862, a trio of British tourists made its maiden canoe voyage on the Red River. By stage they had reached Georgetown in Minnesota, about a hundred and fifty miles south of the Canadian border, and there they chose to continue by river and without a guide. The immediate goal was Fort Garry, now Winnipeg. For six dollars they purchased one birch bark canoe, for two and a half they hired a second. In one went the journal-keeper and physician, Dr. Walter Butler Cheadle, and a Mr. Messiter, identified only as a young Etonian and Oxonian. In the other went the titled member of the party, William Fitzwilliam, Viscount Milton.

The untried voyageurs, wrote Cheadle, had a "jolly feeling of independence" as they took to the river. They learned quickly that a canoe with one paddler moves less rapidly than one with two; but the latter was the rental canoe and a persistent leaker, and three times that first afternoon its crew had to stop to pitch its bottom. All three travellers were soon sunburned, and Lord Milton displayed the spirit that made the Empire great by refusing even then to roll down his sleeves. The next day his arms were so blistered and swollen that he could not paddle; Cheadle and Messiter took his canoe in tow.

Their exploits on the river were a series of all the misadventures that have become the classically amusing aspects of canoe-tripping. There was, of course, a plague of mosquitoes. On the second day someone broke the ax handle. And the food! The pemmican, great staple of canoe travellers, was "utterly condemned." It was as tasty as "chips and tallow."

They were all but swamped by a passing steamer and one night, during the most fearful thunder and lightning storm any of them had ever experienced, they drifted in utter misery in their half-flooded canoes. Cheadle logged this as the longest and most uncomfortable night of his life. They shot a few ducks, but in the heat of July the birds were scarcely edible the following day. In a seeming effort to bring a fitting climax to all their mishaps, one of them broke the frying pan and then the billhook, the only tool for cutting wood they had had since the breaking of the ax.

Salvation came at dawn of the fifteenth day when they were overtaken by the northbound Fort Garry steamer. They spent two days aboard that vessel, luxuriating in fresh, clean clothing and overeating at the ship's well-stocked table. All three agreed it was the best two-day canoe trip possible.

Those who find diversion with guns and rods have been using native watercraft since the first of their kind realized how rich were the wildlife resources of North America. The special qualities of the canoe make it ideal for stalking certain game, for shooting wildfowl, for fishing the difficult waters of fast streams, for moving silently through rush-grown shallows to drop a line where few other boats can reach.

A British visitor to New Brunswick in 1890 reported that, in the capable care of Micmac guides, sportsmen on the tidal rivers could expect to take salmon of from twenty-five to fifty pounds. On the Restigouche River, this fishermen's bark canoe is a Micmac rough-water type, a model at that time quite familiar on the Bay of Chaleur.

229

For the sportsman who has learned the subtler joys of wilderness travel without slaughtering the fauna, the Indian canoe has always played a special role in evoking the romance of an older way of life. For the veteran bush man, growing up to know, to trust, sometimes virtually to live in a bark canoe, there was never a question as to its essential role in his life. For the city man, the once-a-year adventurer who sought a small share of wilderness life, the bark canoe was a magic link to a primitive and soothing world.

Beginning early in the nineteenth century, it was the wilderness country of the state of Maine that drew sportsmen from the eastern United States. For the tourist or the holidayer, this was birch bark canoe country. In northern New York State, the Adirondack region, to many city people known simply as the "North Woods," became about 1830 a great open-air shrine for sportsmen. While the bark canoe was native to Maine, birch trees of adequate size were hard to come by in the Adirondack woods, and hunters and guides brought Indian-made canoes into this increasingly popular wilderness resort. The Adirondack guide boat, a splendid lapstrake rowing-craft, light enough for portaging, was soon to become the distinctive and most familiar boat on these lakes and rivers, but in the earliest years the Indian bark canoe was known to every visitor to the region.

Not one to stray often from his native Concord region, Henry David Thoreau made a sortie to Maine in 1857. In a bark canoe he made an unhurried river tour through the kind of wilderness that even then was becoming increasingly rare in the United States. Insatiably curious about the practicalities of living in the wilds, he spent hours on that trip learning from his Indian companion; but no matter how he tried, one particular thing that eluded him was the art of making from black spruce root the split thread used to sew together a canoe's birch skin.

British army officers, posted to Canada in earlier times, have left entertaining and enlightening accounts of fine fishing and hunting. If garrison life was at times less than exhilarating, Captain Campbell Hardy, stationed in the mid-1800s in Halifax, was able to spend enjoyable hours in the forests and on the rivers of Nova Scotia and New Brunswick. He hired Micmac and Malicete guides and canoemen at a dollar a day and could rent a bark canoe for a half-dollar or could buy one at from eight to twenty dollars. Hardy explained that such charges were far from unreasonable because birch bark was becoming scarce and Indian paddlers were concerned about their vessels: "To see their faces of anxiety on shooting shoal rapids! not from physical fear, but for the canoe; and the agonized look when a long grating rub proclaims contact with the rocks, and how eagerly on reaching shore they turn her over to inspect the bottom bark and ascertain if the cut is deep or not!"

The outdoorsman of today may have to visit a museum to see a bark canoe, but there are some who recall that, perhaps no more than forty years ago, there were opportunities in the eastern woodlands territory to order an Indian-made birch canoe, at a price set according to its length, for a dollar or so per foot. Phillip Goodwin's oil painting of a hunter and his guide in such a canoe provides an evocative recollection of the wilderness vacation of the recent past.

A paddler and his dogs, floating downstream on a golden summer day, may well have been on the water for the sheer joy of moving with grace and in silence through a beautiful land and riverscape. The painting, by Virgil Williams, is View from the West Branch of the Penobscot River. *The canoe appears to be the work of Passamaquoddy Malecites, people of the Maine-New Brunswick border country.*

232

During the visit in 1860 of the Prince of Wales, later King Edward VII, bark canoe racing made an exciting contribution to the "Lumbermen's Regatta," held on the Ottawa River just below the yet incompleted Parliament Buildings of Canada's capital. The drawing is by C. Williams, an amateur artist and a member of the party travelling with the young British heir.

Captain Hardy was a thorough convert to the pleasure and comfort of canoe travel in the company of those eastern Indian guides:

I know of no more delightful life than a canoe expedition through the forest. So many luxuries may be taken; and the position in which one reclines, legs stretched at full length in the bottom, with the back propped up against the blankets and loads, is just the one in which to enjoy the ever changing scenery; and whilst on the water you are blessed by a perfect immunity from the flies.

By 1890 affluent sportsmen dedicated to the pursuit of Atlantic salmon that weighed up to fifty pounds could find handsome and comfortable lodging close by the most likely pools on the Miramichi and Restigouche rivers of New Brunswick. An illustrated British weekly reported that visitors from New York, Boston, Montreal, and Quebec could reach this supreme sporting mecca most conveniently via the Intercolonial Railway. And for the dedicated British fisherman, the correspondent explained that New Brunswick was no more remote than Norway, a favorite resort for salmon-seekers. But Norway, of course, could hardly compare. In New Brunswick the visitor could cast his line in salmon-rich waters while seated in comfort in the bottom of a birch-bark canoe, safely in the hands of a couple of Micmac guides who were equally adept with the paddle and the gaff.

By this date, of course, manufacturers in the United States and Canada were offering at modest prices a varied choice of white man's canoes that were sturdy, safe, and less prone to damage than the Indian bark canoe. But for some outdoorsmen the birch bark remained their first choice. Writing in 1882 for the American readers of *Lippincott's Magazine*, a Canadian extolled the traditional native canoe. The modern substitutes, he suggested, must appeal principally to a novelty market; none of them compared for practicality to the Indian model. He began by quoting Thomas Haliburton, the author who gave his character Sam Slick these words to

say concerning the bark canoe: "With a light hand, a cool head, and a quick eye, you can make them go where a duck can. . . . If I was a gal I'd always be courted in one, for you can't romp there, or you'd be upset. It's the safest place I know of."

To arrange a unique holiday or a quest for trout or deer, the magazine writer urged readers to "drop a line to Chief Joseph or Chief Louis at Oka." He told them they could hire Indian guides for a dollar a day and could buy a canoe for five or six dollars. At the Oka reserve, a small Iroquois community on the lower Ottawa River, his Indian friends favored the author's whim during one visit by making for him a birch bark canoe, using only pre-European tools. Certain stones and a sharp bone replaced knife and ax. A stout thorn became a gimlet and sewing needle and the high technology of a stone age was exercised anew for his benefit.

The completed canoe, eighteen feet long, three in breadth, was for him the perfect craft for woodland waters. "When it lay empty on the water it touched it with an edge like a knife. When we were all in, it only sank about four inches." He recalled the Longfellow epic, in which Hiawatha had smeared his canoe's sides with sturgeon oil to make it swifter in the water, and the writer asked Chief Joseph if he had ever heard of such a practice. The reply, one suspects, was grammatically modified by a city editor to a form thought suitable for a red man: "Well, long time ago I heard my grandfader tell story like dat, and I believe it was use by Indians once. But me think it only superstition."

To early explorers from the Old World, the bark canoe of the New was a fascinating novelty, an intriguing craft of cunning design, and it was to be seen in great numbers. To holidayers at the end of the nineteenth century, it was still intriguing, still a clever design, but a novelty, too, because it was no longer seen in such numbers. The bark canoe was already becoming rare in parts of the woodlands region, and new canoes, made in new ways by the explorers' descendants, were taking its place.

(ABOVE) *Along the Slave River in what is now the southern border country of Canada's Northwest Territories, James W. Tyrrell's government surveying party in 1900 uses Red River carts to portage what were then newly introduced canvas-covered canoes. Even at this relatively late date, the survey trip across 4,600 miles of the north lands would have been impossible without canoes.*

(LEFT) *With a farm-wagon box and household effects straddling a pair of bark canoes, Indian paddlers on moving day cross Leech Lake in northern Minnesota.*

(FOLLOWING PAGE) *In northern Ontario, where the Lady Evelyn River meets the Montreal River, the workhorse vehicles of past and present in wilderness country are moored briefly to the same wharf. The canvas-covered cedar canoe, carrying a crew of campers on vacation, is built on the lines of the old* canot du nord. *The float plane will reach remote lakes more quickly, but it will take a larger aircraft to match this canoe's carrying capacity.*

The Modern Canoe

THE NATIVE BARK CANOE had evolved from a mere flexible envelope to a tough and resilient lightweight craft with superb hydrodynamic lines. The skin boat had been developed into an exquisitely fine and speedy hunting vessel. The dugout, which began as a cumbersome trough, had become the magnificently sculptured and thoroughly seaworthy boat of the Caribbean and the north Pacific coast.

Even so, when Europeans brought more sophisticated tools and new technological ideas, the native peoples continued to modify their varied canoes. Newcomers who took to using the indigenous boats of the continent inevitably strove to eliminate what they saw as shortcomings or faults, sometimes trying to preserve the best traditional features, at other times attempting to turn the original model into something distinctly different. The variety of new types of boat that resulted served to extend the economic use of the canoe and carried the very idea of the canoe into a new era of sporting and recreational use at a time when traditional forms and traditional usage were beginning to decline.

Different building materials and processes were applied to the old dugout, bark, and skin models. Many experimenters must have had a hand in the latter-day evolution of the canoe, but it is not until the early nineteenth century that one begins to see the changes clearly documented in the records.

The continent's outstanding geographer and mapmaker, David Thompson, recorded in March of 1811 that he and his men made a canoe of cedar planks. They had gone westward over the Rockies and then had begun searching for birch to build a canoe to go down the Columbia River. What little bark they found was poor, too thin to sheath a craft that would withstand those rough waters:

We had to turn our thoughts to some other material, and Cedar wood being the lightest and most pliable for a Canoe, we split out thin boards of Cedar wood of about six inches in breadth and builded a Canoe of twenty five feet in length by fifty inches in breadth, of the same form of a common Canoe, using cedar boards instead of Birch Rind, which proved to be equally light and much stronger than Birch Rind, the greatest difficulty we had was sewing the boards to each round the timbers. As we had no nails we had to make use of the fine Roots of the Pine which we split. . . .

Whether Thompson's Columbia River canoe was carvel built, with a smooth hull, or clinker built, with overlapping side planks, is not certain. Since he made no mention in his journal of caulking and gumming, essential if sheathing pieces had been fitted edge to edge, it probably was a clinker, or lapstrake, craft. Thompson had begun his service with the Hudson's Bay Company and was no doubt familiar with the lapstrake boats made by Orkneymen at western posts. An entry in the journal of Robert Stuart, who in 1810 had become a partner in the Pacific Fur Company, indicates that plank canoes were not unfamiliar on the lower Columbia. He described one made of cedar boards a quarter-inch thick, supported inside by "braces or Knees of the same material $3/8$ of an inch to which the boards are sewed with sturgeon twine. . . ."

In 1837, while on a land survey in that belt of Upper Canada (now Ontario) between Georgian Bay and the Ottawa River, Thompson once again found himself making canoes from the raw materials of the forest. "Tin" canoes, made from sheet iron, had been recommended by survey management, but Thompson would have no part of them. He insisted on a cedar-plank canoe and got one, making it clear that such craft had become generally familiar, in that region at least.

By September, working in what is now Algonquin Park, a provincial park and popular canoeing area, Thompson and his men decided they could not complete their assignment before freeze-up unless they divided the party. The solution proposed by the sixty-seven-year-old veteran of more than fifty thousand miles by paddle was to build two smaller canoes to survey the shallow streams. In twelve days they felled cedar trees and split out about a hundred boards. They used their crooked knives to smooth and shape the boards, and then Thompson prepared a canoe bed, just as a bark-canoe builder would. He wrote of first placing a "Bottom" on the canoe bed, suggesting that he used a central single member running full length between bow and stern. The gunwales, spread by "Bars," and the stem pieces were added, and a basic skeleton began to take shape.

In the nineteenth century some wilderness travellers carried a ready-made, waterproofed canvas canoe-skin, such as that designed by Verplanck Colvin, surveyor for the state of New York, while working in the Adirondack region. In the 1870s an Albany manufacturer, R. C. Scott, put the Colvin Canvas Boat on the market. It weighed just over ten pounds and was reinforced with light leather patches to protect the canvas at the points where it was fastened to keelson and gunwale pieces, which were improvised when required. A brass strip riveted to the canvas became a rigid cut-water, and leather thongs bound the unfolded fabric to those gunwales.

Colvin's Adirondack region had long supported white hunters and trappers, many of whom used Indian-made birch bark canoes. By then there were few Indians left in the area, and the woodsmen sometimes had to improvise their own craft. The substitutes they made from various barks were of makeshift quality, and, along with trappers, hunters, surveyors, prospectors, and bush workers in other districts, they began to buy their craft from commercial builders, who would offer them canoes that were both durable and light in weight.

For the businessman of the late years of the nineteenth century, producing canoes of bark was not practicable. For one thing, the process of making them in the traditional manner remained a mystery to most white men. That clever engineering by which a flexible sheath was first prepared and then a framework was fitted into it piece by piece so that the whole was held together by an equilibrium of tensions—that technique was entirely novel to Europeans. The fact that some observers, even those writing late in the nineteenth century, could watch skilled Indian craftsmen at work and yet describe the process as a matter of fitting a bark cover over a pre-built frame makes it clear that many never did understand the advanced technology of the native peoples.

Although David Thompson in 1837 had refused to use a tin canoe, experimenters before the end of the century produced numbers of metal canoes with the same objective as that of the iron-ship designers—greater durability and longer useful life.

Bark canoes gave way gradually to planked craft, and by 1900, on the St. Mary's River, which drains Lake Superior, cedar board canoes were no longer a novelty in the rapids waters, where, for centuries past, the fishing had been a mainstay of the Indians' economy.

"Rib" is a word that doesn't appear in Thompson's journal, but he referred to "Timbers" and "Boards," and he "got in the necessary Timber" before applying the sheathing boards. With few nails on hand, they made wooden pegs to fasten the boards to the frame. Some old "Line" was picked to bits for oakum, and spruce gum was melted and run into the exterior seams. These canoes were probably carvel built, the thin sheathing boards fitted closely together, edge to edge, to make a smooth outer surface.

European cloth was a popular trade item acquired by native peoples from the earliest periods of contact. They used canvas for sail-making and found that fragments of the fabric were excellent for sealing bark seams. Strips of cloth placed over the gummed lacing at the sharp bow and stern made a superior reinforcement at points where the bark skin was particularly vulnerable. Bits of fabric were also used to reinforce the periodic gumming so necessary while travelling. The further inevitable step, of course, was the making of a totally canvas-covered canoe. Indians who made canvas canoes for the Hudson's Bay Company followed the traditional building procedure, fitting the frame pieces into a sewn fabric sheath.

"Tin" canoes reappeared from time to time in the sporting literature of the later nineteenth century and, when a new refining process brought low-cost aluminum to the market after 1886, some canoes of this lightweight metal were made. Even so, it has been only in very recent times, following the Second World War, that extremely durable aluminum canoes have achieved general popularity. Tin, of course, then as now, is a misnomer; the canoe was made from flexible sheets of what was called Russian iron. Today's counterpart is galvanized iron or steel.

The most intriguing of the early experiments was the big sheet-iron canoe built about 1840 for the garrison at Penetanguishene on Ontario's Georgian Bay shore. Lewis Solomon, an old voyageur who died in 1900, recalled that it was made by the community's tinsmith, Toussaint Boucher. Solomon's estimate that it was about forty-five feet long was possibly on the generous side, but the boat certainly matched the largest of the fur-trade canoes: "It carried fourteen paddlers and six passengers, besides the usual attendants, with provisions and supplies. . . . It was rigged for sailing, but was no good in a storm, as it cut through the waves and was in danger of filling, while the bark canoe bounded over them."

The metal canoe remained mainly a novelty in the nineteenth century, but there were other attempts, many never recorded, to adapt old and new boat-building techniques to the making of canoes. A district that contributed significantly to the development of modern canoes is Ontario's Peterborough County. It has been suggested, in fact, that if the canoe had not been a gift from the Amerindians, the sporting folk of Peterborough might have invented it just to enjoy to the fullest the beautiful waterways of their region.

Bark canoes were not unfamiliar but dugouts were more common, and the Missisauga Indians of Rice Lake, on the county's southern edge, used only dugout canoes. For white immigrants, who began arriving in the 1820s, pine-log dugouts became the familiar means of transport and communication along the winding rivers and lakes of this district just on the edge of the Canadian Shield.

In the golden autumn, great expanses of wild rice drew migrating waterfowl by the thousands, and the hunters slipped silently through those watery grain fields in their dugouts. Through rice or rushes or reeds, the dugout, they thought, made less sound than a bark canoe, and they were convinced that it was a more stable vessel to shoot from. Samuel Strickland, newly arrived in 1825, made his own dugout for salmon fishing. It was sixteen feet long, and he was thoroughly proud of it even if "the thing looked more like a hog-trough than a boat."

Hunters wanted a craft more stable than the average Indian-made dugout, and the first change they made was to give it a wide, flat bottom. The kind first acquired from local Indians, just large enough for two hunters and their fowling pieces, almost invariably had a bottom contour that was essentially the natural round of the original log. It was extremely cranky and, for gunners, neither comfortable nor secure.

There were, no doubt, many variations in line and performance between the dugouts made by different hunters and boat-builders in the district, but their combined experimenting with ax and adze was to develop and fix the hull form that later became identified with the open Canadian canoe. Sporting rivalry among builders and users led to racing competitions in which their craft design and their paddling prowess were tested in public. A regatta was staged in neighboring Victoria County at least as early as 1839, and the first regatta primarily for canoes took place on Rice Lake in 1846.

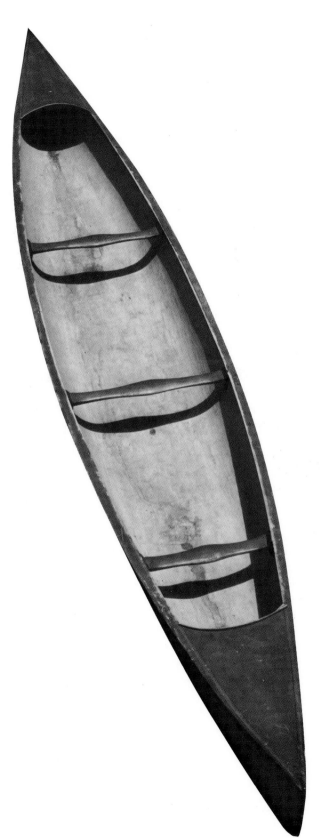

237

A finely shaped, lightweight dugout is one of a pair carved from a single straight-grained basswood trunk in the yard of Payne Brothers lumber mill near Lakefield, Ontario. It is representative of the quality of work attained by settlers in Peterborough County by the middle of the nineteenth century and is a dugout of the type that led directly to the development of the open canoe of the present day.

Although Samuel Strickland had likened his first attempt to a "hog-trough," he and other members of his family at Lakefield at the head of the Otonabee River went on to produce many fine canoes and to paddle them well enough to win many of the prizes in the early regattas. Weight was overcome by shaving down a dugout hull, and Strickland claimed, "My boys and I have made canoes of this sort so light, that one person could easily carry one of them on his head over short portages."

About 1855 his son, George Strickland, reduced dugout-making to a system, so that new boats could be made true to a given model. What he probably did was to take the lines off a particularly fine dugout and make templates from which further canoes, exactly like the prototype, could be shaped. In 1860 George Strickland built the first decked canoe to be seen in the district. It was a slim and shallow butternut dugout, about eighteen feet long and only two feet wide. Butternut decking enclosed nearly two-thirds of its length, leaving a cockpit six feet long. The beautifully sleek canoe was finished with French polish and was presented to the Prince of Wales, who visited and toured Canada in that year.

Folk wisdom has it that John Stephenson, while portaging a waterlogged dugout, resolved that something must be done to lift such burdens from his shoulders and those of fellow sportsmen. At the Peterborough regatta in 1857 he inspected the best of the competing dugouts as well as the birch bark entrants and a canoe of canvas stretched over a light wooden frame. The dugout designs looked best to him, but the dugout was just too heavy. Partner in a local planing mill, he had the tools and the material to undertake any kind of board construction, and in the following year he made several experimental canoes from thin basswood boards.

Basswood is not a wood of the greatest strength, but it is light, a factor that increases in importance with the length of the canoeist's portage. It bends and molds readily, and it has a leathery quality that resists fracture.

Stephenson's experiments led him to choose a rib-and-batten system. For a canoe of sixteen feet, six to eight tapered quarter-inch-thick boards were close-fitted for a smooth outer hull and the seams were covered on the inside by long battens about an inch wide. The ribs, no wider than the battens, were spaced four to six inches apart so that battens and ribs together formed a grid pattern.

Stephenson's basic design was immediately popular, not only among paddlers in the district, but also with three other canoe-makers, who by 1862 were producing their own versions of the board canoe. Stephenson's operation in the village of Ashburnham, a suburb of the town of Peterborough, was later to become the Ontario Canoe Company. The others to take up plank-canoe manufacturing were William English in Peterborough, Thomas Gordon, who was already an established boatbuilder at Lakefield, and Daniel Herald, who had been trained as a shipwright in England and whose shop was at Gore's Landing on Rice Lake.

Working to standardized models, canoe-makers were soon producing the tapered longitudinal planks from patterns and putting the board canoe together over a form, which in the first instance was probably an actual dugout. Sophistication of line, however, particularly the "tumblehome" shape that gave the developing Canadian canoe a wider beam below, rather than at gunwale level, demanded specially made sectional forms or molds. These molds, understandably, were the most jealously prized possessions in each of the canoe-making shops.

The new rib-and-batten canoe did not put an end entirely to the making of dugouts. For many hunters, the flat-bottomed dugout, stable, solid, and proof against damage, remained a firm favorite. It was also the easiest craft to keep clean; the smooth interior finish of a dugout that had carried the bloody carcasses of a couple of deer or a hundred ducks could be washed out quickly.

The first board-sheathed canoes to be made with a smooth interior were disappointing, but in 1871 Dan Herald of Gore's Landing devised a system of making double-skinned cedar canoes true to any model. Two layers of thin white-cedar plank were steamed and bent around the mold, the inner layer set laterally, like a series of very wide ribs set flush together, and the outer layer running longitudinally and presenting an equally smooth outer surface. The two layers were clinched together with nails in the same manner that outer planking had been fastened to ribs. It was an immensely strong hull.

When Herald purchased the *Flying Cloud*, a handsome dugout that had won every race in the Rice Lake regatta of 1865, he took the lines of this speedy dugout for the Herald canoe, about which a writer for *Forest and Stream* said in 1887: "This canoe was as far as model goes the archetype of the Canadian canoe. She had the sharp lines, the broad flat floor, the slight tumble home of the topsides that are to this day the chief characteristic of the Canadian canoe."

Reginald Drayton, a young English immigrant whose family had settled near Gore's Landing, wrote in his diary about this time that he and a friend had ordered a canoe from Herald: "and of course we had to go and see how it was getting on each day. . . . It was not long before our canoe was ready for us. It was 16 feet long and 31 inches wide, smooth inside, built entirely of cedar and we paid $35 for it. We soon had it in the water and found no great difficulty in paddling it, as it was flat on the bottom and fairly steady."

John Stephenson's response was a new cedar-rib canoe. Made without a longitudinal sheath, it was formed entirely of cedar ribs about one inch wide, fastened flush one to another with tongue-and-groove joints. Gunwale strips, keel, and keelson were the only lengthwise members, and so the canoe had a smooth interior. At the same time Stephenson introduced a model with longitudinal planks fastened together by tongue-and-groove joints. This one needed ribs but no battens for the inner surface. Stephenson made both carvel- and clinker-built canoes, and the firms that carried on his business were still offering them at the turn of the century.

238

Devotees of the very popular cedar strip model made by the Lakefield Canoe Company in the earlier years of this century swore that she was faster than any canvas-covered canoe. She was built from long strips no more than an inch wide, secured inside by light, half-round ribs. Wherever regattas were held throughout Ontario vacation country, she was an ever-present paddling competitor and, with leeboards, an excellent sailing craft.

Her lines are, while long, full enough to give her great carrying capacity, and she will rise to a choppy sea without waiting to be expostulated with. Decks she has none, except a pretense thereat, at bow and stern, which is purely ornamental, and her stem is peculiar to herself alone, as are the peculiar curves of her stem and stern piece. Her internal fittings are of the simplest description. If she is a rib and batten, floor boards are buttoned to her bottom, if she has a smooth interior, there is nothing but the thwarts, solid pieces of timber that not only prevent the whole craft from spreading, but that serve as kneeling rests. Her outfit consists of a pair of leeboards, that can be strapped to a thwart when in use and when idle fold into small compass, a lateen mainsail, occasionally a jigger, and a couple of single-bladed paddles.

On the far side of the Atlantic in the 1860s a quite different type of canoe was introduced and popularized. British adventurers much earlier had carried home as curios or trophies numbers of native canoes and kayaks, and the characteristics of Indian and Inuit vessels evidently were familiar to more than a few persons in Britain. Certainly there were canoes of sorts on the Thames by 1850; but the introduction of canoeing as a sport with mass appeal was very much the result of the enthusiasm of one very keen man.

For Americans who chose to paddle a Canadian model, recognized as a distinct type after 1870, a Dan Herald product, frequently noted in the literature as a Rice Lake canoe, was the early favorite. As new enterprises appeared and some of the older disappeared, the names of the first builders in Peterborough faded and the principal firm before 1890 became the Ontario Canoe Company. This name, in turn, disappeared and, in 1892, there first appeared the label of the firm that for many Canadians came to symbolize the lasting standard of canoe manufacture — the Peterborough Canoe Company, Limited.

The dugouts earlier designed for racing in this district had evolved with a hull form closely akin to that of the woodland Indians' bark craft. While the Canadian canoe was derived essentially from a dugout tradition, the very form and character of the craft from the 1860s to the present suggest the profile and the spirit of the birch bark — so much so that in sporting journals before the turn of the century writers referred frequently to the Canadian canoe as an improved birch bark model.

The "Canadian canoe" was described by a reporter for *Forest and Stream* in 1887 at the height of its early popularity:

The typical Canadian canoe, such a craft as may be found on nearly every sheet of water in Canada, is a craft of about 30 in. of beam and 12 in. of depth for 16 ft. of length. She has a flat floor with a quick turn at the bilge, and her topsides generally fall in a little.

John MacGregor's Rob Roy, *a clinker-built solo canoe for use with a double paddle, was adopted and modified by American builders after 1870. In Canton, New York, Henry Rushton called his model the* American Traveling Canoe *and published this illustration in his catalogue.*

John MacGregor, a Scot living in London, devoted a great deal of energy to what at the time was called muscular Christianity, an evangelizing philosophy that sought converts through the example of sportsmanship, physical training, and athletic competition. MacGregor travelled widely in the interests of his faith, and while on a trip to North America in 1859 he had his first experience with canoeing. On the Ottawa River he was introduced to the pleasures of paddling in three different canoes—an Indian-made birch bark, a dugout of some sort, and one made from an India-rubber skin over a rigid, lightweight frame.

MacGregor travelled ultimately as far as Kamchatka, the Siberian peninsula that extends eastward into Bering Sea and all but links Asia to the Americas. While there he was particularly impressed by the qualities of northern kayaks.

Home again in London, he built a canoe that was more akin to the boats of the Arctic than to birch bark or dugout types. But whereas the Arctic kayak was a short-trip craft, most often used for hunting, MacGregor's boat was planned for long-distance cruising. The *Rob Roy*, as he named it, was the hybrid product of European technology and Inuit design. About fifteen feet long, it was clinker-built with a full keel of oak. The strakes were of thinly shaved oak, except for its top strakes of mahogany. The deck was of thin cedar. In cross-section at mid beam it was an almost perfect semicircle.

Like most kayaks, the *Rob Roy* was intended for a lone boatman, who occupied a cockpit, sat right on the bottom, and propelled the craft with a double-bladed paddle. It also carried a mast that rose only four feet nine inches above deck level, and a lugsail with a bamboo yard and boom each of the same length as the mast. With a

tiny jib, the total sail power was of little use except with a following wind. Later models were on the average fourteen feet in length, twenty-six inches wide, and eleven inches deep. Complete with fittings they weighed seventy-one pounds.

MacGregor explained that the *Roy Roy* was designed "to sail steadily, to paddle easily, to float lightly, to turn readily, and to bear rough usage on stones and banks, and in carts, railways, and steamers; to be durable and dry as well as comfortable and safe."

Cruising was his initial objective and cruising he certainly did go. The ample space below deck he packed with his own compact kit and a large supply of religious tracts, and then in 1865 he set off to tour, for nearly three months, rivers and lakes in Germany, France, and Switzerland. MacGregor's position as the pioneer of European canoeing was assured with the publication the following year of his immensely popular account of that one-man journey. *A Thousand Miles in the Rob Roy Canoe* went through many editions and was read avidly by would-be cruisers on each side of the Atlantic. Further touring was followed by further books and many readers became converts to canoeing—more, possibly, than were swayed by his evangelical messages. In 1866, the year his first book was published, this swell of enthusiasm led to the founding of the Royal Canoe Club, the first organization of its kind in the world. The Prince of Wales, who had been fêted at a voyageurs' regatta during his visit to Canada just a few years earlier, became its commodore and a participating paddler.

British canoes were to be seen the following year at the international exhibition at Paris, and the French immediately began making their own canoes and took to paddling on the Seine. Designers in Britain were already making improvements to MacGregor's craft, and Warington Baden-Powell, brother to the founder of the Boy Scout and Girl Guide movements, introduced the *Nautilus*, the first canoe designed primarily for sailing.

The clinker-built *Nautilus* had a hull with considerable sheer, its stem post rising almost two feet above keel level—and this in a vessel only fourteen feet long. With two masts, one before and one aft the cockpit, it carried about sixty square feet of sail, including jib. This appears to have been the first of the sporting canoes to be equipped with a rudder. The extreme sheer made it somewhat difficult to paddle against the wind, and in order to carry full canvas in a breeze, the *Nautilus* required ballast, usually bags of sand or shot.

Like MacGregor, Baden-Powell went cruising under paddle and sail on continental waterways and then added another book of travel experiences to the growing library of canoe literature. About the same time a somewhat similar British boat called the *Pearl* appeared, but it was the simpler and less costly *Rob Roy* that remained the most popular canoe. The fraternity grew rapidly and by 1872 the Royal Canoe Club had a membership of nearly two hundred. An American writer reported to his readers that year that members in the British club owned canoes made of tin, iron, India rubber, and paper, and that one canoe was propelled by steam.

The widespread popularity of canoeing in the United States in the final quarter of the century did not spring from a home-grown enthusiasm for the watercraft of the Indians. Canoeing as an American sport was imported from Britain.

Responding to MacGregor's gospel of the double-bladed paddle, several men in the New York City area by 1869 had acquired British-style canoes, and a contemporary reporter of the canoeing scene later wrote: "A meeting of gentlemen interested in the organization of a canoe club was held at No. 122 William Street, New York City, on a certain Saturday evening in September, 1871."

One of the gentlemen, William L. Alden, then on the staff of *The New York Times*, corresponded that winter with Baden-Powell and obtained from him drawings of *Nautilus No. 3*. The New York Canoe Club members took the plans to a local boat-builder, James Everson of Williamsburg, now part of Brooklyn, and by spring Everson had completed canoes for six of the original ten members. He used white cedar instead of the prototype's oak, but the first boat he completed was a faithful rendering from Baden-Powell's plans.

The club's first regatta was held on October 19, 1872, on Flushing Bay at the city end of Long Island Sound. There were four entries in the only event, a ten-mile contest on a triangular course for canoes under sail. The

victor was Montgomery Schuyler in his *Gretchen*, and the next day the reporter for *The New York Times* provided a full account of the race, including comment on immediate post-race developments:

The pleasures of canoeing in October were practically exemplified by Captain Porter and Rear Commodore Schuyler, as both these gentlemen capsized their canoes immediately after passing the home stakeboat. This manoeuvre was wisely delayed until after the conclusion of the race, as by the rules of the club the crew are not allowed to jump overboard or take soundings during a regatta.

Recruits "anxious to own a cheap and portable yacht" did not appear immediately in such numbers as to overwhelm the membership secretary. The growth of the

Pearl was one of two British sailing canoes which raced for the International Challenge Cup during the 1886 meet of the American Canoe Association, held at Grindstone Island on the St. Lawrence River. In their heavier, ballast-carrying craft, the visitors did not fare well.

reborn sport was slow in these early years, and initially membership in the New York Canoe Club was pretty much a casual commitment. There wasn't another regatta until 1879, and the principal group function of the club was its annual dinner. Most members went canoeing on their own and only in 1879 did they establish a club boathouse at New Brighton on Staten Island.

In 1879 the weekly periodical Scientific American *reported the successful operation of "the steam canoe* Nina," *built by J. Davidson, a New York City designer. Its fourteen-foot hull of hickory, oak, and cedar was patterned after the* Nautilus *canoe model; it had a ten-inch-diameter firebox, a seventeen-inch-diameter boiler, and stowage space for forty pounds of coal.*

In 1875 the Jersey Blue Canoe Club became the second formally organized club in the United States. One of its founders, W. P. Stephens, of Rahway, New Jersey, also became one of the best known of American canoe designers and builders. About the same time, a number of enthusiasts in Newark built their own canvas-covered paddling canoes. The period up to 1880 saw the development of the first new American canoe models in materials both traditional and novel. It was a period, too, of canoe cruising and of testing new models under demanding travel conditions.

The great exploit of 1874 was a cruise by Nathaniel H. Bishop in a paper canoe from Troy, New York, southward on the Hudson River and then along protected coastal waters as far as Florida and the Gulf of Mexico. His vessel was a product of E. Waters and Sons at Troy, a firm that had been making other lightweight watercraft by gluing sheet after sheet of manilla paper over appropriate forms. A stabilizing frame was built into a shell when it came off the mold. That a canoe so constructed could be reliably serviceable was established when Bishop boarded *Maria Theresa* and proceeded to row her the two thousand miles to Florida.

The Voyage of the Paper Canoe was published in 1878, and author Bishop was promptly disparaged by some few hard-nosed members of the official canoeing fraternity. Bishop's sin was to have travelled under oar power; for some of those who had taken up the sport in the MacGregor tradition, whenever the double-bladed paddle was discarded there was some doubt as to the vessel's even being a genuine canoe. But Nathaniel Bishop was a proven hero and overnight became the best-known canoeist in the nation.

His book was one of a number of American volumes to stimulate a wide enthusiasm and support for recreational canoeing. Appearing in the same year as Bishop's account, *Canoeing in Kanuckia* was a light-hearted report of a cruise by four men who made a holiday tour from Lake Champlain down the Richelieu River as far as the St. Lawrence. The authors, John Habberton and C. L. Norton, were members of the New York Canoe Club. They made it very plain that canoeing could be great fun and that advanced sailing and navigating skills were by no means necessary to thoroughly enjoy cruising on inland waterways. Many a reader put down the book only to go shopping immediately for a canoe.

Each of the four holidayers in *Canoeing in Kanuckia* took his own canoe, a sailing rig, and a double-bladed paddle. A recurring theme was a good-natured debate on the respective merits of the decked *Nautilus* type and the open Canadian canoe; two of the men were travelling in the former while the authors of the book preferred the Canadian ribless canoes.

Like most canoeists who went into print in that period, they ridiculed those who rowed, and therefore saw only the landscape already behind them: "the oarsman sways to and fro like the deserted half of a melancholy hinge, which wavers helplessly about in air. . . ."

For many readers who still suspected that canoes were hazardous, the authors claimed "the chance of capsizing a sober canoeist of a week's practice is less than that of falling dead in the street at home."

Economy was a great argument for the canoe. Alden had described it as "a cheap and portable yacht," and Habberton and Norton claimed that a canoe could sail "over tide-mud barely glazed with water" while the occupant enjoyed "every pleasure experienced by the owner of a twenty-thousand dollar yacht."

William Alden, the canoeist from *The Times*, did much to publicize the sport, blending information with entertainment—the former tempered somewhat by his prejudices. In 1877 he joined the published bookmen of canoemanship with *The Canoe and the Flying Proa, or Cheap Cruising and Safe Sailing*. Alden announced therein that the four best cruising canoes were the *Rob Roy*, the *Nautilus*, the *Herald*, and the *Shadow*. The first two were British models and the third was the familiar open Canadian canoe. The *Shadow* was a greatly modified version of the *Nautilus*, in whose design Alden himself had a major hand. In evaluating the canoes, he had no hesitation in placing the *Shadow* well to the fore—this despite the fact that at the time of publication the veteran boat-builder, Everson, did not yet have the prototype ready for the water.

A canoe built after the *Shadow* plans was of the same length and deck breadth as the *Nautilus* family but had a distinct tumblehome, rather like the *Herald*. It broadened to its extreme width about the waterline, and had a floor much closer to flat than any earlier sailing canoe. The sheer of the British design was reduced by about half. These changes made this American canoe much easier to paddle than the *Nautilus*, especially into the wind. It sat light in the water and was a speedy craft under sail.

Alden's book preached to a receptive audience his own tenets of good canoes and good canoeing. John MacGregor had slept at night in the cockpit of his *Rob Roy*, and Alden maintained that a canoe could scarcely be acknowledged such if it did not provide a bed for its captain. "A canoe that cannot be slept in," he wrote, "is not a canoe, but an insufficiently hollow mockery. . . ." Then he went on to condemn the *Rob Roy* itself as a vessel unsuited for sleeping:

The captain, after worming himself into the cabin, must sleep with his head and part of his chest under the deck. As an inevitable consequence, he dreams that he is buried alive in a cheap and ill-fitting coffin, and when he awakes he invariably contuses his nose against the deck carlines. During the cruising season the owner of a "Rob Roy" may always be identified by his nose. A peculiar abrasion, known among anatomists as "MacGregor's line," diversifies the ridge of the nose. . . .

Alden regarded the dugout and birch bark canoes as barbarous and entirely unsuited to modern use. He was almost equally derisive concerning the open Canadian canoe, even if it was the favorite of some members of the New York club. He gave it some points for speed under sail but suggested some tendency towards instability: "when a *Herald* canoe does decide to capsize, the rapidity with which the operation is performed is simply dazzling."

In 1885 W. P. Stephens, by then well established as a canoe-builder, published *Canoe and Boat Building*, which for many years was the standard American reference on canoe construction. Such books as these,

together with a good deal of newspaper and magazine publicity, carried the doctrine of recreational canoeing far and wide. In a canoeing periodical in later years, a writer explained that as a youth, ill and confined to bed, he had been given *Canoeing in Kanuckia* and *The Canoe and the Flying Proa*. According to his testimony, he had been converted while still flat on his back. As soon as he was up and about he acquired a canoe and joined the romantic brotherhood.

For many persons, canoeing was and is an unstructured sport to be enjoyed alone or in the company of a friend or two. Until the New York club established its home boathouse in 1879, even its members more often than not went their separate recreational ways. A watershed event for organized canoeing was a regatta held that same year on Lake George, just south of New York's Adirondack region, at which the earliest of international canoe competitions saw Canadian contestants entering their canoes against those of the New Yorkers and representatives of clubs from Cincinnati, Jersey City, and Boston.

Following this successful regatta, the canoeing marathoner Nathaniel Bishop began discussing with other canoe people plans for a national organization. Bishop was the vigorous advance agent, and it was Bishop who composed and printed "The First Call," the invitation sent to devotees on both sides of the international border.

The National Canoe Congress in August of 1880 was also held on Lake George, and the group that gathered there put together the framework of the American Canoe Association, an organization that still represents recreational canoeing interests in the United States. From the beginning, full membership was also open to amateur canoeists in Canada, although few Canadians appeared for this initial meeting.

New York's William Alden was elected the Association's first commodore. The vice-commodore was Nicholas Longworth from the Cincinnati Canoe Club, and the secretary was Nathaniel H. Bishop.

The constitution drawn up the same year is of special interest because it established for members a definition of the term canoe:

Article 2. — A canoe, in order to be placed on the Association list, and to be entered for races, must be a boat sharp at both ends, and not more than thirty-six inches in width on deck. She may be propelled by sails or paddle, or both; but she must be capable of being efficiently propelled by a double-bladed paddle.

The efforts from time to time over the years to play down racing events have served to remind the more avid competitors that cruising was the principal objective of most members in the American clubs. Still, a program of races has always been a popular part of the annual meeting of the Association, and at that inaugural gathering there were nine contests for craft in five classes. The two leading American canoe-builders, Stephens and J. Henry Rushton, were among the charter members, and each was concerned that his products show to advantage during the races.

The first contest, a sailing race for canoes of the *Rob Roy* class, was won by D. Lucien Wulsin, a Cincinnati member, in a craft made by Rushton. William Stephens in one of his own *Jersey Blue* models came home first in the paddling event for sailing canoes and also in the "Upset" race. In this contest the competitors had to capsize their sailing vessels part way through the course, right them again, and go on to the finish. Major paddling honors went to one of Herald's Rice Lake canoes in the hands of Thomas Henry Wallace from Gore's Landing, Ontario. He won the paddling contest open to all canoes, as well as that restricted to paddling models, and he did so using the single blade. Wallace was identified as "a professional guide," and there may have been some question at the time as to his eligibility. A "Long Distance" paddling race was won by the Reverend Mr. Edward Cressy, a New Hampshire paddler who made his own canoes. A *Rob Roy* placed second, and a New Yorker came in third in one of the two tin canoes at the meet.

244

(OPPOSITE) *By the time its third annual gathering was held in 1882 at Lake George, New York, the American Canoe Association was a genuinely international organization with officers and members from both the United States and Canada. (OPPOSITE) Contenders for the International Challenge Cup gather at the starting point for the major event at the 1886 meet of the American Canoe Association. Robert Gibson in his* Vesper *(second canoe from the left) was the victor. The trend that was to lead to sailing racers unsuited to recreational paddling was already well under way.*

The founding of the A.C.A. and its first regatta received considerable publicity in the daily press and in sporting periodicals. Interest in canoeing increased greatly, and the twenty-three A.C.A. members of 1880 grew to one hundred and seventy the following year and to more than two hundred in 1883. Eight of the members were women, mostly wives of officers, but they held honorary status only.

The second and third annual gatherings, like the first, were held at Lake George. The meet in 1881 drew about seventy canoes representing the clubs on hand the previous year and others from Cleveland, Detroit, Minneapolis, and Hartford, plus a second club from New York City, the Knickerbocker Canoe Club. Canadian members came from clubs in Toronto, Peterborough, and Ottawa.

The canoeing movement's own journal appeared for the first time in 1882. *The American Canoeist* published articles, regatta results, and reports of cruising experiences, and kept widely scattered but keen participants in touch with canoeing activities at large. A reporter for the September 1882 issue suggested that the most striking feature observed at that summer's annual meeting had been the remarkable display of uniforms worn by members:

the Mohicans of Albany won the smiles of the Goddess of Beauty as they in their gray knee breeches and blouse with hat to match were by far the most picturesque. The members of the Peterboro C. C. were also marked by their neat appearance in a plain suit of navy blue and straw hat. . . . the Knickerbockers in their blue shirts and gray knee beeches and stockings . . . Philadelphians in their gray shirt and knee breeches and red stockings.

Two years later some sort of club uniform was virtually the rule, and almost everyone appeared at annual meets and at other regattas in knee breeches and stockings.

Some Canadian members attending the early meetings of the umbrella organization may have been guilty of a degree of that superiority peculiar to those who choose to "rough it." The poorly hidden truth has it that they enjoyed the comforts and cossets that American brethren brought to camp. During the 1882 encampment on Lake George, the Cincinnati Club one evening entertained fellow paddlers and sailors and went to elaborate lengths to provide ice cream for all. In his report of the meet, the special correspondent of *The Toronto Mail* affected some shock at such effete provisioning: "All that detracted from the 'canoebial' simplicity of the repast was the unwonted ice-cream, and the fact that the familiar bread and ham of the canoeist appeared not in chunks, but in the thin layers of the civilized sandwich — with mustard!"

The strong Cincinnati Club placed members first or second in many of the races in the meets of the first few years, although Canadians dominated the single-blade paddling contests. A Peterborough representative, E. B. Edwards, won the open paddling in 1881 and a senior sailing race in 1882. He was elected commodore of the Association that year, the first Canadian to head the international organization. The gathering the next year

eastward run along the Gulf of Mexico as far as Pensacola. In his *Aurora*, Neidé covered 3,300 miles. Kendall pushed on to Tarpon Springs, Florida, adding a further 500 miles to his total.

A sometime clown who wore a large beaver hat as standard canoeing costume, C. Bowyer Vaux was a New York Canoe Club member, a major racing contender, and a regular reporter whose writings today constitute the backbone of the history of organized canoeing in the United States up to 1900. He served for a time as editor of *The American Canoeist*, published a book entitled *Canoe Handling*, and contributed to sporting periodicals a rich store of data on the progress of recreational canoeing.

When the A.C.A. was founded in 1880, one of the first essential tasks was to establish clearly defined competitive classes for the different kinds of vessels in use. For the inaugural meet, the first listing described five: canoes for paddling only, including the birch bark and the open Canadian type; paddling canoes with sailing capacity, primarily the *Rob Roy* type; canoes that were equally suited to paddling or sailing, like the *Shadow*; canoes that were intended primarily for sailing but could be paddled while cruising; and finally, sailing canoes of the heavier *Nautilus No. 5* type, which evidently only just met the paddling specification to qualify it as a canoe by the A.C.A. definition.

The greater press attention was devoted to canoe racing, the results of local, regional, and association regattas, and in the United States the focus of attention was on the glamorous sailing racers. But in more comprehensive reports, there was frequent affirmation that canoe tripping was the highest and noblest aim. Most canoe users, in fact, whether or not members of local clubs or the A.C.A., had no interest at all in racing competition, but it was the keen competitors who raised the greater excitement, who received the constant attention of the press, and who spurred the designers and builders to produce speedier craft.

was held at Stony Lake near Peterborough, the biggest yet for the A.C.A., drawing some four hundred campers and three hundred canoes. Many Canadians brought their families along, and it was here on Stony Lake that a campsite was first reserved for women and was named "Squaw Point."

By 1889 membership in the A.C.A. had grown to 1,625. The annual gatherings, the most important events on the calendar for many canoeists, were held most frequently in the Thousand Islands district of the St. Lawrence River because it offered excellent canoeing right on the U.S.-Canada border. Since 1903 the annual meet has been held each year at Sugar Island, a site the Association purchased just inside Canadian waters. It lies just below the Ontario town of Gananoque.

It is difficult to overestimate in the early period the important role of the printed word in fostering interest in recreational canoeing. A spate of books devoted to the techniques of paddling and sailing, the choosing of or the building of canoes, and the narratives of canoe-borne travellers was read avidly by thousands. Canoe-cruising

experiences and regatta results were reported regularly in daily papers and in the sporting monthlies. In 1882 *The American Canoeist* became the first periodical devoted exclusively to the sport.

Dr. Charles A. Neidé, a dentist who preferred paddling over drilling, and Captain Samuel D. Kendall, a retired seaman, set off at the close of the A.C.A. meet in 1882 and paddled from Lake George, through the Mississippi system to the Gulf of Mexico, and on through salt water to Florida. With *The Canoe Aurora: From the Adirondacks to the Gulf*, published in 1885, Neidé won further converts to active paddling as he described the adventures he and Kendall met on their five-month expedition. Each in his own craft, they passed through Lake Champlain, by canal to the Hudson River, and along the Erie Canal to Buffalo, and then made a railway portage link to the Allegheny River. It was steady downstream paddling and sailing thereafter as they navigated the Ohio and then the Mississippi itself, completing their long journey with the

245

246

Bark canoes on the Penobscot River make it clear that Old Town, Maine, has been familiar with the traditional craft since its founding. The lumbering village of this mid-nineteenth-century view later became the home of the Old Town Canoe Company, which built a reputation for durable and handsome canvas-covered craft. One of its classic models (RIGHT) is now displayed in the Adirondack Museum at Blue Mountain Lake, New York.

The builders were busy in this period as great numbers of the newly converted filed orders for canoes. There was a constant striving for the ultimately satisfying compromise that would result in a canoe that might sail as lightly as wind-driven down, would respond to the paddle like an oarsman's racing shell, would sit firm in choppy waters, would remain dry amidships, and would carry her master safely and comfortably and yet not strain his back when it came time to carry her over a portage trail.

The trouble is that paddling and sailing are two quite different things, and the best results under each means of propulsion are achieved by quite different design solutions. The British *Nautilus* models, after which the first American sailing canoes were designed, were really as much yachts in miniature as they were canoes, and certainly the initial appeal of this sport, both in Britain and in the United States, was to men who were already familiar with sailing and sail racing. In contrast to paddling canoes, those intended partly or primarily for sailing took on weight and size. The inevitable urge to set more and more canvas for speed's sake led to deeper hulls, centerboards, and the use of ballast.

The old Chestnut Canoe Company in Fredericton, dating from the turn of the century, was an important industry in the New Brunswick community. For eighty years it produced canvas canoes that were work boats for trappers and frontier surveyors and pleasure craft for sporting people.

In this shop, the canoe at the rear is about to be removed from the mold or form. In the foreground, with its inwale pieces clamped in position, a canoe of the same model is ready to have its remaining side strakes nailed to the ribs. The overlapping edges of the planking in this type of craft were tapered, so that a lapstrake technique resulted in a canoe with an entirely smooth hull. Such high quality in craftsmanship, as well as in design, was vital to establishing a praiseworthy reputation for a canoe-builder before the mass production period.

When the push for faster paddling craft came, the development was in a quite different direction. Hull resistance, or drag, had to be reduced to a minimum, and so canoes designed for racing—"racing machines" as the cruising men disdainfully dubbed them—became long, low, and shallow. By the 1890s the racing canoe had become a distinct canoe type. But the achievement of superb racing capacity required the sacrifice of much that was pleasing in the traditional paddling canoe. The racing canoe was and is of no use except for racing. Its slight body and meager freeboard dictate that it be used only on calm water. Some clubs, like those accustomed to using Great Lakes shore water, frequently found that conditions were too rough even to launch such a cockle of a craft.

Sailing canoes were fitted with many features familiar in larger vessels. A *Shadow* model built by George Roahr of Harlem appeared at the opening of the 1881 season with a huge spread of sail and a wooden daggerboard fitted into a trunk set amidships. Following a British lead, several American canoes the next year had heavy iron centerboards and carried bags of shot for ballast—up to two hundred pounds. When Neidé made his long cruise, his *Aurora* was fitted with the Atwood folding iron-plate board which earlier had been used in the highly regarded St. Lawrence skiff. The Atwood board consisted of three metal blades whose housing extended only four inches above the canoe floor; increasing the number of metal blades made it possible to diminish their size and thus fit the entire device to the keelson so that nothing projected above the canoe floor.

Heavy boats, sometimes made more so with the addition of ballast, were the safest bet for coastal sailing and certainly were the general rule for canoeing under sail in Britain. But by 1883 the trend was reversed in North America. The A.C.A. 1884 meet at Grindstone Island in the St. Lawrence River saw the last appearance of a major fleet of heavyweight sailing canoes. Laurels for speed at that meet went typically to a lightweight vessel whose captain came out of the cockpit to sail her from a deck position. By shifting his weight from moment to moment while perched to windward on the gunwale, he could take every advantage of a varying wind, compensating with his own shifting weight for the lack of any other stabilizing ballast.

The shift to lighter hulls and sailing from a deck position were principal factors in the victory of American canoeists over British rivals who came in 1886 to compete for the new International Challenge Cup, presented by the New York Canoe Club for an annual race. At the A.C.A. meet, again at Grindstone Island, the challengers were Warington Baden-Powell in his *Nautilus* and Walter Stewart in *Pearl*, another well-known British sailing model. But *Pearl* had suffered in transit, and her seams were leaking; at race time she was hardly a serious contender. *Nautilus* was ballasted with a hundred pounds of shot and a centerplate weighing fifty-six pounds. While the captains of the American canoes rode their decks, the Britishers sat low in their cockpits and when the race came, it was a contest only between American canoes. The challengers finished eighth and ninth.

Winner of the Challenge Cup by only a matter of seconds was Robert W. Gibson, a Mohican Club member whose clinker-built *Vesper* was made by Henry Rushton. The runner-up was E. H. Barney from the Springfield Canoe Club in Massachusetts. His carvel-built *Pecowsic* came from the shop of Fletcher Joyner at Glens Falls, New York. In a consolation contest between the two British canoes and the first two Americans to finish in the challenge race, Barney's *Pecowsic* outsailed *Vesper*. Since each vessel had won a major race, the builders, Rushton and Joyner, each declared himself designer of the international championship canoe. Their advertising claims for some time appeared to be somewhat in conflict.

In races later that summer, Baden-Powell improved his performance by coming out of the cockpit to sail his *Nautilus* from the deck, and during the next year a great many British canoemen followed his lead.

About the same time, Paul Butler from Lowell, Massachusetts, introduced the sliding seat, a device extending beyond the gunwale that enabled the captain to sit well out to windward and yet slide quickly back to the cockpit when necessary. It required the agility of a gymnast but enabled the canoeist to carry yet more sail.

The years immediately following were the high period of the "racing machines." Comfort, cockpit capacity, almost anything was sacrificed to make for a speedier sailing canoe. For different kinds of weather, serious contenders had to have up to five different sets of sails, and most racers laced them to the mast so that, while they might be reefed, they could not be lowered.

Speed and still greater speed was the only consideration in designing canoes for sailing—a trend that inevitably narrowed the field of participants, which in turn reduced interest in this sport. Those who remained major contenders had newly designed or modified canoes each season—something the average canoeist could not afford. In the sporting journals some observers announced that the sport was dead.

Just before the First World War there was some restirring of major interest, and there were some changes, too, in canoe design and standards, including a larger hull, seventeen feet long and with a beam of up to forty-two inches. In 1933 Uffa Fox and Roger DeQuincey, members of the Royal Canoe Club, became the first Britishers to win the International Challenge Cup. The two decked canoes they brought to the United States were seventeen feet long, wide in the beam, and had deep, heavy centerboards. They carried mainsail and jib rig rather than the old yawl rig of mainsail and mizzen that in earlier days had been the standard for all sailing canoes. Following this race, British and American regulations each were modified to help achieve an international standard—to develop an international decked

In Rushton's shop at Canton, New York, planked canoes were sanded to an extremely smooth surface before finishing. A coat of linseed oil preceded several of varnish, the result being a slick hull with an absolute minimum of "drag" in the water.

canoe that would become the equitable standard for staging international races. This first proposal for international standards set a maximum length of 5.20 meters (17 feet, $^{3}/_{4}$ inch) and a sail area of 10 meters (107.64 square feet).

To many paddlers these hundred years past, the modern canoe has meant first and foremost the ribbed and canvas-covered model, like the aging craft (CENTER) that was made by the Peterborough Canoe Company. The fisherman's vessel (BELOW) is from the Old Town Canoe Company, which still manufactures the planked fabric-covered variety as well as models of fiberglass and other complex chemical compounds. Also molded from such tough constituents, the modern sporting kayak (ABOVE) has become widely popular as a craft in which to challenge the hazards of white-water courses. The rugged aluminum canoe, like that being portaged (CENTER BELOW) over a rocky northern Ontario route, has set a latter-day standard for durability in wilderness travel.

The "Sunnyside cruiser" (ABOVE), a cedar-strip model with distinctive ridged bow decking and stem lines, was in the early years of this century an immensely popular pleasure boat made by Walter Dean's firm on the Toronto waterfront. The fiberglass craft (CENTER) is one of many models made by many companies and whose low price has made it the most widely used of present-day canoes in North America. Preserving the character and quality of the canvas-covered craft on which its business was first built, the Old Town Canoe Company today builds planked cedar models (BELOW), but the modern sheathing is increasingly a fiberglass cloth rather than canvas.

252

The simple lateen rig, by which a triangular sail on a long yard can be raised on a short mast, was very popular for cruising canoes. Posing during the 1886 meet of the American Canoe Association are Commodore Robert Shaw (left) and Phillip B. Wackerhagen of Albany's Mohican Canoe Club.

Meanwhile, among pleasure canoeists, there was a growing fondness for the open Canadian canoe. Decked canoes did not entirely disappear among those unconcerned with the racing mania, but photographs from A.C.A. meets just before the turn of the century indicate that open canoes may have predominated by then, and they show too that many open canoes carried a single sail in the bow. Even at A.C.A. meets in the eighties, the solo canoeist realized there was a serious social drawback to his decked vessel; it was the open Canadian model that came to be called the "girling" canoe.

The 1889 meet of the A.C.A. was held again in Thousand Islands waters, this time based on Stave Island. This was the year that the Toronto Canoe Club introduced the large club canoe or war canoe, inspired by the old fur-trade craft.

The manufacturer, the Ontario Canoe Company of Peterborough, had been making large plank canoes for government survey and other exploration parties working in the more northerly regions of Canada. The

Toronto Club's *Unk-ta-hee* (God of the Waters) was a planked craft thirty feet long, manned by sixteen paddlers. There was room for passengers too, and *Forest and Stream* reported that at camp the cargo had consisted of "pretty girls without number."

The large club canoe had a sociable influence, one that made it possible for a smaller club to put its entire membership into one vessel. Of equal importance, it had a democratic influence in the canoeing fraternity. Younger paddlers particularly, some of whom couldn't afford to buy canoes of their own, joined a club to become part of its war-canoe crew.

A number of clubs in the United States were quick to rise to the Toronto challenge. The St. Lawrence River Skiff, Canoe and Steam Launch Company, at Clayton, New York, built an even larger craft, the *Ko-Ko-Ko-Ho*, which the Yonkers Canoe Club introduced at the 1890 meet at Jessup's Neck, Long Island. She was thirty-five feet long, had a beam of fifty-two inches and a depth of twenty-four inches, and could hold a crew of up to eighteen paddlers.

At the 1891 meet on Lake Champlain, the Albany paddlers of the Mohican Canoe Club also came to camp with a big club canoe. The Ontario Canoe Company in its catalogue claimed to have supplied war canoes also to clubs in Montreal, Ottawa, Washington, and Trenton, New Jersey. In 1897 at Grindstone Island, the Rochester Canoe Club appeared with *Huff*, a club vessel carrying two sails, and the Buffalo Club won the one-mile war-canoe race with thirteen paddlers in their *Quid-Pro-Quo*.

Particularly in eastern Ontario, war-canoe racing in the 1890s became the heart and soul of the sport. The town of Brockville alone had three clubs with big canoes and rabidly competitive crews. The club canoe proved a very effective means of channelling youthful exuberance into team effort and, in central Canada, many contending war canoe crews came from community athletic clubs whose activities were by no means limited to canoeing. Such clubs, with more diverse programs, were not, of course, affiliated with the A.C.A., and in order to enter the war-canoe race at its annual meet, a team from some community club was required to pay a camp fee and a membership fee for each of its fifteen paddlers. For those interested only in that one race, what amounted to an entry fee of seventy-five dollars for one canoe seemed a very stiff requirement.

The conflict of interests was increased by some Canadian clubs that wanted to see a larger role in A.C.A. competition for war canoes. While a writer in *Forest and Stream* suggested that a more serious problem was the deterioration of some war canoes to "racing machines," likening one of them to a torpedo boat, representatives from eastern Ontario and the Montreal district met in Brockville in May of 1900 to form a separate league for war-canoe racing.

Before the meeting was over they had agreed to do a great deal more. The nine clubs represented each named a member to the executive committee of a new body to be called the Canadian Canoe Association. Brockville was host to the organization's first regatta, held in August of that year.

The C.C.A. did not become a properly national body overnight. Certainly some of the best Canadian paddlers chose to continue their memberships in the older organization, and until 1921 two out of three of the annual winners of the A.C.A. Paddling Championship Trophy came from north of the border. Partly because the Commodore of the A.C.A. in 1900 was William G. McKendrick, one of their own number, members of the influential Toronto Canoe Club stayed with the A.C.A. for some years. Canadians declared their Association was not established in opposition to the older organization and there has never been an actual bar to prevent them from holding memberships in the two. Even so, there was a major drop in the number of Canadians in the A.C.A. The

Crossing the line to win the International Challenge Cup in 1913 is Leo Friede of New York City in his sailing canoe Mermaid. *His rival that year was Ralph B. Britton of Gananoque, Ontario, in his* Jonah.

253

On the water at Phalen Park in St. Paul, Minnesota, in the 1920s, relaxation was evidently more important than exercise. On a Sunday afternoon in a canvas canoe, a "Victrola" was as much a requisite as a paddle.

Toronto Canoe Club came into the Canadian Association in 1906 and the enrolment in the Northern Division of the A.C.A., which included all of Canada, dropped from 263 in 1900 to only 50 in 1907. The C.C.A. grew to national status, but while the American body has continued a program to encourage and promote pleasure canoeing and cruising, as well as racing, the Canadian Association has been concerned only with flat-water racing.

The war canoe survived the threat of extreme specialization, and although fiberglass models have been introduced, even today most hulls in competition are of planked cedar construction. In years to come these models will be made, like other standardized racing vessels, of the lightest plywood, of fiberglass, or of one of the newer lightweight products of the chemical industry.

In the United States, war-canoe racing became for a period mainly a localized New England event. In Canada, where it remains a national institution, war-canoe competition is on most regatta programs for varying age groups and for both men and women. Races are five hundred and a thousand meters long. Each class uses the one standard canoe—thirty feet long, with a minimum beam of thirty-six inches and a weight of one hundred and ninety pounds (915 cm, 91 cm, and 86 kg). The crew has fourteen paddlers and a cox.

The formation of an independent Canadian organization, distressing to A.C.A. officials at the time, was inevitable. Fifteen years earlier there had been a more serious splintering threat when some one hundred and fifty active canoeists in Ohio, Indiana, and Illinois joined to form the independent Western Canoe Association. The reason, said organizers, was that easterners refused to stage the annual A.C.A. meet outside their own territory.

The Cincinnati Club, an A.C.A. bulwark, joined the new association, and the first annual meeting and regatta was held in 1885 at Ballast Island in Put-in Bay, Lake Erie. The response of the A.C.A. was to promote and encourage the formation of regional divisions that sponsored their own social and athletic events, leading up to the annual A.C.A. meet, which was the culmination of the year's canoeing program. Even so, it was not until 1898 that the breakaway association returned to become the older organization's Western Division.

There was occasionally some slight conflict between the ideals of gentlemen amateurs and any who might even marginally be labelled professionals. Hunting and fishing guides were considered professionals and not normally eligible for A.C.A. competition. In earlier times, a birch bark canoe race between Indian crews was often a highlight of a white man's regatta, but there was evidently a clear understanding that there would be no competition between native and non-native paddlers. After all, Indians were familiar with canoeing from birth; they used canoes in their daily lives, and that made them professionals, so to speak. One wouldn't expect gentlemen who paddled for pleasure to compete with them.

The acceptance of women on any official level by the canoeing organizations of the United States and Canada was a long time coming. They were offered associate membership in the early days of the A.C.A., but that brought with it little more than a ladies'-auxiliary function. Most clubs were male strongholds, but by the turn of the century there were some that encouraged a broader family participation in aquatic recreation. In the early years of this century women were on the way to some recognition as competitive paddlers, but the First World War, which ended so much sporting activity, set back women's interests a further twenty years. By 1930 women's paddling events were once more on the regatta programs of some clubs, more often the broadly based aquatic clubs rather than the traditional canoe-racing and cruising organizations. In a more liberal Europe, women were admitted to the first European paddling championships in 1933 and to the world championship races, also in Europe, begun in 1938. A sequel to this development was the addition of the 500-meter kayak singles for women to the Olympic Games program in

(TOP) Unk-ta-hee, *the Toronto Canoe Club's so-called war canoe, appears as it was sketched for the periodical* Outing *in 1890.*

The rooftop as well as the balcony is thronged with spectators on a regatta day about 1906 at the Toronto Canoe Club. The size of the building, then near the foot of York Street, suggests something of the popularity and importance of recreational canoeing in the period.

1948. World-level participation from North America was minimal, and it was another twenty years before Canada even named a woman paddler to its Olympic team.

With the application in 1943 of fifty-nine canoeists in the Pacific coast states for membership within the A.C.A., that venerable body was backed into a decision long overdue. The western applicants wanted not only a new Pacific Division within the old organization but also full membership for women within that division in which women were already active.

It was impossible, of course, for A.C.A. officers to contemplate dropping the sex bar in one part of a national organization while retaining it in the rest. The request from the coast in succeeding months forced consideration of, and debate on, women's status, and a reexamination of the old rule that membership was open only to persons who were competent swimmers and male. When the decision came to a vote in 1944, the executive committee, by a nine-to-three edge, eliminated the latter of these qualifications.

In Canada women were competing in some local club regattas before 1930, but on the larger official level they went unrecognized until very recent years. After the Second World War the women's war-canoe race was added to C.C.A. regattas, but only as an exhibition event. Not until 1965 were the kayak singles and pairs for women made recognized events. In the years since, kayak fours and war-canoe races have also become official.

When western Europeans took up canoeing, about the time of MacGregor and his *Rob Roy*, it was the beginning of a long-term love affair. Although it had scarcely any contact with paddlers in North America, the continental movement grew at a phenomenal rate. While the decked canoe did not go out of favor to the same extent there, by 1900 the open canoe had been imported from Canada and was widely used, particularly in Britain, France, and Germany. It was everywhere recognized and called the Canadian, and when the open canoe was adopted for Olympic competition it became known officially as the Canadian canoe.

255

Wicker armchairs provide unaccustomed comfort for canoe-ferry passengers in Ontario's lake country about 1910. A motor is mounted between the canoe sterns.

The first international organization to promote and govern canoe racing was organized in 1924 by canoeing associations from Denmark, Austria, Germany, and Sweden. Today, with national association membership from around the world, this body, reorganized in 1946 as the International Canoe Federation, oversees such international competition as the world championships and the canoe program of the Olympic Games.

Paddlers from the United States and Canada were the principals in a racing demonstration during the 1924 Olympics at Paris. They staged a show in singles, doubles, and fours, the American paddlers winning all the double-blade events, the Canadians all the single. Official support was slow to mature, and it was another twelve years before canoeing was added to the Olympics program. The first races for open-canoe and kayak classes, nine events altogether, were held at the 1936 Games in Berlin, and it was there that North Americans learned the Europeans had claimed this sport as their own. Led by paddlers from Austria and Germany, the Europeans captured the greater share of those first Olympic medals. Canada took only one gold, a silver, and a bronze in the Canadian-canoe events and the United States a bronze in the 10,000-meter kayak singles. During the London Olympics in 1948 it was the United States that won a gold, a silver, and a bronze in the Canadian-canoe races, while Canada won only a silver and a bronze. Since these first Games of the postwar period, North Americans have taken home very few canoeing medals. First it was the central and northern Europeans, more recently it has been the eastern Europeans who have dominated paddling events at the Olympics and also at the World Championships, now held annually except for Olympic years.

In addition to national meets in the United States and Canada, an annual regatta is held for North American championships. Canoe racing was added to the Pan American Games in a 1979 decision, and the International Canoe Federation sanctions a further championship meet open to all the Americas.

The exciting appeal of white-water paddling led to the organizing of downriver racing on mountain streams in Switzerland and Austria in the 1930s. Slalom skiing, so familiar there, appears to have had a direct influence, for it was also there that slalom paddling competition first appeared. The first world championships in canoe slalom were held in 1949 in Switzerland, and in 1972, on a turbulent man-made river course at Munich, slalom events for men and women in kayak singles and for men in Canadian-canoe singles and pairs were held for the first time at the Olympic Games.

Although slalom events were not included in the Olympics of 1976, World Championships in both slalom and "wildwater racing" are now held every other year and in 1979 were staged, for the first time outside Europe, on the challenging Rivière aux Sables at Jonquière, Quebec.

A more recent competitive development—this one more particularly a North American phenomenon—is "marathon" canoeing over natural watercourses. In its early stages it appeared in part a trend comparable to the swing away from downhill to cross-country skiing. In the United States and Canada the many marathon canoe events range in length from five to three hundred miles, and the longer contests may be run over a period of two or three days. Cash prizes are offered in many events, and several river marathons have drawn almost a thousand entrants. For the most part, marathon racing first attracted competitors in ordinary pleasure canoes, but increasingly the principal contenders use craft modified for speed and easy portaging.

The canoe-builders have kept pace in supplying the vessels required to meet changing tastes and enthusiasms. In the United States the men who first met the demand for recreational canoes were already recognized boat-builders. Everson, who made most of the canoes for the New York club in its earliest years, was a builder with a solid reputation before he had even seen the plans for a *Rob Roy*. Will Stephens of Rahway, New Jersey, who went on to overshadow the work of Everson, was already in the 1870s a keen canoeist, but he trained in a shipyard before setting up as a designer and builder of canoes.

In both the United States and Canada a variety of canoes was available in the 1870s. A sportsman's guide for 1877 listed every practicable craft then available, including birch bark and dugout canoes. Among those described were several folding canvas canoes made in the United States; when "folded" each could be reduced to the size of a small trunk weighing from forty to seventy-five pounds.

The Berthon Folding Boat, first developed in 1849 and later used as an auxiliary lifeboat by the British Navy, was the inspiration for a collapsible canoe designed by Quebec-born Colonel C. M. Douglas. After duty as an army surgeon in India, he had settled in 1883 at Lakefield, Ontario, and there he worked out a canoe model which could be folded lengthwise and turned its manufacture over to the Ontario Canoe Company.

Resuming his military-surgeon role during the North West Rebellion in 1885, Douglas travelled by rail to Swift Current, Saskatchewan, but there was no rail link to his objective, the field hospital at Saskatoon, more than two hundred miles north. He had in his kit, however, one of his folding canoes.

For a hundred years and more, the Wisconsin Dells in the central part of the state have drawn visitors. Eroded sandstone cliffs flank the Wisconsin River, offering an enchanting waterway whose tourists paddled first in bark, later in canvas, canoes.

258

In the late years of the nineteenth century, recreational canoeing was responsible for introducing great numbers of persons, often in family groups, to outdoor holidaying. Although the annual meet of the American Canoe Association was always an encampment, the wilderness experience was usually tempered by the presence of many urban comforts.

By buckboard and pony he reached the South Saskatchewan River, a prairie drive of some forty miles, where he opened the forty-five-pound, six-inch-thick package from Peterborough into a canvas canoe twelve feet long and thirty inches in beam. With a stiff upper lip and a double-bladed paddle, Douglas covered the two hundred miles through hostile country in six days. He reached Saskatoon just as the first wounded were brought to the field hospital from the battle of Fish Creek. He christened that canoe *Saskatoon*, and in 1895, with one tiny sail and a single paddle, he took it across the English Channel.

The *Qui Vive Canoe*, manufactured by J. F. West in East Orange, New Jersey, had a frame of ash consisting of fifteen ribs and nine main stringers. All of the latter fastened over and outside the ribs so that the covering of No. 10 cotton duck was stretched over and touched only the frame members running fore and aft. A lighter canvas was used for deck covering, and a rubber apron kept water from the cockpit. With mast, standing lug mainsail and a jib, double-bladed paddle, and a staff complete with flag, *Qui Vive* weighed fifty pounds and cost fifty dollars.

Another model available in 1877 appears to have been one of the earliest of the canvas-covered plank canoes. The *Yarmouth Fishing Canoe*, made by W. A. Lawson in Yarmouth, Nova Scotia, was built by first fastening bent pine ribs to the two gunwale pieces. Then thin pine strips, fitted closely together, were fastened to the ribs and a covering of canvas was stretched over the planked hull. A pine keel, a half-inch by one inch, was fastened by screws to the outside, and the entire craft was finished with a blend of shellac and boiled linseed oil.

In Wisconsin, the Racine Boat Company was an early competitor among American producers and had at least one canoe at the first A.C.A. meet in 1880. Towards the end of the century most of the leading canoe-builders of the United States were located in New York State and included Charles Pipenbrink of Albany, E. D. Bowdish of Skaneateles, George W. Ruggles of Charlotte, and Fletcher Joyner of Glens Falls, later of Schenectady. Joyner began work about 1880 and his smooth carvel hulls were in contrast to the lapstrake style of many American-made canoes of the period. By 1890 another serious contender was the St. Lawrence River Skiff, Canoe and Steam Launch Company, first at Clayton, New York, later at Ogdensburg. In 1885, however, the editors of *Forest and Stream* reported that the principal canoe-builder in the United States was J. Henry Rushton in the northern New York town of Canton. He had made his first boat in 1873 and two years later he advertised rowing boats as light as twenty-eight pounds.

Striving for lightweight hulls led him naturally to designing and building canoes. His willingness to experiment, his constant insistence on high-quality material and workmanship, combined with a capacity for making the most of every opportunity for publicity, made his out-of-the-way small-town workshop the most highly respected and one of the busiest canoe-making operations in the country for over twenty years.

The first true canoes he built were thirteen feet long, made of white cedar, of a lapstrake construction with very narrow ribs, and weighed less than thirty-five pounds. They represented a fine merging of clients' specifications with the builder's own design ideas and quality standards.

The Canton builder made improved models of the basic *Rob Roy*, which was much in demand in 1880, and he pioneered in the design of distinctive American sailing canoes. When the open Canadian style became the general paddling favorite in the nineties, Rushton built with great success a variety of models in that class, but the canoes for which he is specially remembered were the all-but-weightless craft he made for George Washington Sears, outdoorsman and outdoors writer.

Under his pen name, "Nessmuk," Sears wrote popular magazine pieces and in 1884 the minor American classic *Woodcraft*, one of the earliest books in its field. He was a small man, never robust, and in 1880 he appealed to the Canton builder for a little craft he could handle easily alone. Rushton's response was an open cedar lapstrake canoe ten feet long and weighing less than twenty pounds. Sears was delighted. For the woodsman's Adirondack tours in following seasons, Rushton produced canoes even lighter, each of them clinker-built. The ultimate product was *Sairy Gamp*, a wraith of a canoe, also ten feet long but weighing only ten and a half pounds.

Ready for a challenge, Felix Sam launches a two-man cedar racing dugout on Chemainus Bay on the lee side of Vancouver Island. At age sixteen, his greatest ambition is to paddle with the Salish men in the big fifty-foot racing canoes.

Late in the century Indians in Maine, where wilderness conditions yet survived, were still making bark canoes for sale to trappers and to a growing number of city people who came for the hunting and fishing. When craftsmen there produced a canvas-covered plank model it quickly became the standard for small sporting craft. The firm that made the name of its community, Old Town, virtually synonymous with the canvas canoe had its beginnings some ten years or so earlier and was incorporated about 1900. It appears to be the only firm on the continent primarily devoted to canoe-building that has survived to the present day. The Old Town Canoe Company now offers craft of latter-day wonder materials, but still manufactures the canvas-covered model that first brought it success.

Following the lead of the Maine builders, William and Harry Chestnut in 1897 began making canvas-covered canoes in Fredericton, New Brunswick. Like the Peterborough Canoe Company in Ontario, the Chestnut Canoe Company found an important market among surveyors, prospectors, trappers, and traders, as well as among sporting canoeists.

By the turn of the century the open canoe was widely available in three main types—the Rice Lake style with wide planking and interior battens; the cedar-strip style with narrow planking nailed to cedar ribs; and the canvas canoe of a planked hull covered with primed and painted fabric. Their various merits have been argued a thousand times, but it is the manner in which they are to be used that settles the argument. Both wooden canoe types must be soaked so that the planks swell to make them watertight. The canvas canoe may be launched and used immediately. The wooden canoes will handle well in white water, but hitting a rock in the rapids usually means serious damage to the planking. Even after very hard knocks, the canvas canoe will generally carry the paddler through to still water.

259

With lateen sails rigged to canvas-covered canoes, a government field party of the Geological Survey of Canada moves smartly along Manitoba's Etchimanish River during a 1910 exploration. Stern men use paddles to steer. In some isolated parts of the country, surveyors today still find canoes invaluable for transport. (OPPOSITE) When mobility during the 1944-5 winter campaign of the Second World War became a major problem in the flooded Netherlands countryside, some Canadian infantrymen took to canoes. In January, men of the Lincoln and Welland Regiment prepare for an attack on Kapelsheveer Harbour. Delayed by ice conditions on the Maas River, they came under severe fire and lost several of the canoes.

260

The canvas-covered model was cheaper than wooden canoes because it demanded less meticulous fitting of the planking. The all-wood types required constant maintenance and professional repairs were relatively expensive, while the canvas canoe would last for years with reasonable care and some occasional painting. The latter was slightly heavier than the former but the economic factors eventually made it the most popular. It was a tribute to its hardy character that so many Inuit hunters adopted it as their outboard-driven craft in waters where ice and rocky beaches are constant hazards.

The canvas canoe was built over a mold. Cedar ribs were shaped and steamed until pliable, then bent around the curve of the mold and nailed to the inner gunwale strips, already in place. The longitudinal planking, usually thin cedar, was butted together and nailed to the ribs. When a metal-sheathed mold was used, the nails driven from the outside were clinched automatically. When the hull came off the mold, minuscule deck pieces were fitted into each end and the thwarts and seats added. The most familiar canvasing procedure was to start with a sort of hammock of the fabric, with each long end securely held some feet apart. The smoothly sanded hull was placed in the hammock loop, right side up and about a foot off the floor. In forcing the hull downward, by so simple a means as wedging a couple of planks between it and the ceiling, the canvas was pulled to a tight fit around the cedar shell. It was nailed along each gunwale, then excess fabric was trimmed and the outer gunwale strips were added. A narrow brass strip was often fitted round the sharp bow and stern to protect the canvas.

One or more coats of filler or size were applied to give the fabric body, and the sequence of painting, varnishing, and curing, essential to guarantee a watertight vessel, varied with each builder. The entire manufacturing process took about four weeks.

Technological advances made during the feverish industrial acceleration of the Second World War period led, in the years immediately following, to canoes made essentially by machine. Today the assembly line satisfies by far the greater part of the market demand for canoes—a market larger than ever before. Aluminum canoes, resistant to damage and never needing paint or varnish, are stamped out in sections by heavy presses, and the pieces are joined by riveting. Production is measured in minutes and not the weeks required for the hand-made craft. The canoe produced in greatest numbers and at the lowest cost is made of fiberglass cloth laid down with a polyester resin, a petrochemical product, on the inner surface of a mold. The bonding of the two components makes an extremely tough and slightly flexible hull. Other plastic and petrochemical products today make possible canoes that are phenomenally tough and unbelievably light in weight. Tomorrow's canoes may be made from synthetic materials yet to be developed.

The popularity of the factory-made open canoe and kayak continues to grow, even while the traditional canoe in a variety of models is still to be found in traditional use among some peoples of this continent. But the bark canoe is little more than a memory on woodland waterways and in the Arctic the skin-covered kayak has been supplanted as a hunting vessel by the factory canoe with a squared stern and an outboard motor. The dugout that still serves the needs of a fisherman in Middle America will not do so for ever. The boat hull molded from synthetic material is increasingly the more familiar one, even in those subtropical regions that yesterday knew only the dugout. The value of wood in world markets makes it less and less likely that in future a mahogany log will be used to form a single dugout when it can be converted to lumber worth a great deal more.

While the traditional canoes of the first peoples of North America may disappear from our waterways, the native concept, the native design, and the native names will survive. The materials from which the open canoe and the kayak are made have changed and will change again, but the basic designs of the most efficient of aboriginal craft survive in their modern counterparts. The well-made canoe of today is much like the well-made canoe of centuries past. A North American paddler out of that past might well approve the durability of the modern model; certainly he would recognize in it the superb design for which he and his peers were responsible.

A Calgary canoeist of 1910 is ready for an outing on any waterway he can reach in his touring auto. His canoe rides on a bicycle-wheel trailer.

Throughout North America in recent years, progressive governments, universities, historical societies, and museums and enthusiastic individuals have done much to save aboriginal watercraft for posterity, to document the techniques of Indian and Inuit canoe and kayak construction, to revive dying crafts among the native peoples, and to stimulate in them a new interest and pride in their maritime heritage.

Among these initiatives has been the reconstruction of Fort William, the old fur trade depot at Thunder Bay at the head of Lake Superior, and the efforts of its managers to make it a living museum, where the public can see bark craft in the process of construction. This project of the Ontario Government has involved the Ojibwa people of the region, who inhabit the native encampment on the site and daily ply their crafts in the manufacture of bark canoes.

Demonstrating the traditional skills of his forebears, an Ojibwa man at Fort William peels the bark from a birch for a new canoe. The bark is laid down on the building bed and extra panels of bark are staked along its sides. An Ojibwa woman peels and splits spruce roots for sewing and lashing. The canoe cover takes shape, with gunwales positioned on both sides of the bark with wedge clamps. The ribs are fitted and forced into place against the inner cedar sheathing and, in anticipation of launching, a young man sits beside a bark lodge, patiently shaping a traditional paddle with a crooked knife.

Close by is a replica of the great canoe sheds of the fur trade era, where twenty-five-foot and thirty-six-foot bark freight canoes are built with the same tools and techniques as in 1800.

Picture Credits

The authors are grateful to many individuals and institutions for collecting and preserving a pictorial record of the canoe. We acknowledge that contribution and we appreciate their courtesy in sharing those illustrations.

Adirondack Museum, Blue Mountain Lake, N.Y., 226, 227, 240, 241, 244, 245, 248, 249

American Airlines, 23 right

American Philosophical Society, Philadelphia, 112 right, 218 left

Warwick Ashley, Ottawa, 36

Authors, ii-iii, 7, 13, 19, 20, 21, 23 left, 24, 25 lower, 32, 49 right, 50, 54, 58-9, 59, 68, 69 right, 72 lower, 100 right, 177, 187, 190, 192 right, 193, 234, 237, 239, 246, 247 left, 250, 251, 259, 266, 274

Eric Ball, through John M. Kochiss, 78

H. H. Bennett Studio, Inc., Wisconsin Dells, 225, 257

Bibliothèque Nationale, Paris, 167

British Columbia Provincial Museum, Victoria, 105 upper, 105 lower, 115, 116 right, 120 upper left, 120 right, 121 upper left, 121 right, 166 right

British Museum, London, vi, 121 lower left, 134

Canadian Pacific Corporate Archives, 188, 236

Carnegie Institution of Washington, 52

Departamento de Artes Plasticas, Morelia, 49 left

Gertrude Duby Blom, 56, 57

Douglas Elliott, Burnsville, N.C., 58 left, 267

Florida Division of Tourism, 63

Geological Survey of Canada, 189

Glenbow-Alberta Foundation, 93, 96, 111, 119, 139 right, 161, 165, 196, 217 lower, 230, 261 lower

Richard Harrington, Toronto, 29, 31 both, 34, 271

James Jerome Hill Reference Library, St. Paul, 164

Bill Holm, Seattle, 102

Peter C. Howorth, Santa Barbara, 126 right, 127, 270

Instituto Guatemalteco de Turismo, 61

Joslyn Art Museum, Omaha, 88

Kanawa International Museum, Minden, Ont., 1, 258

Library of Congress, Washington, 65, 70, 74, 75 right, 83

Lowie Museum of Anthropology, University of California, Berkeley, 11 lower, 117 left, 141

Mariners Museum, Newport News, Va., 76, 77 left, 80, 144, 145

Metropolitan Museum of Art, New York, 89

Metropolitan Toronto Library Board, 8, 17, 22, 41, 53 lower, 110 upper, 148, 170, 179, 182, 224, 255 lower

Middle American Research Institute, Tulane University, New Orleans, 48

Minnesota Historical Society, 233 lower, 254, 268

Museo Nacional de Antropología e Historia, Mexico, 40, 42

Museum fur Volkerkunde, Berlin, 100 left

Museum of the American Indian, Heye Foundation, New York, 10, 11 upper, 12, 75 left, 79, 120 lower left, 139 left

National Anthropological Archives, Smithsonian Institution, Washington, 66, 67, 72 upper, 84, 117 right, 137, 138, 147 upper, 150 left, 153, 265

National Capital Commission, Ottawa, 104 lower, 192 left

National Collection of Fine Arts, Smithsonian Institution, Washington, 86, 231

National Gallery of Canada, Ottawa, 95, 169, 172, 198, 204, 222

National Library of Canada, Ottawa, 101, 112 left, 122, 135, 136, 178

National Museum of Man, Ottawa, 142, 143, 157, 158, 159, 160, 162, 163, 216

Nationalmuseet, København, 140

New York Public Library, Print Division, 69 left

New York State Historical Association, 252, 253

Newberry Library, Edward E. Ayer Collection, Chicago, 85

Old Fort William, Ontario Ministry of Culture and Recreation, 262, 263

Old Town Canoe Company, 250 lower left, 251 lower right

Organization of American States, Washington, 35

Peabody Museum, Salem, Mass., 166 left

Provincial Archives of New Brunswick, Fredericton, 94 lower, 247

Public Archives of Canada, Ottawa, 3, 9, 92, 94 upper, 104 upper, 113 upper, 116 left, 123, 124 lower, 130-1, 132, 146, 150 right, 151, 152, 174, 175, 186, 203, 207, 210, 211, 214-15, 218 right, 232, 233 upper, 256, 260, 261 upper, 269

Radio Times Hulton Picture Library, 28

Royal Ontario Museum, 106-7, 114, 118, 154-5, 180, 201, 202, 206 both

Royal Scottish Museum, Edinburgh, 168

School of American Research, Santa Fe, and University of Utah Press, Salt Lake City, 43 both

Bob Smith, Ottawa, 37

State Historical Society of Wisconsin, 221, 225

Miss L. A. Strickland and Dept. of the Environment, London, on loan to British Embassy, Mexico, 46-7

Richard L. Terry, Houston, 126 left

Thomas Burke Memorial State Museum, Seattle, 108, 109 lower

Tourisme de la Martinique, Fort-de-France, 25 upper

United States National Archives, Washington, 90

University Museum, University of Pennsylvania, 53 upper

University of Oregon, C. L. Andrews Collection, Eugene, 124 upper, 217 upper

Vancouver City Archives, 110 lower, 113 lower

George Wilkes, Ottawa, 62

Winnipeg Art Gallery, loan from Archdiocese of Rupert's Land, Anglican Church of Canada, 219

Bibliography

This bibliography is intended to serve the function of a notes section, as well as to provide the listing of library authority. Care has been taken to identify in the text sources of quotations and other evidence, and these works are then listed — by chapter — in this reference section.

GENERAL REFERENCE WORKS

Adney, Edwin Tappan, and Chapelle, Howard I. *The bark canoes and skin boats of North America.* U.S. National Museum Bulletin 230. Washington: 1964.

Durham, Bill. *Canoes and kayaks of western America.* Seattle: 1960.

Gibbon, John Murray. *The romance of the Canadian canoe.* Toronto: 1951.

Hornell, James. *Water transport, origins and early evolution.* Cambridge: Cambridge University Press, 1946.

Quirke, Terence Thomas. *Canoes the world over.* Urbana: University of Illinois Press, 1952.

Thwaites, Reuben Gold, ed. *The Jesuit Relations and allied documents. Travels and explorations of the Jesuit missionaries in New France, 1610-1791.* 73 vols. Cleveland: 1896-1901.

WHAT IS A CANOE?

Garcilaso de la Vega. *The Florida of the Inca: A history of the Adelantado, Hernando de Soto.* Trans. and ed. by John Grier Varner and Jeannette Johnson Varner. Austin: University of Texas Press, 1951.

RAFTS AND FLOATS

Bancroft, Hubert Howe. "The Maya Nations." *The works of Hubert Howe Bancroft.* Vol. II, pp. 739. San Francisco: 1882-90.

——. "The Nahua nations." *Ibid.* Vol. II, pp. 386-99.

Clavijero, Francisco Javier. *The History of Lower California.* Trans. from Italian and ed. by Sarah E. Lake and A. A. Gray. Riverside, Calif.: 1971.

Simple balsas made of tule rushes served the Pomo needs.

Dampier, William. *Dampier's voyages.* Ed. by John Masefield. 2 vols. London: 1906.

Du Pratz, Antoine Le Page. *The History of Louisiana.* Trans. from French. London: 1774.

Heizer, Robert F., and Massey, William C. *Aboriginal navigation off the coasts of Upper and Baja California.* Bureau of American Ethnology Bulletin 151. Washington: 1953.

Morice, A. G. *The great Déné race.* Vienna: The Press of the Mechithariste, n.d.

Moziño, José Mariano. *Noticias de Nutka; an account of Nootka Sound in 1792.* Trans. and ed. by Iris Higbie Wilson. Toronto: 1970.

Oviedo y Valdés, Gonzalo Fernando de. *Historia general y natural de las Indias....* 4 vols. Madrid: 1851-5.

Shelvocke, George. *A voyage round the world....* London and Toronto: 1928.

Ulloa, Francis de. "The first and second discovery of the Gulfe of California...." In *Voyages of the English Nation to America before the year 1600.* Ed. by Richard Hakluyt. Vol. III, pp. 317-65. Edinburgh: 1889.

Vancouver, George. *A voyage of discovery to the north Pacific Ocean and round the world....* 3 vols. London: 1798.

Villagutierre Soto-Mayor, Juan de. *Historia de la conquista de la provincia de el Itzá....* Madrid: 1701.

Wafer, Lionel. *A new voyage and description of the Isthmus of America.* Ed. by G. P. Winship. Cleveland: 1903.

THE DUGOUT

THE CARIBBEAN

Atwood, Thomas. *The history of the island of Dominica.* London: 1971.

Coke, Thomas. *A history of the West Indies.* Liverpool: 1808.

Du Tertre, Jean Baptiste. *Histoire générale des Antilles habitées par les François...by le r. p. Du Tertre.* 2 vols. Paris: 1667.

Fermor, Patrick Leigh. "The Caribs of Dominica." *The Geographical Magazine,* vol. 23, no. 6, 1950.

Gage, Thomas. *The English-American, his travail by sea and land: or, a new survey of the West India's.* London: 1648.

Jane, Lionel Cecil, comp. and trans. *Select documents illustrating the four voyages of Columbus....* 2 vols. London: Hakluyt Society, 1930-33.

Krieger, Herbert W. "The aborigines of the ancient island of Hispaniola." *Annual report of...the Smithsonian Institution...for 1929.* Washington: 1930, pp. 473-506.

Labat, J.-B. *Voyages aux isles de l'Amérique.* Paris: 1722.

La Borde, Father de. "History of the origins, customs, religion, wars and travels of the Caribs, savages of the Antilles of America." Trans. and ed. by G. J. A. Bosch-Reitz. *Timehri* (Journal of the Royal Agricultural and Commercial Society of British Guiana), vol. 5, 1886.

Landstrom, Bjorn. *Columbus: the story of Don Cristobal Colon, Admiral of the Ocean....* New York: 1966.

Layfield, Doctor. "A large relation of the Porto Ricco voiage; written, as is reported, by...Doctor Layfield...." In *Purchas his pilgrimes,* by Samuel Purchas. Vol. 16, pp. 44-106. Glasgow: 1906.

Lovén, Sven. *Origins of the Tainan culture, West Indies.* Göteborg: 1935.

McCusick, Marshall B. *Aboriginal canoes in the West Indies.* Publications in Anthropology No. 63. New Haven: Yale University, 1960.

Martyr, Peter. *De Orbe Novo, the eight decades of Peter Martyr D'Anghera.* Trans. by Francis A. MacNutt. New York: 1912.

BIBLIOGRAPHY

——. "The first booke of the decades of the ocean." In *A selection of curious, rare, and early voyages, and histories of interesting discoveries, chiefly published by Hakluyt.* Trans. by M. Lok. London: 1812, pp. 367-670.

Méndez, Diego. "An account, given by Diego Méndez, of certain things that occurred on the last voyage of the admiral, Don Christopher Columbus." In *Select documents illustrating the four voyages of Columbus....* London: Hakluyt Society, 1931.

Ober, Frederick A. *Camps in the Caribbees.* Boston: 1899.

Olsen, Fred. *On the trail of the Arawaks.* Norman: University of Oklahoma Press, 1974.

Rochefort, Charles de. *The history of the Caribby-Islands.* Trans. from French by John Davies. London: 1666.

Sheldon, Robert. "Brief account of the Caraibs, who inhabited the Antilles." *Transactions, American Antiquarian Society*, vol. 1, 1820, pp. 365-433.

Southey, Thomas. *Chronological history of the West Indies.* 3 vols. London: 1827.

Stoneman, John. "The voyage of M. Henry Challons intended for the North Plantation of Virginia, 1606...." In *Purchas his pilgrimes*, by Samuel Purchas. Vol. 19, pp. 284-97. Glasgow: 1906.

Taylor, Douglas. *The Caribs of Dominica.* Bureau of American Ethnology Bulletin 119. Washington: Smithsonian Institution, 1938.

Thacher, John Boyd. *Christopher Columbus: his life, his work, his remains as revealed by original printed and manuscript records.* New York: 1903.

CENTRAL AMERICA

Atkins, John. *A voyage to Guinea, Brasil and the West Indies.* London: 1735.

Bard, Samuel A. *Waikna: or, adventures on the Mosquito shore.* New York: 1855.

Byam, George. *Wild life in the interior of Central America.* London: 1849.

Cockburn, John. *The unfortunate Englishman.* London: 1779.

Conzemius, Eduard. *Ethnographical survey of the Miskito and Sumu Indians of Honduras and Nicaragua.* Bureau of American Ethnology Bulletin 106. Washington: Smithsonian Institution, 1932.

Dampier, William. *Dampier's voyages.* Ed. by John Masefield. 2 vols. London: 1906.

Esquemeling, John. *The buccaneers of America.* London: 1911.

Feeney, Corinne B. "Arch-isolationists, the San Blas Indians." *National Geographic Magazine*, vol. 79, 1941.

Helms, Mary W. "Coastal adaptations as contact phenomena among the Miskito and Cuna Indians of lower Central America." In *The economy and ecology of maritime Middle America.* Ed. by Barbara L. Stark and Barbara Voorhies. New York: Academic Press, 1978. pp. 132-5.

Henderson, George. *An account of the British settlement of Honduras....* 2nd ed. London: 1811.

Krieger, Herbert W. *Material culture of the people of southeastern Panama....* United States National Museum Bulletin 134. Washington: 1926.

Martyr, Peter. *De Orbe Novo, the eight decades of Peter Martyr D'Anghera.* Trans. by Francis A. MacNutt. New York: 1912.

——. "The first booke of the decades of the ocean." In *A selection of curious, rare, and early voyages...chiefly published by Hakluyt.* Trans. by M. Lok. London: 1812, pp. 367-670.

Masefield, John. *On the Spanish Main.* London: 1906.

Meyer, Harvey K. *Historical dictionary of Nicaragua.* Metuchen, N.J.: 1972.

Mirsky, Jeannette. *The westward crossings.* New York: 1946.

Radin, Paul. *Indians of South America.* Garden City, N.Y.: 1942.

Roberts, Orlando W. *Narrative of voyages and excursions on the east coast and in the interior of Central America.* Edinburgh: 1827.

Squier, E. G. *Notes on Central America, particularly the states of Honduras and San Salvador.* New York: 1855.

Stout, David B. *The Cuna.* Handbook of South American Indians, Vol. 4. Bureau of American Ethnology Bulletin 143. Washington: 1948.

——. *San Blas Cuna acculturation: an introduction.* New York: 1947.

Wafer, Lionel. *A new voyage and description of the Isthmus of America.* Ed. by G. P. Winship. Cleveland: 1903.

The mariposa dip net and the Tarascan fisherman's dugout are essentially unchanged since pre-Columbian times, but nowadays on Mexico's Lake Pátzcuaro the large "butterfly" net is brought out only for tourist display.

MEXICO: THE AZTECS

Beals, Ralph L. "The Tarascans." In *Handbook of Middle American Indians.* Ed. by Robert Wauchope. Vol. 8, pp. 725-73. Austin: University of Texas Press, 1969.

Cortés, Hernan. *Fernando Cortes; his five letters of relation to the Emperor Charles V.* Trans. and ed. by Francis Augustus MacNutt. 2 vols. Cleveland: 1908.

Craine, Eugene R., and Reindorp, Reginald C., eds. *The chronicles of Michoacán.* Norman: University of Oklahoma Press, 1970.

Díaz del Castillo, Bernal. *The discovery and conquest of Mexico, 1517-1521.* Trans. by A. P. Maudslay and ed. by Genaro García. New York: 1956.

Duran, Diego. *The Aztecs: the history of the Indies of New Spain.* Trans. by Doris Heyden and Fernando Horcasitas. New York: 1964.

García Arroyo, R. *Five Mexican sports.* Mexico: 1969.

Garrett, W. E. "Mexico's little Venice." *National Geographic Magazine*, vol. 133, no. 6, June 1968, pp. 876-88.

Gibson, Charles. *The Aztecs under Spanish rule: A history of the Indians of the Valley of Mexico, 1519-1810.* Stanford: Stanford University Press, 1964.

Leon-Portilla, Miguel, ed. *The broken spears: the Aztec account of the conquest of Mexico.* Ed. and intro. by M. Leon-Portilla. Boston: 1962.

Linné, Sigvald. "Hunting and fishing in the Valley of Mexico in the middle of the sixteenth century." *Ethnos*, vol. 2, 1937, pp. 56-64.

——. "Bird-nets of Lake Texcoco, Mexico Valley." *Ethnos*, vol. 5, 1940, pp. 122-30.

López de Gómara, Francisco. *Cortés; the life of the conqueror by his secretary.* Trans. and ed. by Lesley Byrd Simpson from *Istoria de la conquista de Mexico.* Berkeley and Los Angeles: University of California Press, 1964.

Sahagún, Fray Bernardino de. *Florentine Codex. General history of the things of New Spain.* Trans. with notes by Arthur J. O. Anderson and Charles E. Dibble. Monographs of the School of American Research. No. 14, part 2. Santa Fe: 1950.

Saville, Marshall H. *The wood-carver's art in ancient Mexico.* New York: Museum of the American Indian, Heye Foundation, 1925.

Tylor, Edward B. *Anahuac; or Mexico and the Mexicans, ancient and modern.* London: 1861.

Vaillant, George C. *Aztecs of Mexico: rise and fall of the Aztec nation.* Garden City, N.Y.: 1944.

Bibliography

LANDS OF THE MAYA

Andrews, Anthony P. "The salt trade of the ancient Maya." *Archeology*, vol. 33, no. 4, pp. 24-33.

Blom, Frans. *The conquest of Yucatan.* Boston and New York: 1936.

Chapman, Anne M. "Port of trade enclaves in Aztec and Maya civilizations." In *Trade and market in the early empires.* Ed. by Karl Polanyi, Conrad M. Arensberg, and Harry W. Pearson. Glencoe, Ill.: 1957, pp. 114-53.

Chard, Chester S. *Pre-Columbian trade between North and South America.* Kroeber Anthropological Society Papers No. 1. Berkeley, Calif.: 1950.

Charnay, Désiré. *The ancient cities of the new world.* Trans. from French by J. Gonimo and Helen S. Conant. New York: 1887.

Gann, Thomas W. F. *The Maya Indians of southern Yucatan and northern British Honduras.* Bureau of American Ethnology Bulletin 64. Washington: 1918.

Halle, Louis J., Jr. *River of ruins.* New York: 1941.

Hammond, Norman. "Classic Maya canoes." *International Journal of Nautical Archaeology and Underwater Exploration*, vol. 10, no. 3, 1981, pp. 173-85.

Jane, Lionel Cecil, comp. and trans. *Select documents illustrating the four voyages of Columbus....* 2 vols. London: Hakluyt Society, 1930-33.

Landa, Diego de. *Landa's Relación de las cosas de Yucatan; a translation ed. by Alfred M. Tozzer.* Papers of the Peabody Museum of American Archaeology and Ethnology. Vol. 18, 1941.

Maler, Teobert. *Researches in the central portion of the Usumatsintla Valley.* Memoirs of the Peabody Museum of American Archaeology and Ethnology. Vol. 2, no. 1, 1901.

Maudslay, Anne Cary and Alfred Percival. *A glimpse of Guatemala.* London: 1899.

Means, Philip Ainsworth. *History of the Spanish conquest of Yucatan and the Itzas.* Papers of the Peabody Museum of American Archaeology and Ethnology. Vol. 7, 1917.

Morley, S. G. *The ancient Maya.* Rev. by G. W. Brainerd. Stanford: 1963.

Pendergast, David M., ed. *Palenque; the Walker-Caddy expedition to the ancient Maya city, 1839-1840.* Norman: University of Oklahoma Press, 1967.

Scholes, France V., and Roys, Ralph L. *The Maya Chontal Indians of Acalan-Tixchel; a contribution to the history and ethnography of the Yucatan Peninsula.* Carnegie Institution of Washington, Publication 560. Washington: 1948.

Stephens, John L. *Incidents of travel in Yucatan.* Illus. by Frederick Catherwood. 2 vols. New York: 1963.

Strong, William Duncan. *Archeological investigations in the Bay Islands, Spanish Honduras.* Smithsonian Miscellaneous Collections. Vol. 92, no. 14, 1935.

Thompson, J. Eric S. "Canoes and navigation of the Maya and their neighbours." *Journal of the Royal Anthropological Institute*, vol. 79, parts 1 and 2, 1949, pp. 69-78.

FLORIDA

Acosta, Joseph de. "Observations gathered out of the first, second, third, and fourth bookes of Josephus Acosta...." In *Purchas his pilgrimes*, by Samuel Purchas. Vol. 15, pp. 1-148. Glasgow: 1906.

Bartram, William. *Travels through North and South Carolina, Georgia, East and West Florida....* Dublin: 1793.

Buker, George E. *Swamp sailors: riverine warfare in the Everglades, 1835-1842.* Gainesville: University Presses of Florida, 1975.

Bullen, Adelaide K. *Florida Indians of past and present.* Gainesville: n.d.

Bullen, Ripley P., and Brooks, Harold K. "Two ancient Florida dugout canoes." *Quarterly Journal of the Florida Academy of Sciences*, vol. 30, no. 2, 1967, pp. 97-104.

Capron, Louis. "Florida's 'wild' Indians, the Seminole." *National Geographic Magazine*, vol. 110, no. 6, Dec. 1956, pp. 819-40.

Cushing, Frank H. "Explorations of ancient key dwellers' remains on the Gulf coast of Florida." *Proceedings, American Philosophical Society.* Vol. 35, 1896, pp. 329-432.

Densmore, Frances. *Seminole music.* Bureau of American Ethnology Bulletin 161. Washington: 1956.

Elvas, a gentleman of. "Virginia richly valued, by the description of the maine land of Florida...." In *A selection of curious, rare, and early voyages... chiefly published by Hakluyt...a supplement*, pp. 689-762. London: 1812.

Garcilaso de la Vega. *The Florida of the Inca. A history of the Adelantado, Hernando de Soto....* Trans. and ed. by John Grier Varner and Jeannette Johnson Varner. Austin: University of Texas Press, 1951.

Munroe, Kirk. "A forgotten remnant." *Scribner's Magazine*, vol. 7, 1890, pp. 307-10.

Neill, Wilfred T. "Dugouts of the Mikasuki Seminole." *Florida Anthropologist*, vol. 6, no. 3, Sept. 1953.

——. "Sailing vessels of the Florida Seminole." *Florida Anthropologist*, vol. 9, nos. 3-4, Dec. 1956.

Ribaut, Jean. *The whole and true discoverye of Terra Florida.* Facsimile of London edition of 1563. Gainesville: 1964.

Tebeau, Charlton W. *A history of Florida.* Coral Gables: University of Miami Press, 1971.

Willoughby, Hugh L. *Across the Everglades: a canoe journey of exploration.* Philadelphia: 1904.

THE EASTERN SEABOARD

Alvord, Clarence Walworth, and Bidgood, Lee. *The first explorations of the trans-Allegheny region by the Virginians, 1650-1674.* Cleveland: 1912.

Amadas, Philip, or Barlow, Cumberland. "The first voyage made to the coasts of America, with two barks, wherein were Captaines M. Philip Amadas, and M. Arthur Barlowe, who discovered part of the countrey now called Virginia Anno 1584...." In *The voyages of the English nation to America.* Collected by Richard Hakluyt, ed. by Edmund Goldsmid. Vol. 2, pp. 282-93. Edinburgh: 1889.

Beverley, Robert. *The history and present state of Virginia.* Reprint of 1705 ed. Chapel Hill, N.C.: 1947.

Brewington, M. V. *Chesapeake Bay log canoes and bugeyes.* Cambridge, Maryland: 1963.

Chapelle, Howard I. *American small sailing craft.* New York: 1951.

——. *The migrations of an American boat type.* Contributions from the Museum of History and Technology, United States National Museum Bulletin 228. Washington: 1961.

Dunbar, Seymour. *A history of travel in America.* New York: 1937.

Force, Peter, comp. "A brief account of the establishment of the colony of Georgia under Gen. James Oglethorpe...." *Tracts and papers relating principally to the origin, settlement, and progress of the colonies in North America....* Vol. 1. Washington: 1836.

Hariot, Thomas. *Narrative of the first English plantation of Virginia.* London: 1893.

Hutchinson, Thomas. *The history of the colony and province of Massachusetts-Bay.* Ed. by Lawrence Shaw Mayo. Cambridge: Harvard University Press, 1936.

Jameson, J. Franklin, ed. *Narratives of New Netherlands, 1609-1664.* New York: 1909.

Jones, Charles C., Jr. *Antiquities of the southern Indians, particularly of the Georgia tribes.* Reprinted from 1873 ed. New York: 1973.

Juet, Robert. "The third voyage of Master Henrie Hudson...." In *Purchas his pilgrimes*, by Samuel Purchas. Vol. 13, pp. 333-74. Glasgow: 1906.

Kalm, Peter. *Travels into North America....* London: 1770.

Near the jungle-grown banks of the Usumacinta River in southern Mexico, a modern craftsman shapes the interior of a traditional mahogany log canoe.

Kochiss, John M. *Oystering from New York to Boston.* Middleton, Conn.: 1974.

Lawson, John. *Lawson's history of North Carolina.* Reprint from 1714 ed. Richmond: 1937.

McCary, Ben C. "An Indian dugout canoe, reworked by early settlers." *Quarterly Bulletin of Archeological Society of Virginia*, vol. 19, no. 1, Sept. 1964.

Maloney, John. "Chesapeake odyssey." *National Geographic Magazine*, vol. 76, no. 3, Sept. 1939.

Norwood, Colonel. "A voyage to Virginia...1649." In *Tracts and papers relating to the origin, settlement, and progress of the colonies in North America....* Vol. 3. Coll. by Peter Force. Washington: 1844.

Smith, John. *The generall historie of Virginia, New England & the Summer Isles.* 2 vols. Glasgow: 1907.

Speck, Frank G. "Chapters on the ethnology of the Powhatan tribes of Virginia." In *Indian notes and monographs*, vol. 1, no. 5, pp. 374-81. Ed. by F. W. Hodge. Museum of American Indian, Heye Foundation, New York: 1928.

Strachey, William. *The historie of travell into Virginia Britania (1612).* Ed. by Louis B. Wright and Virginia Freund. Nendeln, Liechtenstein: 1967.

Swanton, John R. *The Indians of the southeastern United States.* Bureau of American Ethnology Bulletin 137. Washington: 1946.

Tyler, D. B. *The bay and river: Delaware, a pictorial history.* Cambridge, Maryland: 1955.

Verrazzano, Giovanni da. "The relation of Iohn de Verrazzano a Florentine, of the land by him discovered...." In *The voyages of the English nation to America.* Collected by Richard Hakluyt, ed. by Edmund Goldsmid. Vol. 2, pp. 389-401. Edinburgh: 1889.

Vlach, John Michael. *The Afro-American tradition in decorative arts.* Cleveland: Cleveland Museum of Art, 1978.

[White, John.] "The fift voyage of M. Iohn White into the West Indies and parts of America called Virginia, in the yeere 1590." In *The voyages of the English nation to America.* Collected by Richard Hakluyt, ed. by Edmund Goldsmid. Vol. 2, pp. 375-88. Edinburgh: 1889.

Wood, Peter H. *Black majority: Negroes in colonial South Carolina.* New York: 1974.

THE MISSISSIPPI AND WESTWARD

Baldwin, Leland D. *The keelboat age on western waters.* Pittsburgh: 1941.

Catlin, George. *Illustrations of the manners, customs, and condition of the North American Indians.* 2 vols. 9th ed. London: 1857.

Cresswell, Nicholas. *The journal of Nicholas Cresswell, 1774-1777.* New York: 1924.

Croghan, George. "A selection of George Croghan's letters and journals...." In *Early western travels, 1748-1846.* Ed. by R. G. Thwaites. Vol. 1, pp. 45-173. Cleveland: 1904.

Du Pratz, Antoine Le Page. *The history of Louisiana.* London: 1774.

Gatschet, Albert S. *The Karankawa Indians....* Archaeological and ethnological papers of the Peabody Museum. Vol. 1, no. 2, 1891.

Gregg, Josiah. "Commerce of the prairies; or, the journal of a Santa Fe trader, 1831-1839." In *Early western travels, 1748-1846.* Ed. by R. G. Thwaites. Vol. 19, pp. 155-349, and Vol. 20, pp. 11-356. Cleveland: 1905.

Hulbert, Archer Butler. *The Ohio River, a course of empire.* New York: 1906.

Joutel, Henri. *Joutel's journal of La Salle's last voyage, 1684-7.* Albany: 1906.

Knipmeyer, William B. "Folk-boats of eastern French Louisiana." Ed. by Henry Glassie. In *American folklife.* Ed. by Don Yoder. Austin: University of Texas Press, 1976.

Laguna, Frederica de. "Eskimo dug-outs." *Pennsylvania University Museum Bulletin*, vol. 5, no. 5, Mar. 1935.

Lewis, Henry. *The valley of the Mississippi illustrated.* Trans. from German by A. Hermina Poatgieter, ed. by Bertha L. Heilbron. St. Paul: Minnesota Historical Society, 1967.

Lewis, Meriwether, and Clark, William. *Letters of the Lewis and Clark expedition with related documents, 1783-1854.* Ed. by Donald Jackson. Urbana: University of Illinois Press, 1962.

Membré, Zenobius. "Narrative of the adventures of La Salle's party...by Father Zenobius Membré, Recollect." In *Discovery and exploration of the Mississippi Valley*, by John Dawson Gilmary Shea. 2nd ed. pp. 151-88. Albany: 1903.

Michaux, François André. "Travels to the west of the Allegheny Mountains." In *Early western travels, 1748-1846.* Ed. by R. G. Thwaites. Vol. 3, pp. 105-306. Cleveland: 1904.

Mirsky, Jeannette. *The westward crossings.* New York: 1946.

Nuttall, Thomas. "A journal of travels into the Arkansas territory during the year 1819." In *Early western travels, 1748-1846.* Ed. by R. G. Thwaites. Vol. 13. Cleveland: 1904.

Poisson, Père du. "Letter from Father du Poisson, missionary to the Akensas...." In *The Jesuit Relations and allied documents.* Ed. by R. G. Thwaites. Vol. 67, pp. 277-309. Cleveland: 1896-1901.

Sinclair, Harold. *The port of New Orleans.* New York: 1942.

Smet, Pierre Jean de. *Life, letters and travels of Father Pierre-Jean De Smet, S. J., 1801-1873.* 4 vols. New York: 1905.

——. "Letters and sketches: with a narrative of a year's residence among the Indian tribes of the Rocky Mountains." In *Early western travels, 1748-1846.* Ed. by R. G. Thwaites. Vol. 27, pp. 123-411. Cleveland: 1906.

Steck, Francis Borgia. *The Jolliett-Marquette expedition, 1673.* Quincy, Ill.: Franciscan Fathers, 1928.

Swanton, John R. *Indian tribes of the lower Mississippi Valley and adjacent coast of the Gulf of Mexico.* Bureau of American Ethnology Bulletin 43. Washington: 1911.

Waldo, Ednard. *The pirogue.* Wildlife Education Bulletin No. 80. Baton Rouge: Louisiana Wild Life and Fisheries Commission, n.d.

Weiser, Conrad. "Conrad Weiser's journal of a tour to the Ohio...." In *Early western travels, 1748-1846.* Ed. by R. G. Thwaites. Vol. 1, pp. 15-44. Cleveland: 1904.

Some nineteenth-century artists with greater romantic and creative capacity than realistic reportorial ability have left us frontier views of very strange aspect. The gondola-like dugouts of the upper Missouri River are the work of one of them.

THE GREAT LAKES AND EASTWARD

Drayton, Reginald. Mss. diary of Reginald Drayton. Archives of Ontario.

Galbreath, Robert. "Dugout canoes in Michigan." *Cranbrook Institute of Science News Letter*, vol. 29, no. 2, Oct. 1959.

Hadfield, Joseph. *An Englishman in America, 1785, being the diary of Joseph Hadfield.* Ed. by Douglas S. Robertson. Toronto: 1933.

"Kanuck." "Bark canoeing in Canada." *Lippincott's Magazine*, old series vol. 30, new series vol. 4, 1882.

La Hontan, Louis-Armand de Lom d'Arce, Baron de. *New voyages to North America....* London: 1703.

Morris, Charles. "Report by Captain Morris to Governor Shirley upon his survey of lands in Nova Scotia...1749." *Archives of Canada report for 1912*, pp. 79-83, 1913.

Radin, Paul. "The Winnebago tribe." *Thirty-seventh annual report of the Bureau of Ethnology, 1915-1916.* Washington: 1923.

Sellar, Robert. *The history of the county of Huntingdon and the seigniories of Chateaugay and Beauharnois.* Huntingdon, P.Q.: 1888.

Wallis, Wilson Dallam and Ruth Otis (Sawtell). *The Micmac Indians of eastern Canada.* Minneapolis: University of Minnesota Press, 1955.

Bibliography

THE NORTH PACIFIC

Aylmer, Fenton. *A cruise in the Pacific. From the log of a naval officer.* London: Hurst and Blackett, 1860.

Boas, Franz. *Kwakiutl ethnology.* Chicago: University of Chicago Press, 1966.

Brown, Vinson. *Peoples of the sea wind: the native Americans of the Pacific Coast.* New York: Macmillan, 1977.

Collins, June McCormick. *The valley of the spirits. The Upper Skagit Indians of western Washington.* Seattle: University of Washington Press, 1974.

Collison, W. H. *In the wake of the war canoe.* London: Seeley, Service & Co., 1915.

Cox, Ross. *Adventures on the Columbia River, including the narrative of a resident of six years on the western side of the Rocky Mountains, among various tribes of Indians hitherto unknown: together with a journey across the American continent.* Vol. I. London: Henry Colburn and Richard Bentley, 1831.

Curtis, Edward S. *The North American Indian... being a series of volumes picturing and describing the Indians of the United States and Alaska.* 20 vols. Cambridge, Mass.: 1907-24.

Duff, Wilson. *The impact of the white man.* The Indian history of British Columbia, vol. 1. B.C. Provincial Museum. Anthropology in British Columbia. Memoir No. 5. Victoria: 1964.

Dunn, John. *History of the Oregon Territory and British North-American fur trade; with an account of the habits and customs of the principal native tribes on the northern continent.* London: Edwards and Hughes, 1844.

Durham, George. "Canoes from cedar logs." *Pacific Northwest Quarterly*, vol. 46, no. 2, Apr. 1955, pp. 33-9.

Ebbutt, Frank. "The canoe in western Canada." *Canadian Geographical Magazine*, vol. III, no. 4, Oct. 1931.

Farnham, Thomas J. *Travels in the great western prairies, the Anahuac Mountains, and in the Oregon Territory.* London: Richard Bentley, 1843.

Harrison, Charles. *Ancient warriors of the North Pacific.* London: H. F. & G. Witherby, 1925.

Holm, Bill. "Carving a Kwakiutl canoe." *The Beaver*, Outfit 292, Summer 1961, pp. 28-35.

Honigmann, John J. *Ethnography and acculturation of the Fort Nelson Slave.* Yale University Publications in Anthropology No. 33. 1946.

Jane, Cecil. trans. *A Spanish voyage to Vancouver and the north-west coast of America; being the narrative of the voyage made in the year 1792 by the schooners Sutil and Mexicana to explore the Strait of Fuca.* London: Argonaut Press, 1931.

Jewitt, John Rodgers. *Adventures and sufferings among the savages of Nootka Sound.* Edinburgh: Constable, 1824.

Johnson, Olga Weydemeyer. *Flathead and Kootenay: the rivers, the tribes and the region's traders.* Glendale, Calif.: Arthur H. Clark, 1969.

Kellogg, Louise Phelps, ed. *Early narratives of the northwest, 1634-1699.* New York: Charles Scribner's Sons, 1917.

Krause, Aurel. *The Tlingit Indians: results of a trip to the northwest coast of America and the Bering Straits.* Trans. Erna Gunther. Seattle: University of Washington Press, 1956.

McFeat, Tom. *Indians of the North Pacific coasts.* The Carleton Library, No. 25. Toronto: McClelland and Stewart, 1966.

McIlwraith, Thomas F. *The Bella Coola Indians.* Toronto: University of Toronto Press, 1948.

McKelvie, B. A. *Fort Langley, outpost of empire.* Toronto: Thomas Nelson and Sons, 1957.

Mason, Otis T., and Hill, Meriden S. "Pointed bark canoes of the Kutenai and Amur." *U.S. National Museum Report 1899*, pp. 523-37.

Mayne, R. C. *Four years in British Columbia and Vancouver Island.* London: John Murray, 1862.

Meares, John. *Voyages made in the years 1788 to 1789, from China to the northwest coast of America.* London: Logographic Press, 1791.

Moziño, José Mariano. *Noticias de Nutka: an account of Nootka Sound in 1792.* Trans. and ed. by Iris Higbie Wilson. Toronto: 1970.

Murphy, John Mortimer. *Rambles in north-western America from the Pacific Ocean to the Rocky Mountains.* London: Chapman and Hall, 1879.

Niblack, Albert P. "The coast Indians of southern Alaska and northern British Columbia." *U.S. National Museum Report, 1888*, pp. 225-386.

Oberg, Kalervo. *The social economy of the Tlingit Indians.* Seattle: University of Washington Press, 1973.

Olsen, Ronald L. *The Quinault Indians.* Washington University Publications in Anthropology. Vol. VI. no. 1, 1936.

——. *Adze, canoe and house types of the northwest coast. Ibid.* Vol. IV, no. 1, 1927.

Ormsby, Margaret A. *British Columbia: a history.* Toronto: Macmillan of Canada, 1958.

The fine lines that can result from spreading a dugout are evident in the small Nootkan canoe.

Pierce, Richard A. "Voznesenskii scientist in Alaska." *The Alaska Journal*, vol. V, no. 1. Winter 1975.

Salisbury, O. M. *The customs and legends of the Thlinget Indians of Alaska.* New York: Bonanza Books, 1962.

Sproat, Gilbert Malcolm. *Scenes and studies of savage life.* London: Smith, Elder & Co., 1868.

Strong, Emory. *Stone age on the Columbia River.* Portland, Ore.: Binford & Mort, 1959.

Stuart, Robert. *The discovery of the Oregon trail, Robert Stuart's narratives of his overland trip eastward from Astoria in 1812-13.... * Ed. by Philip Rollins. New York, London: Charles Scribner's Sons, 1935.

Teit, James. *The Thompson Indians of British Columbia.* American Museum of Natural History, Memoirs, No. 2, 1900.

Wagner, Henry R. *Spanish explorations in the Strait of Juan de Fuca.* Santa Ana, Calif.: 1933.

Waterman, T. T. *The paraphernalia of the Duwamish "spirit-canoe" ceremony.* Museum of the American Indian. Indian Notes. Vol. VII, no. 2, Apr. 1930.

——. "The whaling equipment of the Makah Indians." *University of Washington Publications in Anthropology*, vol. 1, no. 1, pp. 1-67.

——, and Coffin, Geraldine. *Types of Canoes on Puget Sound.* Museum of the American Indian. Notes and Monographs. Misc. 5, 1920.

Waugh, F. W. "Canadian aboriginal canoes." *The Canadian Field Naturalist*, vol. 33, no. 2, May 1919.

Wilkes, Charles. *Narrative of the United States exploring expedition, during the years 1838, 1839, 1840, 1841, 1842.* Philadelphia: Lea & Blanchard, 1845.

Winthrop, Theodore. *The canoe and the saddle, or klallam and klickitat. To which are now first added his western letters and journals.* Ed. by John H. Williams. Tacoma, Wash.: 1913.

Woodcock, George. *Peoples of the coast: the Indians of the Pacific northwest.* Edmonton: Hurtig, 1977.

Work, John. *The journal of John Work, January to October 1835.* Archives of British Columbia, Memoir No. X. Victoria, B.C.: 1945.

Yarrow, H. C. *Study of mortuary customs among the North American Indians.* Washington: Smithsonian Institution, 1880.

In a sunset silhouette on the California coast, modern Chumash canoemen with double-bladed paddles cross the Santa Barbara Channel in a planked tomol.

CALIFORNIA

Costanso, Miguel. *The narrative of the Portola expedition of 1769-1770.* Publications of the Academy of Pacific Coast History. Vol. 1, no. 4. University of California, March 1910. Ed. by Adolph van Hemert-Engert and Frederick J. Teggart.

Grant, Campbell. *The rock paintings of the Chumash: a study of a California Indian culture.* Berkeley and Los Angeles: University of California Press, 1965.

Harrington, John P. *Tomol: Chumash watercraft as described in the ethnographic notes of John P. Harrington.* Ed. by Travis Hudson, Janice Timbrook, and Melissa Rempe. Santa Barbara: a Ballena Press/Santa Barbara Museum of Natural History Cooperative Publication, 1978.

Heizer, Robert F. *Plank canoes of South and North America.* Kroeber Anthropological Society Papers, No. 35, 1966.

——, and Massey, William C. *Aboriginal navigation off the coasts of Upper and Baja California.* Bureau of American Ethnology Bulletin 151. Washington: 1953.

Hornell, James. "The genetic relation of the bark canoe to dug-outs and plank-built boats." *Man*, vol. 40, 1940, pp. 114-19.

Howorth, Peter C. "Voyage of the Helek." *Santa Barbara Quarterly Magazine*, vol. 2, no. 3, pp. 12-16.

Portola, Gaspar de. *Diary of Gaspar de Portola during the California expedition of 1769-1770.* Publications of the Academy of Pacific Coast History. Vol. 1, no. 3. University of California, Oct. 1909.

THE SKIN BOAT

KAYAK AND UMIAK

Amundsen, Roald. *The north west passage.* London: Archibald Constable, 1908.

Arima, Eugene Y. *A contextual study of the Caribou Eskimo kayak.* Canadian Ethnology Service. Mercury Series, No. 25. Ottawa: National Museum of Man, 1975.

——. "Notes on the kayak and its equipment at Ivuyivik, P.Q." *National Museum of Man, Bulletin No. 194*, 1964, pp. 221-61.

Babcock, William H. "Eskimo long-distance voyages." *American Anthropologist*, 15, 1913, pp. 138-41.

Bandi, Hans-Georg. *Eskimo prehistory.* Trans. by Ann E. Keep. University of Alaska Studies of Northern Peoples, No. 2. Juneau: University of Alaska Press, 1969.

Birket-Smith, Kaj, and De Laguna, Frederica. *The Eyak Indians of the Copper River delta, Alaska.* Kobenhavn: Levin & Munksgaard, 1938.

Boas, Franz. *The Eskimo of Baffin Island and Hudson Bay.* American Museum of Natural History, Bulletin, Vol. 15, 1907.

——. "The central Eskimo." *U.S. Bureau of American Ethnology, Sixth Annual Report, 1884-85*, pp. 409-669. Washington: Smithsonian Institution, 1888.

Chappell, Edward. *Narrative of a voyage to Hudson's Bay in his Majesty's Ship Rosamond containing some account of the north-eastern coast of America and the tribes inhabiting that remote region.* London: J. Mawman, 1817.

Clark, Annette McFadyen. *Koyukuk River culture.* National Museum of Man. Canadian Ethnology Service. Mercury Series, No. 18. Ottawa: National Museum of Man, 1974.

Cutter, Donald C. "Malaspina at Yakutat Bay." *Alaska Journal*, vol. 2, no. 4, Autumn 1972.

Davis, John. "A report of Master Iohn Davis of his three voyages for the discoverie of the Northwest Passage, taken out of a treatise of his...." In *Voyages of the English nation to America before the year 1600.* Ed. by Richard Hakluyt. Vol. 1, pp. 270-4. Edinburgh, 1889.

——. "The second voyage attempted by M. Iohn Davis with others, for the discovery of the Northwest Passage, in Anno. 1586." In ibid., pp. 234-46.

Elliott, Henry W. *An Arctic province: Alaska and the Seal Islands.* London: Sampson Low, Marston, Searle & Rivington, 1886.

Freeman, Milton M. R. "Observations on the kayak-complex, Belcher Islands, N.W.T." *National Museum of Canada, Bulletin No. 194*, 1964, pp. 56-91.

[Frobisher, Martin.] "A true report of such things as happened in the second voyage of captaine Frobisher...by the Northwest. Ann. Dom. 1577." In *Voyages of the English nation to America before the year 1600.* Ed. by Richard Hakluyt. Vol. 1, pp. 141-71. Edinburgh: 1889.

——. "A generall and briefe description of the countrey, and conditions of the people, which are found in Meta Incognita." Ibid., pp. 213-19.

Golder, F. A. *Bering's voyages: an account of the efforts of the Russians to determine the relation of Asia and America. vol. 1, the log books and official reports of the first and second expeditions 1725-1730 and 1733-1742.* New York: Octagon Books, 1968.

Guemple, D. L. *The Pacalik kayak of the Belcher Islands.* National Museum of Canada, Bulletin No. 204. Anthropological series no. 70, 1967, pp. 124-90.

Guillemard, F. H. H. *The cruise of the Marchesa to Kamschatka & New Guinea.* London: John Murray, 1886.

Hall, Christopher. "The first voyage of Martine Frobisher to the Northwest...1576." In *Voyages of the English nation to America before the year 1600.* Ed. by Richard Hakluyt. Vol. 1, pp. 74-81. Edinburgh: 1889.

Herbert, Wally. *Eskimos.* Glasgow, London, Toronto, New York: International Library, 1976.

Hoffman, Walter James. "The graphic art of the Eskimos." *Report of the U. S. National Museum for 1895*, pp. 739-968. Washington: Government Printing Office, 1897.

Hooper, C. L. *Report of the cruise of the U.S. Revenue-Steamer Corwin.* Washington: Government Printing Office, 1881.

Janes, John. "The first voyage of M. Iohn Davis, undertaken in Iune 1585 for the discoverie of the Northwest passage, written by m. Iohn Ianes. Merchant." In *Voyages of the English nation to America before the year 1600.* Ed. by Richard Hakluyt. Vol. 1, pp. 224-34. Edinburgh: 1889.

Jochelson, Waldemar. *The Koryak.* Jesup North Pacific Expedition, vol. 6. Memoir of the American Museum of Natural History, vol. 10. New York: E. J. Brill, Leiden, and G. E. Stechert, 1908.

Karr, H. W. Seton. *Shores and alps of Alaska.* London: Sampson Low, Marston, Searle, & Livingston. 1887.

Lantzeff, George V., and Pierce, Richard A. *Eastward to empire: exploration and conquest on the Russian open frontier to 1750.* Montreal: McGill-Queen's University Press, 1973.

McGhee, Robert. *Canadian Arctic prehistory.* National Museums of Canada, Canadian Prehistory Series. Toronto: Van Nostrand Reinhold, 1978.

Miller, Polly and Leon Gordon. *Lost heritage of Alaska: the adventure and art of the Alaskan coastal Indians.* Cleveland and New York: World Publishing, 1967.

Murdock, John. *Ethnological results of the Point Barrow expedition.* U.S. Bureau of Ethnology, Ninth Annual Report, 1887-88. Washington: Smithsonian Institution, 1892.

Palliser, John. *The journals, detailed reports, and observations relative to the exploration, by Captain John Palliser, of that portion of British North America, which in latitude, lies between the British boundary line and the height of land or watershed of the northern or frozen Ocean during the years 1857, 1858, 1859, and 1860.* London: G.E. Eyre and W. Spottiswoode, 1863.

Pike, Warburton. *Through the subarctic forest: a record of a canoe journey from Fort Wrangle to the Pelly Lakes and down the Yukon River to the Behring Sea.* London: 1896.

Renouf, E. "Eskimo kayaks." *The Beaver*, Outfit 260, 1929.

Rymill, J.R. "Watkin's kayak." *The Geographical Journal* 82, 1933, pp. 539-41.

Schwatka, Frederick. *Report of a military reconaissance in Alaska, made in 1883.* Washington: 1885.

——. *Along Alaska's great river....* Chicago: Henry, 1898.

Settle, Dionise. "The second voyage of Martin Frobisher, made to the west and northwest regions, in the yeere 1577...." In *Voyages of the English nation to America before the year 1600.* Ed. by Richard Hakluyt. Vol. 1, pp. 81-97. Edinburgh: 1889.

Sorge, Ernst. *With 'plane, boat & camera in Greenland: an account of the Universal Dr. Franck Greenland Expedition.* London: Hurst & Blackett, 1935.

Stefansson, Vilhjalmur. *My life with the Eskimo.* New York: Macmillan, 1913.

Such, Peter. *Vanished peoples: the archaic Dorset & Beothuk people of Newfoundland.* Toronto: NC Press, 1978.

Taylor, Kenneth I. "The construction and use of kayaks in north-west Greenland: Preliminary Report." *The Polar Record*, vol. 10, no. 68, May 1961, pp. 494-500.

A Greenland kayak sits high on a scaffold safe from hungry dogs.

Turner, Lucien McShaw. "Ethnology of the Ungava District: Hudson Bay Territory." Ed. John Murdock. *U.S. Bureau of Ethnology, 11th Annual Report*, pp. 159-350. Washington: Smithsonian Institution, 1894.

Whymper, Frederick. *Travel and adventure in the Territory of Alaska, formerly Russian America— now ceded to the United States—and in various other parts of the North Pacific.* London: John Murray, 1869.

Wilson, Daniel. *Prehistoric man: researches into the origin of civilization in the old and the new world.* London: Macmillan, 1865.

Wright, J. V. *Six chapters of Canada's prehistory.* Archaeological Survey of Canada, National Museum of Man. Ottawa: National Museums of Canada, 1976.

Zimmerly, David W. "Kayaks: their design and use." In *Wooden shipbuilding & small craft preservation*, pp. 71-4. Washington: The Preservation Press, National Trust for Historic Preservation in the United States, 1976.

———. "An illustrated glossary of kayak terminology." *Canadian Museums Association Gazette*, vol. 9, no. 2, pp. 27-37.

———. "The acquisition and documentation of an artifact." *Canadian Museums Association Gazette*, vol. 10, no. 4, pp. 18-34.

———. *Kayaks of Hooper Bay, Alaska.* Canadian Ethnology Service, Mercury Series, No. 43. Ottawa: National Museum of Man, 1978.

———. *Kayaks of Hooper Bay, Alaska.* Canadian Ethnology Service, Mercury Series, No. 53. Ottawa: National Museum of Man, 1979.

THE BULL BOAT AND OTHERS

Adair, James. *The history of the American Indians.* London: 1775.

Bartram, William. *Travels through North and South Carolina, Georgia, East and West Florida....* Dublin: 1793.

Catlin, George. *Illustrations of the manners, customs, and condition of the North American Indians.* 2 vols. 9th ed. London: 1857.

Cordle, C. G., ed. "The John Tobler manuscripts: an account of German-Swiss emigrants in South Carolina, 1737." *Journal of Southern History*, vol. 5, 1939, pp. 83-97.

Dorsey, James Owen. "Omaha dwellings, furniture, and implements." *13th annual report of the Bureau of Ethnology*, pp. 263-88. Washington: 1896.

Gyles, John. *Nine years a captive; or, John Gyles' experience among the Malicite Indians from 1689 to 1698.* Saint John, N.B.: 1875.

Hunter, John D. *Memoirs of a captivity among the Indians of North America.* 3rd ed. London: 1824.

Jenness, Diamond. *The Indians of Canada.* National Museum of Canada Bulletin 65. Ottawa: 1932.

Johnson, Overton, and Winter, William H. *Route across the Rocky Mountains.* Reprinted from edition of 1846. Princeton, N.J.: Princeton University Press, 1932.

La Hontan, Louis-Armand de Lom d'Arce, Baron de. *New voyages to North-America.* London: 1703.

Larpenteur, Charles. *Forty years a fur trader on the upper Missouri; the personal narrative of Charles Larpenteur, 1833-1872.* Ed. by Elliott Coues. Minneapolis: 1962.

Leechman, J. Douglas. *The Vanta Kutchin.* National Museum of Canada Bulletin No. 130. Ottawa: 1954.

Neill, Wilfred T. "Coracles or skin boats of the southeastern Indians." *The Florida Anthropologist*, vol. 7, no. 4, Dec. 1954, pp. 119-26.

Swan, Caleb. "Position and state of manners and arts in the Creek or Muscogee nation in 1791." In *Historical and statistical information respecting the history, condition, and prospects of the Indian tribes of the United States*, by H. R. Schoolcraft, pp. 253-4. Washington: 1855.

Wyeth, John B. "Oregon; or a short history of a long journey from the Atlantic Ocean to the region of the Pacific by land." In *Early western travels, 1748-1846*, ed. by R. G. Thwaites. Vol. 21. Cleveland: 1904.

Wyeth, Nathaniel J. *The correspondence and journals of Captain Nathaniel J. Wyeth, 1831-6.* Ed. by Frederick G. Young. New York: 1973.

THE BARK CANOE

THE WOODLAND INDIANS

Copway, G. (Kah Ge Ga Gah Bowh). *The traditional history and characteristic sketches of the Ojibway Nation.* London: 1850.

Densmore, Frances. *Chippewà customs.* Bureau of American Ethnology Bulletin 86. Washington: 1929.

Fenton, William N., and Dodge, Ernest Stanley. "An elm bark canoe in the Peabody Museum of Salem." *The American Neptune*, vol. 9, no. 3, July 1949.

Guy, Camil. *The Weymontaching birchbark canoe.* National Museums of Canada, Anthropological Papers, No. 20. 1974.

Jenness, Diamond. *The Indians of Canada.* National Museum of Canada, Bulletin No. 65. Ottawa: King's Printer, 1932.

Kinietz, W. Vernon. *The Indians of the Western Great Lakes, 1615-1760.* Ann Arbor: University of Michigan Press, 1940.

Leechman, J. Douglas. *Native Tribes of Canada.* Toronto: Gage, 1957.

Neill, Edward D. "History of the Ojibways, and their connections with the fur traders...." In *Minnesota Historical Society History of the Ojibway Nation*, 1885, pp. 395-510.

Warren, William W. *History of the Ojibway Nation.* Minneapolis: Ross and Haines, 1957.

THE FRENCH PERIOD

Adams, Arthur T., ed. *The explorations of Pierre Esprit Radisson.* Minneapolis: Ross and Haines, 1961.

Alcock, F. J. "The Long Sault of the Ottawa." *Canadian Geographical Journal*, vol. 45, no. 6, Dec. 1952, pp. 252-61.

Bailey, Alfred Goldworthy. *The conflict of European and eastern Algonquin cultures, 1504-1700.* 2nd ed. Toronto: University of Toronto Press, 1969.

Bayliss, Joseph E., and Estelle L. *The River of Destiny: the Saint Marys.* Detroit: 1955.

Biard, Pierre. *Biard's Relation of 1616.* The Jesuit Relations and allied documents, vol. 3. Ed. by R. G. Thwaites. Cleveland: 1896-1901.

Biggar, Henry Percival. *The voyages of Jacques Cartier.* Ottawa: King's Printer, 1914.

———. *The early trading companies of New France: a contribution to the history of commerce and discovery in North America.* University of Toronto, Studies in History. Toronto: 1901.

271

BIBLIOGRAPHY

Blair, Emma Helen, trans. and ed. *The Indian tribes of the Upper Mississippi Valley and the Great Lakes as described by Nicholas Perrot, French commandant in the northwest; Bacqueville de la Potherie, French Royal Commissioner to Canada; Morrell Marston, American army officer; and Thomas Forsythe, United States agent at Fort Armstrong.* Vol. 1. Cleveland: Arthur H. Clark, 1911.

Bressani, Francesco Giuseppe. *Bressani's Relation of 1653.* The Jesuit Relations and allied documents, vol. 39. Ed. by R. G. Thwaites. Cleveland: 1896-1901.

Buteux, Jacques. *Relation of 1650-51.* The Jesuit Relations and allied documents, vol. 37. Ed. by R. G. Thwaites. Cleveland: 1896-1901.

Butterfield, C. W. *History of Brûlé's discoveries and explorations, 1610-1626....* Cleveland: 1898.

Capp, Edward H. *The story of Baw-a-ting, being the annals of Sault Sainte Marie.* Sault Ste. Marie: 1904.

Cartwright, George. *A journal of transactions and events, during a residence of nearly sixteen years on the coast of Labrador....* 3 vols. Newark, England: D. Estes & Co., 1792.

Champlain, Samuel de. *Works.* Ed. by H. P. Biggar. Toronto: The Champlain Society, 1929. Reprint, Toronto: 1971.

Clark, Andrew Hill. *Acadia: the geography of early Nova Scotia to 1760.* Madison: University of Wisconsin Press, 1968.

Clarke, George Frederick. *Someone before us: our Maritime Indians.* Fredericton: Brunswick Press, 1968.

——. *The birch-bark canoe: its influence on Canadian history.* Collections of the New Brunswick Historical Society, No. 16. Saint John, N.B.: 1961.

Creux, François du. *History of Canada or New France.* Trans. by Percy J. Robinson, ed. by James B. Conacher. Toronto: The Champlain Society, 1951.

Crouse, Nellis M. *Contributions of the Canadian Jesuits to the geographical knowledge of New France, 1632-1675.* Ithaca: 1924.

Dankers, Jasper. "Journal of Jasper Dankers." In *Chronicles of the Hudson...three centuries of travellers' accounts* by Roland Van Zandt. New Brunswick, N.J.: Rutgers University Press, 1971.

Delanglez, Jean. *The life and voyages of Louis Jolliet, 1645-1799.* Chicago: 1948.

Dollier de Casson, François. *A history of Montreal, 1640-1672....* Trans. and ed. by Ralph Flenley. London and Toronto: 1928.

Douglas, R., and Wallace, J. N., eds. *Twenty years of York Factory, 1694-1714. Jérémie's account of Hudson Strait and Bay.* Ottawa: 1926.

Eccles, W. J. *The Canadian frontier, 1534-1760.* New York: Holt, Reinhart and Winston, 1969.

Faillon, E.-M. *Histoire de la colonie française en Canada.* 3 vols. Ville-Marie [Montreal]: 1865-66.

Goulson, Cary F. *Seventeenth-century Canada: source studies.* Toronto: Macmillan of Canada, 1970.

Guy, John. "John Guy's narrative, 1612." In *The Beothucks or red Indians: the aboriginal inhabitants of Newfoundland,* by James P. Howley. Cambridge: Cambridge University Press, 1915, pp. 15-18.

Heidenreich, Conrad. *Huronia: a history and geography of the Huron Indians, 1600-1650.* Toronto: McClelland and Stewart, 1971.

Henday, Anthony. *York Factory to the Blackfeet country, 1754-55.* Ed. by L. J. Burpee. Transactions of the Royal Society of Canada. Toronto: 1907.

Hennepin, Louis. *A new discovery of a vast country in America.* Ed. by R. G. Thwaites. Chicago: A. C. McClurg & Co., 1903.

Howley, James P. *The Beothuks or red Indians, the aboriginal inhabitants of Newfoundland.* Cambridge: Cambridge University Press, 1915.

Innis, Harold A. *The fur trade in Canada.* Revised edition, 1965. Toronto: University of Toronto Press, 1970.

J.C.B. *Travels in New France.* Harrisburg: Pennsylvania Historical Commission, 1941.

Kellogg, Louise P., ed. *Early narratives of the Northwest, 1634-1699.* New York: 1917.

Kidd, Kenneth E. *The excavation of Ste. Marie I.* Toronto: University of Toronto Press, 1949.

Lafitau, Joseph François. *Moeurs des sauvages amériquains comparées aux moeurs des premiers temps.* 2 vols. Paris: 1724.

La Hontan, Louis-Armand de Lom d'Arce, Baron de. *New voyages to North-America....* London: 1703.

La Vérendrye, Pierre Gaultier de Varennes. *Journals and letters of Pierre Gaultier de Varennes, Sieur de la Vérendrye, and his sons....* Ed. by L. J. Burpee. Toronto: The Champlain Society, 1927.

LeBeau, Claude. *Avantures du Sr. C. LeBeau, avocat en parlement; ou, voyage curieux et nouveau, parmi les sauvages de l'Amérique Septentrionale.* 2 vols. Amsterdam: 1738.

Le Clercq, Chrétien. *New relations of Gaspésia....* Trans. and ed. by W. F. Ganong. Toronto: The Champlain Society, 1910.

Le Jeune, Paul. *Le Jeune's Relation 1636.* Jesuit Relations and allied documents, vol. 9. Ed. by R. G. Thwaites. Cleveland: 1896-1901.

——. *Le Jeune's Relation of 1637.* Ibid., vol. 12.

——. *Le Jeune's Relation of 1638.* Ibid., vol. 14.

——. *Relation of 1634.* Ibid., vol. 7.

Lescarbot, Marc. *The History of New France.* Trans. and ed. by W. L. Grant, with an introduction by H. P. Biggar. 3 vols. Toronto: The Champlain Society, 1907-14.

Membré, Zenobius. "Narrative of the adventures of La Salle's party...from February, 1680, to June, 1681, by Father Zenobius Membré, Recollect." In *Discovery and exploration of the Mississippi Valley* by John Dawson Gilmary Shea. 2nd ed., pp. 151-88. Albany: 1903.

Morgan, Lewis H. *League of the Ho-dé-no-sau-nee or Iroquois.* New York: Dodd, Mead, 1904.

Neill, Edward Duffield. *The history of Minnesota, from the earliest French explorations to the present time.* Philadelphia: J.B. Lippincott & Co., 1858.

Norton, Thomas Elliot. *The fur trade in colonial New York, 1686-1776.* Madison: The University of Wisconsin Press, 1974.

Parkins, Almon Ernest. *The historical geography of Detroit.* Lansing: Michigan Historical Commission, 1918.

Perrot, Nicolas. *Mémoire sur les moeurs, coustumes, et relligion des sauvages de l'Amérique Septentrionale....* Ed. by R. P. J. Tailhan. Paris: 1864.

Potherie, Bacqueville de la. *Histoire de l'Amérique Septentrionale.* Paris: 1722.

Preston, Richard A., trans. and ed. *Royal Fort Frontenac.* Toronto: The Champlain Society, 1958.

[Pring, Martin.] "A voyage...for the discoveries of the North part of Virginia, in the yeere 1603." In *Purchas his pilgrimes,* by Samuel Purchas. Vol. 18, pp. 322-9. Glasgow: 1906.

Quaife, Milo Milton. *Chicago and the old Northwest.* Chicago: 1913.

Radisson, Pierre Esprit. *Voyage of Peter Esprit Radisson: being an account of his travels and experiences among the North American Indians, from 1652 to 1684.* Ed. by Gideon D. Scull. Boston: Prince Society, 1885.

Ragueneau, Paul. *Relation of 1657-58.* The Jesuit Relations and allied documents, vol. 44. Ed. by R. G. Thwaites. Cleveland: 1896-1901.

Ray, Arthur J. *Indians in the fur trade: their role as trappers, hunters, and middlemen in the lands southwest of Hudson Bay, 1660-1870.* Toronto: University of Toronto Press, 1974.

Raymond, William O. *The River St. John....* Saint John, N.B.: John A. Bowes, 1910.

Like some other major cities, Chicago owes its beginning to a strategic location on an important canoeing route. Jolliet and Marquette in 1673 were probably the first Europeans to use the vital portage here that linked the Mississippi system to the Great Lakes. This view is from 1820.

Sagard, Gabriel. *The long journey to the country of the Hurons.* Trans. by H. H. Langton and ed. by George M. Wrong. Toronto: The Champlain Society, 1939.

Séguin, Robert-Lionel. *La civilization traditionnelle de l'''habitant'' aux 17e et 18e siècles.* Montreal: Fides (c.1973).

Shea, John Dawson Gilmary, ed. and trans. *Discovery and exploration of the Mississippi Valley.* 2nd ed. Albany: 1903.

Smith, James. *An account of the remarkable occurrences in the life and travels of Col. James Smith…during his captivity with the Indians, in the years 1755, '56, '57, '58, & '59.* Lexington, Ky.: John Bradford, 1799.

Speck, Frank G. *Beothuk and Micmac.* New York: Museum of the American Indian, 1922.

Steck, Francis Borgia. *The Jolliet-Marquette expedition 1673.* Quincy, Ill.: Franciscan Fathers, 1928.

Stites, Sara Henry. *Economics of the Iroquois.* Bryn Mawr College Monographs. Vol. I, no. 3, April 1905.

Sulte, Benjamin. "Canot d'écorce." *Bulletin des recherches historiques,* vol. 22, 1916, pp. 236-41.

——. "Les coureurs de bois au lac Superieur, 1660." Ibid. Third series, vol. 5, 1911, Section I, pp. 249-66.

——. "Le Fort Frontenac, 1668-1678." Ibid. Second series, vol. 7, 1901, Section I, pp. 47-96.

——. *Trois Rivières d'autrefois.* Melange historique: etudes éparses et inédites de Benjamin Sulte. Comp., annotée, et· pub. par Gérard Malchelosse. Montréal: 1918-34.

——. *The valley of the Grand River, 1600-1650.* Transactions of the Royal Society of Canada. Vol. 4, section 2.

Thwaites, R. G. *The French regime in Wisconsin, 1634-1727.* Collections of the State Historical Society of Wisconsin, vol. 16. 1902.

Townsend, John K. *Narrative of a journey across the Rocky Mountains to the Columbia River, and a visit to the Sandwich Island, Chili, &c.* Philadelphia: Henry Perkins, 1839.

Trigger, Bruce G. *The children of Aataentsic I: a history of the Huron people to 1660.* Montreal: McGill-Queen's University Press, 1976.

——. *The Huron farmers of the north.* Holt, Reinhart and Winston, 1969.

Wallis, Wilson D. and Ruth Sawtell. *The Malecite Indians of New Brunswick.* Dept. of Northern Affairs and National Resources Bulletin No. 148, Anthropological Series No. 40. Ottawa: 1957.

——. *The Micmac Indians of eastern Canada.* Minneapolis: University of Minnesota Press, 1955.

Weld, Isaac. *Travels through the states of North America and the provinces of Upper and Lower Canada, during the years 1795, 1796, and 1797.* London: John Stockdale, 1800.

THE BRITISH PERIOD

Agassiz, Louis. *Lake Superior: its physical character, vegetation and animals, compared with those of other similar regions.* Boston: Gould, Kendall and Lincoln, 1850.

Back, George. *Narrative of the Arctic land expedition to the mouth of Great Fish River and along the shores of the Arctic Ocean in the years 1833, 1834, and 1835.* Edmonton: Hurtig, 1970.

Ballantyne, Robert Michael. *Hudson Bay; or, everyday life in the wilds of North America during the six years' residence in the territories of the Hon. Hudson Bay Company.* London: T. Nelson and Sons, 1896.

Barclay, Robert George. "Grey Nuns voyage to Red River." *The Beaver,* Outfit 297, Winter 1966, pp. 15-23.

Barrow, John, ed. *The geography of Hudson's Bay. Being the remarks of Captain W. Coats….* London: The Hakluyt Society, 1852.

Bonnycastle, Richard H. *The Canadas in 1841.* London: Henry Colburn, 1841.

Burpee, L. J. *The search for the western sea: the story of the exploration of northwestern America.* Toronto: Museum Book Co., 1908.

Campbell, Marjorie Wilkins. *McGillivray, lord of the Northwest.* Toronto, Vancouver: Clarke, Irwin & Co., 1962.

Carver, John A. *Travels through the interior parts of North-America, in the years 1766, 1767, and 1768.* London: 1778.

Cocking, Matthew. *An adventure from Hudson Bay: journal of Matthew Cocking from York Factory to the Blackfeet country, 1772-73.* Ed. L. J. Burpee. Royal Society of Canada, Transactions, series 3, vol. 2, 1900, sect. 2, pp. 73-204.

Coues, Elliott. *History of the expedition under the command of Lewis and Clark….* New York: Francis P. Harper, 1893.

Craig, Gerald M., ed. *Early travellers in the Canadas, 1791-1867.* Toronto: Macmillan of Canada, 1955.

Cruikshank, E. A. "Early traders and trade-routes in Ontario and the West, 1760-1783." *Transactions of the Royal Canadian Institute,* vol. 3, pp. 253-74; vol. 4, pp. 299-313.

Davies, K. G., ed. *Letters from Hudson Bay, 1703-40.* Hudson's Bay Record Society, Publications, No. 25, 1965.

——, ed. *Northern Quebec and Labrador journals and correspondence, 1819-35.* Ibid. No. 24, 1963.

Franklin, John. *Narrative of a journey to the shores of the Polar Sea in the years 1819-20-21, and 22.* Edmonton: Hurtig, 1969.

Fraser, Simon. *The letters and journals of Simon Fraser, 1806-1808.* Ed. by W. Kaye Lamb. Toronto: Macmillan of Canada, 1957.

Galbraith, John S. *The little emperor: Governor Simpson of the Hudson's Bay Company.* Toronto: Macmillan of Canada, 1976.

Garry, Nicholas. *Diary of Nicholas Garry, Deputy-Governor of the Hudson's Bay Company from 1822-1835. A detailed narrative of his travels in the Northwest Territories of British North America in 1821.* Royal Society of Canada, Transactions, series 2, vol. 6, 1900, sect. 2, pp. 73-204.

Graham, Andrew. *Andrew Graham's observations on Hudson's Bay, 1767-91.* Ed. by Glyndwr Williams. Publications of the Hudson's Bay Record Society, No. 27. London: 1969.

Harmon, Daniel Williams. *Sixteen years in the Indian country….* Ed. by W. Kaye Lamb. Toronto: Macmillan of Canada, 1957.

Head, Francis B. *The emigrant.* London: John Murray, 1846.

Hearne, Samuel. *A journey from Prince of Wales' Fort in Hudson's Bay to the northern ocean, 1769-72.* Ed. by Richard Glover. Toronto: Macmillan of Canada, 1958.

Heming, Arthur. *The drama of the forests.* Toronto: S. B. Gundy, 1924.

Henry, Alexander. *Travels and adventures in Canada and the Indian territories between the years 1760 and 1776.* New York: I. Riley, 1809.

Innis, H. A. *Peter Pond: fur trader and adventurer.* Toronto: 1930.

Irving, Washington. *Adventures of Captain Bonneville; or scenes beyond the Rocky Mountains of the far west.* London: Richard Bentley, n.d.

——. *Astoria.* New York: 1861.

Jameson, Anna. *Winter studies and summer rambles in Canada.* Toronto: McClelland & Stewart, 1923.

Leechman, J. Douglas. *The Vanta Kutchin.* National Museum of Canada, Bulletin No. 130. Ottawa: Queen's Printer, 1954.

Lizars, K. M. *The valley of the Humber, 1615-1913.* Toronto: McClelland & Stewart, 1913.

MacGregor, J. G. *Peter Fidler: Canada's forgotten surveyor, 1769-1822.* Toronto: McClelland & Stewart, 1966.

MacKay, Douglas. *The Honourable Company: a history of the Hudson's Bay Company.* Toronto: McClelland & Stewart, 1949.

McKenney, Thomas L. *Sketches of a tour to the lakes.* Reprint of 1827 edition. Minneapolis: Ross & Haines, 1959.

Mackenzie, Alexander. *Voyages from Montreal….* Philadelphia: John Morgan, 1802.

Mason, J. Alden. *Notes on the Indians of the Great Slave Lake area….* Yale University Publications in Anthropology, No. 34. New Haven: Yale University Press, 1946.

Morse, Eric W. *Canoe routes of the voyageurs: the geography and logistics of the Canadian fur trade.* Reprint of a series of three articles in the *Canadian Geographical Journal,* May, July, and Aug., 1961.

Mountain, George J. *Journal of the Bishop of Montreal, during a visit to the Church Missionary Society's north-west American mission.* London: Seeley, Burnside, and Seeley; Hatchard and Son, 1845.

Rich, E. E., ed. *James Isham's observations on Hudson's Bay, 1743….* Toronto: The Champlain Society, 1949.

——. *London correspondence inward from Eden Colville, 1849-1852.* London: The Hudson's Bay Record Society, 1956.

——. *Moose Fort journals, 1783-85.* London: The Hudson's Bay Record Society, 1954.

——. *Cumberland House journals and inland journals, 1775-82.* First series, 1775-79. London: Hudson's Bay Record Society, 1951.

——. *Cumberland House journals and inland journals, 1779-82.* Second series, 1779-82. London: The Hudson's Bay Record Society, 1952.

——. *Peter Skene Ogden's Snake country journals, 1824-25 and 1825-26.* London: The Hudson's Bay Record Society, 1950.

Schoolcraft, Henry R. *Narrative journal of travels through the northwestern regions of the United States extending from Detroit…to the sources of the Mississippi River in the year 1820.* East Lansing: Michigan State College Press, 1953.

——. *Information respecting the history, conditions and prospects of the Indian tribes of the United States.* Philadelphia: J. B. Lippincott & Co., 1853-6.

Simcoe, John Graves. *The correspondence of Lieut. Governor John Graves Simcoe, with allied documents relating to his administration of the government of Upper Canada.* Ed. by E. A. Cruickshank. Toronto: Ontario Historical Society, 1923-31.

Simpson, George. *London correspondence inward from Sir George Simpson, 1841-42.* Ed. Glyndwr Williams. London: The Hudson's Bay Record Society, 1973.

——. *Peace River. A canoe voyage from Hudson's Bay to [the] Pacific by the late George Simpson…in 1828.* Ottawa: J. Duris & Son, 1872.

——. *Athabaska journal, 1824-25.* The Hudson's Bay Record Society, 1938.

Thompson, David. *David Thompson's narrative of his explorations in western America, 1784-1812.* Ed. by J. B. Tyrrell. Toronto: The Champlain Society, 1916.

Thomson, Don W. *Men and meridians: the history of surveying and mapping in Canada.* Ottawa: Information Canada, 1966.

Willson, Beckles. *The Great Company, being a history of the honourable company of merchant-adventurers trading into Hudson's Bay.* London: 1900.

Winchell, N. H. *The Aborigines of Minnesota.* A report of the Minnesota Historical Society, 1906-1911. St. Paul: The Pioneer Co., 1911.

TOURISTS AND SPORTSMEN

Arese, Francesco. *A trip to the prairies and in the interior of North America [1837-1838].* Trans. from French by Andrew Evans. New York: 1934.

Beltrami, J. C. *A pilgrimage in Europe and America leading to the discovery of the sources of the Mississippi and Bloody River.* 2 vols. London: 1828.

Bocock, John Paul. "Salmon-fishing in North America." *Illustrated London News*, Aug. 23, Aug. 30, Sept. 6, 1890.

Campbell, Marjorie Wilkins. *McGillivray, lord of the Northwest.* Toronto: 1962.

Catlin, George. *Illustrations of the manners, customs, and condition of the North American Indians.* 2 vols., 9th ed. London: 1857.

Cheadle, Walter Butler. *Cheadle's journal of a trip across Canada, 1862-1863.* Ottawa: 1931.

Hardy, Campbell. *Forest life in Acadie.* London: 1869.

Jameson, Anna. *Sketches in Canada and rambles among the red men.* London: 1852.

Kanuck [pseud.]. "Bark canoeing in Canada." *Lippincott's Magazine*, old series vol. 30, new series vol. 4, 1882.

Murray, William H. H. *Adventures in the wilderness; or, camp-life in the Adirondacks.* Boston: 1869.

Thoreau, Henry David. *The Maine Woods.* New York: 1961.

Wyndham, Windham Thomas, 4th Earl of Dunraven. *The Great Divide.* London: 1876.

Salish dugout-maker Anderson Dick readies a new racing canoe for painting, near Nanaimo, Vancouver Island.

MODERN TIMES

Alden, W. L. *The canoe and the flying proa, or cheap cruising and safe sailing.* New York: 1877.

——. "The perfect canoe." *Harper's New Monthly Magazine*, vol. 56, Apr. 1878, pp. 754-60.

American Canoe Association. Papers, including A. C. A. year books, in library of New York State Historical Association, Cooperstown.

Benedickson, Jamie. "Recreational canoeing in Ontario before the first World War." *Canadian Journal of History of Sport and Physical Education*, vol. 9, no. 2, Dec. 1979, pp. 41-57.

Bishop, Nathaniel H. *The voyage of the paper canoe.* Boston: 1878.

Douglas, C. M. "The lone canoeist of 1885." *The Beaver*, Outfit 281, June 1950, pp. 38-41.

Drayton, Reginald. Mss. diary of Reginald Drayton. Archives of Ontario.

Endicott, Abigail B. "The American Canoe Association, a brief history." *Canoe* (Official publication of Can. Canoe Ass'n.), vol. 1, no. 4, June 1977.

Frazer, Perry D. *Canoe cruising and camping.* New York: 1897.

Hallock, Charles. *The sportsman's gazetteer and general guide.* New York: 1877.

Hoffman, Ronald C. *The history of the American Canoe Association, 1880-1960.* A dissertation presented to the faculty of Springfield College, Springfield, Mass., June 1967.

Johnston, Fred. "History of the Canadian Canoe Association." *Canoe* (Official publication of Can. Canoe Ass'n.), vol. 1, no. 1, Feb. 1976.

——. "The great Canadian canoe was made in the U.S.A.! or where has all our history gone?" *Canoe* (Official publication of Can. Canoe Ass'n.), vol. 1, no. 2, June 1976.

Love, Francis H. "Peterborough…canoe capital of the world." *Forest and Outdoors*. Vol. 45, Sept. 1949, pp. 6-7 and 22.

MacGregor, John. *Our brothers and cousins: a summer tour in Canada and the States.* London: 1859.

——. *A thousand miles in the Rob Roy canoe on rivers and lakes of Europe.* 4th ed. London: 1866.

Manchester, Herbert. *Four centuries of sport in America.* New York: 1968.

Manley, Atwood. *Rushton and his times in American canoeing.* With assistance of Paul F. Jamieson. Syracuse: Adirondack Museum/Syracuse University Press, 1968.

Murray, Florence B., ed. *Muskoka and Haliburton, 1615-1875.* Toronto: Champlain Society, 1963.

New York Times. "The canoe regatta…first annual regatta of the New York Canoe Club." *New York Times*, Oct. 20, 1872.

Norton, C. L., and Habberton, John. *Canoeing in Kanuckia.* New York: 1878.

Osborne, A. C. *The migration of the voyageurs from Drummond Island to Penetanguishene in 1828.* Papers and Records, Ontario Historical Society, vol. 3, 1901.

Peterborough Canoe Co. *The Peterborough Canoe Company Ltd.* 14th year, 9th catalogue (illustrated catalogue). Peterborough: c. 1897.

Porteous, John. "Chestnut, No. 1 in canoes." *The Atlantic Advocate*, July, 1977.

Rogers, Mary Strickland. "The Peterborough canoe." In *Peterborough, land of shining waters; an anthology*, pp. 233-5, Peterborough: 1967.

"Retaw" [pseud.]. "The Canadian Canoe." *Forest and Stream*, vol. 29, no. 23, Dec. 29, 1887.

[Rushton, J. H.] *Pleasure boats and canoes, illustrated catalogue.* J. H. Rushton, Canton, N.Y., c. 1899.

Sears, George Washington ("Nessmuk"). *Woodcraft.* Forest and Stream Pub. Co. New York: 1920.

Stephens, W. P. *Canoe and boat building.* New York: 1885.

Stewart, Hugh. *The story of the Chestnut canoe.* Mimeographed eight-page article from Chestnut Canoe Company, Oromocto, N.B., c. 1978.

Strickland, Samuel. *Twenty-seven years in Canada West.* Ed. by Agnes Strickland. 2 vols. London: 1853.

Strobridge, Henry L. "Modern canoe building for amateurs." *Outing*, vol. 24, Mar. and Apr. 1894.

Thompson, David. *Narrative of…David Thompson.* Ed. by Richard Glover. Toronto: Champlain Society, 1963.

——. Mss. diary of David Thompson. Archives of Ontario.

Tyson, O. S. *Sailing canoes, a brief history.* Pub. for American Canoe Association, 1935.

Vaux, C. Bowyer. "History of American canoeing." *Outing*, vol. 10, June 1887, pp. 259-69; July 1887, pp. 360-9; Aug. 1887, pp. 395-414.

——. "The canoeing of to-day." *Outing*, vol. 16, May 1890, pp. 133-7; June 1890, pp. 214-17.

——. "The modern single-hand cruiser." *Outing*, vol. 22, May 1893, pp. 144-7.

——. "Canoeing." *Outing*, vol. 16, 1890, pp. 495.

Vesper, Hans Egon. *50 years of the International Canoe Federation.* English ed. John Dudderidge. Florence, Italy: I.C.F., [1974].

Index

Italic page numbers refer to picture captions.

276

The text of this book was filmset by
TRIGRAPH, INC. of Toronto,
using 9/12 Zapf Book Medium with
Americana Ultrabold for display.

Color separations were made by
HONG KONG SCANNER CRAFT CO. LTD.,
and the printing & binding were done by
SOUTH CHINA PRINTING CO. Hong Kong,
through SCANNER ART SERVICES, INC. of Toronto.

The endpaper map was prepared by
JAMES LOATES ILLUSTRATING.

Design and production art by
RICHARD MILLER / THE PEPPERMINT PRESS.

The Canoe

This map is a guide to the reader showing Indian and Inuit peoples and the regions they occupied. Tribal locations are largely based on the time period references in the book.

Geographical names are shown in brown

Original peoples are shown in BLUE.

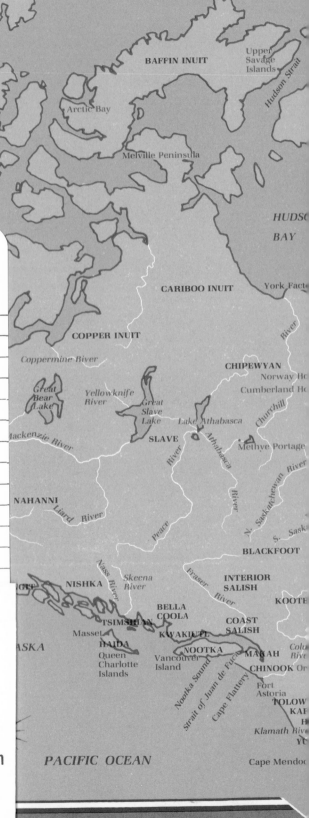